GLORY ENOUGH FOR ALL

Sheridan's
Second Raid
and the Battle of
Trevilian Station

Also by Eric J. Wittenberg

At Custer's Side:
The Civil War Writings of Bvt. Brig. Gen. James H. Kidd,
6th Michigan Cavalry

Under Custer's Command:
The Civil War Journal of James Henry Avery

One of Custer's Wolverines:
The Civil War Letters of Bvt. Brig. Gen. James H. Kidd,
6th Michigan Cavalry

We Have It Damn Hard out Here:
The Civil War Letters of Sergeant Thomas W. Smith,
6th Pennsylvania Cavalry

Gettysburg's Forgotten Cavalry Actions

GLORY ENOUGH FOR ALL

Sheridan's
Second Raid
and the Battle of
Trevilian Station

Eric J. Wittenberg

Foreword by
Gordon C. Rhea

Brassey's
Washington, DC

First paperback edition 2002.

Library of Congress Cataloging-in-Publication Data

Wittenberg, Eric J., 1961–
    Glory enough for all : Sheridan's second raid and the Battle of Trevilian Station / Eric J. Wittenberg ; foreword by Gordon C. Rhea.—1st ed.
      p. cm.
    Includes bibliographical references.
    ISBN 1-57488-353-4 (alk. paper)
    1. Trevilian Station, Battle of, Va., 1864. 2. Sheridan, Philip Henry, 1831–1888. I. Title

    E476.6.W58 2001
    973.7'37–dc21

2001016195

ISBN 1-57488-468-9   (alk. paper)

Printed in the United States of America on acid-free paper that meets the American National Standards Institute Z-39-49 standard.

Brassey's, Inc.
22841 Quicksilver Drive
Dulles, Virginia 20166

First Edition

10 9 8 7 6 5 4 3 2 1

⊷ Dedication ⊶

This book is respectfully dedicated to the memory of the horse soldiers of the Blue and the Gray, who fought, sacrificed, and died at the bloody Battle of Trevilian Station. It is also respectfully dedicated to American soldiers everywhere who are either missing in action, lie under gravestones marked "unknown," or rest in unmarked graves around the world.

The cavalry constitute the eyes and ears of the army. The safety of the entire command depends upon their vigilance and the faithfulness of their reports.

Lieut. Gen. Daniel Harvey Hill
February 25, 1863

During the period of my immediate control of the Cavalry, I tried to carry into effect, as far as possible, the views I had advanced before and during the opening of the Wilderness campaign, i.e., 'that our cavalry ought to fight the enemy's cavalry, and our infantry the enemy's infantry'; for there was great danger of breaking the spirit of the corps if it was to be pitted against the enemy's compact masses of foot-troops posted behind entrenchments, and unless there was some adequate tactical or strategical advantage to be gained, such a use of it would not be justified.

Lieut. Gen. Philip H. Sheridan
Memoirs, Vol. 1 (1888)

An attack of cavalry should be sudden, bold and vigorous. The cavalry which arrives noiselessly but steadily near the enemy, and then, with one loud yell leaps upon him without a note of warning, and giving no time to form or consider anything but the immediate means of flight, pushing him vigorously every step with all the confidence of victory achieved, is the true cavalry; while a body of men equally brave and patriotic, who halt at every picket and reconnoiter until the precious surprise is over, is not cavalry.

Maj. Gen. J. E. B. Stuart
General Order No. 26, Cavalry Tactics
July 20, 1863

"Forward, the Light Brigade!"
Was there a man dismay'd?
Not tho' the soldier knew
Someone had blunder'd:
Their's not to make reply,
Their's not to reason why,
Their's but to do and die:
Into the valley of Death
Rode the six hundred.

"The Charge of the Light Brigade"
Alfred, Lord Tennyson
December 9, 1854

⊸ Contents ⊱

List of Maps   *ix*
Foreword   *xi*
Preface   *xvii*

1   The Union and Confederate Cavalry Forces and the Strategy
    Underlying the June 1864 Trevilian Raid   *1*
2   The Road to Trevilian Station   *37*
3   First Shots: Torbert and Butler Open the Action   *69*
4   Custer's First Last Stand: The Fight for Hampton's Wagons   *97*
5   Union Breakthrough along the Railroad   *133*
6   A Long Night on the Battlefield and a Morning of Destruction
    along the Virginia Central Railroad   *167*
7   Sheridan Is Repulsed at the Bloody Angle: The Second Day
    of the Battle of Trevilian Station   *183*
8   Sheridan's Retreat to White House Landing from Trevilian
    Station   *215*
9   The March from White House Landing to the James River   *249*
10 The Battle of Samaria Church and the End
    of the Trevilian Raid   *263*
11 An Assessment of the Trevilian Raid and the
    Battle of Trevilian Station   *301*

Epilogue   *327*

Appendix A: Order of the Battle   *331*

Appendix B: Union Strengths and Losses at the Battle of Trevilian
Station, June 11, 1864   *337*

Appendix C: Union Strengths and Losses at the Battle of Trevilian
Station, June 12, 1864   *341*

Appendix D: Confederate Strengths and Losses at the
Battle of Trevilian Station   *343*

Bibliography   *347*
Index   *369*
About the Author   *392*

⊷ Maps ⊶

Theater of Operations for Sheridan's Second Raid   24

The Virginia Central Railroad and Locations Pertinent to Sheridan's Second Raid   40

The Camp Sites of the Union and Confederate Forces, June 10, 1864   54

Trevilian Station and Environs, Showing the Battlefields of June 11 and 12, 1864   60

Opening Engagements, Sunrise, June 11, 1864   70

Torbert's Assault along the Fredericksburg Road, Morning, June 11, 1864   85

Custer's "First Last Stand," Mid-Morning, June 11, 1864   99

Torbert Captures Trevilian Station, Late Afternoon, June 11, 1864   145

Positions of the Opposing Forces, Night, June 11, 1864   159

Route of March, Maj. Gen. Fitzhugh Lee's Division, June 12, 1864   173

The Second Day's Battle, June 12, 1864   205

Sheridan's Retreat from Trevilian Station   229

Battle of Samaria Church, June 24, 1864   276

⊰ Foreword ⊱

The Overland Campaign—forty-odd days of fighting and maneuvering in May and June, 1864, that brought Ulysses S. Grant and Robert E. Lee from the Rapidan River to Petersburg—is best known for the brutal slugging matches in the Wilderness, at Spotsylvania Court House, along the North Anna River, and at Cold Harbor. Fights at places such as the Bloody Angle vied for dubious distinction as the most vicious bout of prolonged violence witnessed during the American Civil War. Less well known but every bit as interesting as the infantry engagements was the role that cavalry played while Grant and Lee jockeyed for position. 1864 represented a watershed for Union and Confederate mounted forces in the East.

During the war's early years, Lee's horsemen, adroitly managed by James Ewell Brown "Jeb" Stuart, had ridden circles around their Union counterparts. In 1863, however, the Federal cavalry corps under Alfred Pleasonton began to hold its own. All of that changed during the winter of 1863–64. John Buford, a talented division head, died of typhoid fever; Judson Kilpatrick, heading another division, was sent west after a disastrous raid on Richmond; and Pleasonton became a casualty of the failed Kilpatrick raid and of army politics.

Grant came east that spring and summoned Philip H. Sheridan to head the cavalry corps. Outspoken and highly opinionated, Sheridan possessed little cavalry experience but had impressed Grant with his aggressiveness. Sheridan had a month to reorganize the cavalry corps, and he pitched in with characteristic fervor. By the opening of the campaign on May 4, he had amassed a force of some 12,000 cavalrymen. Heading his three divisions were David M. Gregg, a talented but modest holdover from Pleasonton's tenure; Alfred T. A. Torbert, a former infantry commander with even less cavalry experience than Sheridan; and James H. Wilson, a former aide to Grant who had neither commanded cavalry nor led troops in combat. For all practical purposes, Union cavalry was starting afresh. Whether Sheridan's regime represented an improvement or a disaster remained to be seen.

Lee's cavalry was still in Jeb Stuart's experienced hands. Stuart had 8,000 troopers to Sheridan's 12,000, but continuity in his command structure compensated in large measure for disparity in numbers. Riding into battle with an ostrich feather in his hat and a crimson-lined cape streaming behind him, Stuart was a flamboyant figure who personified the youthful, daring spirit of the rebel horsemen. Despite his foppish appearance, he was a diligent and thoughtful warrior with an uncanny knack for gathering intelligence and bewildering opponents. Stuart, like Sheridan, entered the campaign with three division heads: Wade Hampton, a South Carolina planter with a natural aptitude for combat; Fitzhugh Lee, General Lee's nephew and a professional soldier in his own right; and W. H. F. "Rooney" Lee, General Lee's son, recently returned from imprisonment in the north.

As Grant moved south across the Rapidan River and battled Lee in the Wilderness, Sheridan's new organization floundered. Wilson was supposed to cover the interval between Grant's advancing army and the Confederates but failed to do so, enabling Lee to surprise Grant in the Wilderness. The next day, a single Confederate brigade under dashing Thomas L. Rosser routed Wilson's division. After two days of fruitless combat, Grant shifted south toward the hamlet of Spotsylvania Court House, hoping to interpose between Lee and Richmond. Sheridan's job was to clear the way, and again he botched his assignment. Hampton and Fitzhugh Lee stymied Sheridan north of Spotsylvania Court House at a place called Todd's Tavern. The next morning, Fitzhugh Lee waged a spirited delaying action, deploying his cavalry like infantry and fighting behind barricades stacked across the road. His dogged persistence bought time for Confederate infantry to arrive and halt Grant's advance. May 7 and 8 were two of the rebel mounted arm's finest days.

Tension simmering between Sheridan and his titular boss, George G. Meade, came to a boil on May 8. Meade accused Sheridan of having failed at every turn. Sheridan cursed Meade's infantry and accused the general, who was every bit as temperamental as his cavalry chief, of meddling in the management of his corps. Sheridan stomped from Meade's tent after a heated exchange, demanding that Meade release him to fight Stuart. Expecting Grant to back him, Meade informed the general in chief of Sheridan's boast that he could defeat Stuart. To Meade's chagrin, Grant sided with Sheridan and ordered Meade to let the plucky subordinate try his hand.

The next morning—May 9—Sheridan led the Union cavalry corps on an expedition toward Richmond, hoping to draw Stuart away from Lee's army and defeat him. Sheridan read his opponent to perfection. Stuart followed and intercepted Sheridan on the outskirts of Richmond at Yellow Tavern. Massing his cavalry, Sheridan broke Stuart's line with a ferocious charge orchestrated in large part by George A. Custer, a young Michigan brigadier who matched Stuart not only in daring, but in ostentatious dress as well. Stuart was mortally wounded—he died the next day—and his cavalry was badly scattered. That night, Sheridan pressed toward Richmond, only to become trapped between the city's intermediate defensive line and the Chickahominy River. In another brilliant display of daring, Custer broke through Fitzhugh Lee's strong position at Meadow Bridge and opened an escape route for Sheridan. Having defeated the rebels two days running, Sheridan continued on to the James River, provisioned, and returned to join Grant at the North Anna River.

Sheridan had dramatically altered the pecking order in Virginia. His Richmond raid was a resounding success, and his horsemen knew it. Morale soared, and Sheridan's troopers began to consider themselves invincible. The Confederates were downcast. Stuart was dead, as was his premier brigade commander, James B. Gordon. The cavalry had also lost six colonels, some 1,200 troopers, and thousands of horses, leaving hundreds of men dismounted and hors de combat. Rather than appoint a replacement for Stuart, General Lee decided to bide his time, letting the division commanders report independently to him until he could settle on a suitable corps chief. Fitzhugh Lee's fortunes continued to decline. On May 24 he led an expedition to drive Negro troops from a fort at Wilson's Wharf, on the James. Much to Lee's embarrassment, he was unable to take the garrison and had to retreat after sustaining serious casualties.

On May 28 Grant moved his army across the Pamunkey River, and Sheridan sent Gregg on a reconnaissance in force to locate Lee. Coincidentally, Lee was curious about Grant's whereabouts and sent Hampton on a similar mission. The opposing cavalry collided near an intersection called Haw's Shop. Dismounting his troopers and deploying them behind barricades made from logs and fence rails, Hampton held Gregg at bay all morning. Each side pumped in reinforcements, Hampton drawing on two new South Carolina regiments and Sheridan sending in Torbert's division. After seven hours of brutal combat, Custer broke the impasse with an irresistible charge against the center of the Confederate line. Hampton's men streamed back to the safety of the rebel infantry line.

Both sides claimed victory. Sheridan boasted that he had defeated Hampton and driven him from the field. Jubilant Union cavalrymen viewed the battle as affirmation of their superiority. Here was yet another victory in an unbroken string of successes since Yellow Tavern. Northern newspapers praised Sheridan. "He appears to keep himself so thoroughly informed as to know just how many men to send in to win a fight," a correspondent effused, "or else he is endowed with intuitive judgment in this respect, for he always wins." But in important respects, Hampton had come out ahead. He had thwarted Sheridan's objective—to locate Lee's army—and he had achieved his own goal of determining Grant's whereabouts. Hampton made mistakes, but his troopers were impressed. He understood the efficacy of earthworks and he stood up to Sheridan, giving as well as he took and falling back only when no other choice remained. Confederates could speak of the fight at Haw's Shop with pride, something they could not do of the recent debacles at Yellow Tavern, Meadow Bridge, and Wilson's Wharf. Lee's cavalry needed a commander who gave it prospects of winning, and Haw's Shop suggested that Hampton was that general. "The men of his corps soon had the same unwavering confidence in him that the 'Stonewall Brigade' entertained for their general," a cavalryman later observed. Haw's Shop was a learning experience for Hampton, and he was proving to be an attentive student.

While Grant's and Lee's infantry slugged away at Cold Harbor, cavalry fights sparked along the battlefield's periphery. Torbert's troopers meted out a resounding defeat to Matthew C. Butler's new South Carolina regiments on May 30 at Matadequin Creek. The next day Torbert drove Fitzhugh Lee from an entrenched position at Old Cold Harbor. Then, on June 1, Torbert did himself one better by repelling an attack by Confederate infantry. Things also seemed to be looking up for Wilson, who drove Rooney Lee's division from Hanover Court House and destroyed two railway bridges across the South Anna River. The only bright spot in this dismal tableau for Confederate cavalry came on June 1, when Hampton nearly captured one of Wilson's brigades at Ashland Station. Overall, however, Sheridan seemed undefeatable.

The real test was yet to come. Grant, as was his practice, sent Sheridan to raid west of the armies, his chief purpose being to cut the Virginia Central Railroad and to assist another Union army moving toward Lynchburg. Hampton set off in pursuit, and the two forces met at Trevilian Station. In a two-day, knockdown, drag-out fight, the opposing cavalry forces engaged in a massive test of strength and guile. That fight and its aftermath is the subject of this book.

Like so many 1864 battles, the fight at Trevilian Station has received scant scholarly attention. Perhaps the most vicious cavalry battle of the war, it has long called out for book-length treatment. Eric Wittenberg's labors have finally filled that void. Here, for the first time, are details of the battle told by the soldiers who fought there. And here also is a full assessment of the battle's impact and importance. Hollywood could not conjure up a more absorbing cast of characters than Sheridan, Hampton, Custer, and Butler, pitted here against one another in a thrilling bout of combat replete with all the twists, turns, and surprises of a novel. This book is required reading for anyone wishing to understand the story of cavalry in the American Civil War.

Gordon C. Rhea
Mt. Pleasant, South Carolina

⇜ Preface ⇝

The Battle of Trevilian Station was the largest all-cavalry engagement of the Civil War. This fierce battle, waged over two long, bloody days in mid-June 1864, had all of the elements one expects of intense combat involving horse soldiers. It featured mounted charges with sabres glinting in the bright sunlight, desperate hand to hand fighting, valiant service by the horse artillery, and protracted, brutal dismounted conflict. It was, without question, a pivotal moment in Grant's grand strategy for the summer of 1864. Indeed, the Confederate cavalry scored a decisive victory at Trevilian Station; a Union victory undoubtedly would have hastened the end of the war. Participants on both sides recalled this battle as the hardest and most brutal cavalry fight of the war.

One South Carolina trooper, writing at the turn of the century, recalled: "It was, pure and simple, a cavalry duel, which put to test the relative military ability and fighting ability of the antagonists. It thus possesses a picturesque, romantic charm derived from the isolation of the combatants as they wrestled for mastery, far separated from their armies, as if they had sought out this solitude to settle, uninterrupted, their quarrel by wager of battle." Maj. James H. Kidd, the chronicler of the Army of the Potomac's Michigan Cavalry Brigade, observed of Trevilian Station in 1910: "Then came Trevilian Station, that battle about which so much has been written and so little of the truth is really known. . . . The planning and fighting of the battle, with its artful maneuvers and tactical stratagems, have been compared to a game of chess. To my mind, no cavalry engagement of the Civil War had more points of resemblance to the moves of knights and pawns upon the chessboard than did the first day at Trevilian Station."

Five years ago, when I commenced this project, I had no preconceived notions. I knew that only the most dedicated cavalry scholars had any knowledge of this large, bloody battle. Gens. Philip H. Sheridan and Wade Hampton, the antagonists at Trevilian Station, were two of the great heroes of the American Civil War. After completing this long and arduous task, I have realized that Wade Hampton richly deserves both the accolades and the reputation he has been given.

However, as a result of my work, I have reassessed Phil Sheridan's role in history. I started out believing that Sheridan was a great hero, but I am no longer persuaded that he deserves the lofty reputation bestowed upon him by history. Sheridan's record on the field of combat does not support the reputation as a cavalry commander he now possesses. In fact, Sheridan lost almost every battle in which he commanded the Army of the Potomac's Cavalry Corps. While he deserves credit for being an effective army commander and motivator of men, he lacked the depth of experience and strategic view to be a great cavalry commander.

A close review of the record also demonstrates that Sheridan either had convenient memory lapses, or he often failed to tell the truth about his role in history. This study examines this tendency. His inclination to misstate the truth is, perhaps, nowhere more evident than in his accounts of the Trevilian raid.

History has largely forgotten the Battle of Trevilian Station. It represents a major defeat for Sheridan's troopers, and a major victory for Hampton. Trevilian Station marked the gifted South Carolinian's ascendance to command of the Army of Northern Virginia's Cavalry Corps in the wake of Maj. Gen. J. E. B. Stuart's mortal wounding exactly one month earlier. By thrashing Sheridan's horsemen at Trevilian Station, Hampton proved himself more than a worthy successor to the lamented plumed cavalier. To date, there has been no detailed or comprehensive book-length tactical study of this crucial campaign.

This story will be told in the level of detail it deserves, and wherever possible, will allow the participants to tell their stories in their own words. The tactical details are described as well as the myriad of human interest stories involved with this important raid. I portray the grueling marches to and from Trevilian Station and focus on the toll taken on both men and horses as a result. It is sometimes easy to forget that man and horse were a team and that their fates were interdependent. There are many tales of honor and courage on the Confederate side that will be related in these pages. Six blue-clad troopers, including three hard-bitten career Regular soldiers, earned Medals of Honor for their valor at Trevilian Station, and two more earned it at the short but brutal fight at Samaria Church on June 24, 1864. These compelling stories deserve to be told. The maps and photographs that grace these pages should assist the reader in deciphering the fluid and widely ranging combat that marked the Battle of Trevilian Station.

This extremely fluid and complex battle ranged over nearly 7,000 acres of heavily wooded countryside in three major, separate engagements spread over the course of two days. No better example of its nature may be found than that of the fighting that raged in the fields near Trevilian Station on the morning of June 11. The troopers of Brig. Gen. George A. Custer's Michigan Brigade were deployed in a triangular position. His vaunted Michigan Cavalry Brigade was completely surrounded by the enemy, who was moving in for the kill. Only the combination of Custer's legendary good luck and desperate fighting by his hardy veterans saved the Boy General and his men from annihilation that day. On June 11, 1864, Custer faced a situation not unlike the one that cost him his life twelve years later on the banks of the Little Big Horn River. Extraordinary good luck, however, saved him at Trevilian Station.

The South Carolina Brigade of Brig. Gen. Matthew C. Butler bore the brunt of the fighting on the Confederate side, with Butler and his Palmetto troopers performing brilliantly on both days of the battle. Unfortunately, their feats have been largely forgotten. Theirs is the great untold story of the battle. I hope in my telling of the story I have done these South Carolinians justice.

Trevilian Station is a complicated engagement, which may explain why there has been no modern detailed tactical study of this fight. I have done my best to make sense of the campaign and believe that my assessment is accurate. I have also provided the first modern detailed interpretation of the short but bloody fight at Samaria Church on June 24, 1864, a fight of great intensity that has been entirely overlooked by historians. All of the interpretations set forth herein are solely my own, and I accept responsibility for them as such. I can only hope that I have done these men and their deeds justice in telling their stories. I intend to honor their memories by finally bringing their stories to light.

One other important item needs to be pointed out. Those interested in seeing the ground as it looks today should keep in mind that the area has changed significantly over the years. As an example, the Trevilian intersection of the Gordonsville and Charlottesville roads that existed in 1864 is not near the current intersection, and the road that connected them no longer exists. Today, these two important roads intersect a few hundred yards west of the Trevilian train station. As another example, Carpenter's Ford, the place where Sheridan crossed the North Anna River twice, no longer exists. In the 1970s, the U.S. Army Corps of Engineers dammed the river and built Lake Anna, a major recreational facility. The damming of the river obliterated the ford; it took quite a bit of research in musty legal records in Louisa County to pin down the specific location of the ford. Finally, the visitor should be aware that the United Daughters of the Confederacy marker on the battlefield proper is historically inaccurate and should not be relied on, as it misplaces the scene of the primary portion of the battle.

As with nearly every project of this type, I am deeply indebted to a myriad of people. While I hope that I have remembered all of them, I sincerely hope that I will be forgiven if I neglect anyone. I owe the greatest debt of gratitude of all to Col. Jerry F. Meyers (U.S. Army Ret.), who has done more hard work to interpret the Battle of Trevilian Station than anyone I know. Jerry, who has also written a thorough and intriguing analysis of the battle, spent several days sharing a combat engineer's perspective on this battle, lending greatly to my understanding of the fighting at Trevilian. We also spent a day visiting the forgotten battlefield at Samaria Church. In addition, Jerry shared the fruits of his labors in researching the interesting social history of the area surrounding Trevilian Station, greatly adding to the quality of my work. After consultation, Jerry and I agreed on names for important sites from the Battle of Trevilian Station. We did this to assure some consistency and continuity in differing interpretations of the same battle.

I also owe a deep debt of gratitude to Steve L. Zerbe, my researcher and friend. Without Steve's help, I could not have gathered the large volume of primary source material that makes up this book. Likewise, my friend Tonia J. Smith assisted with obtaining Confederate materials only available in Virginia and also kindly allowed me to use her lovely house in Fredericksburg as a home away from home while I studied the Trevilian Station battlefield. Melody Callahan allowed me to use her home as a base of operations during an extended visit to the battlefield. Thomas A. Canfield scoured a number of the Empire State's many newspapers for me, searching for useful material on the roles played by New York cavalrymen. Gifted historian Gregory A. Coco provided me with the diary of Sgt. Louis Fitch of the Fifth Michigan Cavalry, which provided good insight into the mind set of one of George Custer's orderlies. Richard Reeves contributed an interesting letter from an officer of the Phillips Legion. Prof. Thomas D. Mays of Quincy College provided me with the letters of James M. Barr of the Fifth South Carolina Cavalry. Dan Lorello did some very valuable research on the role of the Ninth New York Cavalry at Trevilian Station that added insight to the analysis. Dusty Eisenburg portrays the Seventh Georgia Cavalry in living history events. Dusty kindly shared the results of years of his research and filled some major gaps on the role of the Seventh Georgia Cavalry for me. Risher Fairey helped me obtain crucial material on the Confederate cavalry.

Dr. Daniel Beattie graciously gave his time and effort to take me on my first tour of the Trevilian Station battlefield. Douglas Cubbison, of White Star Consulting, made a trip to Washington, D.C., on my behalf to obtain photographs and important records. Bryce A. Suderow gave me the benefit of his knowledge of operations during 1864, shared several valuable accounts, and also shared his thorough and groundbreaking assessment of the true strengths and losses of both sides in the two brutal days of fighting at Trevilian Station. Bryce's work along these lines provides the only truly comprehensive analysis of the forces that clashed at Trevilian Station those two long, hot, bloody days in June 1864. He has generously allowed me to reproduce this work in three appendices to this book, which shed light on the ferocity of the fighting. Bryce combed a number of obscure newspapers for me, turning up more obscure accounts of the battle. Finally, Bryce gave my manuscript a thorough and detailed reading, offering useful and insightful comments.

Karla Jean Husby kindly granted me permission to quote her ancestor, Sergeant James H. Avery of the Fifth Michigan Cavalry. I have reviewed more than 400 sources and accounts of the Battle of Trevilian Station, but Sergeant Avery's is unique. It is the only account I have seen that covers the trials and tribulations of a small contingent of the Fifth Michigan. Cut off from the main body of Sheridan's command on the first day of the Battle of Trevilian Station, these men spent two long, hard weeks hiking cross-country to safety in the main lines of the Army of the Potomac. Avery's account sheds light on a neglected but important aspect of the human side of war. I am very grateful to Karla for allowing me to use this account. Likewise, Keith Kehlbeck shared the saga of the Towles brothers with me and provided the photograph of Sgt. Robert C. Towles that graces this book. Steve Donahue of Richmond shared his ancestor's story about the Battle of Trevilian Station. Carolyn Clay Swiggart of Westport, Connecticut, provided me with the only known photograph of her ancestor, Lt. Col. Joseph L. McAllister of the Seventh Georgia Cavalry. Ernie Iler provided data on his ancestor, Sgt. Adam J. Iler, as well as the photograph that appears here, and Jack Wynn provided material on his ancestor, Capt. Francis W. Hokpkins of the Seventh Georgia Cavalry. Dona J. Sauerburger shared the letters of her ancestor, Lt. Thomas Lucas of the First Pennsylvania Cavalry, adding to the depth of the analysis. Andrew W. German provided me with useful information and insights on the Battle of Samaria Church that add to the richness of the narrative.

I am likewise indebted to Marc Ramsey and Ed Crebbs of the Trevilian Station Battlefield Foundation. In addition to their zealous efforts to preserve the battlefield at Trevilian Station, these two gentlemen arranged for me to have access to private land on crucial parts of the battlefield, and helped me to understand the importance of the terrain to the outcome of the battle. Ed pointed out many important but obscure corners of the vast and wide-ranging battlefield. Marc generously provided useful and obscure resources and reviewing and commenting on my interpretation of the battle. I salute the members of the Trevilian Station Battlefield Foundation. Their efforts have honored the memory of the men who fought and died in June 1864.

My friend and mentor, Brian C. Pohanka, gave of his encyclopedic knowledge of the Civil War. Robert F. O'Neill Jr., Horace H. Mewborn, and Jeffry D. Wert read the manuscript and contributed to this project. Prof. Gregory J. W. Urwin, a leading scholar of George Armstrong Custer's career in the Civil War, gave me the benefit of his extensive knowledge of cavalry operations and of Custer's role in this pivotal battle. David F. Wieck, a gifted editor, gave the manuscript a detailed and thorough read. Robert J. Trout, the leading authority on Confederate horse artillery, provided me with important material on the Southern cannoneers. Gordon C. Rhea, a scholar whose work on Grant's Overland Campaign I greatly admire, read the manuscript, and wrote the excellent foreword for this book. Col. Walbrook D. Swank (USAF Ret.) has done more to preserve the memory of the deeds of the brave troopers who served at Trevilian Station than anyone else. Colonel Swank generously provided information from his extensive collection of primary sources and read my work.

Blake A. Magner accompanied me to the battlefield and prepared the fine maps scattered throughout this volume. I am also indebted to John R. Sickles, who generously gave me permission to use several images from his large collection and also tipped me off about the interesting stories of John Hertz, Charles Fitzsimmons, and William Onweller of the Sixth Michigan Cavalry. These compelling stories had to be included in this work. I am further indebted to Cathy Marinacci, who granted me permission to use the images of Philip H. Sheridan and George A. Custer that grace these pages. Finally, a number of archivists at various institutions assisted in locating illustrations for this book, and I am most grateful to all of them.

I am grateful to Don McKeon, the publisher at Brassey's, for his faith in this project. This is now the second book project that we have done together, and I am pleased to be part of Brassey's stable of Civil War authors. David Arthur, my editor at Brassey's, provided good guidance as well as friendship as we wound our way through the labyrinthine maze of the publication process. The fine folks at Brassey's did an outstanding job of making my dream come true, and I thank them for it.

Last, but certainly not least, I owe the largest debt of gratitude of all to my best friend, traveling companion, and beloved wife, Susan Skilken Wittenberg. Without Susan's love, support, and endless patience with my addiction to the stories of the horse soldiers of the Civil War, none of this would have been possible. Susan, as always, I thank you for your love and support.

The Union and Confederate Cavalry Forces and the Strategy Underlying the June 1864 Trevilian Raid

[N]othing pleases a cavalryman so much as the idea of a raid.

The winter of 1863–64 was Abraham Lincoln's winter of discontent. His primary army commander in the East, Maj. Gen. George G. Meade, greatly frustrated him. Lincoln believed that Meade had failed to follow up on his signal victory over Gen. Robert E. Lee's Army of Northern Virginia at Gettysburg. When Meade went into winter camp, the president's irritation grew. Lincoln realized that the Northern public had grown weary and needed victories. Something had to change.

Maj. Gen. Ulysses S. Grant, commander of the Federal Western forces, brought the necessary change. Grant was a grim, determined warrior who had never lost a major engagement. In November 1863 his armies had broken the Confederate siege at Chattanooga and chased his Southern opponent, Gen. Braxton Bragg, into northern Georgia. Grant's political patron, Rep. Elihu Washburne, had introduced legislation to revive the long dormant rank of lieutenant general in the United States army. Washburne intended Grant to hold that lofty rank, making the quiet Illinoisian the highest-ranking officer in Federal service and commander of all the nation's armies. Grant could then shape grand strategy in all the war's theatres.

On March 4, 1864, Grant wrote his dear friend and chief lieutenant, Maj. Gen. William T. Sherman, that "the bill reviving the grade of lieutenant general in the army has become a law, and my name has been sent to the Senate." He had received orders "to report at Washington immediately *in person*, which indicates either a confirmation or likelihood of confirmation."[1]

Grant proved to be correct. Politicians greeted him in the nation's capital as the man who would lead the country to long-awaited victory over the rebellious South. The Army of the Potomac's grizzled quartermaster, Brig. Gen. Rufus Ingalls, Grant's roommate at West Point, predicted to Meade, "Grant means business."[2] Grant's old friend, Lt. Gen. James Longstreet, the Confederate Army of Northern Virginia's senior corps commander, echoed the same sentiment. "That man will fight us every day and every hour until the end of the war," he warned.[3] Lt. Col. Theodore Lyman, a staff officer with the Army of the Potomac, described the grim-faced new commanding general eloquently: "He habitually wears an expression as if he had deter-mined to drive his head through a brick wall, and was about to do it."[4] That single-minded determination changed the face of war in Virginia.

Congress quickly approved Grant's promotion, and the new lieutenant general set about crafting a strategy for the coming campaigns. Grant realized that the only way the North could win the war was to wear out the South, a tactic that required year-round campaigning and constant pressure on a Confederacy already straining its war-making capacity. To that end, Grant decided to coordinate the efforts of all of the Federal armies in the field, bringing all of the Union's resources to bear.[5]

Grant planned a series of coordinated assaults on all fronts. In the West, Sherman would launch a campaign aimed at destroying Gen. Joseph E. Johnston's Army of Tennessee. Maj. Gen. Nathaniel P. Banks would lead an expedition designed to capture the important manufacturing town of Shreveport, Louisiana, an operation already planned and approved before Grant's promotion. Banks was then to advance on the critical port city of Mobile, Alabama. Other Federal forces would move on Charleston, South Carolina, pinning down the Confederate coastal garrisons.

In the East, Maj. Gen. Franz Sigel, a politically influential German immigrant, was to clear the crucial Shenandoah Valley of Virginia of Confed-erates, then advance on Richmond from the west. Meanwhile, the Army of the James, commanded by Maj. Gen. Benjamin F. Butler, would advance on Richmond from the east. Grant intended to travel with the main army in the Eastern Theater, the Army of the Potomac, which would bear the brunt of the fighting in the center, flanked by Sigel and Butler.[6]

Meade, nominally the commander of the Army of the Potomac, received peremptory orders from Grant—Lee's army was to be his objective point, wherever Lee went Meade was to go also.[7] Before the spring's grand campaign began, Meade reorganized the Army of the Potomac into three large corps, the Second, Fifth, and Sixth Army Corps. The Cavalry Corps also underwent major changes in organization and leadership.

During the winter of 1863–64, the ambitious Brig. Gen. Judson Kilpatrick had taken a large mounted force on a raid toward Richmond to free Union soldiers in the notorious Libby and Belle Isle prisons. Kilpatrick commanded one column of the raid, while Col. Ulric Dahlgren, a dashing twenty-one-year-old colonel, led the other. The expedition left Dahlgren dead, fulfilled none of its objectives, and largely wrecked the Army of the Potomac's fine Third Cavalry Division. Maj. Gen. Alfred Pleasonton, commanding the Cavalry Corps, shouldered much of the blame for this failure, even though he had opposed the plan.

Dissatisfied with the performance of the army's mounted arm, Meade, with the approval of Secretary of War Edwin Stanton, promptly relieved Pleasonton of command.[8] One cavalry officer noted that "Even [Pleasonton's] success and the proofs he had given of the value of the cavalry, when properly used and led, were not sufficient to overcome the force of traditions and customs, and among higher authorities the idea still prevailed that the mounted force was secondary to, and should be used for the protection, convenience and relief of the infantry." He continued, "Serious differences of opinion on these questions between Generals Meade and Pleasonton had from time to time occurred, and at last had gone so far that the latter . . . could no longer retain his command."[9]

Brig. Gen. John Buford, the Army of the Potomac's most able cavalry officer, had died of typhoid fever in December 1863, and Second Cavalry Division commander Brig. Gen. David M. Gregg was not a highly aggressive officer. There were no other good candidates within the existing officer cadre.[10] In an early interview with Lincoln, Grant expressed his dissatisfaction with "the little that had been accomplished by the cavalry so far in the war, and the belief that it was capable of accomplishing much more than it had done under a thorough leader. I said I wanted the very best man in the army for that command." The army's chief of staff, Maj. Gen. Henry W. Halleck, asked, "How would Sheridan do?" Grant replied, "The very man I want."[11]

Maj. Gen. Philip Henry Sheridan was largely unknown to the new command. Col. Charles Wainwright, a pithy artillerist, reflected in his diary,

"I know nothing . . . of . . . [Sheridan], but a change I think was needed; neither Pleasonton nor [Maj. Gen. George] Stoneman proved themselves equal to the position."[12] Brig. Gen. Henry E. Davies, who commanded a brigade in the First Cavalry Division, observed that in the Cavalry Corps only the fittest leaders survived. This system ensured that its prior leadership had come from within the ranks of the corps. As a result, little was known of Sheridan's service in the West. Davies continued, "It was not known that he had ever served with or in command of cavalry, and the prejudice . . . among mounted troops against being placed under the orders of an officer whose experiences from which the Army of the Potomac had previously suffered had not induced the belief that the West was the point of the compass from which the advent of wise men bringing rich gifts of victory and success was to confidently expected."[13]

Sheridan was not, at first blush, the best choice to command the Cavalry Corps. Born in Albany, New York, on March 6, 1831, the diminutive Irishman was a member of the West Point class of 1853, ranking in the bottom third of his class. He had served as a second lieutenant in the Fourth Infantry, and after service as a staff officer in the early days of the war, was appointed colonel of the Second Michigan Cavalry, a command he held for only three months. He then was promoted to brigadier general and assumed command of an infantry division. He performed well in leading his foot soldiers in many of the Western Theater's primary battles. His bravery and aggressiveness in assaulting the strong Confederate position at Chattanooga in November 1863 caught Grant's eye, and the commanding general marked the young man for advancement.[14]

Col. Horace Porter, one of Grant's staff officers, wrote that the new cavalry chief "had been worn down almost to a shadow by hard work and exposure . . . he looked anything but formidable as a candidate for a cavalry leader."[15] Maj. James H. Kidd, commander of the Sixth Michigan Cavalry, recorded his observations:

> [Sheridan] was square of shoulder and there was plenty of room for the display of a major general's buttons on his broad chest. His face was strong, with a firm jaw, a keen eye, and extraordinary firmness in every lineament. In his manner there was an alertness, evinced rather in look than in movement. Nothing escaped his eye, which was brilliant and searching and at the same time emitted flashes of kindly good nature. When riding past or among his

troopers, he had a way of casting quick, comprehensive glances to the right and left and in all directions. He overlooked nothing. One had a feeling that he was under close and critical observation, that Sheridan had his eye on him, was mentally taking his measure and would remember and recognize him the next time. No introduction was needed.[16]

The bandy-legged little Irishman did not make a good first impression on Lincoln, who commented that Sheridan was "a brown, chunky little chap, with a long body, short legs, not enough neck to hang him, and such long arms that if his ankles itch he can scratch them without stooping." Grant quickly replied, "You will find him big enough for the purpose before we get through with him."[17]

The Army of the Potomac's Cavalry Corps consisted of three divisions. Two of those divisions, the Second and Third, had two brigades each, and the First Division had three. With the exception of one brigade, the Reserve Brigade, assigned to the First Division, all of these units were made up of volunteer cavalry. The Reserve Brigade included four small regiments of Regular Army cavalry assigned to service with the Army of the Potomac, providing a solid, professional nucleus to the Cavalry Corps. Batteries of Regular Army horse artillery attached to specific brigades supported each division. The Northern horsemen were typically armed with pistols, sabres, and a variety of breech-loading carbines, some with the seven-shot Spencer repeating carbine.

After the disastrous Richmond raid, Kilpatrick was exiled to the Western Theater. At Grant's insistence, Sheridan assigned brash young Brig. Gen. James H. Wilson to command of Kilpatrick's Third Cavalry Division. The choice enraged Brig. Gen. George A. Custer, who had briefly commanded the Third Division in the summer and fall of 1863 and outranked Wilson, who had no previous experience commanding troops. The other brigadier general assigned to the Third Division, Davies, also outranked Wilson, so Sheridan assigned him to a brigade in the Second Division, replacing the injured Col. John B. McIntosh. Custer's brigade moved to the First Division, and Col. George Chapman's brigade transferred from the First Division to the Third.

Another outsider, Brig. Gen. Alfred T. A. Torbert of Delaware, a member of the West Point class of 1855, was given command of the First Division, displacing its senior brigadier, Wesley Merritt. Torbert's "qualifications as a cavalry commander were not remarkable,"[18] a staff officer recalled. "He was a handsome, dashing fellow, at this time, a beautiful horseman, and as brave as a lion; but his abilities were hardly equal to such large commands."[19] Torbert had commanded New Jersey infantrymen with competence, but he had never commanded cavalry. Custer nonetheless seemed pleased with his new commander. "Everything is arranged satisfactorily now; I take my Brigade and join the First Division Cavalry Corps under General Torbert, an old and intimate friend of mine, and a very worthy gentleman," he wrote to his new bride.[20] Custer and his four fine regiments of Michigan cavalry—the First, Fifth, Sixth, and Seventh Michigan—achieved great things while attached to the First Division.

Custer, at the tender age of twenty-four, was on the way to a spectacular career. Graduating at the bottom of his West Point class in 1861, Custer's legendary good luck placed him in a coveted staff billet with the army's first commander, Maj. Gen. George B. McClellan. He was then assigned to Pleasonton's staff, where his boldness and courage caught the cavalry chieftain's eye. Shortly after Pleasonton assumed corps command, he arranged for Custer's promotion from temporary captain to brigadier general of volunteers on June 29, 1863. Tall, brash, handsome, athletic, and a born horseman, the "Boy General with the Golden Locks," as Custer was known, had not disappointed. A man in the Seventh Michigan adoringly described his brigadier as "the idol of his troopers and the terror of his foes."[21] Kidd, commanding one of Custer's regiments, wrote his father in May 1864: "So brave a man I never saw and as competent as brave. Under him a man is ashamed to be cowardly. Under him our men can achieve wonders."[22] One of Sheridan's staff officers, Capt. Frederic C. Newhall, described Custer as "quick as a flash, daring and reckless almost without equal, yet showing coolness and judgment in some tight places."[23] His "Wolverines," as he called his Michigan men, had performed spectacular service at Gettysburg and in the months following. His brigade was the envy of the Army of the Potomac.[24]

The First Division also contained the fine veteran brigade of Col. Thomas C. Devin, known as either "Buford's Hard Hitter" or "Old Warhorse." Devin had been a house painter before the war, and his military training was in the New York militia, where he commanded a company of cavalry. "I can't teach Col. Devin anything about cavalry," Buford once said. "He knows more about the tactics than I do."[25] Another said of Devin that he was "of the school of Polonius, a little slow sometimes in entrance to a fight, but, being in, as slow to leave a point for which the enemy is trying."[26] Perhaps the finest accolade paid him was that "Colonel Devin knew how to take his men into action and also how to bring them out."[27] At forty-one, Devin was older than the other cavalry commanders, and he was long overdue for promotion. Buford's death cost Devin his strongest advocate, and his lack of professional military training also probably held him back.

Devin's veteran brigade consisted of his own Sixth New York Cavalry, the Fourth New York Cavalry, the Ninth New York Cavalry, and the Seventeenth Pennsylvania Cavalry, all veteran commands. Only the Fourth New York Cavalry had a bad reputation, having lost its regimental colors for failing to meet expectations in battle.

The Third, or Reserve or Regular Brigade, consisted of the First, Second, and Fifth U.S. Cavalry, the Sixth Pennsylvania Cavalry, and the Nineteenth New York Cavalry, also known as the First New York Dragoons. This brigade originally had only Regular Army cavalry regiments assigned to the Army of the Potomac; the Sixth Pennsylvania Cavalry joined the brigade in the spring of 1863, and the First New York Dragoons joined that fall. Many Regulars had accepted commissions in volunteer regiments. They had not been used well in the early phases of the war, and their ranks were thin. One regiment, the Sixth U.S. Cavalry, became so depleted during the Gettysburg Campaign that it ceased to be an effective fighting unit and served as the Cavalry Corps's headquarters escort for the balance of the war. In the spring of 1863, Buford was assigned to command the Reserve Brigade. He had reorganized and trained them, casting them in his own mold—steady, competent, and reliable. One Regular described the brigade as the Army of the Potomac's "Old Guard."[28]

Thirty-year-old Wesley Merritt commanded the Regulars. Merritt was every bit Buford's protégé. The talented, modest professional soldier was a member of the West Point class of 1860.[29] He rose through the ranks quickly and was promoted from captain to brigadier general on June 29, 1863. After Buford's death, Merritt commanded the First Division until Torbert's assignment, then returned to command of the Reserve Brigade. Bigger and better things awaited this fine young officer—he was to have a forty-three-year career in the Regular Army, retiring as major general after triumphantly accepting the surrender of Manila in the Spanish-American War. A staff officer recorded that he "had a constitution of iron, and underneath a rather passive demeanor concealed a fiery ambition. He was and is, I am glad to say, a successful and very able soldier, and well deserves the high rank he now holds in the regular army of the United States."[30]

Capt. Theophilus F. Rodenbough, who served under Merritt's command in the Second U.S. Cavalry, thought Merritt was "the embodiment of force." Rodenbough considered him "one of those rare men whose faculties are sharpened and whose view is cleared on the battlefield. His decisions were delivered with the rapidity of thought and were as clear as if they had been studied for weeks. He always said that he never found that his first judgment gained by time and reflection. In him a fiery soul was held in thrall to will. Never disturbed by doubt, or moved by fear, neither circumspect nor rash, he never missed an opportunity or made a mistake."[31] One of Custer's officers noted, "Modesty which fitted him like a garment, charming manners, the demeanor of a gentleman, cool but fearless bearing in action, were his distinguishing characteristics."[32]

Brig. Gen. David M. Gregg, another professional soldier, commanded the Second Division. Gregg and Torbert were West Point classmates, and the modest Pennsylvanian was a cousin of Andrew Gregg Curtin, the wartime governor of the Keystone State. When war broke out, Gregg was a first lieutenant in the First Dragoons. He was transferred to the newly formed Sixth U.S. Cavalry in the fall of 1861. On January 24, 1862, he became colonel of the Eighth Pennsylvania Cavalry, and then was named brigadier general of volunteers on November 29, 1862. By the spring of 1864, at age thirty-one, Gregg had already commanded a division for more than a year. "He was the only division commander I had whose experience had been almost exclusively derived from the cavalry arm," Sheridan noted.[33]

Gregg was remembered fondly as "tall and spare, of notable activity, capable of the greatest exertion and exposure; gentle in manner but bold and resolute in action. Firm and just in discipline he was a favorite of his troopers and ever held, for he deserved, their affection and entire confidence." Gregg knew the principles of war and was always ready and eager to apply them. Endowed "with a natural genius of high order, he [was] universally hailed as the finest type of cavalry leader. A man of unimpeachable personal character, in private life affable and genial but not demonstrative, he fulfilled with modesty and honor all the duties of the citizen and head of an interesting and devoted family."[34] Calm, quiet, modest, and highly competent, Gregg's forethought and good execution led to a spectacular Federal victory over the vaunted Confederate cavalry at Gettysburg on July 3, 1863. A former officer later commented that Gregg's "modesty kept him from the notoriety that many gained through the newspapers; but in the army the testimony of all officers who knew him was the same. Brave, prudent, dashing when occasion required dash, and firm as a rock, he was looked upon, both as a regimental commander and afterwards as Major-General, as a man in whose hands any troops were safe."[35]

Gregg's division consisted of two brigades. The First Brigade, consisting of the First Massachusetts Cavalry, the First New Jersey Cavalry, the Sixth Ohio Cavalry, and First Pennsylvania Cavalry, was a veteran unit commanded by Davies. A twenty-eight-year-old lawyer from New York City, Davies had served with the Fifth New York Infantry. He was later appointed major of the Second New York Cavalry, in which he served under Kilpatrick's command. Davies advanced quickly through the ranks of lieutenant colonel and colonel, and was promoted to brigadier general in the fall of 1863. Rodenbough described Davies as "polished, genial and gallant."[36] Newhall remembered him as "earnest and dashing, always getting horses killed and balls through his boots; a strict disciplinarian and efficient in camp and field."[37] Davies was eventually promoted to major general of volunteers and rendered outstanding service in the closing days of the war.

Gregg's Second Brigade was commanded by his first cousin, Col. John Irvin Gregg. The thirty-seven-year-old Gregg was not a soldier by trade. When war broke out with Mexico in 1846, J. I. Gregg enlisted in a Pennsylvania volunteer infantry regiment. He quickly became an officer. After honorable service in the Mexican War, Gregg returned to Pennsylvania, where he owned an iron foundry. When the Civil War began, he joined his cousin in the newly formed Third U.S. Cavalry, where he was commissioned a captain. The Third U.S. Cavalry was redesignated as the Sixth U.S. Cavalry in the fall of 1861. In November 1862 he was appointed colonel of the Sixteenth Pennsylvania Cavalry and served with distinction. He assumed command of a brigade under his cousin's direction. By the spring of 1864, he had commanded a brigade for nearly a year and had done well in combat, earning a reputation for being "steadfast" and "cool as a clock, looking out from under his broad slouch-hat on any phase of battle."[38] His veteran brigade consisted of the First Maine Cavalry, Tenth New York Cavalry, Second Pennsylvania Cavalry, Fourth Pennsylvania Cavalry, Eighth Pennsylvania Cavalry, Thirteenth Pennsylvania Cavalry, and his own Sixteenth Pennsylvania Cavalry.

Thus Sheridan inherited a command that had been forged in battle that was led mostly by competent veteran officers who had proven their mettle during 1863's long months of hard-fought campaigning. The Army of the Potomac's Cavalry Corps had refuted the old cliché, "Whoever saw a dead cavalryman?" The Yankee troopers were reasonably well mounted and superbly equipped. Many of them carried seven-shot, breechloading Spencer carbines. One Regular officer noted of the Spencers: "The workmanship of this gun was indifferent, but it did, notwithstanding, excellent service and gave an immense advantage to the troops armed with it. [They] could throw in a tremendous fire when necessary, with great effect upon the enemy, who was naturally very often deceived in his estimate of the force opposed to him, judging by the unintermitting, incessant rattle along the line that he was contending with at least a division" when only a brigade was involved.[39] A South Carolinian, Edward Laight Wells of Charleston, later observed that troops armed with Spencers "ought to have been equal to at least double their number carrying only muzzle-loaders."[40] Another Rebel trooper, less elegant in his presentation, described the Spencers, "You'ns load in the morning and fire all day."[41] Compared with the single-shot muzzle-loaders carried by most gray-clad horse soldiers, Yankee troopers had a significant advantage in firepower.

Unlike their Southern counterparts, the Federals also had plenty of supplies, including remounts. Excessive winter picketing, combined with the tribulations of the Kilpatrick/Dahlgren Raid, took a severe toll on the Cavalry Corps's mounts. Sheridan quickly noticed the state of the horses in the spring of 1864. Just after the conclusion of the Gettysburg Campaign, the Army had created a Cavalry Bureau, which provided plenty of mounts for the burgeoning ranks of the Federal horse soldiers. While not a perfect institution by any means, the Cavalry Bureau successfully supplied ample fresh horseflesh to the federal mounted arm.

Their gray-clad counterparts faced different problems. If a trooper lost his mount, he either had to arrange for a replacement or join the dreaded ranks of "Company Q," dismounted cavalrymen assigned to either intermediate duties or subject to transfer to the infantry, a horrible fate for a Southern cavalier.[42] Vicissitudes of hard service in the field had likewise taken their toll on the Confederate horses. As a result, the effective strength of Lee's cavalry was much reduced by the inability to obtain adequate replacements for the growing ranks of the dismounted.

For more than two years, the Confederate cavalry chieftain, Maj. Gen. James Ewell Brown "Jeb" Stuart, and his gray-clad cavaliers rode rings around their Yankee counterparts. However, by the summer of 1863, the Yankee cavalry had grown into a formidable adversary. Stuart began suffering defeats at the hands of an enemy he had been able to laugh off only months earlier.

Northern tactics and leadership had caught up to Stuart's command, and Northern technology had given the Yankee troopers an edge in firepower and logistics. Further, much of Stuart's command was understrength. His command was widely scattered during the winter of 1863–64 and did not reunite until the Overland Campaign was nearly over. As a result, Maj. Gen. W. H. F. "Rooney" Lee's division had only one brigade until early June 1864. Although reinforcements were forthcoming from the Deep South, the spring of 1864 would cost Stuart dearly.

Heavy casualties in the Army of Northern Virginia's officer corps forced a reorganization in the fall of 1863. The new command structure had two divisions under Maj. Gens. Fitzhugh Lee and Wade Hampton. In March 1864, Rooney Lee, who had been captured while recuperating from a combat wound in June 1863, was exchanged and returned to the Army of Northern Virginia. Lee was then promoted to major general. A third division of cavalry was formed to provide him with a command by taking a brigade from each of the other two divisions.

Fitz Lee was Robert E. Lee's nephew. In 1864 he was twenty-nine years old. He graduated from West Point in 1856. The young Fitz Lee served in the Regular Army's mounted arm before the war. He suffered a serious wound in a fight with Comanche Indians, taking an arrow through the lung. When the Civil War broke out, Lee resigned his commission and accepted one in the Confederate army. By July 1862 he was a brigadier general, and was made a major general on August 3, 1863. Articulate and witty, he was Stuart's favorite subordinate. While Lee was a competent tactical commander, his performance to date consisted of flashes of brilliance punctuating sometimes lackluster and disappointing miscues. He probably achieved high rank because of his family connections.[43]

Lee's division consisted of Brig. Gens. Williams C. Wickham's and Lunsford L. Lomax's veteran brigades. Wickham, an influential Virginia lawyer, planter, and politician, was forty-four years old. Brave in battle, Wickham had suffered a severe wound at the Battle of Williamsburg in 1862. He continuously commanded a brigade of cavalry under Fitz Lee until he resigned his commission to take a seat in the Confederate States of America Congress in November 1864. Wickham was fortunate to have serving under him a very competent senior colonel, Thomas T. Munford of the Second Virginia Cavalry. Munford, a thirty-three-year-old graduate of the Virginia Military Institute, was long overdue for promotion to general. One biographer noted that Munford's "career as a cavalry officer was brilliant and notable," despite his failure to achieve the high rank that he deserved.[44] Wickham's veteran brigade contained some of the finest mounted units in either army: Stuart's and Fitz Lee's old command, the First Virginia Cavalry, Munford's Second Virginia Cavalry, the Third Virginia Cavalry, and the Fourth Virginia Cavalry, all hard-fighting, veteran units.[45]

Lomax, another member of an old-line Virginia family, commanded Lee's other brigade. The twenty-nine-year-old Lomax was a West Point classmate of Fitz Lee's and had served on the frontier in the Regular Army. Lomax resigned his commission in the spring of 1861 and was commissioned a captain in the Confederate service. In the spring of 1863, after staff assignments in both theaters of the war, Lomax was appointed colonel of the Eleventh Virginia Cavalry. He served competently in the Gettysburg Campaign. In August 1863 he was promoted to brigadier general and assigned to brigade command. Capable and steady, Lomax commanded the Fifth, Sixth, and Fifteenth Virginia Cavalry. Col. Bradley T. Johnson's First Maryland Cavalry Battalion and the Baltimore Light Artillery battery, which were part of the Maryland Line, and which operated as an independent command, were attached to Lomax's brigade. These veteran units had seen much hard fighting and hard marching throughout the war.

The Second Division commander, Wade Hampton, is one of the under-rated heroes of the American Civil War. "Hampton I think is superior to Stuart in prudence, good judgment and in military affairs," Col. Richard

H. Dulany of the Seventh Virginia Cavalry recounted, "not the extreme dash and perseverance for which Genl. Stuart was remarkable."[46] The son and grandson of generals (also named Wade Hampton), Hampton had no formal military training. Perhaps the wealthiest man in the South, Hampton personally raised and equipped a combined arms unit known as the Hampton Legion when his native South Carolina seceded in the spring of 1861. Slightly wounded at First Bull Run in July 1861 and badly hurt at Fair Oaks on May 31, 1862, Hampton was brave and extremely competent. At age forty-six, he was older than Stuart. He was not part of the Virginia "in" crowd and was always treated as an outsider, although no one disputed either his courage or competence. Perhaps as a result of many years spent hunting bears, Hampton was utterly fearless, preferring to lead pell-mell charges himself.[47]

In July 1862 he was a brigadier general. While leading his brigade, he was badly wounded at Gettysburg on July 3, 1863. By the spring of 1864, Hampton had recuperated and resumed command of his large and veteran division. Big, handsome, and amiable, "his lack of . . . military training would prove an impediment at first, until practical experience in the field, developing the natural bent, had supplied its place."[48] One Northern officer suggested that while Hampton was an unschooled soldier who had probably never even read a book on tactics, he "knew how to maneuver the units of his command so as to occupy for offensive or defensive action the strongest points of the battlefield, and that is about all there is in tactics." To be considered a successful strategist, an officer needed a broader field for the employment of his military talents. Hampton "appeared possessed of almost an instinctive topographical talent. He could take in the strong strategic points in the field of his operations with an accuracy of judgment that was surprising to his comrades. . . . He would hunt his antagonist as he would hunt big game in the forest. The celerity and audacity of his movements against the front, sometimes on the flank, then again in the rear, kept his enemies in a constant state of uncertainty and anxiety as to where and when they might expect him." The Yankee officer concluded, "With his wonderful powers of physical endurance, his alert, vigilant mind, his matchless horsemanship, no obstacles seemed to baffle his audacity or thwart his purpose."[49]

Hampton's division had two veteran brigades. Brig. Gen. Pierce M. B.

Young, of the West Point class of 1861, normally commanded the First Brigade. When Young went to South Carolina to assist in moving the South Carolina cavalry brigade to Virginia, his senior colonel, Col. Gilbert J. Wright of the Cobb Legion Cavalry, commanded his brigade. After Brig. Gen. James B. Gordon was killed in May 1864, Young temporarily assumed command of Gordon's brigade of North Carolinians and was badly wounded at Ashland on June 1, 1864. Young's wound left Wright at the helm of the brigade, which contained the Cobb Georgia Legion, the Phillips Legion of Georgia, and the Jeff Davis Legion of Mississippi, all veteran units. In addition, the Seventh Georgia Cavalry and the Twentieth Georgia Cavalry (Partisan Rangers Battalion), large regiments sent north from the defenses of Charleston, South Carolina, were assigned to this brigade on June 7, 1864.

"Gid" Wright, a tall thirty-nine-year-old Georgian, was a paradox—a practicing attorney, he had killed a close friend in a drunken brawl before the Civil War. This wounded combat veteran of the Mexican War served as judge and mayor of Albany, Georgia. His "unique personality . . . vigorous intellect and . . . untiring energy made a remarkable impression upon all with whom he came into contact."[50] While not a professional soldier, Wright possessed a "bulldog courage" and "stentorian voice" that were conspicuous in battle, and "he was seriously wounded several times, but before his wounds ever healed he would be again on the field of battle."[51] He rose through the ranks of the Cobb Legion from lieutenant to colonel, commanding the regiment.[52]

Brig. Gen. Thomas L. Rosser, a big twenty-eight-year-old Texan who was a special favorite of Stuart's, commanded the other veteran brigade.[53] Rosser was a member of West Point's class of 1861, but resigned two weeks before graduation to accept a commission in the Confederate artillery. After serving as an artillery battery commander, Rosser was promoted to colonel of the Fifth Virginia Cavalry in 1862. He was wounded in action at Mechanicsville during the Seven Days Battles in June 1862, and again at the Battle of Kelly's Ford on March 17, 1863. Despite the wounds, Rosser led his regiment with great success until his promotion to brigadier general in September 1863. When Rosser was passed over for promotion in the summer of 1863, he turned on Stuart, believing that Stuart had deceived him. Although Stuart probably never knew the depth of Rosser's loathing, the two men were never close again.[54]

Rosser was a close friend of Custer's. The two men had a healthy and friendly rivalry that became especially significant in 1864. "Tall, broad-shouldered and muscular, with black hair and mustache, dark brown eyes, strong jaw, and a countenance denoting self-confidence, a good horseman and always superbly mounted, the men of the brigade recognized in their new commander the typical soldier."[55] Rosser also was apparently prone to periodic drinking binges that earned him notoriety in the army.[56]

In the winter of 1863–64, after Rosser took command of his brigade, he dubbed it "The Laurel Brigade." Perhaps the finest cavalry brigade in Confederate service, the Laurel Brigade consisted of hard-fighting and hard-riding veterans accustomed to the trials and tribulations of cavalry service. The Laurel Brigade consisted of the Seventh, Eleventh, and Twelfth regiments of Virginia Cavalry and the Thirty-fifth Battalion of Virginia Cavalry and had borne the brunt of the mounted and dismounted combat of 1863's campaigns. Raised by the legendary Brig. Gen. Turner Ashby, and trained by the now-departed Brig. Gen. William E. "Grumble" Jones, these troopers had won nearly every engagement they pitched into.

In April 1864 Hampton proudly claimed of his division, "They have done their duty in the fullest sense, and deserved the praise of their country. I have seen [them] sleeping upon the frozen ground without tents, shoes, overshoes or blankets, only waiting for the morning's light to attack the enemy, whose fires lighted our own bivouac, and yet I have never heard a murmur" of complaint or protest.[57] These tough, veteran troopers had proven their mettle on every field and were the flower of the Army of Northern Virginia's vaunted Cavalry Corps.

The Third Division, commanded by Robert E. Lee's middle son, Rooney Lee, was also a new command. This division remained with the body of Lee's army as the federal cavalry set off on its grand excursion on June 7, missing the great battle of Trevilian Station. Elements of this division joined the pursuit of Sheridan after the battle, although Rooney Lee did not participate.

Unlike their Northern counterparts, the Southern horsemen were not well equipped. Since they rode their own horses in battle, their mounts were in various states of health. There was no uniformity in accoutrements, and many Confederates used captured saddles, bridles, and halters. Hampton's men carried a hodgepodge of weapons, including pistols and some captured single-shot breech-loading carbines. Only Rosser's Laurels had a significant number of repeating weapons, all of which had been captured or scavenged from Union horsemen.[58]

Once the reorganization of the Cavalry Corps was completed, Sheridan assessed the status of the Federal cavalry. Appalled by the state of his command and by the wretched condition of its mounts, Sheridan faulted excessive picketing during the winter months that took a severe toll on man and beast. Consequently, the Cavalry Corps's horses "were thin and very much worn out by excessive, and, it seemed to me, unnecessary picket duty." Sheridan continued, "However, shortly after my taking command, much of the picketing was done away with, and we had two weeks of leisure time to nurse the horses, on which so much depended."[59] As the horses rested, Sheridan developed a new approach for his troopers.

In his memoirs, Sheridan alleged that he faced resistance from Meade. According to Sheridan, he laid out his "idea as to what the cavalry should do, the main purport of which was that it ought to be concentrated to fight the enemy's cavalry. Heretofore, the commander of the Cavalry Corps had been, virtually, but an adjunct at army headquarters—a sort of chief of cavalry—and my proposition seemed to stagger General Meade not a little." Little Phil continued, "I knew that it would be difficult to overcome the recognized custom of using the cavalry for the protection of trains and the establishment of cordons around the infantry corps, and so far as subordinating its operations to the main movements of the main army that in name was it a corps at all, but I still thought it my duty to try."[60]

In fact, Meade opposed Sheridan at every juncture. When the Army of the Potomac set out for its spring campaign in the first days of May 1864, it had one of the largest and most powerful fighting cavalry commands the world had ever seen. With a well-equipped, well-led, and well-mounted force of more than 10,000 horsemen, Sheridan champed at the bit to pitch into the Confederate cavalry.

The Army of the Potomac moved out of its winter camps before midnight on May 3. The two armies clashed in the dense thickets of the Wilderness for two days on May 5–6, inflicting massive casualties on each other. Instead of pulling back as his predecessors in the East had done, Grant moved around Lee's flank, hoping to interpose between Lee and Richmond. The move triggered a race for the critical crossroads town of Spotsylvania Court

House. In the vanguard of the Northern advance, Sheridan's horsemen fought and scouted, and lost crucial engagements along the Plank Road on May 5 and at Todd's Tavern on May 7. As a result, the shortest route from the Wilderness to Spotsylvania remained in Confederate hands.[61] Meade and Sheridan both issued orders to Gregg, confusing the division commander and infuriating the mercurial Sheridan. Sheridan's failure to act promptly after receiving orders for May 8 prevented the road to Spotsylvania Court House from being cleared.[62] When Meade failed to beat Lee to the important crossroads town of Spotsylvania Court House, the two armies fell into a brutal and bloody stalemate, slugging it out there for nearly two weeks.

Annoyed by the cavalry's failure, Meade summoned Sheridan to his headquarters. Sheridan, in turn, was furious that Meade had issued direct orders to one of his subordinates outside the chain of command. There, "a very acrimonious dispute took place between the two generals." Meade told Sheridan in no uncertain terms that he was unhappy with the performance of his cavalry, and an extended argument took place.[63] Sheridan later recounted telling Meade that he "had broken up my combinations, exposed Wilson's division and kept Gregg unnecessarily idle, and . . . such disjointed operations as he had been requiring of the cavalry . . . would render the corps inefficient and useless."

According to Little Phil, the discussion took on a loud and ominous tone, "One word brought on another until, finally I told him that I could whip Stuart if he (Meade) would only let me, but since he insisted on giving the cavalry directions without consulting or even notifying me, he could thenceforth command the Cavalry Corps himself—that I would not give it another order."[64] In a towering rage, Sheridan stomped out of the meeting. Meade, perhaps wanting to relieve the little Irishman of command for insubordination, went directly to Grant's nearby tent and recounted what had occurred to the commanding general. When Grant heard Sheridan's remarks about whipping Stuart, he responded, "Did Sheridan say that? Well, he generally knows what he is talking about. Let him start right out and do it."[65]

With his entire corps in tow, Sheridan set out to whip Jeb Stuart and his vaunted cavalry on May 9. When word of Sheridan's departure reached Stuart, he rallied part of his command for a forced march and intercepted Sheridan's line of advance at a place called Yellow Tavern. During a day of intense fighting on May 11, Stuart was mortally wounded. The plumed cavalier died in Richmond the next day while the Army of Northern Virginia fought at the Bloody Angle at the Battle of Spotsylvania Court House. Stuart's death created problems within the command hierarchy of the Army of Northern Virginia's cavalry that had far-reaching implications. It also meant that Robert E. Lee was left without his good right arm—he reportedly wept upon hearing the news of his cavalry chieftain's death, lamenting, "He never brought me a piece of false information."[66] William L. Wilson of the Twelfth Virginia Cavalry of the Laurel Brigade rued the dashing cavalier's passing, "The Cavalry corps has lost its great leader the unequalled Stuart. We miss him much. Hampton is a good officer but Stuart's equal does not exist."[67]

As a result of Stuart's death, Lee faced a difficult situation. There was a smoldering rivalry and even dislike building between his nephew Fitz and Hampton. One of Fitz Lee's troopers staked his hero's claim: "The mantle of Stuart finally came to Fitzhugh Lee," he asserted. "This was but natural. Stuart and Fitz Lee had fought side by side, and planned cavalry campaigns together, and Fitz was Stuart's trusted officer to carry out the boldest maneuvers. The cavalry of the Army of Northern Virginia wanted no other leader than Fitz Lee after Stuart's death."[68]

However, Hampton was senior in rank to Fitz Lee, which presented problems. "Hampton's seniority in rank was based upon his commission as brigadier two months ahead of Fitz, and the listing of his name immediately above Fitz's in the recommendations for promotion to major-general," Hampton's biographer commented. "This was a margin so narrow as perhaps to seem no margin at all to Fitz and his friends."[69] There was also bad blood between Hampton and Wickham. Hampton blamed Wickham for the death of his brother, Lt. Col. Frank Hampton, at Brandy Station in June 1863.[70] Because of this conflict and tension, General Lee elected not to appoint a new corps commander, and instead maintained the three divisions as independent commands, each division commander reporting directly to him.[71] While this was probably a good move politically, it created its own problems, as there was no clear chain of command in the field. These problems were exacerbated when Fitz Lee chose to act on his own, a tendency that became painfully evident during June 1864.

While the Army of Northern Virginia grimly hung on at Spotsylvania, the Confederates drove Sheridan away from Richmond, diverting his column onto the Peninsula. Though Sheridan won the fight at Yellow Tavern, his raid failed to achieve its objectives. In the process of conducting the raid, Sheridan earned a reputation as a "vicious" cavalry leader with the Confederates.[72] Since he did not rejoin the main body of the Army of the Potomac until May 25, Meade had only one small brigade of his cavalry force available for more than two weeks. The absence of the Army of the Potomac's Cavalry Corps may have cost Grant a prime opportunity to win the war at the North Anna, for he was left to grope blindly for his adversary.

The unusually hot spring of 1864 took a further toll on Sheridan's horses during the lengthy May raid. Additional refitting was required before another major raid could be attempted. Despite a leisurely pace of march, poor worn out beasts dropped by the score. Rather than allowing broken-down horses to fall into Confederate hands, where they could be nursed back to health and put back into service, the Richmond raid marked a new and harsher turn to the war. As horses broke down by the side of the road, they were shot by the Yankee troopers, who then trudged off, saddles and equipment slung over their shoulders.[73] Despite these losses and the fearful toll taken on the horses by the long and grueling raid, the Cavalry Bureau still provided sufficient remounts and reinforcements to keep a large and effective force in the field. With no similar mechanism for providing remounts, Robert E. Lee's mounted arm was worn down by attrition. More and more men joined the swelling ranks of Company Q.

As the Richmond raid wound down, the Confederate cavalry received reinforcements in the form of a brigade of South Carolinians sent north from the defenses of Charleston, largely at the behest of Hampton, who wanted to bring this large force to bear in the fighting in Virginia. Brig. Gen. Matthew Calbraith Butler, a twenty-seven-year-old lawyer with no formal military training, commanded this brigade. Butler, however, had a fine military pedigree; he was a nephew of War of 1812 naval hero Commodore Oliver Hazard Perry, and his father was a naval surgeon. Married to the daughter of South Carolina governor F. W. Pickens, Butler's future in the Palmetto State's politics seemed bright. At the height of his fame, in battle, he led his men with only a silver mounted riding whip in his hand.[74]

A protégé of fellow South Carolinian, Hampton, Butler, then a colonel, was horribly wounded at the Battle of Brandy Station on June 9, 1863, when a solid artillery shot carried away his right foot. One of his troopers said of Butler, "It used to be said his skin glanced bullets, and that it required a twelve-pounder to carry away" the foot lost at Brandy Station.[75] J. Russell Wright of the Sixth South Carolina Cavalry noted that Butler showed "no emotion as he scanned the field" of battle, calmly taking in the situation and carefully planning a response.[76] One historian remarked of Butler, "so fine was his courage, so unshaken his nerve, that, if he realized danger, he scorned it and his chiseled face never so handsome as when cold-set for battle, never showed if or not his soul was in tumult." He was the sort of leader who sat his horse quietly while shot and shell stormed around him and other men ran for shelter.[77]

Returning to duty in September of that year, he was promoted to brigadier general and was assigned to command a brigade consisting of the Fourth, Fifth, and Sixth South Carolina Cavalry. These three regiments were formerly assigned to coastal defense duty, performing well in that capacity. This brigade, which had not seen any large-scale cavalry-on-cavalry combat before Haw's Shop, numbered nearly 1,300 men. It was the largest cavalry brigade assigned to the Army of Northern Virginia.[78] Armed with muzzle-loading Enfield rifles, these men were more like mounted infantry than cavalry.[79] They would not join the Army of Northern Virginia until the end of May 1864, but they would immediately make their presence felt.[80]

On May 28 Sheridan faced Hampton's gray-clad cavalry force at the bloody battle of Haw's Shop. It was a long and brutal day of fighting primarily involving David Gregg's veterans, and it was remembered by some veterans as the most severe cavalry fighting of the war. Butler's newly arrived men carried the burden of the fighting for the Confederate victory. The aftermath of the battled effectively removed three brigades of Sheridan's Cavalry Corps from the war for two days while they rested and refitted. Maj. Gen. Gouverneur K. Warren's Fifth Corps successfully crossed the Totopotomoy Creek on May 29, but a want of cavalry support cost Meade the opportunity to crush Lee's vulnerable right flank the next day. Nevertheless, a few days after Haw's Shop, a Federal staff officer noted, "Our cavalry is full of confidence and does wonders."[81] The new confidence, bordering on arrogance, was Phil Sheridan's major contribution to the Army of the Potomac's Cavalry Corps.

As part of his grand strategy, Grant had sent an army under the command of Maj. Gen. Franz Sigel up the Shenandoah Valley, with the intent of depriving Lee of his primary source of rations and provender. When a scratch Confederate forced defeated Sigel at New Market on May 15, Grant replaced him with Maj. Gen. David "Black Dave" Hunter, a man derisively described by Confederate cavalry general John D. Imboden as "a human hyena".[82] Hunter consolidated his command, and then advanced up the Valley toward Staunton, intending to destroy the vital railroad depot there. Once he had completed his mission at Staunton, he would then advance on Charlottesville.[83]

By May 19 the bulk of the brutal fighting at Spotsylvania was over. That day Grant ordered Meade to move his entire army to the banks of the North Anna River. On May 21 the Army of the Potomac attempted to cross the North Anna but was thwarted by a stout Confederate defense. Rebuffed, Grant instead withdrew, a move that led to the fight at Haw's Shop. Then, on the 30th, the Army of the Potomac advanced to a strategic crossroads on the Peninsula called Cold Harbor, where the two armies entrenched and fought a bloody battle. On June 3 Meade ordered a massive assault that failed miserably, costing his army heavy casualties in only a matter of minutes in exchange for only light Confederate losses.[84] Years later, Grant candidly admitted: "I have always regretted that the last frontal assault at Cold Harbor was ever made . . . no advantage whatever was gained to compensate for the heavy loss we sustained. Indeed, the advantages other than those of relative losses, were on the Confederate side."[85]

Finally realizing that the terrain around Richmond left little room for maneuver, and aware that the rebel works at Cold Harbor were too strong to be broken, Grant revised his strategy entirely. He decided to cross the James River and advance on the crucial railroad junction town of Petersburg, twenty-five miles south of Richmond. Petersburg had great strategic significance as the junction of the major southern railroads supplying the Confederate capital. If Grant could capture Petersburg and Hunter Lynchburg, Lee's army would be entirely cut off from its lines of supply and would have to come out and fight, surrender, or attempt to flee. Grant believed that the move south of the James had to be hidden from Robert E. Lee's active and vigilant cavalry. With Federal armies on both sides of the James River, Grant knew that the safety of the Confederate capital would be "a matter of the first consideration with executive, legislative and judicial branches of the so-called Confederate government, if it was not with the military commanders. But I took all the precaution I knew of to guard against all dangers."[86]

While commanding in the West, Grant had learned and exploited the importance of the strategic cavalry raid as an effective means of distracting the enemy's attention from his movements. To screen his crossing of the Mississippi below the bluffs at Vicksburg, Grant had ordered Col. Benjamin Grierson to lead a daring cavalry raid deep into the heart of Mississippi, with the assigned task of destroying railroad lines and telegraph wires and creating havoc in the enemy's rear. Spectacularly successful, Grierson drew away much of the enemy's attention and badly distracted Rebel Lt. Gen. John C. Pemberton, commander of Vicksburg's defenses. This diversion permitted Grant to make a nearly uncontested crossing of the river, prompting William T. Sherman to proclaim the exploit "the most brilliant expedition of the war."[87] Sheridan's May Richmond raid diverted enemy attention and drew off a large portion of Lee's cavalry, thereby clearing the way for Meade's advance toward Spotsylvania.

Having used this tactic so successfully in the past, Grant decided to try it again. On June 6 Hunter defeated a small Confederate army commanded by Brig. Gen. William E. "Grumble" Jones at Piedmont. Jones was killed in the fighting, and his force withdrew. After hearing of Hunter's victory at Piedmont, Grant ordered Sheridan to lead another audacious strategic raid designed to distract the enemy. Sheridan was to take Torbert's and Gregg's divisions, march along the course of the North Anna River, and fall upon the important rail junction at Charlottesville. The horsemen would then join Hunter's advancing army near Charlottesville. The combined force would march east to join the main body of the Army of the Potomac, which Grant hoped would be safely across the James River and moving on Petersburg.[88] Grant ordered the destruction of the railroad at Charlottesville, Lynchburg, and Gordonsville as the raid's primary mission. On the return trip, Sheridan was to remain on the course of the railroads until "every rail on the road destroyed should be so bent and twisted as to make it impossible to repair the road without supplying new rails," until "driven off by a superior force."[89]

After receiving written orders from Meade, Sheridan spoke with Grant about the raid. He recalled that Grant instructed Hunter to advance as far as Charlottesville, and that Grant expected Sheridan to unite with Hunter there. After joining forces, the two commands were to destroy the James River Canal and the Virginia Central Railroad, and then link up with the Army of the Potomac. Accordingly, Sheridan recounted, "in view of what was anticipated, it would be well to break up the railroad as possible on my way westward."[90]

When he penned his report of the 1864 campaigns after the war, Sheridan commented, "There also appeared to be another object, viz, to remove the enemy's cavalry from the south side of the Chickahominy, as, in case we attempted to cross to the James River, this large cavalry force could make such resistance at the difficult crossings as to give the enemy time to transfer his force to oppose the movement."[91] While this statement appears to be the product of hindsight, it nevertheless raises a valid point; drawing off the attention of the Confederate cavalry is wholly consistent with Grant's vision for his strategic cavalry raid. Wilson's division would remain with the main body of the army so that some cavalry could screen the move across the James. Further, Sheridan directed all of his dismounted men, a significant contingent of his command, to report to Wilson.

Hunter was directed that the destruction of both the railroad and the canal were of the highest importance to the Federal high command. Hunter was to advance to Lynchburg and then turn east, with the hope that he would take Lynchburg in a single day. Grant's order suggested that Lynchburg had "so much importance to the enemy, that in attempting to get it such resistance may be met as to defeat your getting onto the road or canal at all." If Hunter did not receive his instructions until his army was already in the valley between Staunton and Lynchburg, he was to turn east by the most practicable road until he struck the Lynchburg branch of the Virginia Central Railroad. Having done that, Hunter was to move eastward along the line of the railroad, destroying it completely and thoroughly, until his command joined Sheridan's. The orders concluded, "After the work laid out for General Sheridan and yourself is thoroughly done, proceed to join the Army of the Potomac by the route laid out in General Sheridan's instructions."[92]

Sheridan's force was not at full strength. The hard service of the May raid on Richmond and the heavy combat at Haw's Shop cost his command many of its horses, meaning that the number of dismounted men was large.

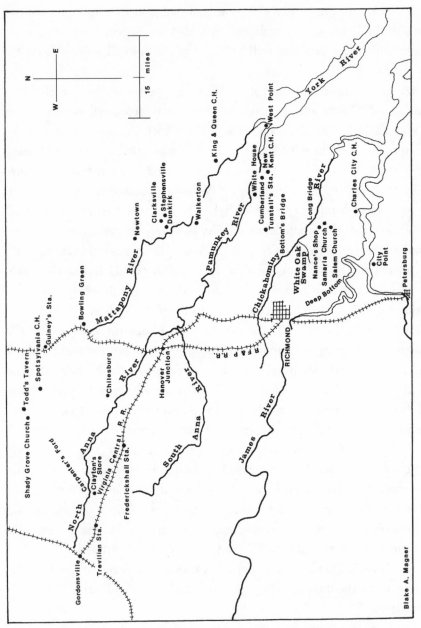

Theater of Operations for Sheridan's Second Raid

Blake A. Magner

It also meant that his command's strength had been much reduced by men killed or wounded during the same period. He claimed, "The effective mounted force of my two divisions was therefore much diminished, they mustering only about six thousand officers and men when concentrated on June 6 at New Castle Ferry."[93]

The precise size of Sheridan's command has been the subject of disagreement. A recent treatment of the battle estimated the size of Sheridan's force at 10,200 cavalrymen present for duty based on the number of mounts reported by the two brigades of the Army of the Potomac's Cavalry Corps.[94] Confederate General Butler believed that Sheridan had 10,337 effectives available.[95] Using the regimental returns for June 1864, it appears that Sheridan's force consisted of approximately 9,300 men, and that Sheridan's own memory of the size of his force was flawed.[96] No matter the precise size of Sheridan's command, it significantly outnumbered the enemy force.

In addition, Sheridan brought along an entire brigade of horse artillery including Capt. Alanson M. Randol's First United States, Batteries H and I (combined), Lt. Edward Heaton's Second United States, Batteries B and L (combined), Lt. Edward B. Williston's Second United States, Battery D, and Capt. Alexander C. M. Pennington's Second United States, Battery M, totaling approximately 20 guns and 300 men.[97] These batteries typically consisted of two sections of two guns per battery, and were equipped with excellent three-inch ordnance rifles, a lightweight but very effective weapon, or twelve-pound Napoleon smoothbores. Further, experienced Regular Army officers commanded these batteries, all of which had been repeatedly tested in battle by the spring of 1864.

After studying the lay of the land, Sheridan decided to pursue a course along the north bank of the North Anna River, marching westward nearly sixty miles from Richmond. He would cross the river at Carpenter's Ford, striking the Virginia Central at an obscure stop located at Trevilian Station, six miles west of Louisa Court House, in Louisa County, approximately six miles east of Gordonsville. He intended to destroy the railroad between Trevilian Station and Louisa and then bypass Gordonsville, striking the railroad again at Cobham's Station and destroying it from there to Charlottesville, where he would link up with Hunter's advancing army. The march west would cover nearly 100 miles.[98]

Sheridan wanted to travel light. He ordered his command to carry only three days' rations, intended to last five days, and two days' grain for his horses, along with only 100 rounds of ammunition, of which 40 would be carried by the soldiers in their cartridge boxes. Finally, he would take a pontoon train, only 1 medical wagon, 8 ambulances, and 1 wagon each for division and brigade headquarters, for a total of approximately 125 wagons.[99] The force was to march early on the morning of June 7.

Word of the impending raid spread quickly among the Federal horse soldiers. Regimental officers received orders to relieve themselves and their men of all unnecessary encumbrances, and all were warned not to expect to find themselves near any depot or other resting place for as many as twelve days.[100] Bugler Carlos McDonald of the Sixth Ohio Cavalry prophesied, "This means that we are to have some long marches away from our base of supplies, and in all probability some fighting."[101] The two divisions were concentrated at New Castle Ferry, the jumping-off point for the grand raid. A trooper of the First New York Dragoons of Merritt's brigade inscribed in his diary, "Marched this morning to Ruffins Farm near Hanovertown and drew rations and ammunition for a raid as we expect."[102] A few stray Confederate shells fell on the assembling Yankee troopers, annoying them but causing no harm.[103]

That day, Sheridan left Old Church Tavern and encamped at New Castle Ferry on the Pamunkey River. While riding toward New Castle Ferry, he was joined by soldiers of the Fiftieth New York Engineers, their bridge train in tow. The Pontoniers arrived at New Castle Ferry and laid the bridge across the river in preparation for the coming raid. Gregg's division came up from its position near Bottom's Bridge on the Chickahominy after being relieved by Wilson's men. Nathaniel Davidson, a correspondent of the *New York Herald*, traveling with Sheridan's command, noted, "Every one knew now that something was up—another raid probably—and nothing pleases a cavalryman so much as the idea of a raid, if it only be through a country where supplies may be obtained."[104] One Pennsylvanian wrote, "The principal duties which Gen. Sheridan's cavalry are called upon to perform are to make raids into the enemy's country, destroy communications, and harass and annoy the enemy as much as possible."[105] This attitude marked a dramatic change from the prior philosophic approach of the Federal Cavalry Corps.

On the night of June 6, Custer scribbled a hasty note to his new bride, writing: "Again I am called on to bid you adieu for a short period. To-morrow morning two Divisions, 1 and 2, of this Corps set out on another raid. We may be gone two or three weeks. I will write, the first opportunity.

Keep up a stout heart, and remember the successful issue of the past. God and success have hitherto attended us. May we not hope for a continuance of His blessing?"[106] A member of the Ninth New York Cavalry of Devin's brigade recalled, "Much reticence was observed by the officers since Grant had taken command and only division commanders were informed of contemplated movements before their execution. To the men and subordinate officers this move was an enigma."[107]

Lt. Noble D. Preston, commissary officer of the Tenth New York Cavalry, led a detail of men to the vast Federal supply base at White House Landing to obtain provisions on the morning of June 6. When Preston and his contingent arrived, some of the infantry officers garrisoned there informed Preston that a cavalry raid was in the offing. He did not take the news seriously, "So little credence did I give the rumor that I made no unusual haste to return, finally leaving White House a little before dark to rejoin the command near Bottom bridge." Struggling with the rugged terrain, Preston and his small command had a tough march after they learned from stragglers that the cavalry had indeed moved to a different spot. Wandering aimlessly, looking for the blue-clad horde gathering for the raid, Preston and his contingent grew increasingly tired as the night wore on, finally stopping to rest a bit in a shady grove. Rousing themselves, Preston and another trooper set out to find the rest of the corps. Finally spotting the bustling cavalry encampment on the banks of the Pamunkey at New Castle, Preston spurred ahead, finding that his own brigade had already crossed the river. There, "we now received verification of what our infantry friends had told us at White House, and which he had listened to with so much indifference because we felt that so important a matter would hardly be known to the entire army."[108]

Sgt. Samuel Cormany, one of J. I. Gregg's men, recorded in his diary for June 6, "I had a fine time today—got as much milk as I wanted to drink—and was kind of free and easy—at 11 p.m. we quartered for the night."[109] It would be the last free and easy day the Yankee troopers would enjoy for quite a while.

Notes

1. William S. McFeely, *Grant: A Biography* (New York: W. W. Norton & Co., 1982), 151.

2. Bruce Catton, *Grant Takes Command* (Boston: Little, Brown, 1968), 163.

3. Horace Porter, *Campaigning with Grant* (Bloomington: Indiana University Press, 1961), 46–47.

4. George R. Agassiz, ed., *Meade's Headquarters, 1863–1865: Letters of Col. Theodore Lyman from the Wilderness to Appomattox* (Boston: Atlantic Monthly Press, 1922), ix.

5. *The War of the Rebellion: A Compilation of the Official Records of the Union and Confederate Armies*, 128 volumes in 3 series (Washington, D.C.: U.S. Government Printing Office, 1880–1891), series 1, vol. 36, part 1, 12. (Further references will be to the "O.R." In addition, unless otherwise noted, all further references will be to Series 1 of the O.R.).

6. *Ibid.*, 14–18.

7. *Ibid.*, 15.

8. George Meade, ed., *The Life and Letters of General George Gordon Meade*, 2 vols. (New York: Charles Scribner's Sons, 1913), 2:185. There is some dispute over precisely who was responsible for Pleasonton's relief from corps command.

9. Henry E. Davies, *General Sheridan* (New York: D. Appleton & Co., 1895), 92–93.

10. Gregg may well have resented being passed over for corps command. When he realized that Sheridan was not competent to command the Cavalry Corps, his resentment may have boiled over. Gregg resigned his commission in the winter of 1865, just before the war's final campaign, and never fully explained his reasons. Exasperation with being passed over for command undoubtedly factored into that decision.

11. Ulysses S. Grant, *Personal Memoirs of U. S. Grant*, vol. 2 (New York: Charles L. Webster & Co., 1885), 133.

12. Alan Nevins, ed., *A Diary of Battle: The Personal Journals of Colonel Charles S. Wainwright, 1861–1865* (New York: Harcourt, Brace & World, 1962), 341.

13. Davies, *General Sheridan*, 93–95.

14. Roy Morris Jr., *Sheridan: The Life and Wars of General Phil Sheridan* (New York: Crown Publishers, Inc., 1992). For more on Sheridan's critical role in the Battle of Chattanooga, see Wiley Sword, *Mountains Touched with Fire* (New York: St. Martin's Press, 1995).

15. Porter, *Campaigning with Grant*, 23.

16. James H. Kidd, *Personal Recollections of a Cavalryman in Custer's Michigan Brigade* (Ionia, Mich.: Sentinel Printing Co., 1908), 298.

17. Morris, *Sheridan*, 1.

18. Kidd, *Personal Recollections*, 261.

19. E. R. Hagemann, ed. *Fighting Rebels and Redskins: Experiences in Army Life of Colonel George B. Sanford 1861–1892* (Norman: University of Oklahoma Press, 1969), 224.

20. George A. Custer to Elizabeth Bacon Custer, April 16, 1864, in *The Custer*

Story: The Life and Letters of General George A. Custer and his Wife Elizabeth, Marguerite Merrington, ed., (New York: Devin-Adair Co., 1950), 89.

21. William F. Kenfield, "Trevilian's Station," in *Personal and Historical Sketches and Facial History of and by Members of the Seventh Regiment Michigan Volunteer Cavalry, 1862–1865*, compil. William O. Lee (Detroit: Ralston Co., 1901), 239.

22. James H. Kidd to James M. Kidd, June 3, 1864, James H. Kidd Papers, Bentley Historical Library, University of Michigan, Ann Arbor.

23. Frederic C. Newhall, *With General Sheridan in Lee's Last Campaign* (Philadelphia: J. B. Lippincott, 1866), 228.

24. There are, of course, dozens of biographies of George A. Custer. There are so many, in fact, that it is hard to keep them straight. For those interested in a balanced but thorough treatment of Custer's life and career, the author recommends Jeffry D. Wert, *Custer: The Controversial Life of George Armstrong Custer* (New York: Simon & Schuster, 1996). For those interested in a detailed study of Custer's exploits in the Civil War, there is no better source than Gregory J. W. Urwin, *Custer Victorious: The Civil War Battles of George Armstrong Custer* (East Brunswick, N. J.: Associated University Presses, 1983).

25. Edward G. Longacre, *The Cavalry at Gettysburg: A Tactical Study of Mounted Operations during the Civil War's Pivotal Campaign, 9 June–14 July 1863* (Rutherford, N. J.: Fairleigh Dickinson University Press, 1986), 51.

26. Newhall, *With General Sheridan*, 228.

27. Ezra J. Warner, *Generals in Blue: The Lives of the Union Commanders* (Baton Rouge: Louisiana State University Press, 1964), 124. That long overdue promotion did not come until the winter of 1865, well after John Buford's death.

28. Theophilus F. Rodenbough, "Sheridan's Richmond Raid," in *Battles and Leaders of the Civil War*, vol. 4, eds. Robert U. Johnson and Clarence C. Buel (New York: Century, 1884–88), 188 (unless otherwise noted, the four-volume set of *Battles and Leaders* will hereinafter referred to as "B&L").

29. Kidd, *Personal Recollections*, 237. The only full-length biography of Merritt is Don E. Alberts, *Brandy Station to Manila Bay: A Biography of General Wesley Merritt* (Austin, Tex.: Presidial Press, 1980).

30. Hagemann, *Fighting Rebels and Redskins*, 225.

31. Theophilus F. Rodenbough, "Some Cavalry Leaders," in *The Photographic History of the Civil War*, vol. 10, ed. Francis Trevelyan Miller (New York: The Review of Reviews Co., 1911), 278.

32. Kidd, *Personal Recollections*, 238–239.

33. Philip H. Sheridan, *Personal Memoirs of P. H. Sheridan*, vol. 1 (New York: Charles L. Webster & Co., 1888), 352.

34. "David McMurtrie Gregg," Circular No. 6, Series of 1917, Military Order of the Loyal Legion of the United States, Commandery of Pennsylvania, May 3, 1917, 2.

35. Samuel P. Bates, *Martial Deeds of Pennsylvania* (Philadelphia: T. H. Davis & Co., 1875), 772. There is no satisfactory biography of David M. Gregg available. The only published biography is Milton V. Burgess, *David Gregg: Pennsylvania Cavalryman* (privately published, 1984).

36. Rodenbough, "Sheridan's Richmond Raid," 188.

37. Newhall, *With General Sheridan*, 229.

38. Rodenbough, "Sheridan's Richmond Raid," 188; Newhall, *With General Sheridan*, 229.

39. Louis Henry Carpenter, "Sheridan's Expedition Around Richmond May 9–25, 1864," *Journal of the United States Cavalry Association*, 1 (1888): 301.

40. Edward L. Wells, *Hampton and His Cavalry in '64* (Richmond, Va.: B. F. Johnson Publishing Co., 1899), 95.

41. Samuel Harris, *Personal Reminiscences of Samuel Harris* (Chicago: The Robinson Press, 1897), 31.

42. Samuel Carter, III, *The Last Cavaliers: Confederate and Union Cavalry in the Civil War* (New York: St. Martin's Press, 1979), 10. Stuart formally eliminated Company Q in the fall of 1863, but the hardships of service in the field led to more and more men being dismounted. Although Company Q no longer existed formally, it was still a factor to be considered, and a fate to be dreaded. The term "Company Q" is used throughout the manuscript to describe dismounted men of either army.

43. Ezra J. Warner, *Generals in Gray: The Lives of the Confederate Commanders* (Baton Rouge: Louisiana State University Press, 1959), 178. There is only one biography of Fitz Lee, and it is somewhat disappointing, choosing only to portray those positive aspects of Lee's life and career. For more, see, James L. Nichols, *General Fitzhugh Lee: A Biography* (Lynchburg, Va.: H. E. Howard Co., 1989).

44. Bennett H. Young, *Confederate Wizards of the Saddle* (Boston: Chapple Publishing Co., 1914), 510.

45. Both men were experienced commanders. Munford had commanded Fitz Lee's brigade at Brandy Station and the battle of Aldie, and Wickham commanded Fitz's division in the Shenandoah Valley in the fall of 1864, when Lee assumed command of all of the Army of the Valley's cavalry. Lee was then wounded at the Battle of Third Winchester on September 19, and missed much of the rest of the war. Wickham helped block Torbert's advance in the Luray Valley, thwarting Sheridan's chances for an even more decisive victory at Fisher's Hill.

46. Margaret Ann Vogtsberger, *The Dulanys of Welbourne: A Family in Mosby's Confederacy* (Lexington, Va.: Rockbridge Publishing, 1995), 219.

47. James G. Holmes, "The Fighting Qualities of Generals Hampton, Butler and Others Related by Adjutant-General Holmes of Charleston," *The Sunny South* (June 13, 1896).

48. Wells, *Hampton and His Cavalry*, 76. There is, unfortunately, no satisfying

modern biography of Hampton available. The only one is dated and lacks depth. However, it remains the only full-length treatment of Hampton's life and extensive military and political careers. See Manly Wade Wellman, *Giant in Gray: A Biography of Wade Hampton of South Carolina* (1949; reprint, Dayton, Ohio: Morningside, 1988).

49. Rodenbough, "Some Cavalry Leaders," pp. 2:275–6. Rodenbough would be awarded the Medal of Honor for his performance at Trevilian Station.

50. William J. Northern, ed., *Men of Mark in Georgia*, vol. 3 (Atlanta: A. B. Chapman, 1907–1912), 352–353.

51. *Ibid.*, 353; Atlanta *Constitution*, June 4, 1895.

52. Robert K. Krick, *Lee's Colonels: A Biographical Register of the Field Officers of the Army of Northern Virginia* (Dayton, Ohio: Morningside, 1992), 409.

53. In fact, Stuart's support of Rosser stirred up a great deal of controversy. Lt. Col. Henry Clay Pate felt he was entitled to command of the Fifth Virginia Cavalry, and not Rosser. Pate ended up a defendant in a general court-martial. See Emory N. Thomas, *Bold Dragoon: The Life of J. E. B. Stuart* (New York: Vintage Books, 1988), 202.

54. *Ibid.*, 261–262.

55. William N. McDonald, *A History of the Laurel Brigade* (Baltimore, Md.: Sun Job Printing Office, 1907), 196–97. The only full-length biography of Rosser is Millard Kessler Bushong and Dean McKain, *Fightin' Tom Rosser, C.S.A.* (Shippensburg, Pa.: Beidel Printing House, 1983).

56. Thomas, *Bold Dragoon*, 202.

57. Supplement to the *Columbia South Carolinian*, April 23, 1864.

58. Thomas L. Rosser to Edward L. Wells, March 11, 1898, Edward L. Wells Correspondence, South Carolina Historical Society, Charleston, South Carolina.

59. O.R. vol. 36, part 1, 787.

60. Sheridan, *Personal Memoirs*, vol. 1, 354–5.

61. Little has been written on the critical fighting at and near Todd's Tavern, the substance of which goes far beyond the scope of this work. For the most comprehensive treatment done to date, see Gordon C. Rhea, *The Battle of the Wilderness, May 5–6, 1864* (Baton Rouge: Louisiana State University Press, 1994).

62. Andrew A. Humphreys, *The Virginia Campaign of 1864 and 1865: The Army of the Potomac and the Army of the James*, vol. 1 (New York: Charles Scribner's Sons, 1883), 60–72.

63. Porter, *Campaigning with Grant*, 83–84.

64. Sheridan, *Personal Memoirs*, vol. 1, 368–69. In fact, Sheridan had a legitimate point. Of all the commanders of the Army of the Potomac, Meade probably had the least understanding of either the proper role or proper usage of cavalry. His record as an army commander is replete with examples of his clear misunderstanding of the proper usage for his mounted arm. Instead of using it as a striking force, his

focus was almost entirely on using it to scout and screen, which, while important, is a less effective use of a large and powerful force such as the one commanded by Phil Sheridan in the spring of 1864.

65. Porter, *Campaigning with Grant*, 84. There is no evidence that Meade specifically intended to relieve Sheridan and replace him with Brig. Gen. David M. Gregg, the senior division commander. This may have been the case. Sheridan was not Meade's choice, and the two men had already had some friction in their relationship. Meade probably saw Sheridan's actions as a direct challenge to his authority, and reacted strongly. Further, Sheridan had failed in his mission to clear the way for the infantry's advance on Spotsylvania via Todd's Tavern. Grant obviously did not agree with the army commander's assessment, something that undoubtedly angered Meade a great deal. An early account, written by Bvt. Lt. Col. Carswell McClellan, a cavalry staff officer, accused Sheridan of being both a liar and insubordinate, and that his insubordination in refusing to obey the lawful orders of his commanding officer, Meade, was rewarded by Grant, who permitted him to cut loose from the army in independent command. See Carswell McClellan, *Notes on the Personal Memoirs of P. H. Sheridan* (St. Paul, Minn.: Press of Wm. E. Banning Jr., 1889), 25.

66. Thomas, *Bold Dragoon*, 297. For a detailed study of Sheridan's Richmond Raid and the Battle of Yellow Tavern, see either Carpenter, "Sheridan's Expedition around Richmond," 300–324 and Rodenbough, "Sheridan's Richmond Raid," 188–193.

67. Festus P. Summers, ed., *A Borderland Confederate* (Pittsburgh, Pa.: University of Pittsburgh Press, 1962), 80; Tracy Power, *Lee's Miserables: Life in the Army of Northern Virginia from the Wilderness to Appomattox* (Chapel Hill: University of North Carolina Press, 1998), 57.

68. G. T. Cralle, "The Bold Horsemen," *Richmond Dispatch*, January 7, 1900.

69. Wellman, *Giant in Gray*, 140. Southern historian Douglas Southall Freeman observed, "In combat [Hampton] undeniably was the peer if he was not the superior of Fitz Lee, though Hampton was not as resourceful as Fitz in finding provender for the horses. Fitz, on the other hand, had been closer to Stuart personally and had much of 'Jeb's' joy of battle. The difficulty was that Hampton and Fitz Lee were secret rivals. They never were pitted against each other. Outwardly, they were on good terms. At heart, Fitz Lee represented and Wade Hampton challenged the Virginia domination of the cavalry Corps, and, some would say, of the entire Army of Northern Virginia. Advancement of one man over the other might, at the moment, be demoralizing. Time must try and perhaps time would resolve the differences between the two." Douglas Southall Freeman, *Lee's Lieutenants: A Study in Command*, vol. 3 (New York: Charles Scribner's Sons, 1942), 436.

70. Wellman, *Giant in Gray*, 109. The courtly Hampton, who was almost invariably diplomatic in his dealings with his fellow officers, publicly criticized Wickham. "But for the fact," he said, "that the Fourth Virginia Cavalry, under the Command

of Colonel Wickham, broke and ran, my brother, Frank Hampton, would not have been killed that day."

71. O.R., vol. 36, part 2, 1001 ("[u]ntil further orders, the three Divisions of Cavalry serving with this Army will constitute separate commands and will report directly to and receive orders from these headquarters."); Lloyd Halliburton, ed., *Saddle Soldiers: The Civil War Correspondence of General William Stokes of the 4th South Carolina Cavalry* (Orangeburg, S.C.: Sandlapper Publishing Co., 1993), 139 ("Since Stuart has been killed I hear there will be no more Cavalry Corps, but that each of the Major Generals will have a division and report direct to General Lee.").

72. Thomas Nelson Conrad, *The Rebel Scout: A Thrilling History of Scouting Life in the Southern Army* (Washington, D.C.: The National Publishing Co., 1904), 109.

73. Carpenter, "Sheridan's Expedition around Richmond," 321.

74. Walbrook Davis Swank, *The Battle of Trevilian Station: The Civil War's Greatest and Bloodiest All Cavalry Battle* (Shippensburg, Pa.: Burd Street Press, 1994), 43.

75. Edward Laight Wells, "A Morning Call on Kilpatrick," *Southern Historical Society Papers* 12 (March 1884): 127.

76. J. Russell Wright, "Battle of Trevilian," *Recollections and Reminiscences 1861–1865*, vol. 6 (Charleston: South Carolina Division of the United Daughters of the Confederacy, 1995), 372.

77. Holmes, "The Fighting Qualities."

78. Matthew C. Butler to Edward L. Wells, June 7, 1888, Wells correspondence.

79. Butler himself observed, "[m]y brigade . . . was armed with long-range Enfield rifles, and was, in fact, mounted infantry, but for our sabres." Matthew C. Butler, "The Cavalry Fight at Trevilian Station," *B&L*, vol. 4, 237.

80. For a detailed study, see U. R. Brooks, *Butler and His Cavalry in the War of Secession 1861–1865* (Columbia, S.C.: The State Co., 1909).

81. Agassiz, *Meade's Headquarters*, 131.

82. John D. Imboden to I. Marshall McCue, October 1, 1883, Imboden Papers, Museum of the Confederacy, Richmond, Virginia. For more on the campaign in the Valley, see Richard R. Duncan, *Lee's Endangered Left: The Civil War in Western Virginia, Spring of 1864* (Baton Rouge: Louisiana State University Press, 1999).

83. O.R., vol. 37, part 1, 485–6.

84. *Ibid.*, vol. 36, part 1, 18–22. The fighting at Cold Harbor and Petersburg foreshadowed the ghastly trench warfare of World War I, featuring direct frontal assaults against strongly entrenched enemy positions marked by appalling casualties.

85. Grant, *Personal Memoirs*, 588.

86. *Ibid.*, 591.

87. Edward G. Longacre, *Mounted Raids of the Civil War* (Lincoln, Nebr.: University of Nebraska Press, 1975), 122. For more on Grierson's spectacular raid, see D. Alexander Brown, *Grierson's Raid: A Cavalry Adventure of the Civil War* (Urbana:

University of Illinois Press, 1954). A similar diversion by a brigade of mounted infantry under command of Col. Abel Streight earlier in the campaign also drew off Maj. Gen. Nathan Bedford Forrest's cavalry, thereby allowing Grant freedom of maneuver. Unfortunately, Streight's raid was nowhere near as successful as that of Grierson.

88. O.R., vol. 36, part 1, 22.

89. *Ibid.*, part 3, 598.

90. Sheridan, *Personal Memoirs*, vol. 1, 415.

91. O.R., vol. 36, part 1, 795. This may be a bit of twenty-twenty hindsight on Sheridan's part.

92. *Ibid.*, vol. 37, part 1, 598.

93. Sheridan, *Personal Memoirs*, vol. 1, 417.

94. See Jerry Meyers, "Trevilian!," *Louisa County Historical Magazine* 30, no. 1 (Spring, 1999): 31. This number was determined by the author's detailed analysis of Union losses as reported in the Official Records from the estimated strength of the Cavalry Corps on May 26, after it was reinforced by four regiments and replacements for losses sustained in the May campaigning. Meyers estimates Torbert's strength at 5,300 and Gregg's at 4,900. Capt. Theodore H. Bean of the Seventeenth Pennsylvania Cavalry estimated Sheridan's command at between 7,000 and 8,000 in an account written in 1887. See Theodore H. Bean, "Sheridan at Trevilian," *Philadelphia Weekly Times*, June 11, 1887.

95. Butler, "The Cavalry Fight at Trevilian Station," 239. Butler derived his number from a review of the Cavalry Corps's consolidated returns of May 31, 1864.

96. Historian Bryce A. Suderow has done the first detailed analysis of the comparative strengths and losses of both sides at Trevilian Station. After combing through many records, Suderow determined that the actual strength of Sheridan's column was 9,286 effectives. Suderow's analysis appears as Appendices B, C, and D to this book. See, also, RG 94, Entry 653, Box 28, "Lists of Casualties in the Cavalry Corps," and the various documents there.

97. There is some dispute over the precise number of guns accompanying Sheridan's raid. One of his officers very clearly noted in a letter home just after the raid that twenty-four pieces of artillery accompanied the march. However, at four guns per battery and only five batteries along on the march, it is doubtful whether more than twenty guns made the trip with Sheridan. Further, a note about horse artillery is probably appropriate. Horse artillerymen did all of their marching mounted on horses, instead of on foot, as the regular artillery did. Its men were assigned the specific task of serving with the cavalry as so-called "flying batteries." They used lightweight ordnance in order to keep their traveling weight down, thereby minimizing the strain on their horses. By 1864, the Federal horse artillery had become a very formidable force for the Confederates to reckon with.

98. Sheridan, *Personal Memoirs*, vol. 1, 417–418. The precise location of Carpen-

ter's Ford is impossible to pin down today, as that crossing is now under water, part of the Lake Anna dam complex built for flood-control, reservoir, and recreational purposes during the latter half of the twentieth century.

99. O.R., vol. 36, part 1, 795; *New York Herald*, June 21, 1864.

100. Henry Pyne, *Ride to War: The History of the First New Jersey Cavalry* (New Brunswick, N. J.: Rutgers University Press, 1961), 217.

101. Carlos McDonald diary, entry for June 6, 1864, included in *Report of the Forty-Sixth Annual Reunion of the Sixth Ohio Veteran Volunteer Cavalry Association* (Warren, Ohio: Wm. Ritezel & Co., 1911), 54.

102. Diary of Howard M. Smith, entry for June 6, 1864, Howard M. Smith Papers, Manuscripts Division, Library of Congress, Washington, D. C. Smith refers to the farm of the fire-eating secessionist, Edmund Ruffin, who had so vigorously advocated the beginning of the war in 1861, and who fired one of the first shots at Fort Sumter.

103. William P. Lloyd, *History of the First Regiment Pennsylvania Reserve Cavalry, from Its Organization, August 1861, to September 1864, with List of Names of All Officers and Enlisted Men Who Have Ever Belonged to the Regiment, and Remarks Attached to Each Name, Noting Change* (Philadelphia: King & Baird, 1864), 97.

104. *New York Herald*, June 21, 1864.

105. *Philadelphia Press*, July 4, 1864.

106. George A. Custer to Elizabeth B. Custer, June 6, 1864, included in Merington, *The Custer Story*, 193.

107. Newell Cheney, *History of the Ninth Regiment, New York Volunteer Cavalry, War of 1861 to 1865* (Poland Center, N.Y.: privately published, 1901), 184. The same sentiment was echoed by the regimental historian of another of Devin's units, the Seventeenth Pennsylvania Cavalry, bugler Henry P. Moyer, who noted, "To the subordinate officers and men this move looked like another raid. Much reticence was observed, and evidently but very few were informed of the contemplated movement." Henry P. Moyer, *History of the Seventeenth Regiment, Pennsylvania Volunteer Cavalry* (Lebanon, Pa.: n.p., 1911), 84.

108. Noble D. Preston, "The Battle of Trevilian," *Philadelphia Weekly Times*, August 28, 1880.

109. James C. Mohr and Richard C. Winslow, eds., *The Cormany Diaries: A Northern Family in the Civil War* (Pittsburgh, Pa.: University of Pittsburgh Press, 1982), 433.

⊷ 2 ⊷

The Road to Trevilian Station

I think Genl H. is going after Sheridan.

On the morning of Tuesday, June 7, 1864, with everything in readiness, Sheridan's command marched. At daylight, bugles blared "Boots and Saddles," followed by "To Horse" at 5:00.[1] Blue-clad horsemen received orders to proceed quietly through the Virginia countryside.[2] Rumors buzzed up and down the Federal column, with some troopers speculating that they were heading to Maryland to head off a reported raid by Fitz Lee's division.[3] Gen. David M. Gregg's Second Division took the lead, followed by Gen. Alfred T. A. Torbert's three brigades. Moving at four miles per hour, the long column passed through Aylett's Crossroads, Sharon Church, and Brandywine and then continued along the south bank of the Mattapony River to Dunkirk. One of Custer's troopers estimated that the column covered only about fifteen miles, not a full day's march.[4] Sheridan himself traversed the entire eight-mile line, making sure that horses were not overworked in the unpleasant conditions. The historian of the First New Jersey Cavalry recalled that, "the horses had to be watched carefully to save them as much as possible from the effect of overexhaustion and of reckless riding."[5] Capt. Theodore H. Bean of the Seventeenth Pennsylvania Cavalry observed that, "The march was unmolested by the enemy, although it was evident that our movement was closely observed, as occasionally we could see and exchange shots with their scouts on our flank, but at considerable distance from the main column."[6]

The weather was hot, and billowing clouds of dust plagued the march. Lt. Asa Isham, one of Custer's Michiganders, painted this vivid portrait:

> There is nothing particularly exciting or delightful in thumping along at a trot in a cavalry column. The clouds of dust, sent up by the thousands of

hoof-beats, fill eyes, nose, and air passages, give external surfaces a uniform, dirty gray color, and form such an impenetrable veil, that, for many minutes together, you can not see even your hand before you. Apparently, just at the point of impending suffocation, a gentle sigh of wind makes a rift, and a free breath is inspired. Dust and horse-hairs permeate everywhere. Working under the clothing to the skin, and fixed by sweat, the sensation is as though one was covered by a creeping mass of insects. Accumulations occur in the pockets; the rations come in for their full share, and with the bacon, particularly, so thoroughly do dirt and horse-hairs become incorporated, that no process of cleansing can remove them. But there is no better appetizer than horseback jolting, and little squeamishness with genuine hunger, A hunk of dirty, raw bacon, with "hard tack," on a campaign, are partaken with keener relish and enjoyment than "a good square meal," when engaged in less arduous duty.[7]

Sheridan's horses began breaking down just hours into the raid, even though the march was being conducted at a walk in an effort to conserve horseflesh. Following the pattern established during the Richmond raid in May, broken-down horses were shot and left alongside the road, their riders trudging off either to search the countryside for a fresh mount, or to join the forlorn ranks of the dismounted.

For Edward P. McKinney of the Sixth New York Cavalry, the march was especially trying. McKinney usually messed with his commanding officer, Lt. Col. William H. Crocker, and they had packed a six-day supply of coffee. They promptly lost the benefit of their good planning when runaway slaves—known as "contrabands"—who were traveling with the column, boiled all of it at breakfast on the first day. "This was a serious loss and can be appreciated only by those who have had like experience," McKinney wryly noted. "We relied on coffee more than on solid food."[8]

As the column plodded along, foragers spread out on the flanks, searching for provisions. Because of strict orders not to take horses out of column, most of this foraging was done dismounted. Adventurous and hungry boys would start off on foot in advance of the column in the morning," Edward P. Tobie of the First Maine Cavalry recalled, "and scour along the line of march as well as they could, leaving their horses to be led along in the column by comrades, recompensing the comrades for this trouble by dividing the spoils with them on their return, which oftentimes was not till the command had halted for the night."[9] Angry bands of locals buzzed around the fringes of the marching horse soldiers, and the recklessness of the Federal foragers often cost them their lives or a trip to Richmond as prisoners of war. Maj. William P. Hall of the Sixth New York Cavalry was captured from the column's rear guard, joining other unfortunate comrades for the long and unhappy journey into captivity.[10]

Ella Washington, a Virginian who had struck up a friendship with Custer, complained about the efforts of the foragers in her diary, "Heard that Sheridans command crossed at Newcastle into King William [County]," she wrote. "Where can they be going. We heard the drums all night beating constantly. . . . I wish most heartily they were all moved off, there will not be a living thing that is eatable in all this country. We see them passing all day with sheep, hogs, veal and fowls; with quarters of mutton and beef hung to poles which they carry between them. They have even taken the servants fowls and pigs. Certainly there was never such an army of demons collected before, outside the infernal regions."[11]

The blue-clad troopers bivouacked for the night at the farm of a Confederate officer named Douglas, who hastily fled just moments before the Federals arrived. Once the Yankees settled in, the ladies of the Douglas household "treated us very kindly and one of them consented to play the piano for our entertainment," reported Lt. Louis H. Carpenter, of Sheridan's headquarters escort.[12] As the Tenth New York posted its pickets, a small column from another of Gregg's regiments spotted them. Mistaking these troopers for the enemy, the two Northern regiments charged each other and had a brief melee that cost four men slightly wounded. Red-faced, both contingents retreated, and an uneasy truce fell over the two camps as Sheridan's troopers settled down for the night.[13] The correspondent from the *New York Herald* blandly noted, "Nothing of interest occurred on the first day."[14]

"Assembly" sounded at 5:00 A.M. the next morning, and sleepy Yankee horse soldiers roused themselves for breakfast. By 8:00 the hot and dusty march westward resumed, this time with Torbert's First Division leading. The Federals covered twenty-five miles that day, reaching Pole Cat Station on the Richmond, Fredericksburg, and Potomac Railroad about 4:00 in the afternoon.[15] A member of the Sixth Ohio Cavalry recalled passing "through a beautiful section of country."[16] Commenting on the terrain, Lieutenant Carpenter sniffed, "We waded a few insignificant streams on the road dignified by the name of Morgan Swamp and Rudy Swamp, where we watered

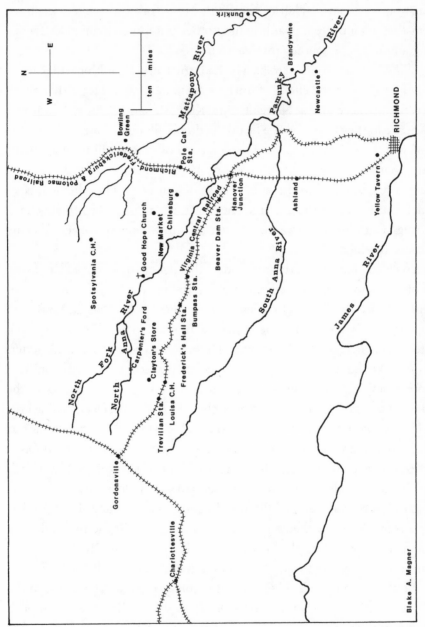

The Virginia Central Railroad and Locations Pertinent to Sheridan's Second Raid

Blake A. Magner

before arriving at the railroad." A little more than two miles beyond the station, Sheridan ordered his troopers to pitch camp for the night in large fields of fine clover. Merritt's Reserve Brigade drew the task of tearing up railroad lines for a considerable distance.[17] That job completed, the First New York Dragoons of the Reserve Brigade went on picket duty. Everything was quiet that night.[18]

The march again took its toll on Sheridan's horses. "Some horses began to give out and drop by the wayside, forcing their riders to accompany the command for the rest of the journey on foot," the First New Jersey's historian commented. "The route which we traveled had been marched over by our infantry and army trains, so that there was no forage to be obtained in it; and our horses were obliged to live on the amount carried on the saddles."[19] Deducing from the growing ranks of dismounted men that increasing num-bers of horses were breaking down, Sheridan issued orders to shoot all horses unable to keep up with the command.[20] Saddles and other equipment were gathered up and thrown into wagons. The Northern column lengthened as dismounted men struggled to keep up.[21]

Not long after the day's trek began, Brig. Gen. Henry E. Davies dispatched Lt. Col. B. F. Sceva of the Tenth New York Cavalry to take a small force and search for a Confederate mail wagon that had recently passed through the area. Finding the wagon and its small Rebel escort, Sceva ordered a charge. He failed, and lost his hat in the bargain. Searching for a replacement, he found a silk hat of "very ancient construction and style," giving him "something of the appearance of William Penn, as illustrated in the old time school books." Hurrying to catch up with his troopers, Sceva passed General Davies, who was aghast at Sceva's appearance. "Imagine his surprise and consternation at being placed in arrest by General Davies for a breach of discipline," a witness reminisced. "He hastened to explain matters and was released with the admonition that he should make a change in chapeau to more nearly conform to the army regulations at as early a moment as possible."[22]

The men of the Sixth Pennsylvania Cavalry of Merritt's Reserve Brigade kept a sharp eye for delicacies. Passing a large farmhouse, they noticed several beehives in the yard. A trooper unfamiliar with the ways of bees took his tin cup and ran over to the hives, intending to pour himself a cup of honey. He quickly discovered the error of his ways, as "the next moment he looked more like a bee hive himself than he did like a soldier, and was glad to beat a hasty retreat," to the mocking laughter of his comrades. Saddler Edgar B. Strang of Company M, a country boy from Chester County, Pennsylvania, thought he knew more about bees. Strang spotted a calico dress and an old sunbonnet lying nearby. After donning this protective gear, Strang launched his attack on the beehive. Slipping a large bag over one of the hives, he grabbed it, carried it to a stream, and dumped it into the water, expecting to drown the hive's occupants. The strategy for this assault was solid, but Strang did not hold the hive underwater long enough to kill all the bees.

Still wearing the calico dress and sunbonnet, he mounted his horse sidesaddle, holding the bag of bees in his lap. "Dar goes Miss Sallie with the Yankee soldiers!" a slave remarked. Strang noted that "the wrapper and sun bonnet belonged to Miss Sallie and they thought that she was inside of them, and it was not long before I wished she was, for in the language of the poet I could say, 'Still so gently o'er me creeping.' " He described his battle with the enemy bees: "Those that I had not succeeded in drowning, had crawled out of the bag and were creeping up my sleeves and down my back, and it was not long before I was not only glad to get out of Miss Sallie's wrapper and bonnet, but I got out of as many of my own clothes as I could, in order to convince them that I was not a hive." Faced with this furious counterattack, poor Strang had no alternative but to admit his defeat and moved on to safer forage.[23]

Bugler Carlos McDonald of the Sixth Ohio Cavalry brought back corn meal, flour, and bacon. However, the unfamiliar and heavily wooded terrain disoriented the Buckeye and his companion, who did not locate their camp until well after dark.[24] One of Irvin Gregg's officers was also successful, getting "lots of Corn, Meat, Meal, Milk, &c., &c."[25] So far, the excursion had been nothing but a joyride for the Yankee troopers. One remembered that he and his comrades "actually began to forget that we were at war."[26] Things were about to change.

Word of the raid had reached Hampton by the morning of June 8. Capt. Thomas N. Conrad, chaplain of the Third Virginia Cavalry, had a real gift for scouting. Conrad reconnoitered the Confederate left that morning, and spotted a lone bluecoat approaching. Conrad rode out, expecting a contest, but soon realized that the rider was a lone mulatto dressed in a Federal uniform. The man approached and asked Conrad if he was a Confederate officer. When Conrad confirmed that he was, the young man informed Conrad that "he had just escaped from Sheridan's headquarters and had information that was very important for us to know." The servant had attended Rosser in the early days of the war, and upon reaching the Confederate picket lines, he asked to be taken to Rosser. Conrad asked what the nature of the information was and learned that "while at General Sheridan's headquarters that morning he had heard much about the raid, to what points they were going to."

Conrad led the mulatto to Rosser's headquarters. Rosser recognized the man immediately and heard the report.[27] "He reached me late at night," Rosser recalled, "and in a clear and straightforward manner related all that had occurred in Sheridan's camp preparatory for this expedition, and this information was of great service to us."[28] Rosser sent the man on to Hampton, which "seemed a revelation." Conrad later noted, "The capture of the mulatto and his information enabled Hampton and Rosser to get in position in front of Sheridan and prepare for his coming. What a Godsend!"[29]

Hampton's scouts kept in constant contact with headquarters, informing the Army of Northern Virginia's high command about Little Phil's progress.[30] Isaac S. Curtis, of the Ninth Virginia Cavalry of Rooney Lee's Division, left Hanover on the night of the June 7, rode along the North Anna River, and found the Yankee column, capturing two soldiers and learning that they were carrying rations for several days. Curtis sent his friend Zack Scott back to Hampton with a note "telling him my idea was that Sheridan was making a raid to cut all our armys cummunications north and return to the Army; west of Petersburg this was correct."[31] Other scouts reported "that a large body of Yankee cavalry had moved out from behind Grant's lines and was then crossing the Pamunkey at a point headed northward."[32] Hampton immediately notified General Lee of the status of Sheridan's slow westward trek and received orders to take "one division in addition to my own and follow him."[33]

That night General Lee reported to Confederate Secretary of War James Seddon, "Two divisions of . . . cavalry under Genl Sheridan are reported to have crossed the Pamunkey yesterday at New Castle Ferry and to have encamped last night at Dunkirk and Aylett's on the Mattapony. They were accompanied by artillery, ambulances, wagons and beef cattle."[34] Butler estimated the strength of the combined forces of Fitz Lee's and Hampton's divisions at 5,000 sabres.[35] Recent research indicates that Hampton brought approximately 6,000 mounted troopers with him.[36] Hampton also took four batteries of horse artillery—the Washington Artillery of South Carolina (Capt. James H. Hart commanding), the Ashby Virginia Battery (Capt. James Thomson commanding), the Lynchburg Beauregards Artillery (Capt. John J. Shoemaker commanding), and one section of the Stuart Horse Artillery (Capt. Philip P. Johnston commanding), for a total of 15 guns and 400 men, giving him a total strength of 6,400, considerably fewer men than Sheridan.

Guessing that Sheridan's objectives were the railroad junctions at Gordonsville and Charlottesville, Hampton knew that a quick response was critical. "I moved rapidly with my division so as to interpose my command between [Sheridan] and [Gordonsville and Charlottesville]," he recorded, "at the same time directing Maj. Gen. Fitzhugh Lee to follow as speedily as possible."[37] Hampton ordered his command to assemble at 2:00 A.M. on June 9. By then the Federals would have a head start of two full days, and the Confederates had a lot of ground to make up. Many of the Virginia troopers were familiar with the terrain, and the gray-clad horse soldiers also had the benefit of shorter, more direct lines of march and communications.

Preparations began immediately. "Receive information that Sheridan had crossed the Pamunkey with a large body of cavalry and had encamped near Aylett's on the Matapony; and orders to be prepared to move after him," Maj. James D. Ferguson, Fitz Lee's assistant adjutant general, recorded in his diary. "Our Division and one Brigade from W. H. F. Lee ordered to march after dark."[38] Horatio Nelson of Company A, Fourth Virginia Cavalry of Wickham's brigade, noted in his diary on June 8, "The Confederates received information that General Sheridan with a large force was moving north with the possible intention of combining with General David Hunter's expedition against Lynchburg. After being relieved by W. H. F. Lee's Division during the day, Fitz Lee moved that night to the aid of General Hampton who was moving toward Trevilian's Station."[39]

One of Butler's officers wrote home, "I think Genl H. is going after Sheridan, who is said to be on the Pamunky committing depredation."[40] Gunner George Neese of Chew's Battery recorded in his diary, "The Yankee cavalry disappeared from our front yesterday and it seems they have gone in force on an extensive raid toward the Blue Ridge. I suppose they are trying to nose around to our rear and go into the railroad-destroying business, or perhaps they intend to perpetrate some other devilment that would be more damaging to Dixie than railroad cutting."[41]

William Ball of the Eleventh Virginia Cavalry recalled, "Suddenly we were issued an order to cook three days rations and be ready to march. Said rations were musty cornmeal and bacon about four inches thick with not a streak of lean in it. By this time I had a well developed case of typhoid fever and didn't know it, didn't want to know it. I had been feeling wretched for a week, with no appetite, headaches and dizziness, but my ardor was great enough to overcome almost any sickness."[42] Things were quiet in the camp of the Laurel Brigade—the night before, they had learned of the death of their former leader, Grumble Jones, on June 5. Further, their horses were in bad shape. "Citizen thinks we should leave his grass alone. Will give $250 to be divided among the soldiers if we will not graze his clover. Vain entreaty. Starved cavalry horses must be fed," observed Pvt. James F. Wood of the Seventh Virginia.[43]

Private Edward L. Wells of the Charleston Light Dragoons, Company K, Fourth South Carolina Cavalry of Butler's brigade, recalled that there was a great deal of uncertainty and speculation surrounding the orders to march, as nobody knew the intended destination, and because only five days' rations had been issued. He noted, "Certainly a raid, or expedition of some kind was intended, but neither officers nor men had the slightest idea of where they were going. Change is certainly welcome, and the mystery added a charm to the expected movement. Some said they were going to Washington; others perhaps looked forward to dancing in Baltimore, but no one doubted that there would be, at all events, plenty of 'music' of a certain kind."[44]

Lt. Col. J. Fred Waring, the thirty-two-year-old commander of the Jeff Davis Legion of Hampton's division, echoed the same uncertainty, scrawling in his diary, "Can Hampton be intending to make a raid?"[45] Neese observed, "General Hampton with a good force of cavalry is after the raiders in hot pursuit, and when he strikes a warm trail there is usually some blood left in the track and some game bagged."[46] One Georgian of Wright's command even speculated that Sheridan was chasing John Hunt Morgan's Confederate raiders in Tennessee.[47] Prepared for the march, the Confederate horse soldiers tried to catch a few hours of that rarest of all commodities for the soldier on campaign—sleep.[48]

Bugles blared and Confederate troopers swung into their saddles and moved at a steady walk. Hampton's division, consisting of Rosser's, Butler's, and Wright's brigades, led the march, with the Cobb Legion in front. Lee's division followed.[49] Sgt. Charles McVicar, another of Chew's gunners, noted, "Bugle sounded for marching at 3 o'c., we are moving by Yellow Tavern, five miles from Richmond. Turned to the right on Telegraph Road on to the Central RR by Bumpass and Fredericks Hall Stations and halted. Never have I seen it rain harder."[50] Trooper William Ball of the Eleventh Virginia pointed out that the rain began almost as soon as the column moved out and that it continued all night. He recalled, "When we stopped for feed and rest, I was fortunate enough to secure two flat rails and leaning them against a stump, with blanket and oilcloth over me, I had a fairly comfortable night. We resumed march at daybreak, and I felt weak and hungry, but with the bread only a little less sour than vinegar and the bacon rancid, I could only nibble at it as we marched along."[51]

The column moved at a steady walk. Because only two rest breaks per day were allowed, Hampton's force covered nearly thirty miles that first day. Fitz Lee stayed in contact with his uncle's headquarters by telegraph. Writing from Ashland, he reported, "Head of column reached this place at 12 m. today. It is reliably reported that Sheridan . . . is moving today toward Chilesburg. His advance reached that place at 2 P.M. Prisoners taken from him say that he is going to assist Hunter to join Grant."[52] This intelligence was remarkably accurate. As the gray-clad cavalry snaked across the Virginia countryside, Pres. Jefferson Davis wrote to General Lee: "The indications are that Grant, despairing of a direct attack, is now seeking to embarrass you by flank movements. If our cavalry, concentrated, could meet that of the enemy, it would have moral as well as physical effects, which are desirable."[53]

Lee responded with an accurate assessment of the expedition. "I have received no definite information as to his purpose," wrote Lee to Davis, "but conjecture that his object is to cooperate with Genl Hunter, and endeavor to reach the James, breaking the railroads &c. as he passes, and probably to descend on the south side of that river." The army commander continued, "I think it necessary to be on our guard and make every arrangement in our power to thwart his purpose and protect our communications and country. I have directed Genls Hampton and Fitz Lee with their divisions to proceed in the direction of Hanover Junction, and thence, if the information they receive justifies it, along the Central Railroad, keeping the enemy on their right, and shape their course according to his." Lee accurately predicted, "The pause in the operations of Genl Grant induces me to believe that he is awaiting the effect of movements in some other quarter to make us change our position, and renders the suggestion I make with reference to the intention and destination of Genl Sheridan more probable."[54]

Blissfully unaware that he was being pursued, Little Phil resumed his leisurely advance on the morning of June 9, leaving his camp at 8:00. His troopers passed through Chilesburg and crossed East North East Creek, halting at the plantation of a Mr. De Jarnette, a relative of a member of the Confederate Congress. The Yankee troopers industriously set about foraging, much to the chagrin of the local citizenry. That night, Sheridan pitched his tent in the yard, placing his headquarters guard in the immediate vicinity.[55]

One New Yorker complained, "Marched about 24 miles today—weather intensely hot—and but little water to be found for man or beast. A thunderstorm came up just after going into camp, but little rain fell however."[56] Lieutenant Carpenter noted, "No rain having fallen for some time, the roads have been excessively dusty today and horses and men suffered much."[57] The regimental historian of the Sixth New York Cavalry concurred: "The horses were beginning to show the strain of the hard service, 150 of them in the division giving out in the afternoon's march."[58] This day was the anniversary of a seminal event in the history of the Federal cavalry, the crucial battle of Brandy Station, the opening engagement of the previous summer's Gettysburg Campaign. The correspondent from the *New York Herald* related, "June 9 was remembered by the command most vividly as being the anniversary of the battles of Beverly Ford and Brandy Station. Many of those present had been wounded or made prisoners in that sanguinary fight, and they were not likely very soon to forget the date."[59]

Hampton's Scouts continually skirmished with the rear guard of the blue-clad column. E. C. Moncure and two other scouts shadowed Sheridan's column the entire day. Moncure spotted a Federal foraging and "put a load of buckshot" into his back. The Southerners ordered the Yankee to dismount, but the man instead turned and tried to make a run for it. "This man made his escape by jumping his horse from the ledge of a rock about ten feet to a sandbar beneath." Later that day, the gray-clad scouts spotted Sheridan's rearmost squadron resting and decided to have some fun with the Yankee horsemen. The three scouts drew their sabers and charged, the Rebel yell ringing. Moncure and his friends opened fire, and the startled Yankees withdrew; they "seemed to be panic-stricken and retreated up the road without firing a gun."[60]

Sheridan learned from a captured scout that Hampton had left his positions north of the Chickahominy, and that Fitz Lee and Butler had left their positions south of the river, and that they were pursuing him along the route of the Virginia Central Railroad. A Northern scouting party sent to cut the telegraph wires along the railroad track confirmed the unwelcome news. Sheridan wrote, "Breckinridge had been ordered back to the valley by General Lee as soon as he heard of Hunter's victory near Staunton, but now that my expedition had been discovered, the movement of Breckinridge's troops on the railroad was being timed to correspond with the marches of my command till Hampton could get more nearly parallel with me."[61]

The area covered by Sheridan's raid had been the subject of numerous marches by both Northern infantry and cavalry, and was well picked over. On either side of Sheridan's line of march, parties fanned out, searching for supplies, mules, and horses. These contingents had to cover considerable ground, straining the endurance of man and beast. Yet "these supplies had to be secured; and at the expense of a few animals the rest were kept alive."[62]

Henry Avery, a commissary sergeant of the Fifth Michigan Cavalry, led a column of foragers. Spotting a handsome farm, the foragers stopped to look for food and hidden weapons. The residents had tried to hide their bounty under cornhusks, but the Wolverines found the large supply of corn stashed beneath the husks. Avery approached the farmhouse, where "I found not only comfort, but splendor, and hanging on the wall was a life size portrait of General George Washington." Avery told the woman of the house that it was a wonder that the portrait "did not take life and curse them for trying to break up the Union." Avery thought that the picture of the Father of the Country must have served as a guard against roving bands of pillagers, so Avery and his men searched the house for weapons. Finding none, Avery and his men withdrew, leaving "all things unmolested."[63]

As the long blue column marched westward, its tail grew as large numbers of contraband and runaway slaves joined it. Near dusk, the head of the column emerged from a wood, and advance elements spotted a large group of blacks congregated by the side of the road. The First New Jersey Cavalry, regimental colors flying, led the way. The blacks, spotting the U.S. flag, sent up "joyous songs and shouts." Because the Yankee troopers were dust covered, the fugitives could not make a positive identification of the column until the flag was spotted, prompting one to say, "Golly, Mas'r, when we seed dat flag we know'd we'se all right." Their day of jubilee having arrived, the blacks "fell into line in the rear and commenced the tramp, they hardly knew whither."[64]

Temporary hospitals containing convalescing wounded Union prisoners of war dotted the countryside. The Seventeenth Pennsylvania Cavalry of Devin's brigade was detached for the day to scour the area and bring in wounded Union soldiers who were able to march and also to parole any Confederates captured in the process. That night, as the Pennsylvanians moved to rejoin the main column, concealed partisans attacked the head of the column. "Quick as I can write it a dozen carbineers jumped from their horses, some of them smarting from wounds of bird shot, and made a dash for these 'bushwhackers'," Captain Bean recounted. "The chase was a short one. Two men were overtaken with shotguns in their hands. They were not asked to surrender but were riddled with bullets and left where they fell. With inexperienced troops attacks of this kind by night often lead to serious trouble and sometimes to confusion, but with trained veterans they will make short work of those rash enough to molest them on the march."[65]

Also that night, a detachment of the First Maine Cavalry reconnoitered the road leading from Newmarket to Bumpass Station on the Virginia Central. This excursion was the only portion of Sheridan's command to cross the North Anna River before June 10. At Bumpass Station, the Maine men cut the telegraph wires to Richmond, temporarily impairing Rebel communications. They also took two of Mr. Bumpass's horses.[66]

The pursuit resumed on the morning of June 10. The Confederates got an early start, marching to Fredericks Hall Station, resting there, and then continuing on. Lee's division followed a few miles behind Hampton's. Waring recorded, "Began march at 2 A.M. Caught up with the front Brigade. Marched all day long, reaching Louisa C. H. at 3 P.M. Here watered our horses, the first time in 24 hours." He reported Yankee raiding parties on the other side of the North Anna. "A party of them crossed & visited Bumpass's Station, robbing Bumpass of two horses. Our movement they did not discover till this afternoon, near Trevellyan Station. They came very near to Louisa C. H. But did not advance on Louisa to-day. . . . I suppose we will meet the enemy tomorrow."[67]

Wells of the Fourth South Carolina recalled that about noon, during a short rest, Butler sent the regimental adjutant of the Fourth South Carolina Cavalry with a message to a member of Wells's company. Those men with failing horses were to fall quietly out of ranks and return to the Confederate cavalry's Reserve Camp near Atlee's Station to join the rest of the division's contingent of dismounted men. "This incident was thought to indicate a long expedition," Wells noted, "but at that time [Butler] himself was not aware of his destination."[68]

Earlier that afternoon, near Louisa, the men of the Twentieth Battalion of Georgia Cavalry stopped for a break, blocking the road. They spotted a party of mounted men approaching their position, and Sgt. Charles Paine Hansell of Company E realized that unless the Georgians moved, the mounted party would be forced off the road into a fence line. The leader of the small column rode to the head of the Georgians and said, "in a most pleasant manner and with the softness of a lady—'Gentlemen, let me pass please.' " Recognizing the officer as Hampton, the Georgians "pulled back with such vigor and earnestness as almost to throw their horses on their haunches. Had the manner and tone been other than they were, a military order instead of a request, there would have been a way made, but a very different one." Inspired by their commander, the tired and thirsty Georgians pressed on.[69]

Sgt. George M. Neese, a member of Capt. James Thomson's Virginia Battery, recalled that his unit marched until nearly midnight on the Tenth, finally camping on the Charlottesville Road about five miles west of Trevilian Station. He noted in his diary, "The Yankee raiders are not far from this section of country, for we scented them and heard from them to-day; about tomorrow they will try to do something and we will be ready to assist them with the job."[70] Arriving at Louisa, Hampton's men learned that the Union column was marching along the north bank of the North Anna River and aiming for the junction of the railroads at Gordonsville.[71]

Lt. John Bauskett of Company B, Sixth South Carolina Cavalry, commanded the rear guard of Hampton's division. Bauskett complained to Col. Hugh Aiken, his commanding officer, that he did not want to command the rear guard if it appeared that the column would get into a fight. Aiken told Bauskett that he knew his men would fight, and the disgruntled lieutenant obeyed the order. Bauskett had an unpleasant evening, remembering, "Under fire we took cover in the thick of an oak thicket that night without fires. I didn't unsaddle. I took an oak root as my pillow, and the ground for a [mattress], and the shade of [his horse] for cover."[72] Another South Carolinian echoed a similar sentiment, commenting, "soon weary riders and horses were stretched on the ground asleep, both equally careless of what the morrow would bring forth."[73] Close to the Federal lines, Butler's men spent an uncomfortable night in the thick Virginia woods.

Finally feeling better, Trooper Ball of the Eleventh Virginia Cavalry enjoyed the friendly countryside's bounties. The regiment passed through Louisa and halted to rest and feed their horses. Ball's brother sent word that he and Col. Elijah V. White of the Thirty-fifth Battalion of Virginia Cavalry, also of Rosser's brigade, had been invited to dinner at a private house and that William must join them. Ball recalled that "It was a fine meal and I was nearly famished, and especially remember one dish, fried onions, which I greatly relished, alas, too well and it was many a year after that meal, before I ate another fried onion!"[74]

Hampton's command passed through Louisa. Rosser's Laurels camped several miles west of the train station astride both the Virginia Central and the direct route to Gordonsville.[75] Wright's and Butler's brigades camped east of Trevilian Station, but not as far out as Rosser's outpost, which was intended to guard against potential threats from Hunter's troops in the Valley. Fitz Lee's men bivouacked within a half-mile of Louisa, on the Virginia Central.[76] Hampton's persistence had paid off. His command was planted firmly across Sheridan's line of march along the Virginia Central. That night he wired General Lee, "I am getting between him and Gordonsville. Everything going well."[77] General Lee passed this information on to Secretary Seddon: "My first impression was that the object of the expedition was to cooperate with the forces under Genl Hunter in the Valley, and there is nothing as yet in their movements inconsistent with this idea." He continued, "They may intend to strike for the James River above Richmond, and cross to the south side to destroy the Danville Road . . . and should he turn towards the river our cavalry under Genl Hampton will endeavor to protect the bridges, and if unable to do so, will aid the parties charged with burning them."[78]

The problem, however, was a four-mile gap between Hampton's and Fitz Lee's positions. The main road from Carpenter's Ford to Louisa, the Marquis Road, ran right through that gap.

Apparently unconcerned with these haphazard dispositions, the gray-clad horse soldiers rested. "Few of [the Confederate cavalrymen] will ever forget the occasion; the quiet summer evening, the cool crisp air, so grateful after the heat and well-nigh unendurable dust of the two days' march, and the blue mountain-ridges in the distance looking peaceful and pretty, and refreshing to the eyes," observed Wells.[79] J. Russell Wright, another of Butler's men, recalled, "All night long my comrade, Jim Quattlebaum, and I were on picket, with our jaded horses by our side, saddled and bridled, pawing the ground impatiently and shaking their bits as if they shared the eagerness of our purpose, though they knew not its meaning."[80] Charles M. Calhoun of the Sixth South Carolina Cavalry recalled, "That night we could hear the drums of the enemy, off in the distance, and it seemed we had got ahead of them but kept very quiet and not allowed to have any fire."[81] Butler stated, "On the night of June 10th my orders were to be prepared the next morning at daylight for action."[82] His brigade of 1,300 South Carolinians would bear the brunt of the next day's fighting.

The Yankees maintained their steady advance. Moving at 5:00 A.M. on the 10th, they enjoyed "the coolness of the atmosphere at this early hour, the command made the most of it, and pushed on at a rapid rate."[83] They crossed the North Fork of the North Anna at Young's Mill, passed Good Hope Church, and continued west. They then turned south and crossed the North Anna at Carpenter's Ford, about six miles northeast of Louisa.[84] At Good Hope Church, nine miles from Spotsylvania Court House, they discovered a large Confederate field hospital containing Union wounded. Devin sent the Seventeenth Pennsylvania Cavalry and a staff officer to investigate. The Seventeenth did not return to the main body until late on the 11th, missing the next day's excitement and bringing back no prisoners for their troubles.[85]

The extended marching in the June heat was taking a serious toll on the Federal horses. Captain Bean of the Seventeenth Pennsylvania Cavalry commanded the rear guard on June 10. He remembered an intensely hot, sultry day with extremely dusty roads. Between the beginning of the day's march and 10:00, the rear guard had already shot several horses. By 11:00, exhausted animals could be found in groups of three and four. Because these horses could not be driven to take another step, the men of the rear guard dismounted and shot them through the head. Bean recounted, "By noon, and from that on until 4 o'clock P.M., this duty became distressing. Upwards of five hundred horses were lost on this day, and all were shot." As a result, it was not unusual for him to see a dozen of these poor, suffering beasts huddled together under a roadside shade tree, "abandoned by their riders because they finally staggered and fell and would go no further. Relieved of their burden, with saddle and bridle removed, they would get upon their feet and find shade, if near at hand. Their heads would droop almost to the ground, their ears seemed motionless, their eyes dull and glassy. Panting and covered with flies, they seemed insensible to the cruel slaughter of their numbers as one after another fell to the crack of pistol and carbine." While most of these animals would have recovered had they been given rest and ordinary care, they would have fallen into enemy hands. Their newly dismounted riders immediately sought new mounts, as "No cavalryman will walk if he can find a horse or a mule."[86]

Sheridan detached part of his rear guard to prevent straggling and to see that the dismounted men kept pace. A member of Company Q, after being urged to go faster, replied that he "was pretty well played out as well as his horse, and if they wanted him to go faster he might as well shoot himself at once." Believing that these remarks were made in jest, the officer commanding the rear guard urged the trooper forward again. Obviously not jesting, the dismounted man placed his revolver to his head "and blew out his brains."[87]

That night, Sheridan pitched his camp near Clayton's Store, at Ravenwood, the home of Dr. William A. Gillespie, a local physician.[88] The Regulars set up camp at the farm of Buck Chiles, six miles north of Trevilian Station. Devin's brigade passed Clayton's Store and camped at the Woolfolk plantation, known as "Walnut Grove," five miles northeast of the train station. Custer's Wolverines camped on a prominent ridgeline along the Louisa road, between White and Nunn's Creeks, approximately three and a half miles north of Louisa. Only the First Division was up; David M. Gregg's

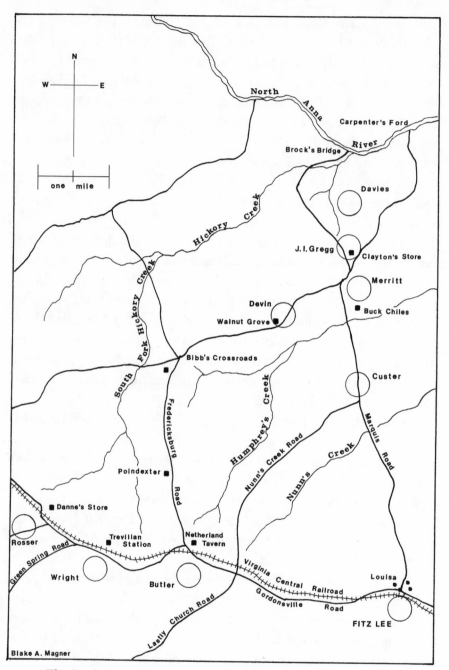

The Camp Sites of the Union and Confederate Forces, June 10, 1864

division was strung out along the roads from Carpenter's Ford, screening the advance of the wagon train.

J. Irvin Gregg's brigade brought up the Federal rear, far from the head of Sheridan's column. The men of this brigade were aware of increased Confederate activity that night; Capt. Isaac Ressler, commanding Company L of the Sixteenth Pennsylvania Cavalry, commented in his diary, "16th went on picket. Captured horse and saddle. Capt. Walker shot in rear. Capt. Rush sent short order for captured horse and saddle." Ressler mistakenly claimed, "Rear guard fired upon by guerrillas."[89] Lieutenant Cormany of the Sixteenth Pennsylvania also observed, "Our foraging parties are being fired into very much."[90] In fact, there were no organized partisans or home guards in the area; angry local citizens, Hampton's Iron Scouts, or some combination of both probably constituted this annoying enemy force.

Dr. Joe Baker, a wounded Confederate soldier from Louisa County recuperating at his home, heard that the Union cavalry were advancing toward Clayton's Store from Carpenter's Ford. Borrowing an old rifle, Baker hid behind a fallen log near Bibb's Store and watched the Union divisions march by. Along with two local boys, Hawes and Rupert Powell, he waited for stragglers to pass by, and was soon rewarded for his diligence. Three stray cavalrymen headed toward his hiding place. Baker raised his gun and demanded the surrender of the Northerners, who gave up when they spotted the two local boys behind them. They turned the disarmed prisoners over to Confederate forces at Louisa Court House. The Powell boys, having gotten a taste of guerrilla warfare, later joined Col. John S. Mosby's Forty-third Battalion of Virginia Cavalry.[91]

Lindsay Wallace Cave owned a handsome brick house overlooking Carpenter's Ford. His younger brother, Reuben, a Confederate soldier, was recuperating at his brother's house from wounds received in the Battle of Spotsylvania Court House when Sheridan's column began splashing across the North Anna. Although still weak from his wounds, Reuben Cave rose from his sickbed, borrowed a horse from his brother, and rode off to raise the alarm. A Yankee mounted on a white horse spotted Cave and sent several bullets whizzing by Cave's ear. With the mounted Federal hot on his tail, Cave galloped off until he found a contingent of Hampton's Iron Scouts. The Scouts wheeled, pitched into the pursuing Northerners, and drove them off. Cave's report confirmed that Yankees were moving toward

Trevilian Station. Years later, Reuben Cave, then a noted minister in Nashville, invited a number of delegates to a Baptist convention to his home for dinner, and the conversation turned to Cave's experiences in the Civil War. When he related the story of his narrow escape on June 10, 1864, one of his dinner guests, a minister from Chicago named Wilkerson, piped up and said, "Why, sir, I was the man on the white horse." Reverend Cave and the visiting minister shook hands across the table, bringing a happy ending to their wartime encounter.[92]

Yankees nearer to the front lines also noticed a marked increase in Confederates buzzing around the fringes of the Federal column. The increasing aggressiveness of the Confederates prompted Sheridan to claim, two years later, and with the benefit of clear hindsight, "During the night of the 10th the boldness of the enemy's scouting parties, which we had encountered more or less every day, indicated the presence of a large force."[93] Private William G. Hills of the Ninth New York Cavalry recounted, "We . . . were attacked by a small squad of rebs who charged on our pickets but soon got out of way of the Reserve." Ominously, Hills concluded, "Hampton's cavalry reported on our track."[94]

Describing the same incident, Torbert reported that the head of his column was attacked by a contingent of ten or twelve of the enemy, who quickly retreated. He wrote, "This was the first time we had seen the enemy during this trip."[95] Hampton's Iron Scouts, out feeling for the Federal positions, harassed Sheridan's advance. One of Butler's men interviewed a captured Federal trooper and learned that the Federals were "entirely unaware that Hampton was in the neighborhood, and in quest of him," and that the Federal commander "had incautiously placed behind himself a river, supposing that he would have an undisputed march." The blue-clad prisoner made it clear that Sheridan was "so completely . . . in the dark about Hampton's movements, that when his advance guard came into collision the next morning with the Confederate force, he mistook the latter for some local militia endeavoring to protect their homes."[96]

Little Phil's troopers were tired and hungry. One Regular recalled, "On that day our regiment had been in the rear, and you know, to be in the rear of a few thousand cavalry was to be in a very barren country, with nothing eatable within two miles on either side. Our officers had been unusually strict on foragers, but when I saw others eating, after feeding my horse, I started to look for something. It began to get dusk and while I was standing in the road trying to decide which way to strike out a small colored boy about twelve years old approached me." The boy, a slave on a local farm, told the trooper that there was food on his master's farm. The Regulars rode off, and soon discovered "a regular commissary, containing large quantities of flour and tobacco." Shouldering several bags of booty and a jug of molasses, the Yankee trooper carried his prize back to camp, where he and his friends savored their flapjacks late into the night.[97]

Other Yankees also enjoyed the countryside's bounty. Pennsylvanian Strang, recovered from his defeat at the hands of the Confederate bees, had luck foraging on the evening of June 9 and prepared his own feast of flapjacks to celebrate his 26th birthday, which was the next day. Strang feasted on the captured flour, shared his good fortune with friends, and saved enough flour for their breakfast the next morning. Sated, Strang lay down and was "soon enjoying a good sleep," blissfully unaware of the large Rebel force camped nearby.[98]

After establishing a picket line, the First Maine Cavalry unsaddled their horses to rub them down and rest them. As the Maine men tended their mounts and prepared their suppers, rifle shots rang out from the direction of the vidette line. Col. Charles H. Smith, the regimental commander, was resting under a nearby tree when he heard the shots. Startled, the colonel jumped to his feet, calling out "Attention!" As the men scurried to saddle their mounts, an orderly rode up and had a few quiet words with the colonel. Smith coolly turned around, and "with military voice and manner" gave an entirely different order: "Go on with your Apple sauce!" This was a strange command "which was long remembered." The tension broken, the men obeyed this odd order, "and hilarity ran rampant for a few moments. It appeared that the commander of the pickets found near his line some fine, fat cattle, and wisely judged they would do his men good, so he concluded to shoot one or two of them, first sending an orderly to notify Colonel Smith, that no alarm might be created." Unfortunately, the orderly got lost, and the officer, believing he had waited long enough, gave the order to fire. The men recalled this incident fondly years after the end of the war, still chortling over their colonel's strange command.[99]

Sgt. Nathan B. Webb of Company D of the First Maine Cavalry remembered the plentiful and sweet cherries along the line of march, a rare delicacy that he and his friends enthusiastically enjoyed. He observed, "We have passed through a most lovely country. Crops look beautiful and everything is fresh and green. It seems a great pity that such fine fields should be laid waste, but such is war."[100]

Lieutenant Noble D. Preston of the Tenth New York led a far tougher foraging expedition. Not long after crossing the North Anna, Preston took a detachment from his regiment and went in search of supplies. An old slave told them of a large supply of bacon and grain not far away. The owner of the farm claimed to be a loyal Union man when confronted by the Yankees. Seeing only ladies' dresses and accoutrements instead of forage, the useful items were distributed and the return march began. As the troopers passed the farm of the "loyal Union man," shots rang out. The New Yorkers, alarmed by the fire into their flank, galloped off in pursuit, getting lost in the dense woods.

Preston and his men had to dismount in the darkness of the thick forest and feel the ground for hoof prints, looking for evidence of the passage of a large body of horsemen. Finally, sentries of the First Maine Cavalry, who were wary of the approaching troopers, greeted them. When the commander of the picket post called out, "One will advance from your party," Preston rode forward. The Maine officer recognized him and greeted him warmly. Preston's little band returned safely to their camp without much to show for their efforts.[101]

Sheridan's large mounted horde swept across central Virginia like a plague of locusts. Once quiet and peaceful, rural Louisa County turned into a place where ugly incident followed ugly incident, both sides committing atrocities. One officer of the Fourth Pennsylvania Cavalry recalled that Sheridan's troopers literally "cleaned out" everything edible for man or beast, "operating over strips of country for miles wide, all along the line of march, both right and left. There were rather rough deeds perpetrated by us in Virginia, at this time, out of sheer necessity." The residents were often entirely destitute of provisions, leaving them with "fair prospects of famine. We were obliged to appropriate to our own uses, all they had. We came down upon them like swarms of locusts, eating up the very seed for their next harvest."

As a result, the enraged citizenry "hovered around in the shape of guerrillas, picking up any stray foragers they found, and making summary examples of them. In consequence it was no uncommon sight to see our dead comrades suspended conspicuously from the limbs of trees along our line of march, and labeled 'Such will be the fate of every forager caught!' " Efforts of the local citizenry to fight back only enraged the marauding Federals: "These scare-crows, horrible and revolting as they were, only whetted the operations of our men, giving to their movements a slight coloring of vengeance. Several of the bodies I saw suspended in this manner, I recognized as those of well-remembered soldiers from our command."[102] As the Union horsemen settled in for the night on June 10, they faced both the Confederate cavalry and an angry local population. They could not have found themselves in more hostile circumstances.

Custer's brigade camped near the Buck Chiles farm, just off the Marquis Road, about three miles from the town. They would be in closest proximity to the Rebels, now known to be nearby in large numbers. Custer established vidette posts along the road to Louisa, waiting for the morning, when he would advance toward the town along the Marquis Road. Custer did not know that this route would take his brigade through the gap between Hampton's and Lee's positions.[103]

Hampton and Sheridan both planned movements the next day. Sheridan developed a simple plan: At sunrise on June 11, Torbert would converge on the important railroad depot at Trevilian Station from two directions. Custer would take his brigade along a wood road running atop a ridgeline, reportedly a direct route to the train station. Merritt and the Regulars would advance on the Fredericksburg Road, followed by Devin's brigade. Torbert's division would then unite at the station and continue west toward Mechanicsville. David M. Gregg's division would bring up the Federal wagon train and guard the flanks in the direction of Louisa.[104] Captain Theophilus F. Rodenbough, commander of the Second U.S. Cavalry, recounted, "Sheridan's intention was to cut the main line of the Virginia Central at Trevilian Station, and the Lynchburg branch of the Charlottesville" railroad.[105] Sheridan did not know that Hampton was in his front with such a large force, and he was also unaware that Lee's Confederates occupied Louisa Court House in strength.[106] Perhaps this explains why Sheridan did not order Gregg to move closer to Torbert's so as to support his advance the next morning.

The pugnacious Hampton saw a rare opportunity to catch his opponent off guard and unprepared. One of Butler's men eloquently described the

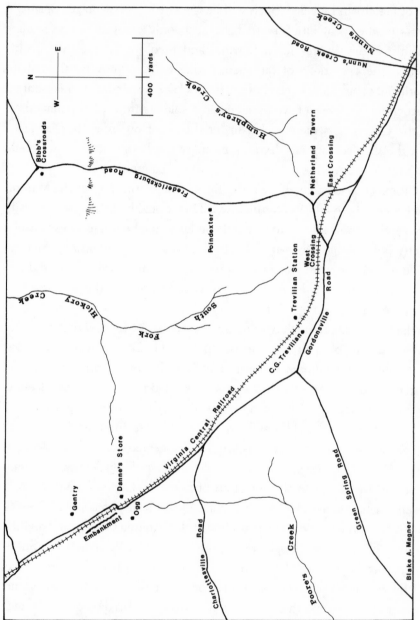

Trevilian Station and Environs, Showing the Battlefields of June 11 and 12, 1864

Blake A. Magner

commanding general's apparent mind-set: "The moment had come not merely for checking his adversary, but for absolutely destroying him; surprised and driven back upon the river, his entire force would be devoted to ruin."[107] Hampton determined to attack the Yankees at dawn. Butler and Wright would advance north along the Fredericksburg Road toward Clayton's Store, while Rosser covered the left flank on the Gordonsville Road. Fitz Lee would move north from Louisa on the Marquis Road, thereby covering Hampton's right flank. The two divisions would unite near Clayton's Store.[108]

In this scenario, Hampton's Division would drive the enemy in his front while Lee flanked Sheridan, pinning the Yankee cavalry against the banks of the North Anna River, and dealing a "*coup-de-grace* to Sheridan's host. The plan was simple, and admirable."[109] When he finally penned his after-action report after the end of the war, Fitz Lee noted, "The converging point, however, was too distant, and before I could reach its vicinity the enemy had passed it."[110]

As events unfolded, neither plan prevailed.

Most of the terrain north of Trevilian Station is not well suited to mounted operations. Trevilian Station is situated between two rivers. Rolling hills and ridges also fill this area. In 1864 thick secondary undergrowth like that in the nearby Wilderness clogged the passage of horse soldiers. Typically, the only breaks in the woods occurred where homesteads and farms had been carved out of the forest. Louisa County only held a population of 6,183 whites and about 11,000 blacks. The widely scattered farms meant that there were more woodlands than open fields. Bricks, lumber, livestock, grain, fruit, and vegetables marked the various items produced in the community, and the environs were a scenic and well-known resort area.[111] The primary physical features were the Louisa Court House–Gordonsville Road, winding its way along the course of the Virginia Central Railroad, crossing over the tracks twelve different times between Louisa and Gordonsville.[112] The Netherland Tavern sat on a knoll at the third crossing, commanding the area surrounding the train station. A fourth crossing separated Netherland Tavern and Trevilian Station. Fifty yards from the train station sat Charles Goodall Trevilian's plantation house.[113]

Author Jerry Meyers points out that the Trevilian Station battlefield "features triangular battlefields, triangular key terrain, and rarely used triangular defensive formations." The train station, the town of Louisa Court

House and Clayton's Store represented the three points of the four-by-four-mile right triangle, with Clayton's Store at the northern end of the triangle and the Gordonsville road as its base. A second key triangular position, located within the boundaries of the first, began at the crossing over the railroad tracks about a quarter of a mile from Netherland Tavern (the "East Crossing"). It continued to the road intersection at the tavern, about 175 yards to the north, and ended with a local road south of the tracks (the "West Crossing").

Finally, where Green Spring Road intersected the Gordonsville Road a quarter of a mile west of the Trevilian house rested the point of an inverted triangular position that played a critical role in the second day's fighting. The road to Mechanicsville intersected the Gordonsville Road, and was a second leg of the triangle. The third leg was the Green Spring Road, angling off to the west. This triangle became the focus of the fighting on June 12.[114] With the heavy woods only broken up by buildings, roads, and the railroad, the area offered far from ideal terrain for extensive mounted operations.

Both Yankee and Rebel horse soldiers tried to catch a few fleeting moments of sleep. The next day, June 11, would see the largest all-cavalry battle of the Civil War.

Notes

1. Carlos McDonald "Diary," *Report of the Forty-Sixth Annual Reunion of the Sixth Ohio Cavalry* (Warren, Ohio: Wm. Ritezel & Co., 1911), 54.

2. William Hyndman, *History of a Cavalry Company: A Complete Record of Company "A", Fourth Pennsylvania Cavalry* (Philadelphia: James B. Rogers Co., 1870), 124.

3. Matthew W. King, *To Horse: With the Cavalry of the Army of the Potomac, 1861–65* (Cheboygan, Mich.: n.p., 1926), 11.

4. The 1910 War Department Field Service Regulations address the speed of march of cavalry. As the Army had no mechanized components at all, and as all of the army's transportation was still based on the horse, the same sort of analysis probably applies. These regulations prescribe a rate of four miles per hour for the walk, eight miles per hour for the trot, and twelve miles per hour for the gallop. The average walk of a horse is at a rate of one mile in sixteen minutes, or 3.75 miles per hour. In the field, the usual gait is the walk of 3.75 miles per hour, including halts. Under favorable conditions, the walk and trot alternate, with the trot not exceeding fifteen minutes per hour marched. The first and last two miles

should be made at an easy walk. The average march for veteran cavalry should cover twenty-five miles per day. War Department, Office of the Chief of Staff, *Field Service Regulations, United States Army, 1910*, War Department Doc. No. 363 (Washington, D.C.: United States Government Printing Office, 1910): Section 147, 94. These rates of march will be assumed appropriate for the analysis set forth in this book. See also Frank D. Grommon diary, entry for June 7, 1864, Bentley Historical Library, University of Michigan, Ann Arbor.

5. Pyne, *Ride to War*, 218.

6. Bean, "Sheridan at Trevilian."

7. Asa B. Isham, "Through the Wilderness to Richmond," *Sketches of War History, 1861–1865: Papers Prepared for the Ohio Commandery of MOLLUS*, vol. 1 (1884), 207–208. When he wrote this, Isham specifically describe d the May 1864 Richmond raid, in which he was captured. While the Trevilian raid took place, Isham was a prisoner of war in Richmond's Libby Prison. Nevertheless, the description is, undoubtedly, accurate for the June raid as well as for the May raid.

8. Edward P. McKinney, *Life in Tent and Field, 1861–1865* (Boston: Richard G. Badger, 1922), 117.

9. Edward P. Tobie, *History of the First Maine Cavalry, 1861–1865* (Boston: Press of Emery & Hughes, 1887), 282.

10. Preston, "The Battle of Trevilian"; Hillman A. Hall, ed., *History of the Sixth New York Cavalry (Second Ira Harris Guard), Second Brigade, First Division, Cavalry Corps, Army of the Potomac, 1861–1865* (Worcester, Mass.: Blanchard Press, 1908), 196.

11. James O. Hall, ed., "An Army of Devils: The Diary of Ella Washington," *Civil War Times Illustrated* (February 1978), 24.

12. Carpenter to his father, June 22, 1864.

13. Preston, "The Battle of Trevilian."

14. *New York Herald*, June 21, 1864.

15. Grommon diary, entry for June 8, 1864.

16. Carlos McDonald diary, entry for June 8, 1864, *Report of the Proceedings of the Sixth Ohio Cavalry*, 55.

17. Samuel L. Gracey, *Annals of the Sixth Pennsylvania Cavalry* (Philadelphia: E. H. Butler & Co., 1868), 258.

18. Carpenter to his father, June 24, 1864; Howard M. Smith diary, entry for June 8, 1864.

19. Pyne, *Ride to War*, 218.

20. Bean, "Sheridan at Trevilian."

21. Hyndman, *History of a Cavalry Company*, 125.

22. Preston, "The Battle of Trevilian."

23. E. B. Strang, *Sunshine and Shadows of the Late Civil War* (Philadelphia: privately published, 1898), 48–49.

24. Carlos McDonald diary, entry for June 8, 1864.

25. Mohr and Winslow, *The Cormany Diaries*, 433.

26. Hagemann, *Fighting Rebels and Redskins*, 241.

27. Conrad, *The Rebel Scout*, 109–110.

28. Thomas L. Rosser, *Riding with Rosser*, Roger S. Keller, ed. (Shippensburg, Pa.: Burd Street Press, 1997), 36.

29. Conrad, *The Rebel Scout*, 110–111.

30. Rosser, *Riding with Rosser*, 36.

31. Swank, *The Battle of Trevilian Station*, 92.

32. Ulysses R. Brooks, *Butler and His Cavalry in the War of Secession, 1861–1865* (Columbia, S.C.: The State Co., 1909), 238.

33. O.R., vol. 36, part 1, 1095.

34. Clifford Dowdey, ed., *The War Time Papers of Robert E. Lee* (Richmond: Virginia Civil War Commission, 1961), 769.

35. Butler, "The Cavalry Fight at Trevilian Station." Author Jerry Meyers believes that the actual strength of these two combined forces was closer to 6,000 sabres. His estimate is based on subtracting the estimated losses from estimated strength after the arrival of Butler's Brigade, Seventh Georgia Cavalry, Twentieth Battalion of Georgia Cavalry, and First Maryland Battalion, adding it to Fitz Lee's estimated strength. Meyers, "Trevilian!," 43, n. 12.

36. Suderow has also researched Confederate strengths and losses. His analysis may be found in Appendix D to this book. The sources for his research are either records in the National Archives, or reports of the action that appeared in various Confederate newspapers. See, as an example, letter from Young's brigade, date June 17, 1864, in the *Savannah Republican*, June 27, 1864, p. 1, col. 3, or the *Richmond Daily Dispatch*, July 1, 1864, p. 1, col. 5. This is groundbreaking and tedious research, but it has brought about the only truly accurate picture of the relative strengths and losses of both sides in this crucial battle.

37. Butler, "The Cavalry Fight at Trevilian Station."

38. Diary of J. D. Ferguson, entry for June 8, 1864, Munford-Ellis Family Papers, T. T. Munford Division, Box 17, Special Collections Department, William R. Perkins Library, Duke University, Durham, North Carolina.

39. Horatio Nelson, *"If I Am Killed on This Trip, I Want My Horse Kept for My Brother": The Diary of Last Weeks In the Life of a Young Confederate Cavalryman*, Harold E. Howard, ed. (Manassas, Va.: United Daughters of the Confederacy, 1980), 17.

40. Halliburton, *Saddle Soldiers*, 146.

41. George M. Neese, *Three Years in the Confederate Horse Artillery* (New York: Neale Publishing Co., 1911), 282. Neese's memoir is the finest single source on the Confederate horse artillery.

42. William Ball memoir, Virginia Historical Society, Richmond, Virginia, 36.

43. James F. Wood diary, entries for June 7 and 8, 1864, Virginia State Archives, Richmond, Virginia.

44. Edward L. Wells, *A Sketch of the Charleston Light Dragoons* (Charleston, S.C.: Lucas, Richardson & Co., 1888), 50. Wells was, perhaps, Wade Hampton's most ardent supporter. He spent the rest of his life writing about and encouraging the memory of Wade Hampton as the greatest of the Southern cavaliers, not Jeb Stuart. His writings, which are extensive and easily accessible, make for an interesting and partisan read.

45. Diary of Joseph F. Waring, entry for June 8, 1864, Southern Historical Collection, Wilson Library, University of North Carolina, Chapel Hill.

46. Neese, *Three Years*, 282–283.

47. William B. Burroughs to his mother, June 12, 1864, William B. Burroughs letters, Southern Historical Collection, University of North Carolina, Chapel Hill, North Carolina.

48. Waring diary, entry for June 9.

49. Brooks, *Butler and His Cavalry*, 238.

50. Diary of Charles McVicar, entry for June 9, 1864, Manuscripts Division, Library of Congress, Washington, D.C.

51. Ball memoir, 36–37.

52. O.R., vol. 51, part 2, 998.

53. *Ibid.*, 996.

54. Dowdey, *Wartime Papers*, 771. Lee recounted the story of the escaped servant who reported the movement to Rosser, and further responded, "It was stated by a prisoner captured yesterday belonging to Genl Sheridan's command, that they had heard that Genl [John Hunt] Morgan was in Pennsylvania and that they were going in pursuit."

55. *New York Herald*, June 21, 1864.

56. Howard M. Smith diary, entry for June 9, 1864.

57. Carpenter to his father, June 22, 1864.

58. Hall, *History of the Sixth New York Cavalry*, 196.

59. *New York Herald*, June 21, 1864. This anniversary was not lost on the Confederates, either. Private Noble J. Brooks of the Cobb Legion noted in his diary on June 9, "This day a year ago I was captured near Beverly's ford on the Rappahannock a sharp shooting." Noble Brooks diary, entry for June 9, 1864, Southern Historical Collection, Library of the University of North Carolina, Chapel Hill. James F. Wood of the Seventh Virginia Cavalry noted in his diary, "Anniversary of the great cavalry fight at Brandy Station one year ago." Wood diary, entry for June 9, 1864.

60. E. C. Moncure, *Reminiscences of the Civil War* (Caroline County, Va.: privately published, 1924), 16.

61. Sheridan, *Personal Memoirs*, vol. 1, 418–419. In reality, Breckinridge's divi-

sion was actually at Waynesboro in the Shenandoah Valley by the time Sheridan learned Hampton was pursuing him.

62. Pyne, *Ride to War*, 218.

63. Karla Jean Husby and Eric J. Wittenberg, eds., *Under Custer's Command: The Civil War Memoir of James Henry Avery* (Washington, D.C.: Brassey's, 2000), 87.

64. Preston, "The Battle of Trevilian." The presence of these contrabands would become a serious logistical problem for Sheridan as the raid continued. Their ranks constantly swelling, these poor fugitives only extended Sheridan's column and stretched it out further across the Virginia countryside.

65. Bean, "Sheridan at Trevilian." Interestingly, there is no mention of this incident in the regimental history of the Seventeenth Pennsylvania Cavalry.

66. Tobie, *First Maine Cavalry*, 282; *New York Herald*, June 21, 1864.

67. Waring diary, entry for June 10, 1864. Waring also makes an interesting observation about the men of the Seventh Georgia Cavalry in this entry: "The 7th marches very badly. They gallop too much. McAllister [colonel of the Seventh Georgia] & Anderson are determined to do something with them."

68. Wells, *Charleston Light Dragoons*, 59.

69. Charles Paine Hansell memoir, Civil War Miscellany, Personal Papers, Georgia Department of Archives and History, Atlanta, Georgia.

70. Neese, *Three Years*, 283–284.

71. Frank M. Myers, *The Comanches: A History of White's Battalion, Virginia Cavalry* (Baltimore, Md.: Kelly, Piet & Co.,1871), 294. Wells reported that the men of Butler's brigade did not learn these facts until that night, after the brigade had gone into camp for the night. Wells, *Charleston Light Dragoons*, 59.

72. Memoir of Capt. John Bauskett, John C. Calhoun collection, Indianapolis, Indiana.

73. Wells, *Hampton and His Cavalry*, 194.

74. Ball memoir, 37.

75. The real Green Spring Valley is actually farther south and holds the headwaters of the South Anna River.

76. O.R., vol. 36, part 1, 1095; Rosser, *Riding with Rosser*, 37.

77. *Ibid.*, vol. 51, part 1, 1003.

78. Dowdey, *Wartime Papers*, 773. Lee recommended to Seddon that small parties of men be sent out to protect against such a foray.

79. Wells, *Charleston Light Dragoons*, 59.

80. Russell, "Battle of Trevilian," 372.

81. Charles M. Calhoun, *Liberty Dethroned: A Concise History of Some of the Most Startling Events before, during, and since the Civil War* (Greenwood, S.C.: privately published, 1903), 124.

82. Butler, "The Cavalry Fight at Trevilian Station," 237.

83. Carpenter to his father, June 22, 1864.

84. O.R., vol. 36, part 1, 796. The precise location of Carpenter's Ford has been a challenge to locate. The damming of the North Anna River obliterated the ford. Only through a review of Chancery Court records in Louisa County, and with the assistance of Louisa attorney John Gilmer, was the author able to ascertain that the ford was located along modern-day State Route 641, which connects the location of the ford and Clayton's Store. See *Carson S. Winston v. John P. Bisese, et al.,* Circuit Court of Louisa County, Virginia, Case No. 1457, April 1, 1974. The same court case also indicates that Meriwether's Bridge and Carpenter's Ford were ostensibly located at the same place. This research resolves uncertainty that has existed as to the precise location of the ford for many years. The author is grateful to Mr. Gilmer for his assistance with unwinding this mystery.

85. *New York Herald,* June 21, 1864; O.R., vol. 36, part 1, 807.

86. Bean, "Sheridan at Trevilian."

87. *New York Herald,* June 21, 1864. The *Herald* correspondent who filed the report was unable to identify this distraught casualty of hard campaigning, indicating only that he thought that the man had come from one of Custer's Michigan regiments. There is no other mention of this episode that the author has been able to locate.

88. Claudia Anderson Chisholm and Ellen Gray Lillie, *Old Home Places of Louisa County* (Louisa, Va.: Louisa County Historical Society, 1979), 160.

89. Ressler diary, entry for June 10, 1864.

90. Mohr and Winslow, *The Cormany Diaries,* 434.

91. Walbrook D. Swank, *The War in Louisa County, 1861–1865* (Charlottesville, Va.: Papercraft Printing & Design Co., 1986), 153; Walbrook D. Swank to the author, January 29, 2000; James J. Williamson, *Mosby's Rangers: A Record of the Operations of the Forty-third Battalion Virginia Cavalry, from Its Organization to the Surrender* (New York: Ralph B. Kenyon, 1896), 484; Hugh C. Keen and Horace Mewborn, *43rd Battalion Virginia Cavalry, Mosby's Command* (Lynchburg, Va.: H. E. Howard Co., 1993), 357. The Powell boys both joined Company F of Mosby's Rangers. Hawes Powell was the great grandfather of Colonel Swank's wife, Frances.

92. Walbrook D. Swank, "Federal Troops Invade Our County," unpublished article provided to the author. Cave was a grandfather of Col. Swank's wife, Frances.

93. O.R., vol. 36, part 1, 796.

94. William G. Hills diary, entry for June 10, 1864, Manuscripts Division, Library of Congress, Washington, D.C.

95. O.R., vol. 36, part 1, 807.

96. Wells, *Charleston Light Dragoons,* 62.

97. Eli H. Lawyer, "Sheridan's Trevilian Raid," *The National Tribune,* April 13, 1911.

98. Edgar B. Strang, *Sunshine and Shadows of the Late Civil War* (Philadelphia: privately published, 1898), 50–51.

99. Tobie, *First Maine Cavalry*, 283.

100. Nathan Webb diary, entry for June 11, 1864, Schoff Civil War Collection, Clements Library, University of Michigan, Ann Arbor.

101. Noble D. Preston, *History of the Tenth Regiment of Cavalry, New York State Volunteers, August 1861 to August 1865* (New York: D. Appleton, 1892), 196–197.

102. Hyndman, *History of a Cavalry Company*, 125–126.

103. O.R., vol. 36, part 1, 823; Hagemann, *Fighting Rebels and Redskins*, 242.

104. Kidd, *Personal Recollections*, 346–347.

105. Rodenbough, "Sheridan's Trevilian Raid," *B&L*, vol. 4 (New York: Century Publishing Co., 1888), 233.

106. O.R., vol. 36, part 3, 735–736.

107. Wells, *Charleston Light Dragoons*, 63.

108. O.R., vol. 36, part 1, 1095.

109. Wells, *Charleston Light Dragoons*, 63.

110. Report of Fitzhugh Lee, December 20, 1866, Fitzhugh Lee Papers, Eleanor S. Brockenbrough Library, Museum of the Confederacy, Richmond, Virginia.

111. Alvin Jewett Johnson, *New Illustrated Family Atlas, with Descriptions, Geographical, Statistical, and Historical* (New York: Johnson & Ward, 1859), 74.

112. This road is modern-day U.S. Route 33, which passes through the heart of the Trevilian Station battlefield. The railroad is still there, and much of Route 33 follows the original road trace through that area.

113. Traditional accounts indicate that the Danne family house was south of the railroad tracks, across from the train station. However, recent discoveries by Jerry Meyers and Ed Crebbs, who have spent many hours on the battlefield at Trevilian Station, have indicated that the house always thought to be the Danne house is actually a Trevilian family home, one of several in the general area. The Trevilian house was acquired by Charles Danne Jr. in 1873, and is generally known to locals as the Danne house, even though it was actually Charles Goodall Trevilian's home. Most of the prior accounts of the Battle of Trevilian Station misidentify this house as the Danne house. The author is grateful to Meyers and Crebbs for their diligence in researching these issues and for sharing the results of their labors with him.

114. Meyers, "Trevilian!," 31–32. Meyers, a combat engineer, has spent countless hours examining the ground and using his years of military training and experience to divine this information. He was kind enough to show the author these features and to assist in the author's understanding of the critical role played by the local terrain in this battle. The author is very grateful to Jerry Meyers, not only for sharing this information, but also for allowing those who wish to understand the Battle of Trevilian Station to share in it as well.

3

First Shots: Torbert and Butler Open the Action

I propose to fight.

Confederate Brig. Gen. Thomas L. Rosser arose early on Saturday, June 11, 1864. As the first fingers of daylight crept across the morning sky, the restless twenty-eight-year-old general swung into his saddle and rode to the headquarters of his close friend, Brig. Gen. Matthew C. Butler. Arriving there, Rosser inquired, "Butler, what is Hampton going to do here today?" Butler responded, "Damned if I know. We have been up mounted since daylight and my men and horses are being worsted by non-action." Rosser suggested that the two generals ride to Hampton's headquarters at the Netherlands Tavern and find out what was expected of them. After ordering his men to dismount and stand to horse, Butler agreed. The pair rode off to find their commanding general.[1] In the meantime, Butler's brigade, "quietly, without blast of bugle or other needless sound . . . was in ranks of readiness to advance to the attack." As they sat waiting, the South Carolinians heard the blare of reveille wafting from Sheridan's nearby camps.[2]

The Netherland Tavern sat just north of the intersection of the Fredericksburg and Gordonsville roads, overlooking the railroad. Built in 1822, the sturdy wood frame two-story building had a stone foundation and brick chimneys at either end. For a number of years, it had served as the principal inn for the railroad station and the Virginia Central's weary travelers.[3] Centrally located between the scattered elements of Hampton's command, it was the logical choice for his headquarters. The tavern became a focus of the day's action.

Arriving at Hampton's headquarters, the two young brigadiers found their commanding general, still fully clothed, sound asleep on a carpenter's

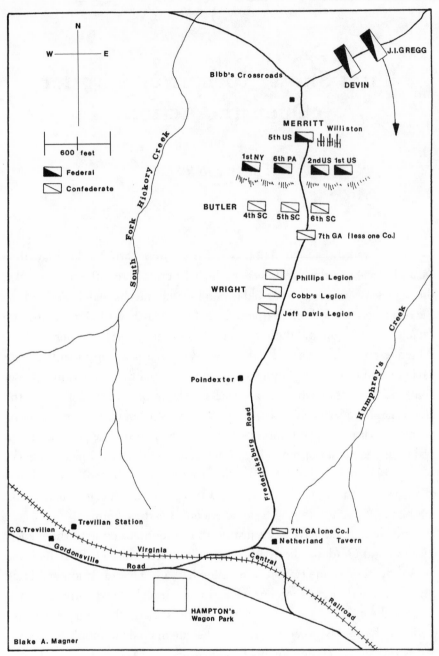

Opening Engagements, Sunrise, June 11, 1864

bench outside the front door of the tavern. Roused, Hampton greeted his subordinates cheerfully, prompting Rosser to ask, "General, what do you propose to do here today, if I may inquire?" Nonchalantly, Hampton replied, "I propose to fight." Butler remarked "that the surrounding country being thickly wooded, did not seem a suitable field for the operation and maneuver of cavalry," to which Hampton responded, "Well, let's ride out and reconnoiter a little." As Rosser rode back to prepare the Laurel Brigade for action, the two South Carolinians, followed by their staffs, mounted and headed off toward Butler's picket posts, the Confederate positions closest to the Yankee camps.[4]

The little band had not gone far when it encountered Capt. Abner B. Mulligan's squadron of the Fourth South Carolina Cavalry, which was rapidly coming in from the distant vidette line. Mulligan, a trader from Charleston, reported that his pickets had been driven in by a strong force of Yankee cavalry near Bibb's Crossroads, north of the railroad station. J. V. Baxley of the Sixth South Carolina Cavalry had been on the vidette line that morning with three of his comrades. When Baxley spotted the Yankee advance, he had to uproot the bush he had hitched his horse to, as the enemy column was so close that he lacked time to untie his mount. When he mounted, the advancing Federals were only fifty yards away. Baxley put spurs to horse and rode off to find Hampton.[5]

As the South Carolinians prepared to go into battle, the morning was chilly and the clover dripped with dew. A cool breeze came off the Piedmont to the west. Trooper Edward L. Wells noted that, "a small piece of musty corn-bread hastily munched represented the only available substitute for breakfast," and observed that not all of the men had that luxury as they readied to do battle. "Happy then would have been that mythical personage, who, it is said, 'would rather fight than eat,' but he would have mustered very few disciples among all those fellows with empty stomachs."[6] They would not have long to wait, as Merritt's Regulars, marching in column of fours and unprepared for battle, were advancing on Butler's position in strength.

In the meantime, Lt. Louis H. Carpenter of the Sixth U.S. Cavalry noted, "we took . . . the dusty road again. The sun seemed particularly warm today and the clouds of dust were suffocating. Our men looked like a set of rebels, gray as they were with the fine dust."[7] The order to march had come early that morning. One member of the Second U.S. Cavalry recalled, "before we got our coffee boiled, it was 'Fall in, boys.' "[8] Merritt's Regulars led Sheridan's advance, with the Second U.S. Cavalry in the van of the blue-clad column. Torbert rode with the Regulars. Twenty-five-year-old Capt. Theophilus F. Rodenbough commanded the Second U.S., a storied regiment with a long and proud history. A native of Pennsylvania, Rodenbough was not a West Pointer. When war broke out in the spring of 1861, the young graduate of Lafayette College received a commission as a second lieutenant in the Second U.S. By the time of Gettysburg, he was a captain, and then assumed command of the regiment upon Merritt's promotion to general. The popular Rodenbough had proved himself capable and competent, prompting Torbert to call him "one of the most deserving young officers of the cavalry." Moreover, Torbert knew that Rodenbough would "not disappoint any trust reposed in him."[9]

At 5:00 A.M. on June 11, Rodenbough led the Reserve Brigade's advance toward Gordonsville. Southwest of Bibb's Crossroads on the Gordonsville Road, Rodenbough's Regulars made the first contact with Butler's men, driving in Rebel pickets and forcing Hampton to deploy Butler. Merritt later remembered that he personally directed Rodenbough to send a squadron forward to capture and hold the train depot at Trevilian Station, which he believed was only about two miles distant. Temporarily leaving another officer in command of the regiment, Rodenbough led the squadron toward the station at a trot and then turned back to resume command of the regiment. A moment later, the Confederates charged, repulsing the Regulars. Spurring forward to the head of the squadron sent to capture the station, Rodenbough led the Regulars in a headlong charge, driving the Confederates back and holding them in place while the rest of the brigade came up.

That morning Hampton ordered Fitz Lee's division to move up the Marquis Road from Louisa toward Clayton's Store. Rosser's Laurel Brigade guarded the western flank and was available as reinforcements. He ordered the division's wagon trains consolidated on a knoll near the train station, getting them out of the way of the fighting developing north of the station.[10] News of the fighting galvanized Hampton, who immediately ordered Butler to bring up his brigade and attack Sheridan. Hampton held Wright's brigade in reserve to support Butler's flanks.

Butler promptly ordered his Palmetto men to "Dismount to fight—action left and action right!"[11] Captain Samuel J. Snowden of the Fourth South Carolina charged with his squadron, hoping to develop the strength of the enemy. Snowden's little force came back nearly as quickly as it went up, reporting the presence of a strong Yankee force. Butler realized that he had met an entire brigade. He expected support from Fitz Lee's division, which supposedly was advancing toward Clayton's Store. The one-legged general dismounted his entire command, except one squadron of the Fourth South Carolina Cavalry, commanded by Capt. John C. Calhoun, a grandson of the great Southern politician.[12] "Butler's men began to dismount, and every fourth man was sent to take the horses to the rear. I was counted as the fourth, but, as Lide Law, my younger cousin, hadn't been in service long," remembered Pvt. William A. Law of the Sixth South Carolina Cavalry, "I handed him the reins and took his place in battle."[13]

Butler ordered his men forward, and they drove the Second U.S. Cavalry back nearly three-quarters of a mile through dense woods. One account described this action as "almost hand to hand." W. H. Dowling of Company B, Fifth South Carolina Cavalry, recalled that he and his comrade Sgt. A. R. Richardson were side by side during this phase of the fighting, their elbows touching. Dowling and Richardson each fired forty rounds that morning "before we let our rifles cool." Dowling and Richardson saw the majesty of the mountains towering to the west for the first time that morning, prompting Richardson to remark, "The old Blue Ridge is looking down on the scene." The two Palmetto troopers fired shot after shot at the advancing Yankee masses. Dowling recalled, "Some of the boys wondered how we could be so cool. The Yankees were reinforced—the fighting is desperate— Kiah Sadier is killed—Capt. Skinner, commanding our squadron, walks up and down encouraging the men: not one of us thought of giving back an inch."[14]

During Merritt's savage attack, Col. Hugh Aiken, commander of the Sixth South Carolina, received a severe wound when a Yankee bullet passed through his body and grazed a lung along the way. The regimental surgeon believed the wound mortal. They left the colonel in the hands of the Union doctors, who considered his condition hopeless and did not attempt to remove him. The Northern surgeons left him on the field to be taken in by a local man. Despite the terrible wound, Col. Aiken recovered.[15]

Pvt. Gabriel Manigault, a messenger sent to find the wounded colonel, rode crouching low to keep out of harm's way. Manigault met a Confederate who indicated that he knew where Aiken could be found. Thanking the gray-clad trooper for the information, Manigault rode on, coming face to face with two Northerners concealed in the high grass. Carbines loaded and cocked, the Federals demanded Manigault's surrender. Recognizing that he had no alternative, and trembling with fear, Manigault handed over his revolver and marched to the rear, his battle ended almost before it began.[16]

Charles M. Calhoun, another trooper of the Sixth South Carolina, recalled, "We gradually fell back firing and contesting every inch of ground." He watched Col. Aiken go down. He then saw a Yankee ball kill the regimental sergeant major, Oscar Sheppard. Receiving orders to lie down and face at right angles to their original position, Butler's men assumed a position along an old rotten wooden fence. They had an open space in front of them with woods to their rear. It was a defensible position, but Calhoun knew that they would not be able to stay there long.[17]

Lt. John Bauskett of the Sixth South Carolina was near Aiken when the colonel fell. Along with six other men, Bauskett found himself cut off and almost surrounded, with firing all around. He told his men to find what shelter they could behind trees and to shoot back. Worried about being captured, the lieutenant was relieved to see a squadron of his regiment advancing toward him. The commander of that squadron, a Captain McGuire, was lost and searching for the main body. Bauskett asked McGuire to take a position on his flank, but McGuire refused, indicating that he preferred high ground behind the lieutenant's position. Maj. Thomas Ferguson, now commanding the regiment after Aiken's fall, also was disoriented. He rode up, took charge of the small force, and ordered McGuire to deploy on Bauskett's left. A severe firefight developed, with the South Carolinians holding their position until one of Butler's staff officers, crawling up on his hands and knees, told them to come out quietly, mount, and report to Hampton.[18]

Another Fourth South Carolina squadron, heavily pressed by Yankee troopers, was on the verge of giving way when Butler and his staff galloped up. Rallying the men, Butler realigned the regiment and pushed it forward again. As the gray-clad horse soldiers advanced, they found a lone Federal officer, Capt. Charles Loeser of the Second U.S. Cavalry. The Confederate charge had cut Loeser off from the rest of his regiment. Two of Butler's couriers called for Loeser's surrender. When Loeser did not respond quickly, the Confederates threatened to shoot him down. Butler countermanded the order and called to Loeser to surrender.

Loeser obeyed and rode out to meet Butler, who took Loeser prisoner. Butler told the captain that he would have to surrender his horse and equipment. Loeser, mortified at his predicament, asked Butler for permission to break his sword, but Butler refused. Butler asked the Yankee how he had become separated from his command. Loeser answered that he had been cut off during the countercharge of the Fourth South Carolina. The humiliated Northerner inquired whether his West Point classmate General Rosser was nearby. Loeser said that he was afraid of being robbed while a prisoner and that he expected better treatment in the hands of his old schoolmate. Butler promised Loeser that he was safe in his charge, but nevertheless offered to send him to Rosser under guard if he gave up his horse and weapons. Loeser agreed, telling Butler that his sorrel mare was "played out." Butler's brother and aide-de-camp, Capt. Nat "Pick" Butler, took Loeser to Rosser, carrying orders to see to it that the Yankee not be robbed as he began his long, lonely ride toward Libby Prison. However, poor Loeser lost his fine pair of boots to one of Hampton's horse artillerists, fulfilling his fears of being robbed.[19]

Private Eli Lawyer rode with Rodenbough's command that day. Suspecting a trap, the Federals slowed to a walk in the thick woods. Lawyer saw two enemy troopers come around a curve in the road, followed by a body coming forward at a charge. Lawyer and his companions retreated, but a downed horse blocked their way. Lawyer spotted a gray-clad horseman bearing down on him, sabre at the ready. He hunkered down on his horse, dug in his spurs, and rode to the safety of the next squadron in line. Turning about, the Regulars received the Confederate charge and ran "into those in front with such force as to dismount a number of them," capturing fifteen to twenty Confederates. Lawyer also noted that "quite a number of our boys got severe sabre cuts in their heads that laid them up some time."[20]

A South Carolinian made his way through this line of Federals and rode right up to Rodenbough just as the captain turned to give orders to the next squadron in line. The rebel shot the Pennsylvanian at point-blank range. "We dared not shoot, as our men stood in range," Lawyer recalled. "But as he passed us a number of us fired and wounded him seriously in the side. He fell into our hands and said he was 17 years old. Many would call that a brave and daring act. I would call it a most foolish one."[21] Rodenbough, severely wounded, turned over command of the regiment to Capt. Daniel S. Gordon.

Merritt praised his subordinate. "Had Rodenbough simply detached the squadron, transmitted the orders through his adjutant and remained with his regiment he would have executed my order in the customary way. As it was I judged of his action then as I have since regarded it as especially distinguished and of great benefit, as an example of valor, as well as leading quickly to an important result."[22] Sheridan urged Rodenbough's promotion as a result of his valor on June 11, leading to Rodenbough's appointment as colonel of the Eighteenth Pennsylvania Cavalry later in the summer. In 1894, thirty years after the battle, he received the Medal of Honor "for distinguished gallantry in action at Trevilian Station while handling his regiment with great skill and unexampled valor."[23]

The rest of the Reserve Brigade formed into line of battle, facing Butler. A brisk firefight broke out, shattering the crisp morning air. Lt. Michael "Paddy" Lawless of the Second U.S., one of the bravest and most popular officers of the regiment, always sought out the heaviest fighting. About 10:00 that morning, he ordered a squadron of the Second U.S. to rush across a small open space to drive the enemy out of a thicket in the woods ahead. The troopers crept forward, calling for Lawless to come back from the open space, but the Irish-born officer would not listen. Instead, he called in his thick Irish brogue, "Forwards! There's no inemy here!" A Confederate volley mortally wounded Lawless. He staggered forward a few steps and fell, pleading, "Come and get my watch." Half an hour after being carried to the rear, the beloved Irishman died holding his rescued watch.[24] Merritt mourned Lawless, eulogizing him, "He was a fearless, honest, and eminently trustworthy soldier, 'God's truth' being the standard by which he measured all his actions."[25]

Merritt advanced his battle line, the First U.S. Cavalry on the left, the Sixth Pennsylvania and the Second U.S. in the center, and the First New York Dragoons on the right. The Fifth U.S., held in reserve, supported Lt. Edward B. Williston's battery, which had come up while the fighting developed. Capt. George B. Sanford of the First U.S. Cavalry remembered that "The whole brigade was immediately deployed into one of the thickest tangles of brush that I have ever seen. We were so close to the enemy that we could hear every word of command as distinctly as those of our own people, but the woods were so dense that we could see no one."[26] Merritt ordered his Regulars forward, and with a yell, they advanced, driving Butler's men before them. The regimental historian of the Sixth Pennsylvania noted, "From carbines they came to pistols; from pistols to sabres, and a desperate hand to hand fight ensued. Lieutenant [Patrick W.] Horrigan [of the Fifth U.S. Cavalry] crossed sabres in a fight with a rebel officer, and after wounding him, compelled his surrender." The wounded Horrigan received a brevet for his valor that day.[27]

Their breakfast interrupted, the First New York Dragoons went into battle that morning at the behest of their commander, Col. Alfred Gibbs, a man described as "courteous, jolly and hospitable, always ready . . . for whatever fortune found for him to do."[28] Alarmed by the closeness of Butler's men, Gibbs leapt onto his horse, calling "Hey, there, you men! Climb on them horses damned quick!" The Dragoons promptly obeyed the order and moved out, with Lt. Col. Thomas J. Thorp leading the regiment into battle. Reaching the front, Thorp loudly ordered his men to dismount and advance at the double-quick. One officer of the Dragoons noted, "The vigilant enemy was on hand, and gave us a warm reception, killing and wounding several in a very short time, besides capturing prisoners, Colonel Thorp being among the captured." Later, a Confederate prisoner reported that "We-uns allers know'd when them dogon Dragoons were comin' when that yelling officer [Thorp] began to whoop; and when we hard that 'Forward, double-quick!' and you-uns began pumping the bullets out-en them shooting irons of yourn we know'd 'twas time to git." Despite the loss of the popular officer, the Dragoons pressed forward, maintaining a galling fire.[29]

As the Dragoons advanced, an officer rode to the rear of their line and shouted, "Forward on the right and take those led horses!" The squadron on the right obeyed, crossing a gully and heading toward a group of horses hitched to straggly pine trees. Three gray-clad troopers appeared, Enfields at the ready, yelling, "Halt, you Yankee sons of bitches!" Union Private C. L. Cuddebec remembered, "You bet my mind worked quick, my Spencer repeater was already cocked, and quicker than it can be told I aimed, fired, and jumped for the bushes. They also fired, one ball cutting through my whiskers and coat collar." After crossing the stream and heading for the horses, Cuddebec encountered about a dozen Confederates, who fired a ragged volley at him. Realizing he had been separated from the rest of his squadron, Cuddebec searched for familiar blue uniforms. Cuddebec found a few other Union troopers and a wounded enemy horseman, shot through the bowels. Although the wounded man begged to be taken to a hospital, the New Yorkers gave him water and left him propped against a tree. "We-uns thought we'd got you-uns sure," the Rebel said. Cuddebec and his companions returned to the main body, their mission of capturing the led horses a failure.[30]

Saddler Edgar B. Strang of Company M of the Sixth Pennsylvania Cavalry, he of the bees and the pancakes, celebrated his twenty-sixth birthday that day. After a celebratory feast the night before, Strang and his tentmate, Pvt. John Butcher, tried to grab some much-needed sleep. "When our advanced pickets were attacked, and we were ordered to mount and were taken to the front at a gallop, where we were dismounted and ordered to prepare to fight on foot, and in less than two hours poor Butcher, my tent-mate, was lying silent in death." Strang never forgot that birthday celebration.[31]

Pvt. Eli Lawyer of the Second U.S. moved along the left side of the road in thick timber. A woven fence ran alongside the road. Recognizing that he might have to beat a hasty retreat and that the thick fence might prove a hindrance, Lawyer put down his carbine to pull down a section of the fence. As he heaved a plank across the road, a Confederate bullet whizzed by his ear and hit a nearby black oak tree with a splat. Lawyer dropped behind a rotten log and spotted the rebels about 100 yards away, carrying rails. He recalled, "I had a good position, and must have made the splinters fly among those rails, as I could see but little more of them moving about." Finally, orders arrived for Lawyer's company to move off to the right. Lawyer obeyed, seeking shelter behind a large tree. He and his sergeant fired on a party of Confederates. Another soldier politely asked the two Federals to move, as he was afraid that he might shoot them during an exchange with Butler's men. After complying with the request, Lawyer and his sergeant saw the soldier fall dead, a Confederate bullet in his brain.[32]

Another of the Regulars, C. W. Stanton of Company C of the Second U.S. was shot during the fighting in the dense woods. Both bones in his left leg shattered just below the knee, Stanton went down in a painful heap.

Knowing that the Federal battle line might advance and leave him behind, Stanton resolved to make his way back, first using his carbine as a crutch, and then crawling on his good leg and both hands. Finally reaching safety, Stanton was taken to a field hospital, his war over.[33]

Lt. Charles H. Veil of the First U.S. held the extreme left of Merritt's line with a force of dismounted men. As the attack pressed the Confederates back, Veil came to a fence previously defended by Butler's men. There, Veil saw "one of the most gruesome sights I ever saw." A big Rebel trooper sat on the inside corner of the fence with his carbine in his hands. A solid artillery shot had torn his head off, and Veil remembered "the skin of his lower jaw was hanging down on his breast. He evidently had a long beard for that was hanging down almost covering his breast."

Turning away from the horrible sight, Veil focused on the task at hand. A farmhouse that served as a refuge for the retreating Confederates stood in front of his position. Veil ordered his men to rush the farmhouse, calling for its occupants to surrender. When he got to the door, the men inside handed out their weapons until a small pile lay in front of Veil. After determining that all weapons had been surrendered, Veil pushed inside, where he found wounded Southern horse soldiers. One of the "wounded" men looked unusually healthy to Veil, who realized that the elderly woman who occupied the house had persuaded a healthy soldier to feign wounding in the hope that he might get away. Veil recounted, "I got the best of him and he had to go along," and Veil led the man into captivity.[34]

Col. B. Huger Rutledge, commanding the Fourth South Carolina, reported to Butler that he was being flanked and needed reinforcements. Butler turned to the courier and calmly said, "Give my compliments to Colonel Rutledge and tell him to flank back." Rutledge commented that this it was the cheekiest order he had ever heard, that he was in the woods with his line stretched out to its limit, and that he was doing his best to hold back the enemy, let alone to flank him.[35] Butler reported his predicament to Hampton, who ordered Wright's Brigade and a section of Capt. James Hart's South Carolina battery of horse artillery sent to support the South Carolinians.

As dawn broke, the sound of gunfire roused the sleepy men of the Seventh Georgia Cavalry. Hastily breaking camp, the men of the Seventh Georgia stood to horse awaiting orders. About 6:00, the Georgians received orders to dismount and picket their horses near Trevilian Station, leaving a small guard with the animals. The Georgians spent the morning "marching and countermarching until quite weary," commented Maj. Edward Anderson, the regiment's second-ranking officer.[36] One member of the regiment reported, "We were then marched to the scene of action, and I do truthfully say that I have never seen men go into a fight more willingly and more calmly than the Seventh Georgia Cavalry." He continued, "A smile lit up the countenance of every man from the right to the extreme left of the line." Committed to the fight, the Seventh Georgia led Wright's counterattack, blunting the Federal advance. A member of the Seventh Georgia noted, "We drove them back in every charge, notwithstanding the advantageous ground which they were occupying. Their ranks were broken, and they fled precipitously. Soon, however, the rally was sounded, and having received large reinforcements, they charged us, numbering us nearly ten to our one. We contested every inch of ground with them, and even held them in check for a time."[37]

Sgt. Charles P. Hansell of the Twentieth Battalion of Georgia Cavalry, of Wright's brigade, recalled that, "we left the pike and turned square off to the left or northward, rode by a large two story house, through a small piece of woods, and then halted and remained here for some time, sitting on our horses and listening to the firing in front where the Seventh [Georgia Cavalry] dismounted and Butler's Brig. were engaging the enemy." Hansell found the angry sounds of Yankee carbine balls whizzing by most disconcerting and worried that being mounted would elevate him into the path of a Federal bullet. To his relief, his dismounted squadron reported to Capt. James Nichols of the Phillips Legion. Nichols led them through the woods and across a small field to a fence near the apex of the firestorm. Because of thick vegetation, the Georgians could not see anything in front of them, but soon received orders from Nichols to fall back and mount up to meet another crisis. Hansell and his mystified comrades soon found out why their services were needed elsewhere—Yankees were reportedly in Hampton's rear.[38]

The advancing Regulars now partly enveloped Butler's line. Pvt. J. V. Baxley of the Sixth South Carolina, who had been cut off by the Yankee attack and was looking for friendly faces, mounted and set off to find his unit. Instead, he found Federal troopers who demanded his surrender. The

Northerners were so dust-covered and grimy that Baxley mistook them for friends, announcing that he was no damned Yankee. To his great surprise, the men in front responded, "Yes, but we are!" Baxley began his journey to a prisoner of war camp, his fine horse appropriated by a Union officer.[39]

Thirty-six-year-old Pvt. James M. Barr, a farmer from Lexington, South Carolina, served in Company I of the Fifth South Carolina Cavalry. He was out on the firing line that morning, and had knelt down as the Federals began their flanking movement. While Barr was on his knees, a Yankee ball dealt him "a tremendous lick" on the inside of the right leg, about an inch and a half below the kneecap. The ball "hit the bone, passing down and around through the Calf of the leg, coming out on the other side, making a wound eight inches long. I don't see what prevented the ball from smashing the bone to pieces," reported Barr to his wife, Rebecca. The ugly wound incapacitated Barr, and he had to be carried from the field about an hour after he fell. The wound left him unable to use the leg. He was taken to a hospital in Charlottesville. He seemed to be recuperating and was optimistic about his chances for recovery, but an infection soon set in. After two amputations, the infection claimed Barr's life on August 29.[40]

As Wright's brigade arrived on the field, Butler sent them to fall in alongside the Fourth South Carolina Cavalry, holding the left flank. Butler later recorded that "Colonel Wright had some difficulty in the thick under-growth in finding his position on Rutledge's left, the enemy meantime pounding us with all his might."[41]

Lieutenant Colonel J. Fred Waring, commander of the Jeff Davis Legion, dismounted a "good many men to support General Butler."[42] As Waring's command and the Georgians of the Twentieth Battalion of Georgia Cavalry pitched into the fray, so too did most of the men of the Seventh Georgia Cavalry and Cobb's Legion. Lt. Wiley C. Howard of Company C of Cobb's Legion had a badly inflamed throat and a severe cough. Under doctor's orders, Howard stayed with the led horses while the balance of the command moved out dismounted. He watched the men advancing, wondering whether they would drive back Torbert's column. He soon found out.[43] The additional men made an immediate impact. Hampton later noted that "these two brigades pushed the enemy steadily back, and I hoped to effect a junction with Lee's division at Clayton's Store in a short time."[44]

Thomson's gunners waited for action that morning. Private D. M. Deck recalled, "Early in the morning we were ready for business and on the road leading from the west toward Trevilian Station and awaiting orders. We had not long to wait." Neese noted, "The fields around the little station were destined to become the arena on which the mastership of the present raiding business was to be decided, and determine who is to be the boss of the expedition."[45] As the Federals advanced steadily toward the train station, Thomson received orders to move his battery forward. Deck, judging from the direction of firing, assumed the battery had taken a position left of the road. He recalled that the day "was clear and hot, without a cloud to be seen save that made by the batteries of the Stuart Horse Artillery as they belched forth their missiles of destruction into the ranks of the Union cavalry, advancing on our lines."[46] Thomson detached Neese's section and sent it toward Gordonsville to find Rosser's brigade, which occupied a blocking position along the Charlottesville road about five miles from Trevilian Station. These guns faced west to protect against forays from the Valley by Hunter's command.

Maj. Roger P. Chew, commander of the Confederate horse artillery battalion, later remembered that "during the fight the guns I had the honor to command held a conspicuous position on top of a hill. Early in the morning, and during the entire day we had a view of the whole battlefield, and it was a most delightful fight for us." He continued, "We were firing all day at them, and our guns did good execution. We fired to kill. That is war. It is a serious business. When you go into a fight, it means wounds, death and destruction."[47]

During this fierce counterattack, Pvt. Thomas Lining, color bearer of the Charleston Light Dragoons, Fourth South Carolina Cavalry, chafed at the idea of remaining with the led horses. Lining exchanged places with an ill man, taking his rifle and cartridge box and falling in with the rest of the company. Lining quickly bled to death when a Yankee ball severed his femoral artery.[48]

Torbert responded by committing Devin's brigade. The Old War Horse sent the Fourth and Ninth New York Cavalry into the fray. Thirty-five-year-old Col. William Sackett, a well-regarded veteran officer, commanded the Ninth New York, an experienced unit that had participated in most of the Army of the Potomac's cavalry engagements. The New Yorkers connected with Merritt's right flank, deploying to the right of the First New

York Dragoons and connecting on the left with a small detachment of thirty men of the Second U.S. Cavalry. Devin committed the Fourth New York, which also deployed into line of battle, connecting with the Regulars of the First U.S. Cavalry. In addition, Devin brought Lt. Edward Heaton's battery into action and detailed three squadrons of the Sixth New York to support the guns.[49] The Northern artillerists took a position back off the crest of the ridge, "so that the muzzles of the guns just cleared the top of the hill."[50] As the New Yorkers deployed, Torbert learned that J. Irvin Gregg's brigade of the Second Division had been sent to his aid. Torbert postponed the attack to wait for the arrival of Gregg's men. The reinforced command would assault the Confederate left.

Gregg's brigade also got an early start that day, the First Maine Cavalry leading the way. John P. Tobie of the First Maine recalled that "skirmishing commenced between six and seven o'clock in the morning, and the engagement soon became general and severe."[51] About half an hour after they moved out, and only about two miles from the train station, Sheridan, who had ridden out to consult with J. Irvin Gregg, halted the column to send out scouting parties. Sgt. Nathan Webb of the First Maine noted, "it became evident that Wade Hampton with his command was in our front. And I have no doubt that when Gen. Sheridan ascertained that fact he was glad. For it was our boast that we were now the superiors of even that famous chieftain's command." One of Gregg's men thought that it took Gregg's brigade nearly two hours to complete its reconnaissance and to form into line of battle.[52] The regimental historian counted six different instances where the regiment prepared to fight on foot. The Maine men never fired a shot, but instead moved around the battlefield supporting Capt. Alanson M. Randol's Batteries H & I (combined), First U.S. Artillery and plugging holes in the line.[53]

After deploying, Randol's guns, which came up from the rear of the column, opened on the Confederates, causing gray-clad troopers to scurry out of harm's way. Webb praised the Regular artillerymen. "I don't think I ever saw more accurate artillery shooting," he wrote. "Every shot told and soon they retired to the edge of the woods." Precise Federal firing blunted Butler's counterattack.

The fighting intensified as Torbert awaited Gregg's arrival. The two foes slugged it out, each side taking heavy casualties. Butler later recalled that his brigade and Wright's "were thus struggling with a superior force in my front, and the stubborn fight [was] kept up at close quarters for several hours."[54] The Confederate troopers made a stand at the Poindexter house, about a mile from the train station. The house occupied a ridge well back from the road in an apple orchard that was surrounded by a large clearing. Behind the clearing stood more dense woods, hiding the Southerners gathering there. Hampton also placed Hart's battery there in a position selected by Chew. Butler now had his first opportunity to forge a cohesive battle line.[55]

Hart's Confederate gunners opened severe counter-battery fire on Heaton's position. "The enemy had a battery on a . . . crest about a mile distant," recalled Trooper Edward P. McKinney of the Sixth New York Cavalry, assigned to support Heaton's guns. "We remained dismounted behind the battery, holding our horses, far enough down the hill so that most of the shells passed over us although we had some casualties. Having to lie still for such a long time, and listen to the shells coming close over our heads, was more trying to the nerves than active fighting."[56] Heaton's gunners got the better of the exchange. Lt. William T. Adams, one of Hart's section commanders, received a painful wound, and three privates of Adams's section were killed in the artillery duel.[57]

Torbert realized that a delay gave Butler opportunity to strengthen his defensive position. Torbert hoped to prevent the South Carolinian from doing so. Sheridan, patrolling his lines that morning, rode up to Devin and asked the Old War Horse if he had a regiment that could break Hampton's line in the woods. Devin replied, "Yes, I have. Where's the Ninth New York?" Colonel Sackett received orders to take his 220 officers and men and advance cautiously into the woods toward the Poindexter house and orchard, which were located on the west side of the Fredericksburg Road. Hearing the warning to be cautious, Sackett boasted, "All hell can't stop my men—they were never known to be on the line five minutes without charging," and gave the order for the regiment to go forward.[58] The men went into the thick brush with a yell, unable to see the enemy positions. Unfortunately, these brave men soon found Butler's position "by his rapid fire and the singing of his bullets."[59] Trooper William Bradshaw described the Rebel volley, "As the line reached Merritt's line, all at once, without warning, such a blast and withering fire, so close the heat from the guns was like a blast from a furnace, or from the infernal regions."[60]

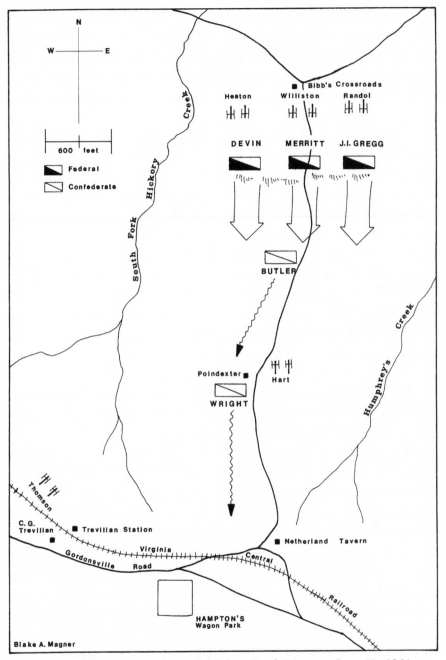

Torbert's Assault along the Fredericksburg Road, Morning, June 11, 1864

Sackett fell mortally wounded, and about forty other officers and men also fell. Undeterred, and cheering as they advanced, the New Yorkers took advantage of the thick foliage that had protected Butler's men. They shattered the South Carolinian's line of battle. Sgt. Edward P. Gifford had enlisted in the Ninth New York at the time of its formation, and served in all of its campaigns. In February 1864, he enlisted for a second three-year term, determined to see the war through. Gifford was killed instantly by a Confederate ball that struck him in the breast. "A braver or truer soldier than Sergt. Gifford . . . never laid down his life for his country," lamented a correspondent. "Unflinching in battle, beloved by his comrades, faithful in the discharge of his duties, ever sober and reliable, his friends at the town of Dunkirk may well feel proud of him."[61]

This small force, joined by the Fourth New York and some of Regulars, pushed Butler's and Wright's brigades, which were already breaking contact with Torbert's troopers, back toward Netherland Tavern. The men of the First Division forced the enemy out of their position in the dense woods, ran them across an open field, two laterals that fed Hickory Creek and another open field. The men of the First Division drove the Confederates almost all the way back to the train station, a distance of nearly two miles.

The New Yorkers captured more than 80 prisoners, including one intrepid Rebel major who, with a few men, tried to defend his position in the woods instead of falling back. "Well, this beats hell," the Southern major said. "I was at headquarters this morning and they said they were surely going to bag the Yankees before night—sure as hell this looks like it, don't it?"[62] Trooper Bradshaw proudly pointed out that this single regiment had accomplished what five regiments of the Reserve Brigade had failed to do: break the lines of Butler and Wright. He crowed that the regiment "had done the unexpected" in executing Devin's orders to assault the woods.[63] Cpl. Nelson Taylor of the Ninth New York, who seized the Fifth South Carolina Cavalry's battle flag from a captured wagon, remembered the fray as "one of the hardest Cavalry fights of the war." Sadly, Taylor lamented that he held little hope for the popular Sackett's recovery.[64] The Federals took a total of 380 Southern prisoners during the assault. The Union troopers suffered heavy casualties, too. Sackett died on June 14. He received a posthumous brevet to brigadier general of volunteers in honor of his coura-geous assault that morning. One of his men wrote, "Col. Sackett's loss will be severely felt by the regiment. His dauntless courage, and constant care for the welfare of his regiment had endeared him to all."[65] He was buried in the yard of the Bibb house, next to Bibb's Crossroads.[66]

A Virginian remembered that "the raiders made a gallant and desperate charge on General Hampton's line, and for a while the conflict raged furiously; at one place the blue line swept over the field with such a bold and fearless courage that some of our cavalry, under a heavy fire of the oncoming exultant foe, wavered and fell back in a regular mixed-up flinch."[67] Lt. Col. William Stokes of the Fourth South Carolina reported to his wife that "we lost a good many [prisoners], who were surrounded and went into the enemy's lines [mistaking them] for ours."[68] The retreating Confederates also left most of their dead and wounded in Northern hands.[69]

Sheridan, unable to resist the call of the firing lines, rode to the front accompanied by his staff officers, "where shot and shell flew unceremoniously close, but where he could personally superintend all movements."[70] Captain Sanford recalled that Sheridan's "influence on his men was like an electric shock, and he was the only commander I have ever met whose personal appearance in the field was an immediate and positive stimulus to battle."[71] Inspired by their commander's presence, the Federals resumed their push to break the lines of Butler and Wright and to clear the path to Trevilian Station.

Butler realized that he was in danger of being flanked, and ordered his men and Wright's brigade to fall back. They retreated in good order and took up a position behind a fence. They resisted the advance, laying down a heavy fire, "determined to make a desperate stand, but we soon found that the Yankees know of our strong formidable position and refused to advance."[72] Hampton rode by and praised the Georgians, crying out, "Boys, you have fought nobly and desperately; you have fought as if you had all the fighting to do yourselves."

The retreat of the outflanked men of the Seventh Georgia Cavalry surprised Private Noble Brooks of Company E, Cobb's Legion. The men of Cobb's Legion mounted and drew sabres, hoping to stem the tide. They failed, yielding to the momentum and size of Torbert's assault. Brooks recalled that his company commander drew his sabre and threatened to use it on the men of the Seventh Georgia, but to no avail. Two panicked Georgians ran into Brooks's horse, nearly knocking him from the saddle and causing him to drop his gun. Brooks dismounted to retrieve the carbine, but before he could remount his horse, the Yankees came up at full speed, firing as they came. The firing so excited Brooks's horse that Brooks could not climb aboard the frightened animal. Brooks turned him loose instead and sought shelter in the railroad cut.

While hiding, Brooks heard two passing Federals laughing. "We are giving them fits now," they said. He noted in his diary, "the joke was soon turned for our pickets farther on down the road fired into them and turned them back. They retreated as fast as they advanced. The rear-most man dismounted and fired a shot back in five feet of me." Brooks had lost his weapons and could not capture the lone Yankee. Instead, he hid in a workshop not far from the railroad.[73]

Lt. Wiley C. Howard had a similar experience. When the Seventh Georgia came flying back, Howard remained with the led horses while Cobb's Legion exchanged fire with the Northern horsemen. Soon, a body of Federals got into his rear and spooked the horses, which stampeded. The Yankees chased Howard for nearly a mile. He jumped his horse over a pile of shells from a wrecked caisson and tried to negotiate a ravine. The animal fell, throwing him. Howard tried to escape on foot with Federals in pursuit. One of them caught up to him, calling for his surrender, but Howard refused. Instead he pressed on, scrambling over a fence as the ping of Northern bullets whistled in his ears. Sheridan's troopers used him for target practice, but to Howard's great surprise, no bullets hit him. Finally reaching the shelter of a forest, the panting officer fell in with a member of the Jeff Davis Legion. The two men hid, waiting to see what would happen. Lieutenant Howard tried to suppress the wracking coughs that had placed him on sick call that morning.[74]

Private Wells of the Fourth South Carolina Cavalry was in the front line resisting Torbert's advance. As fighting raged, a Northern bullet badly wounded Wells in the leg. Lying where he fell, the advancing Yankees took him prisoner. He survived the wound to become the most prominent chronicler of the exploits of Hampton's cavalry.[75] Wells' commanding officer, Lieutenant Colonel Stokes, was nearly bagged when he mistook Heaton's guns for a Confederate battery. Because he did not know the ground, he became disoriented and only "made a narrow escape in getting off."[76]

Private Ulysses R. Brooks of the Sixth South Carolina, aged eighteen, fought alongside his older brother, Whitfield Butler Brooks. The Brooks boys were cousins of General Butler, sharing a common great grandfather. They proudly served under their kinsman's command. The siblings "wanted to have a good time and joined the Confederate cavalry." They had seen action in the coastal defenses of South Carolina and at Haw's Shop. The older brother, Whitfield, at nineteen, was known for being "ever at his post and never failing at his duty." They steadfastly did their duty on June 11, too. One of them had one day left to live.[77]

The South Carolinians put up a stout defense. Trying a counterattack against Devin's assault, some members of the Sixth South Carolina charged. A few paces into their attack, though, one of the regiment's orderlies, John Clowney, was shot in the bowels. Charles Calhoun avenged the orderly's death, killing the blue-clad trooper who had fired the fatal shot. Clowney lingered until the next day, and died knowing that Calhoun had avenged his death. Calhoun watched another member of his company draw a bead on a Federal trooper. As the Southerner pulled the trigger, a Yankee ball "riddled the stock of his rifle cutting off the end of one of his fingers, he thinking he was wounded in the bowels fell down and hollowed manfully. Some of the boys carried him to the rear and found out nothing was wrong only his finger was shot off, but he was sent to the hospital, took gangrene in the wound and died."[78]

J. Irvin Gregg's men arrived and connected with Devin's left, bringing Randol's battery with them. Torbert now had three brigades and two batteries to press the attack. Only two enemy brigades opposed him. Confederate artillerist Neese recalled that the Yankee troopers "made a fierce and stubborn onset right at Trevilian Station, and for a while they fought like fury, as if they intended to do something this time sure enough, and they came very near doing it."[79] An officer of the Sixteenth Pennsylvania Cavalry recalled, "by 9:30 the fight rages furiously."[80] Sergeant Webb of the First Maine noticed that the brigade's position risked being flanked. As the firing grew heavier, Colonel Gregg and General Sheridan galloped by the men of the First Maine, and Gregg bellowed at their commander, Col. Charles H. Smith, "Have your command in readiness, Colonel!" In order to meet the threat, a few Maine men crossed a ravine that formed the headwaters of White Creek, forcing the Confederate lines back once again. That small action eliminated the threat.[81]

Torbert recorded, "The enemy undoubtedly seeing these dispositions, commenced to withdraw from my front, which I immediately followed up so closely that he had no time to form again till he was beyond the station, and I stopped the pursuit."[82] So far, things had gone well for the Federal advance. Torbert's training and experience as an infantry officer had paid dividends. He recognized that thick undergrowth and forests made mounted operations largely impossible. Torbert had used his dismounted troopers like foot soldiers, effectively employing infantry tactics against Butler and Wright. Advancing like infantry and supported by fire from Heaton's guns, his men drove the Confederates for two miles, inflicting heavy casualties and taking large numbers of prisoners.

The morning's success, however, had been costly. Torbert's division took heavy casualties in the fighting with Butler's men, who were armed with long-range Enfield rifle-muskets. Two of Torbert's regimental commanders were down: Col. Sackett of the Ninth New York with a mortal wound, and Capt. Rodenbough of the Second U.S., seriously wounded in the opening minutes of the battle. Despite these losses, if the opening phases of the fight foretold the prospects for the afternoon, June 11 was going to be successful for Northern arms.

About noon, a lull fell across the battlefield, as the two sides consolidated their positions. Sergeant Webb spotted Sheridan sitting on his horse near Randol's guns, his hat off, relaxing in the shade of a cherry tree. Webb surmised that the commanding general was "apparently waiting for something to be done or a certain time to come." The respite gave some enterprising troopers a chance to boil coffee and plunder nearby cherry trees.[83]

Despite his success so far, Torbert was uneasy. He had ordered Custer and his Wolverines to take a different route to Trevilian Station than that taken by his other two brigades. Torbert learned from local inhabitants that a country road branching off the Marquis Road south of the Buck Chiles farm led directly to the main highway east of the train station. The division commander dispatched his aide-de-camp, Capt. John J. Coppinger of the Fourteenth U.S. Infantry, with orders for Custer to advance by that route, to arrive at Trevilian Station at 8:00 A.M., and to hold the crucial station until the rest of the division arrived.[84] Custer was directed "as he neared the station to connect or communicate with the command on his right," and had moved out around 5:00 when the rest of the division began its march. Neither Custer nor Torbert knew the road. This created problems, and Custer lost contact with the rest of Torbert's command.[85] Lt. Robert C. Wallace, commissioned as an officer in the Fifth Michigan Cavalry, but serving on Torbert's staff, remembered that Custer "was separated from our Command and his whereabouts was not known."[86] By 10:00, Torbert had had no word from the Wolverines.

Worried for their safety, the general sat pondering his next move when he heard loud firing exploding in his front, coming from the direction of the train station.[87] The next chapter in the Battle of Trevilian Station was about to begin. This new and dangerous episode nearly cost George Custer both his life and his brigade, and also foreshadowed another hot June day twelve years later on the bluffs overlooking the Little Big Horn River.[88]

Notes

1. Brooks, *Butler and His Cavalry*, pp. 239–240; Butler, "The Cavalry Fight at Trevilian Station," 237.

2. Wells, *Hampton and His Cavalry*, 194.

3. Chisholm and Lillie, *Old Home Places of Louisa County*, 155. The tavern stood well into the twentieth century, but was eventually torn down. The present landowner has constructed a replica near the site of the original that is accessible to the public. William A. Netherland and his wife Martha Jane Netherland are buried nearby.

4. Brooks, *Butler and His Cavalry*, 240.

5. J. V. Baxley, "Some of the Experiences of J. V. Baxley, a Confederate Veteran, as told by him," in *Recollections and Reminiscences 1861–1865 through World War I* (Columbia, S.C.: United Daughters of the Confederacy, 1990), 98. Mulligan was described by one of Butler's staff officers as possessing "unflinching courage and highly effective soldiership." Mulligan was badly wounded in October 1864. The injury prevented his promotion to colonel of the Fourth South Carolina Cavalry. Clement Anselm Evans, ed., *Confederate Military History: A Library of Confederate States History in Thirteen Volumes Written by Distinguished Men of the South*, vol. 5 (Atlanta: Confederate Publishing Co., 1899), 768–770.

6. Wells, *Charleston Light Dragoons*, 63.

7. Carpenter to his father, June 22, 1864.

8. Lawyer, "Sheridan's Trevilian Raid."

9. Francis F. Heitman, *Historical Register and Dictionary of the United States Army*, vol. 1 (Washington, D.C.: U.S. Government Printing Office, 1904), 841; Roger D. Hunt and Jack R. Brown, *Brevet Brigadier Generals in Blue* (Gaithersburg, Md.:

Olde Soldier Books, 1989), 515; Alfred T. A. Torbert to Edwin M. Stanton, October 25, 1864, included in Theophilus F. Rodenbough Medal of Honor file, RG 94, File No. 9750PRD1893, the National Archives, Washington, D. C. Rodenbough's story is a fascinating one. Later in 1864, he was appointed colonel of the Eighteenth Pennsylvania Cavalry, and, while leading his men in the grand cavalry charge that decided the Third Battle of Winchester on September 19, 1864, he was badly wounded in the arm, which required amputation. In the spring of 1865, he received a brevet to brigadier general of volunteers and another brevet to brigadier general in the United States Army in recognition of his gallant and meritorious service. After the war, he stayed in the Regular Army and retired in 1879 as a full colonel. After his active military career ended, he became the most prominent American cavalry historian of the nineteenth century, leaving a rich and prolific legacy behind, including a fine regimental history of his old regiment, the Second U.S. Cavalry. He died in 1912 after a long and interesting life spent either in the service of his country, or in documenting the deeds of those in service of their country.

10. O.R., vol. 36, part 1, 1095; McDonald, *History of the Laurel Brigade*, 251. Butler contended that there were actually several different wagon train parks, but it appears that the train was assembled in one place near Trevilian Station. Butler, "The Cavalry Fight at Trevilian Station," 237.

11. O.R., vol. 36, part 1, 1095; Brooks, *Butler and His Cavalry*, p. 240; Abner B. Mulligan, *"My Dear Mother and Sister": Civil War Letters of Capt. A. B. Mulligan, Co. B, 5th South Carolina Cavalry, Butler's Division of Hampton's Corps, 1861–1865* (Spartanburg, S.C.: Reprint Co., 1992), 183.

12. Butler, "The Cavalry Fight at Trevilian Station," 237.

13. Swank, *The Battle of Trevilian Station*, 98.

14. Mulligan, *"My Dear Mother and Sisters,"* 183.

15. "Additional Sketches Illustrating the Services of Officers, Privates and Patriotic Citizens of Louisiana," *Confederate Military History* 13:323.

16. Lucius Manigault Family Papers, Manuscripts Division, Library of Congress, Washington, D.C.

17. Calhoun, *Liberty Dethroned*, 124–25.

18. Bauskett memoir.

19. Brooks, *Butler and His Cavalry*, 241–242; Charles Loeser, "Personal Recollections-Prison Life," in *From Everglade to Canon with the Second Dragoons*, ed. Theophilus F. Rodenbough (New York: D. Van Nostrand, 1875), 315–18.

20. Lawyer, "Sheridan's Trevilian Raid."

21. *Ibid*.

22. Wesley Merritt to Adjutant General, U. S. Army, September 2, 1893, Theophilus F. Rodenbough Medal of Honor File, RG 94, File No. 9750PRD1893, the National Archives, Washington, D.C.

23. Theophilus F. Rodenbough Medal of Honor Citation, RG 94, File No. 9750PRD1893, the National Archives, Washington, D.C.

24. C. W. Stanton, "Sheridan's Trevilian Raid," *National Tribune*, November 30, 1911.

25. O.R., vol. 36, part 1, 849.

26. Hagemann, *Fighting Rebels and Redskins*, 242.

27. Gracey, *Annals of the Sixth Pennsylvania Cavalry*, 260; Heitman, *Historical Register*, 543.

28. Newhall, *With General Sheridan*, 11.

29. James R. Bowen, *Regimental History of the First New York Dragoons, with Lists of Names, Post-Office Addresses, Casualties of Officers and Men, and Number of Prisoners, Trophies, &c.* (Washington, D.C.: Gibson Bros., 1865), 198, 187.

30. *Ibid.*, 194–95.

31. Strang, *Sunshine and Shadows*, 51.

32. Lawyer, "Sheridan's Trevilian Raid."

33. Stanton, "Sheridan's Trevilian Raid."

34. Charles H. Veil, *The Memoirs of Charles Henry Veil: A Soldier's Recollections of the Civil War and the Arizona Territory* (New York: Orion Books, 1993), 45. Then a sergeant, Veil had been Maj. Gen. John F. Reynolds's orderly at the time that Reynolds was killed at the Battle of Gettysburg, and had been commissioned an officer as a reward for his dutiful care of his slain commander.

35. Brooks, *Butler and His Cavalry*, 243.

36. Carolyn Clay Swiggart, *Shades of Gray: The Clay and McAllister Families of Bryan Count, Georgia* (Darien, Conn.: Two Bytes Publishing, 1999), 73.

37. "From the Seventh Ga. Cavalry," *Savannah Republican*, July 8, 1864.

38. Hansell memoir.

39. Baxley, "Some of the Experiences of J. V. Baxley," 167–68.

40. James M. Barr to My Dear Rebecca, June 14, 1864 and June 16, 1864, in James Michael Barr, *Let Us Meet in Heaven: The Civil War Letters of James Michael Barr, 5th South Carolina Cavalry*, ed. Thomas D. Mays. Unpublished book manuscript. Chapter 7, 4–11. The author is grateful to Prof. Thomas D. Mays of Quincy College who provided him with the pertinent chapter of his as-yet unpublished book manuscript of Barr's letters.

41. Butler, "The Cavalry Fight at Trevilian Station," 237. It is difficult to find this spot today.

42. Waring diary, entry for June 11, 1864.

43. Wiley C. Howard, *Sketch of Cobb Legion Cavalry and Some Incidents and Scenes Remembered* (Atlanta: privately published, 1901), 14.

44. O.R., vol. 36, part 1, 1095.

45. Neese, *Three Years*, 284.

46. D. M. Deck, "Captured at Trevilian Station," *Confederate Veteran*, 24 (1916): 123.

47. R. P. Chew, "The Fight at Trevilian," typescript, Roger Preston Chew Papers, Jefferson County Museum, Jefferson County, Virginia, 1.

48. Wells, *Charleston Light Dragoons*, 64.

49. O.R., vol. 36, part 1, 840. One of the two remaining squadrons of the Sixth New York was sent to try to communicate with Custer's brigade, and the other remaining squadron was held in the rear, guarding the wagon trains. Thus, Devin committed to battle with a command that was not up to its normal size or strength.

50. McKinney, *Life in Tent and Field*, 117.

51. Tobie, *First Maine Cavalry*, 283.

52. Webb diary, entry for June 12, 1864.

53. Tobie, *First Maine Cavalry*, 284.

54. Butler, "The Cavalry Fight at Trevilian Station," 237.

55. Chew, "The Battle of Trevilians," 5–6. Maj. Chew remembered that the positioning of Thomson's guns was the first support that Butler had that morning.

56. McKinney, *Life in Tent and Field*, 117–18.

57. U. R. Brooks, *Stories of the Confederacy* (Columbia, S.C.: The State Company, 1912), 267.

58. William Bradshaw, *The Ninth New York Cavalry: A Forlorn Hope, the Battle of Trevilian Station, June 11, 1864* (Washington, D. C.: privately published, 1864), 9.

59. Cheney, *Ninth New York Cavalry*, 184; William G. Hills diary, entry for June 11, 1864.

60. Bradshaw, *A Forlorn Hope*, 9.

61. *Fredonia Censor*, June 29, 1864.

62. Cheney, *Ninth New York Cavalry*, 185.

63. Bradshaw, *A Forlorn Hope*, 11.

64. Gray Nelson Taylor, *Saddle and Sabre: The Letters of Civil War Cavalryman Corporal Nelson Taylor* (Bowie, Md.: Heritage Books, 1993), 159.

65. *Fredonia Censor*, June 29, 1864.

66. Hunt and Brown, *Brevet Brigadier Generals in Blue*, 515.

67. Neese, *Three Years*, 284–85.

68. Halliburton, *Saddle Soldiers*, 146.

69. Hall, *History of the Sixth New York Cavalry*, 197.

70. Gracey, *Annals of the Sixth Pennsylvania Cavalry*, 260.

71. Hagemann, *Fighting Rebels and Redskins*, 222.

72. Thomas Gamble, "The McAllister Family," included in the Gamble Collection, Savannah Public Library, Savannah, Georgia, 3.

73. Noble P. Brooks diary, entry for June 11, 1864.

74. Howard, *Sketch of Cobb Legion Cavalry*, 14–15.

75. Edward L. Wells, handwritten reminiscences, Wells Correspondence, 23. Wells eventually was admitted to the bar in South Carolina, maintaining a legal practice in Charleston. He spent the rest of his life chronicling the accomplishments of Hampton's cavalrymen, and was a prolific writer, producing two well-respected books, *Hampton and His Cavalry in '64* and *A Sketch of the Charleston Light Dragoons,*

as well as numerous articles and voluminous correspondence, all of which is essential to anyone attempting to research the Confederate cavalry in 1864.

76. Halliburton, *Saddle Soldiers*, 146.

77. Brooks, *Butler and His Cavalry*, flyleaf and pages 7–10. Ulysses Brooks, who dedicated his fine work, *Butler and His Cavalry in the War of Secession*, to the memory of his beloved brother Whitfield, also spent the balance of his life documenting the exploits of Matthew C. Butler's gallant cavalry as well as South Carolina's contributions to the Civil War. A lawyer by training, Brooks went on to serve as clerk of the Supreme Court of South Carolina in the years after the Civil War. Again, his works are standard references on their subjects. It is interesting that Brooks and Wells fought together on the same fields, but probably did not know each other, even though both made major contributions to the body of Civil War history.

78. Calhoun, *Liberty Dethroned*, 125.

79. Neese, *Three Years*, 284.

80. Mohr and Winslow, *The Cormany Diaries*, 434.

81. Webb diary, entry for June 12, 1864.

82. O.R., vol. 36, Part 1, p. 807.

83. Webb diary, entry for June 12, 1864.

84. Carle Woodruff to Adjutant General, United States Army, July 3, 1892, John Kennedy Medal of Honor File, RG 94, File No. 18184PRD1891, the National Archives, Washington, D.C.

85. Kidd, *Personal Recollections*, 348–49.

86. Robert C. Wallace, *A Few Memories of a Long Life* (Fairfield, Wash.: Ye Galleon Press, 1988), 37.

87. O.R., vol. 36, part 1, 807.

88. Ironically, the man most often blamed for the disaster that befell Custer at the Little Big Horn, Maj. Marcus A. Reno, was also present at Trevilian Station. Reno served as a staff officer with Torbert. Thus, Reno was an eyewitness to the two most trying days of Custer's life and death.

4

Custer's First Last Stand:
The Fight for Hampton's Wagons

Where in hell is the rear?

Custer's Michigan Cavalry Brigade spent the night of June 10 encamped a mile south of the Buck Chiles farm along the Marquis Road and a nearby wood road. The Boy General had a comfortable camp, surrounded by his staff officers and two personal servants, including young Johnnie Cisco, a waif who washed the general's shirts, waited on his table, and held his extra horses in battle. His other servant was a runaway slave named Eliza Brown. She cooked Custer's meals and was beloved by the young general, his new bride, and the men of the Michigan Brigade, who appreciated Eliza's sense of humor and sauciness. She followed the Boy General closely in a rattletrap carriage that had undoubtedly been liberated from a Southern plantation, earning her the endearing sobriquet, "The Queen of Sheba."[1]

Torbert sent a staff officer to Custer with orders for his brigade to march at once, about daylight, or around 5:00 A.M. The Fifth Michigan, at the head of Custer's column, moved out a few minutes later, followed by Lt. Alexander Pennington's battery and the Sixth Michigan.[2] To guard against Confederate activity, Custer assigned the men of Maj. Melvin Brewer's Seventh Michigan Cavalry to picket the road.[3] Brewer's troopers spent an anxious night, huddling for warmth in the light summer drizzle and waiting to see whether the Southerners would attack. A Michigan man recalled that "the morning was cloudy and mist lay low so we could not see very far."[4]

Fitz Lee ordered Wickham's Virginia brigade to sortie up the Marquis Road and find the enemy. Wickham's men swung into their saddles around 3:00 A.M. and advanced tentatively up the road. They did not reach the main Union picket lines until daylight. About a mile north of Louisa, Wickham's troopers spotted Maj. Alexander Walker's videttes on the north bank of a creek, drew sabres, and charged, capturing three of Custer's scouts.[5] They continued on until they reached the Wolverines' main line and pitched into Custer's camps.

Many of the Michiganders were preparing their breakfasts when the Virginians slammed into them.[6] "The firing continued for some time, and a report was received by Gen. Custer to the effect that he was attacked by at least a brigade of cavalry. "This was the first we had encountered since we left the army, and told us that the rebels had not only overtaken us, but had gotten around in our front," recounted one of the Wolverines.[7] Capt. Robert J. Sproul, commanding Company C of the Seventh Michigan, recalled that "the Rebels began charging the picket reserves of the Seventh Michigan Cavalry . . . and soon after were repulsed by our men."[8] Lt. Harmon Smith, commanding Company F, remembered that his company repulsed Wickham's charge.[9] Sgt. Lewis Fitch of the Fifth Michigan Cavalry heard the firing, noting in his diary, "there was some skirmishing, the Rebs attacked the Seventh pickets & there was a little fighting."[10] Pvt. Horatio Nelson of Company A of the Fourth Virginia Cavalry described it as "a considerable fight."[11]

Hearing gunfire from the Seventh Michigan pickets, Custer sent Col. Peter Stagg's First Michigan Cavalry back to support Brewer. Stagg's veterans rode to the sound of the firing, dismounted, and formed a line of battle, firing a few shots.[12] After about an hour of skirmishing, the Virginians withdrew down the Marquis Road to Louisa Court House. When they did not follow up on their attack, Custer ordered his Wolverines to continue their advance on Trevilian Station.[13]

Custer had the entire Michigan Brigade in their saddles and moving by 6:00 A.M. Wickham's rear guard threw some shots at the advancing Wolverines.[14] In his after-action report, Custer remembered that "the other brigades of the division had already moved by another road, and I was ordered to connect with them at the station."[15] After the fight, Custer bragged to his wife Libbie: "As usual the Michigan Brigade was detached from the main body, for the purpose of turning the enemy flank and, if possible, attacking him in the rear. I was ordered to go to Trevilian Station, there to form a junction with two other brigades. I carried out instructions

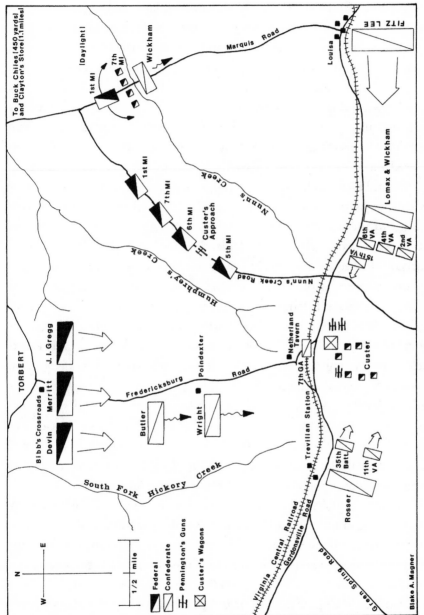

Custer's "First Last Stand," Mid-Morning, June 11, 1864

Blake A. Magner

to the letter, but the others were three hours behind me."[16] Although Custer complained about the delay, it worked to his advantage. Because of the skirmish with Wickham, Custer's command was late reaching the Gordonsville Road. Meanwhile, the engagement along the Fredericksburg Road had begun to intensify, drawing the Georgians of Wright's brigade into the action. But for the skirmish with Wickham, the Wolverines would have run into Wright's brigade as they advanced toward the train station.[17]

Led by Col. Russell A. Alger's Fifth Michigan Cavalry, the advance was steady and unmolested. Custer and his staff marched immediately behind the Fifth Michigan, and Pennington's Battery M, Second U.S. Artillery, followed Alger. Next came the Sixth Michigan Cavalry, followed by the Seventh and First Michigan, which trailed as a rear guard protecting against further attacks by Wickham, whose cavalry harassed the Wolverines, skirmishing all the way.[18] Custer noted that, although rebel pickets remained within pistol shot on their left flank, the "force by which we had been attacked followed us up, but did not press my rear very close."[19]

Twenty-four-year-old Maj. James H. Kidd, of Ionia, Michigan, commander of the Sixth Michigan Cavalry, made an unfortunate choice. When a fellow officer asked for help, Kidd agreed to exchange horses. Instead of riding his reliable war horse, Bay Billy, the major rode "a spirited and nervous black horse belonging to the latter [the other officer], intending, as he expressed it, 'To take the ginger out of him.'" Rather than the regulation McClellan saddle, Kidd's skittish mount carried only a small saddle like that used by jockeys, an attractive rig, "but not such a one as a cavalry officer with a sound mind would select for close work on the battle line." With his bugler John Hertz by his side, Major Kidd blithely rode off, leading his regiment down the country road toward Trevilian Station.[20]

The column snaked along until it intersected the Gordonsville Road at Mills Crossing, a mile and a half east of Trevilian Station. Hearing gunfire, the Wolverines halted and formed line of battle in an opening, facing south. When it became apparent that there would be no immediate fighting, the Michigan men moved out again, heading west on the Gordonsville Road about 8:00 A.M.[21] Capt. Smith H. Hastings, commanding the lead squadron of the Fifth Michigan Cavalry, sent back word of a large wagon train to the east of the train station. Recognizing an opportunity to capture some Southern prizes, Custer ordered the entire Fifth Michigan to charge the wagon train, near the West Crossing. The Boy General then spurred ahead to see the prize.[22]

Alger, a twenty-eight-year-old former lawyer and lumber merchant, was originally commissioned a captain in the Second Michigan Cavalry. He apparently persuaded the governor of Michigan to appoint Capt. Philip H. Sheridan colonel of the regiment. In the summer of 1862, Alger became lieutenant colonel of the Sixth Michigan Cavalry. When the colonel of the Fifth Michigan, Joseph T. Copeland, was promoted to brigadier general, Alger was transferred to the Fifth and promoted to colonel. He had performed competently to date, and was by 1864 the Michigan Brigade's senior regimental commander. Great things awaited Russell Alger after the close of the war, when he would receive brevets to brigadier and major general of volunteers in recognition of his service. He would serve as secretary of war under President William McKinley, spearheading the American victory in the Spanish-American War, and would serve a term in the United State Senate after McKinley's assassination.[23] June 11, 1864, would be a day of danger and trial for the Michigander.

As the 441 officers and men of the Fifth Michigan drew sabres and charged, they rode past Custer and his staff. Alger engaged with Confederate skirmishers sent forward to protect the wagon train and the led horses of Butler's and Young's men, fighting a mile or so to the northeast of the station. Putting spurs to horses, Alger's men pitched into the enemy skirmishers. "After a desperate resistance for a moment [the enemy] was routed," a Michigan man reported, "and the fight became a running one, kept up for a distance of 4 miles."[24] Alger led the charge, accompanied by the brigade commissary officer, Captain Brewster, and one of Custer's staff officers, Lieutenant Shanahan, who was sent back to report to Custer. Swooping down on largely defenseless wagons and horses, the Fifth Michigan bagged several hundred prisoners, 1,500 horses, a stand of colors, 6 caissons, 40 ambulances, and 50 army wagons. Many Confederates broke their weapons upon surrendering rather than give them up.[25] Others dropped their weapons until they realized that the Fifth Michigan was unsupported. They then picked up their arms again and fired into the rear of the Wolverines.[26] One Confederate officer recalled that "Custer charged with his whole brigade and went through our center like a thunderbolt."[27]

The commotion in the rear alerted Butler. He sent some of his South

Carolinians back toward the station to see what was going on in his rear. Their presence, combined with the Seventh Georgia Cavalry dispatched by Hampton earlier to protect the wagon trains, bought valuable minutes.[28] The Twentieth Georgia Cavalry of Wright's command was also sent back to stem the tide. Sgt. Charles P. Hansell of the Twentieth Georgia had a clear view of the wagon train's capture while waiting for orders to pitch into the fray. With nothing to do and no orders, Hansell and his comrades dismounted and turned their horses out to graze. He would not have long to wait.[29]

Alger, unaware that the Confederates were already reacting to cut him off from the rest of the Michigan Brigade, posted guards. He sent Captain Brewster back to Custer to ask for support. The Boy General dispatched another staff officer to send Major Kidd's Sixth Michigan forward to support the attack of the Fifth. The head of Kidd's column, still in files, had barely reached the woods along the edge of the road when the staff officer flew by, shouting to Kidd, "Take the gallop and pass the battery!" Kidd promptly ordered: "Form fours, gallop, march," and with a touch of his spurs sent his skittish black steed forward at full gallop, followed closely by the regiment's first squadron. Kidd left a regimental staff officer behind to repeat the orders to the remaining squadrons as they came forward.

Arriving at Mills's Crossroads, Kidd watched Custer and his staff shooting at the enemy near the East Crossing, who were attempting to check the advance of the Wolverines into Hampton's unprotected rear. "Custer never lost his nerve under any circumstances," Kidd said. "He was, however, unmistakably excited. 'Charge them' was his laconic command; and it was repeated with emphasis."[30]

Kidd checked to make sure that the leading squadron was close behind and ordered his men to draw sabres. Still in column of fours, with Kidd leading the way, a portion of the Sixth Michigan charged straight at the Seventh Georgia, which had fallen back to defend the wagon train. Only one squadron made the charge; Custer held the other two in reserve. The Wolverines crashed through the thin Confederate line, scattering the enemy. The momentum of their charge carried Kidd and his Sixth Michigan several hundred yards toward the train station. The absence of further enemy resistance perplexed "Bob" Kidd, who was unaware that the Fifth Michigan had charged, or that Alger's men had routed the enemy. "The obvious course," Kidd noted, "was to halt, rally, reform, see what was going on in rear, rejoin the brigade commander, get the regiment all together, for work where we were most needed."

Realizing that he required both hands to check his imperious steed, Kidd holstered his revolver and began struggling with his black mount. As Capt. Harvey H. Vinton, commanding the first squadron, came alongside, Kidd twice gave Vinton the command to halt. Kidd's skittish stallion veered and halted only after entering the woods. As he brought the horse to a halt, the major heard the clatter of hoofs behind him. Expecting to see Vinton and his men, the stunned Kidd instead found himself accompanied only by his bugler, John Hertz, and surrounded by Confederates. "A well mounted and sturdy" Rebel officer of Wright's brigade demanded the major's surrender. The Southerner addressed Kidd "in language both profane and apparently designed to cast reflections on my ancestry, declared that if I did not comply instantly with his polite request he would complete the front cut on my head." Kidd pondered his plight for a moment and made a wise choice: "Now it is a maxim that no cavalry officer may surrender so long as he is not unhorsed. But in the situation in which I found myself there did not seem to be an available alternative. I surrendered, gave up the black horse and the jockey saddle, and never saw either of them afterwards. After the experience described I was glad to be rid of them on most any terms."[31]

Four Rebel troopers escorted Kidd and Hertz toward the Trevilian house. However, Kidd, anticipating that Custer would follow up the charge, managed to delay the guards for as long as possible. He had gone only about a hundred yards when a commotion signaled that "the curtain had risen on the second scene of our little drama." Capt. Manning D. Birge's squadron of the Sixth Michigan, sent in by Custer, put Kidd's little escort to flight, and the major escaped through the thick undergrowth, angry enemy bullets whizzing by. Kidd later gratefully wrote: "looking back across the years, I can see and freely acknowledge that to no man on this earth am I under greater obligations than to Manning D. Birge. But for his approach it might not have been possible for us to successfully make our break for freedom." Kidd was a prisoner of war for only about ten minutes.[32]

Hertz was not so fortunate. By the time of the Battle of Trevilian Station, he was already a hero. At Falling Water, West Virginia, during the heavy fighting that marked the retreat from Gettysburg, Hertz (misidentified in several published accounts as "John Hetz") swam across the rain-swollen Potomac River on July 4, 1863. Covered by Northern carbine fire, the bugler cut loose the pontoon bridge used by the Army of the Northern Virginia to cross the river during the advance into Pennsylvania. With Hertz clinging to the bridge, the current swept the end of the bridge to the Maryland side of the roaring river, enabling a detachment of Union cavalry to cross and attack the enemy rear guard. After bringing back a few prisoners, the Union troopers destroyed the bridge, trapping Lee's army against the banks of the swollen river, and giving Meade the opportunity to bring Lee to bay. Hertz escaped that engagement unharmed.[33]

Separated from Kidd at Trevilian Station, the twenty-one-year-old bugler ended up in the notorious Confederate prison at Andersonville, where he suffered for nearly a year until the end of the war liberated him from his purgatory. Obviously blessed with good fortune, Hertz not only endured the horrors of the notorious Confederate stockade, but he also safely came through the explosion and sinking of the badly overloaded troop transport ship *Sultana* on April 27, 1865. This tragedy killed more than 1,000 of the men who had endured the hell of the Georgia prison camp.[34]

The road cleared, albeit temporarily, Custer attempted to capture a section of Thomson's battery that had been left unattended near Netherland Tavern. Sgt. Charles McVicar of Thomson's battery had noted in his diary that the situation facing the gunners was desperate: "we have no support, we are completely surrounded. They have opened an enfilading fire from all points, we are now completely flanked. There was nothing left but hard fighting and we had plenty of that."[35]

The First and Seventh Michigan, bringing up the rear of Custer's column, filtered onto the Gordonsville Road and closed the gap with the rest of the brigade. Recognizing that his position was exposed, Custer ordered Kidd's men to begin building a barricade across the road not far from the East Crossing and the intersection of Nunn's Creek and Gordonsville Roads. One squadron of the Sixth Michigan, commanded by Capt. Don G. Lovell, remained mounted and sheltered in the wood line, ready for action. Just then, a sergeant came up with a prisoner from the Seventh Georgia Cavalry. Upon dismounting, the forlorn captive patted his horse fondly and said, with a tear in his eye, "That is the best horse in the Seventh Georgia Cavalry." Kidd found himself with a new mount, a beautiful black. "Handsome as a picture, kind and well broken, sound, spirited but tractable, with a glossy coat of silky luster, he was a mount that a real cavalryman would become attached to and be proud of."[36]

As Custer consolidated his position and his prizes of war, word reached Wade Hampton that a large force of Yankees was in his rear and that his trains had been captured. As the historian of the Laurel Brigade aptly put it, the enemy "in Hampton's rear meant general disaster. What was to be done, had to be done quickly. Seldom did a duty of heavy responsibility where promptness of decision in the leader, and ready valor in the men was needed."[37] Calling for Rosser's brigade, Hampton ordered his lines consolidated around Netherland Tavern. The big South Carolinian ordered Col. J. Fred Waring of the Jeff Davis Legion to move back and charge the Yankees.[38] He ordered Butler to send the Sixth South Carolina and the Phillips Legion to reinforce the position near the train station. These regiments charged and drove Custer's men back from the railroad. "The losses in our regiment have been very small," a captain of the Phillips Legion later wrote home, "though we narrowly escaped having the whole regiment captured at Trevilian Station, having been almost surrounded by the Yankees."[39]

Worried and frustrated by the tardiness of his other division, Hampton sent a messenger to Fitz Lee with orders for the Virginian to join Hampton as soon as possible.[40] Lee later wrote, "Quickly retracing my steps, I moved at once for Trevilian," but it is not clear that he moved promptly.[41] His tardiness nearly proved fatal for Confederate arms at Trevilian Station, because the delay permitted Custer to drive a wedge between Lee's and Hampton's divisions.

Tom Rosser, unlike Lee, did not wait for Hampton's orders. Itching for action, he rode forward, looking for opportunity. An escaping Confederate picket, galloping away from Trevilian Station hatless and sporting a sabre cut on his face, had reported that Custer was in the rear and wreaking havoc. Rosser called his brigade forward at a gallop.[42] It responded quickly, closing ranks and following its general toward the firing. "A glance at the victorious Federals, accompanied with captured trains and ambulances filled with prisoners, only quickened the rush as the brigade swept with shouts to the rescue."[43] As they rode toward the chaotic scene playing out amidst the wagons, the Laurels saw that "the Yankees swarmed over the whole country."[44] Rosser was pleasantly surprised to find that Custer had neglected to picket the road; with the nearly impenetrable undergrowth masking his approach, he aimed to crash into Custer's flank undetected.[45] Pvt. James Wood of the Seventh Virginia recalled that Rosser's men had a "splendid position" and that they "made good use of it."[46]

As the Laurels sped toward the crisis, Confederate Major Roger P. Chew reacted quickly to save Thomson's guns from capture. Chew had ridden back toward the Netherland Tavern to bring a section of Thomson's guns to bear in the fight against the rest of Torbert's command when he encountered Hampton in the road. The general told Chew that the enemy had gotten into the rear, and advised Chew to go back and do the best he could with his guns. Spotting some high ground that faced the train station, Chew deployed six guns on a knoll overlooking a large field. He "got by chance, in the best position I could have found, and it was a delightful fight, because no one fired at us. I reckon it was the most delightful fight I was ever in, because we were shooting at the Yankees all the time, and they never fired back."[47] Chew considered himself fortunate. In his official report of the action, he said, "The road at this point makes a curve so that our position was almost encircled by the enemy, who were moving towards Gordonsville to secure their capture. The guns were supported by but a squadron of cavalry, but the enemy, evidently intimidated by the fire of the guns, made no effort to charge them."[48] McVicar recalled that he and his fellow artillerists "opened right, left, and front. We are pouring shell on them as fast as they break cover at any point."[49]

Colonel Waring promptly complied with Hampton's orders to pitch into the Federals. Hastily gathering a number of men from his regiment, the colonel directed his troopers to draw sabres. With Rebel yells piercing the morning air, the men of the Jeff Davis Legion flew at the Yankee troopers who were plundering the wagon train. Waring reported in his diary, "We charged the enemy & were in turn charged by the enemy in our rear. Turned off to the right, crossed the railroad & moved up to get to Gen. Hampton."[50] One of Rosser's troopers described the comic scene that played out in front of him: "A regiment of Yankees went tearing down the road, and into the dust which rose in clouds around them darted Col. Waring with his Jeff Davis Legion, in hot pursuit. Close on his rear pressed another Yankee regiment, followed by one of Rosser's—all thundering along together!"[51]

Blunted by the countercharge of the Wolverines, and unable to find Hampton in the thick and confusing woods, the men of the Jeff Davis Legion headed for Thomson's guns, posted on a nearby knoll. Waring was frustrated; from his vantage point, he could see the Northern horsemen marching off with the wagon train, but because the guns were unsupported, Waring decided that it was more important for him to stay and support them than to give chase.[52]

Chew's guns fell silent, though, as Rosser's charge came within range of their blasts. With Rosser leading the attack, the yelling Laurels pitched into Custer's ranks. The Eleventh Virginia Cavalry led on the right, and White's Comanches led on the left.[53] "Sabers clashed, pistols and carbines crashed, and for a short while, it looked like a free fight," one of Chew's gunners recalled. "The firing was quick and heavy for a short time; I heard the din of the conflict as we were hastening to the fray."[54] "Then commenced a cavalry fight in earnest, which for spirit and excitement has rarely been surpassed. The Yankees, attacked on the flank and astounded at this temerity, scattered in all directions, some of them trying to cut their way back, and others taking to the bush," described one of the Laurels.[55] Sergeant Hansell of the Twentieth Georgia described "a headlong charge" that drove Custer back and recaptured all that had been lost a few minutes earlier.

Itching for action, Hansell continued, "It was certainly a grand and most gratifying thing to us to watch this, but meanwhile what we were to do?"[56] Finding Custer's bluecoats "chasing and 'gobbling up' the scattered Confederates," the Laurels gave the Wolverines the cold steel of their sabres, breaking Custer's thin line and driving the Yankee troopers back. The careening Laurels tried to avoid prisoners of Wright's brigade, who sent up mixed yells of "don't shoot this way!" and "hurrah! You 'uns has saved we 'uns again!"[57] As Capt. Frank Myers of the Comanches recalled, "Pretty soon the tide was turned, and in a perfect whirlwind of dust and smoke the 'Comanches' pushed hotly after the retreating enemy, many of whom they captured and sent to the rear," liberating Custer's prizes.[58]

In the meantime, Pennington's gunners went into battery. As they unlimbered, dismounted Rebels moved down to the railroad bed and started shooting into the ranks of the Yankee artillerists, who raised the cry, "Here they come!" The Southern horse soldiers made a rush for the guns, and Custer, sitting his horse, found himself surrounded by enemy troopers. An observer recalled, "Gen. Custer was entirely surrounded, but with his usual daring rode at the nearest rebels, and thanks to the audacity of the act, escaped unharmed, and in an instant after was rallying his men and getting his pieces into a safe position. He opened on the rebels and quickly drove them back, and following them closely soon regained all the ground he had temporarily lost."[59]

Recognizing Custer's desperate predicament, Rosser ordered Col. Lige White's Comanches, the Thirty-fifth Battalion of Virginia Cavalry, to charge again. Hampton wisely countermanded the order, and the Comanches retired to the safety of a nearby dense wood line, where they got "the first actual view of cannon-shot we have ever *enjoyed*." Pennington's guns threw shot after shot at them, one of which, striking the solid ground about an eighth of a mile from the position taken by the Comanches, bounced and spun wildly past Colonel White's horse, barely missing both man and beast. White ordered his men back farther, where they joined the main battle line of the Laurel Brigade. Yet another solid artillery shot from one of Pennington's rifles struck the ground in front of the Comanches and bounced over them, landing and bouncing again, this time clearing the Twelfth Virginia Cavalry. Miraculously, the heavy iron ball made yet one more jump, finally clearing the led horses of the brigade and coming to a stop.[60]

Startled Wolverines scattered into the woods to the right, looking for safety in the dense undergrowth. Rosser's column splintered as detachments rode off looking for these fugitives. Having ridden past the wagon park to reconnoiter near the train station with a small party of forty officers and men, Alger was cut off by the impetuosity of Rosser's charge, during which many troopers of the Fifth Michigan Cavalry were captured. Turning back, Alger found his escape route blocked by the Laurels. Sidling to his right, he entered a narrow strip of woods. He noticed that the enemy was moving on both sides of the strip of woods, very near his position. A Rebel officer spotted the small group of Wolverines and inquired, "What command do you belong to?" Capt. Robert F. Judson, riding with Alger, responded, "Hampton's." Bluffed, the Confederate officer replied, "All right," and rejoined his column.

The reprieve, however, was brief. Alger called a halt in a small stand of trees, and the forty men with him discussed the available options as heavy columns of enemy troopers passed by.[61] Another party of the Laurels soon discovered Alger's little group and charged the Michigan men as they moved off toward Louisa in the thick undergrowth. Given no alternative, Alger ordered his little band to draw sabres and charge. Alger and ten of his men slashed through the Rebels, leaving behind twenty-eight of their number and the contingent of Confederate prisoners taken during the charge on the wagons. Lost in this melee was the Fifth Michigan's regimental commissary, Lt. Dwight B. Pendleton. Alger and his fugitives rode nearly twenty miles before finding safety inside friendly lines near where his regiment had camped on the night of June 10. Not long after the war, Alger proudly wrote, "This was my hardest fight . . . I had a horse killed and two holes shot in my coat in this fight."[62]

The twenty-eight men and their handful of Confederate prisoners that Alger left in the woods also had quite an adventure. Abandoning their horses, they remained hidden for two days before starting out on foot to find the rest of their regiment. Crossing the Rapidan River at Morton's Ford, they made for Alexandria, where they arrived after a week of hard night marches. These enterprising men spent their days hiding and foraging, subsisting on small amounts of corn meal scavenged from friendly slaves.[63]

Other elements of the Fifth Michigan faced similar obstacles. Lt. James Allen of Company E was guarding the intersection where Custer's column had emerged from the wood road and had to cut his way to safety. Capts. Horace Dodge and George Drake and Lt. Walter Stevenson, along with men sent with them, were cut off from the regiment during the charge for the wagons. Alger noted that both Dodge and Drake "escaped with portions of their commands and reported to the general commanding." He continued, "In this engagement my loss was very heavy in prisoners captured while guarding prisoners, together with the greater portion of the captures made by my regiment."[64] He later stated that he lost 171 of the 300 men who had followed him into battle that morning.[65]

Pvt. James K. Lowden was one of those captured that morning. Remembering June 11, 1864, he commented that at Trevilian Station "a great many of us wished we could have lost the time instead of losing ourselves." Lowden blamed Custer for the Fifth Michigan's losses that day. "It was on this field, and in this engagement, that we were taught to think that our regiment was not as well handled as it had been sometimes before, or as well as it might have been," he complained. "If any have the right to think so it certainly is the men who were made prisoners there." He concluded, "I firmly believe, and know, that Col. Alger was—by the act of another, and not by a pardonable zeal or by his own volition—placed by positive orders from his superior in a spot where his regiment must suffer a loss of one-half of its strength."[66] Indeed, the Boy General's desire to snatch the prize of Hampton's wagon train had sacrificed a major portion of a fine regiment.

Those elements of Wright's brigade fighting near the train station experienced varying degrees of adversity. Spotting Sergeant Hansell and his Georgians idly watching the fight just a few yards away, an officer shouted orders for them to mount up and pitch in. "You damned fools," he yelled, "what do you mean by grazing your horses and the Yankees right on! Form fours, draw sabres, and if you get out of this you'll have to cut your way out!" Hansell quickly mounted, and the Twentieth Georgia moved out, passing the beaten Seventh Georgia Cavalry. As Hansell and his company advanced, they saw the carnage wrought by Pennington's guns, and the sergeant grew worried for his safety. His company commander, Lt. Tom Heeth, also fretted, commenting to Hansell, "Charlie this looks like a mighty tight place." Heeth was killed moments later. Hansell led the company to one of Chew's batteries, where they supported the battery.

The sergeant found a riderless horse in the road, still festooned with all of its equipment. A hasty examination convinced Hansell that the animal belonged to an unfortunate member of the Seventh Georgia Cavalry. He was contemplating what to do with the beast when a Yankee artillery shell exploded a few feet away, severely injuring the horse and knocking the sergeant senseless. As he moved off, his commanding officer, Maj. Ivy F. Lewis of the Jeff Davis Legion (who had been assigned to command the Twentieth Georgia's battalion), asked, "Where are you going, Sergeant?" Shaken from his funk, Hansell rode back, with Lewis kindly saying, "No, come on we will all leave here."

That same artillery shell killed two of Rosser's men and severely wounded Pvt. Willie Hayes of the Twentieth Georgia. Hansell watched as Hayes strode up to Wade Hampton and demanded treatment of his injured arm. General Hampton asked a nearby surgeon to treat the boy, whose arm had to be amputated. As Hayes passed through a group of captured Wolverines, one inquired of Hayes, "Buddie, won't you have some chicken?" Furious, Hayes retorted, "You God damned blue-bellied son of a bitch, I wouldn't have anything you've got!"

Major Lewis then led Hansell and his men down a road until they had passed out of range of the Yankee artillery. They halted, glad to be safe from the shells. Hansell's joy was fleeting, for a moment later, the major said, "Sergt., go back yonder and see if any of your men are still there." Hansell's reaction was predictable: "That looked hard, very hard. We had just left the place because it was too dangerous to stay there; but orders must be obeyed." Reluctantly, he turned back and found none of his men. He did, however, spot several other members of the battalion that had been cut off and gave up his horse to a wounded man, Leonard Sims.

As the little band moved off, a bullet fired by a Michigan sergeant whizzed past Hansell's ear. The lone Wolverine demanded the surrender of the six men. Hansell handed over his gun, and the Yankee asked where his lines were. When Hansell refused to answer, the blue-clad horse soldier said, "If I get you to our lines you are my prisoners; but if I run into your lines, I am your prisoner." The Georgians decided to confuse their lone captor. Hearing the clatter of hooves, Hansell said, "There are your men now!" "No," replied the Yankee sergeant, "They are yours!" Hansell demanded the sergeant's pistol, and the Yankee was soon taken away by some of Rosser's men, who were combing the woods for other isolated pockets of Northerners.

Hansell finally found the rest of the members of his unit, who regaled him with stories. One of the Georgians was briefly a prisoner and had his hat taken by a Michigan trooper, who handed the Georgian his own cap. When Rosser's charge freed the Georgian, he was left with the blue kepi and not his own hat. Another Southerner told a story of how he and his friends watched horrified as some of Custer's men shot holes in a barrel of fine Michigan whiskey, which began draining. Not eager to let the good spirits go to waste, the Georgians scurried forward to fill their canteens from the barrel.

Hansell's day ended. He and his friends withdrew, enjoying a fine meal of griddle cakes made from flour purchased from a friendly woman in a nearby house.[67]

As Alger and his band of fugitives sought safety, Col. Lige White, commander of the Comanches, spotted a battery near the West Crossing and resolved to go support it. White also noticed a large number of the enemy seeking shelter near a brick kiln to the left of the guns. White ordered a plank fence lining the road torn down and made ready to charge. As the guns were only 200 yards away, and the force of Yankees sheltering behind the brick kiln was increasing in size each minute, White was impatient. At that moment, Hampton rode up and asked, "Colonel White, what are you going to do?" "Going to support that battery," responded the colonel. "Get away from here, Colonel, it's a Yankee battery," replied Hampton, prompting White to obey the order posthaste.[68]

The hard-charging Laurels, their sabres glinting in the bright morning sun, spotted Custer's line of battle deployed just to the west of the intersection of the Nunn's Creek and Gordonsville Roads. Custer was supported by Pennington's battery. Not long after Alger's headlong charge, a section of Pennington's gunners ran a gauntlet of mounted Confederate troopers. Separated by a high board fence that lined the Gordonsville Road, the Yankee gunners tore down a portion of the fence, deployed, and went into action.[69] Custer had chosen his position wisely. He took up a compact position a little over a mile to the east of the station, where he could resist the enemy's attacks under the protection of Pennington's guns, which roared constantly over the heads of the Wolverines.[70] Spotting this strong position, Rosser wisely called off the pursuit in order to reorganize and consolidate his scattered brigade. Covered by Chew's guns on higher ground above them, Rosser used the large field as a staging area to rally his scattered command. Some troopers found an abandoned keg of Northern applejack and were busily filling their canteens when Pennington's guns opened on them. A single shell wounded or killed six of White's men and two of his horses. As Captain Myers noted, "Seldom has such execution been done by a single shell."[71]

The shelling by Chew's guns, safely perched atop a knoll and firing down on Custer's position, jeopardized the captured wagon train. Under heavy fire, the officer commanding the wagon train approached Custer and asked if he might take the wagons and other booty to the rear and safety. Distracted, the Boy General replied, "Yes, by all means." Relieved, the officer left to lead the wagons to safety. Just after the officer rode off, Custer snapped out of his reverie, looked all around, and inquired, "Where in hell is the rear?"[72] That question required no answer; it was immediately obvious to all those who cared to look that there was no rear.

Custer was furious at the unnamed officer for leading his prize away. When he penned his after-action account of the battle, Custer wrote, "In doing so, [the unnamed officer in charge of the train] conducted [the wagons] into the lines of the enemy, where they were captured. In causing this mishap he acted on his own responsibility, impelled by fear alone, and I might add that for his conduct on this occasion the President of the United States has dismissed him from the service for cowardice and treachery."[73]

Fitz Lee's lead elements were also trotting onto the field, meaning that Custer's beleaguered command would soon be hemmed in on three sides, leaving the Wolverines caught "on the inside of a living triangle," as one of Merritt's Regulars, watching the action unfold, described it.[74] Lee's adjutant, Maj. James D. Ferguson, noted that when Fitz's division moved through Louisa to join Hampton at the train station, they were surprised to find Custer's brigade wedged between them and their objective. Maj. Robert F. Mason, one of Lee's staff officers, went to Lunsford Lomax with orders to report for duty and was promptly placed in command of one of Lomax's regiments, the Fifteenth Virginia Cavalry. That morning Lomax had relieved Lt. Col. John Critcher of command of the Fifteenth Virginia. "I have become satisfied that he cannot command," he stated, asserting that he had acted in the "interests of the service" in relieving Critcher "before there was any certainty that the Regt. would be engaged." Critcher resigned his commission in a huff the next day.[75]

Leading Lomax's advance, Mason, "an officer distinguished for his dashing gallantry upon every occasion where engaged during the war," ordered the men of the Fifteenth Virginia to draw sabres and charge. Crashing into Custer's flank, the Virginians scattered the men of the First Michigan Cavalry to the east of the train station. Their "handsome charge" recaptured nearly all of the wagons that had been lost earlier, and also bagged five of Pennington's caissons as well as Custer's headquarters wagon and the ramshackle coach of his faithful cook, Eliza.[76]

The Queen of Sheba, realizing that the wagon would be taken, tried in vain to save her general's personal effects. Custer later moaned to his wife, "Would you like to know what they have captured from me? *Everything except my toothbrush.*" Perhaps trying to play down the magnitude of his loss, Custer misstated the number of wagons taken by the Confederates: "They only captured one wagon from me, but contained my all—bedding, desk, sword-belt, underclothing, and my commission as General which only arrived a few days before; also dress coat, pants and one blue shirt." Custer also lost three horses, including a favorite stallion named "Clift." Most humiliating, however, was the loss of intimate love letters from his wife, some of which were later published in the Richmond newspapers, to his great embarrassment. A correspondent of the *Richmond Examiner* prissily commented, "His letters show a depravity in Northern society beyond anything our people could imagine; and if they would be published, they would fully expose the villainy of high officers in Yankee commands."[77] "The letters show him to be a man of very loose morals," sniffed one of Rosser's men.[78]

Stung, the Boy General chided his bride, "I regret the loss of your letters more than all else. I enjoyed every word you wrote, but do not relish the idea of others amusing themselves with them, particularly as some of the expressions employed . . . Somebody must be more careful hereafter in the use of *double entendu*."[79]

Libbie, for her part, responded a few days later: "I suppose some rebel is devouring my epistles, but I am too grateful to feel badly about that. Let me unburden my mind about the matter, since your letter implies chiding, tho the slightest and kindliest. No Southerner could say, if they are *gentlemen* that I lacked refinement. There can be nothing low between man and wife if they love each other. What I wrote was holy and sacred. Only cruel people would not understand the spirit in which I wrote it." She continued, "How I laughed when I heard that the inevitable toothbrush had not been taken!"[80]

Eliza was captured by the Virginians. Although she failed to save the Boy General's personal baggage from capture, she somehow managed to save her own. When a Confederate ordered her to mount the horse behind him, she saucily retorted, "I don't see it!" This prompted one of her captors to sneer, "Ain't she damned impudent!" Taken nearly two miles behind enemy lines, she somehow managed to escape and made her way back to Custer's camp that night, to the delight and acclaim of the Wolverines, who thought for certain that they had seen the last of the Queen of Sheba.[81] One of the Wolverines, with tongue planted firmly in cheek, noted bitterly, "One half the pluck and energy displayed by her would if possessed by the employees of the train could have saved it entirely."[82] Custer's other devoted servant, young Johnnie Cisco, was not so lucky. He and several of the Boy General's orderlies were captured by the impetuous charge of the Virginians.

Custer's assistant adjutant general, Capt. Jacob L. Greene, was also bagged. Carrying orders from Custer and searching for the captured wagon train, Greene asked a private of the First Michigan Cavalry where it might be found. Following the enlisted man, Greene passed through a heavy stand of woods. Riding toward the sound of gunfire, and hoping to find the men of the First Michigan, stationed along the road to Louisa, Greene heard voices ahead. Emerging from the woods, he found not the wagon train, "but two squadrons of the Lomax cavalry just making a charge in my direction." Because the Virginians were on top of him, the captain was unable to turn his horse or escape. He quickly found himself "completely surrounded and facing more pistols and carbines at my head than were at all suggestive of. long life." Surrendering, he was dismounted and disarmed "so quick that my head swam."

Greene discovered why he had been unable to find the train when a captor informed him that it had already been retaken and moved to the rear. In a letter to Custer, Greene observed, "what on earth possessed them to take it into such a place as it was where it would have been almost impossible to get it away if attacked either in our rear on either flank & pushed at all. Some officer is responsible for the loss of it." From his vantage point, Greene could see Fitz Lee's entire division forming for the attack on Custer's position. He was then taken to Hampton's headquarters, where he was interrogated and his spurs and flute were taken. "You have the spurs of General Custer's Adjutant-General," he said.

The captain began his journey to military prison in Charleston, South Carolina, the next day, but not before having a long talk with Fitz Lee "of which I have some amusing things to tell you. Some rich jokes." Greene also reported that Col. Thomas T. Munford of the Second Virginia Cavalry had paid him a visit and promised to send the young captain's valise to him at Richmond. Munford informed Green that he was in possession of the Boy General's property and promised to try to return the commission and personal baggage to Custer at the earliest opportunity.[83]

Custer did not have time to mourn the loss of his headquarters wagon, personal effects, and servants. Wickham's Fourth Virginia and Lomax's Sixth Virginia had joined the fray, supporting the triumphant Fifteenth Virginia. Serious business was at hand. The rest of Lee's division was filtering onto the field, on an angle with Hampton's flank, and the fighting rapidly grew heavy.[84] With Rosser pressing from the west, the Wolverines were completely encircled, and the enemy troops were moving in for the kill. "I was fighting every man I had against two Divisions of the enemy Cavalry," Custer later wrote Libbie. "My Brigade was completely surrounded, and attacked on all sides. I had captured over 1500 horses with saddles, complete; 6 caissons of artillery filled with ammunition, 250 wagons & several hundred prisoners, but, against overwhelming odds and lack of support, could not retain our captures. . . . Never has the Brigade fought so long or so desperately."[85]

The Second Virginia Cavalry received orders to support Maj. Robert Breathed's gunners. However, Colonel Munford spotted a significant portion of Custer's brigade nearby and ordered Breathed's batteries to open fire. Without waiting for further orders, Munford pitched into the fray. With Munford leading his regiment's charge, the Virginians crashed into the Wolverines, "scattering them like sheep," and bore down on Pennington's guns.[86]

Lt. Charles H. Almond of the Second Virginia recalled that his regiment struck the right and rear of Custer's precarious position, where it bagged countless led horses and mules. As the Virginians fell out to gather prizes, Lieutenant Almond and his squadron rode on, aiming for a section of Federal artillery posted on a knoll, near the wood line. The guns were supported by dismounted troopers, and made an attractive target. Almond watched the charge scatter the dismounted supports, but was surprised to see the attack peter out, allowing the gunners to reman their guns and lay down an effective fire on the gray-clad horsemen. "Those who were in advance could not get out of the way," recalled Almond. "We had come in without exposing ourselves to this Grape & Canister and took up a little ravine or depression leading by the side or rear of these guns to the woods in which the dismounted men were and found ourselves between them & the caissons & 60 men of the battery, battery wagon & Custer's HqQrts wagon." He continued, "No one calling on us to surrender, some one suggested that we take these fellows and their 'impedimenta' out, We called on the men to mount; which they promptly did and we started on the full run to get out of the woods." Bringing along sixty prisoners, a battery wagon, four caissons, and some horses, Munford ordered Almond to take his prizes to safety in Louisa, an order that Almond promptly obeyed.[87]

Capt. Reuben Boston, commanding the Fifth Virginia Cavalry of Lomax's brigade, was briefly captured by one of the Wolverines. After being placed in the custody of a Michigan sergeant, the captain offered his guard "some old Virginia weed." While they enjoyed their smoke, the sergeant carelessly set his revolver aside, prompting Captain Boston to make a successful dash for freedom. A few days later, he was promoted to colonel.[88]

Determined to hold on until supports arrived, Custer grimly set about resisting the numerous desperate assaults launched on his little band. "The enemy made repeated and desperate efforts to break our lines at different points, and in doing so compelled us to change the positions of our batteries," he noted. "The smallness of my force compelled me to adopt very contracted lines." He continued, "from the nature of the ground and the character of the attacks that were made upon me our lines resembled very nearly a circle. The space over which we fought was so limited that there was actually no place which could be called under cover, or in other words the entire ground was in range of the enemy's guns."[89] Kidd remembered that "for a time there was a melee that had no parallel in the annals of cavalry fighting in the Civil War. Custer's line was in the form of a circle and he was fighting an enterprising foe on either flank and both flank and rear."[90] Trooper Frank Grommon wrote in his diary that night, "Fought all day. Our little brigade was surrounded."[91] One of Rosser's men claimed that the Laurel Brigade repulsed seventeen different charges during the course of the vicious fighting.[92]

Pvt. Daniel Eldridge of the Seventh Michigan recalled, "We met and resisted charge after charge. . . . In one of the charges some sixty or eighty of us were cut off and forced to the south. I think there was a whole division of the rebels, and as soon as we were cut off from the main body of our command, they pursued us most vigorously." Eldridge captured a Confederate battle flag in the melee but failed to tear it from its standard. During his headlong flight, the standard became a burden. After carrying it nearly two miles, Eldridge finally "threw it into the brush, only caring to save myself." Eluding capture, Eldridge and his little band wandered the dense woods. They stumbled upon the Michigan Brigade's picket line near daybreak.[93]

Major Kidd's Sixth Michigan Cavalry took heavy casualties. Kidd's second-in-command, Capt. Don G. Lovell, a squadron commander, fell with a serious wound, as did Lt. Luther C. Canouse.[94] One of the enlisted men who fell was Pvt. William Onweller of Company B of the Sixth Michigan. The nineteen-year-old, who had only enlisted in January of 1864, was wounded and taken to the Cavalry Corps hospital at City Point, Virginia, where he contracted typhoid fever and died on July 29, 1864.[95] Thirty-five-year-old Bugler John Fitzgerald of Company C of the Sixth Michigan was wounded during the jumbled fighting and captured by one of the Virginians. Fitzgerald's journey into captivity ended at Jacksonville, Florida, where he was held until April 28, 1865.[96]

Many Wolverines were captured during this wild melee. Pvt. Oscar Wood of Company A of the Fifth Michigan was taken when his company was attacked in the rear and cut off. His war over, Wood's greatest battle would become survival in captivity.[97] Pvt. Dexter Macomber of the First Michigan Cavalry had a similar experience. His diary entry for June 11, 1864, tells the story: "we charge and break through their lines several times it is the most mixed up fight I ever saw. . . . Edward Haver and myself being cut off flee about 4 ms to reach our lines but run into the rebel pickets that are stationed in the woods and are captured by men of the rebel battalion that was commanded by [Col. Elijah V. White]." Macomber continued, "we are dismounted & marched to Gen Rosser who commands us to be taken to the rear of his brigade, we march about one mile towards [Charlottesville] & stop another squad of prisoners come in . . . we will stand by each other through prison life." His battle was over.[98]

The hard fighting took a significant toll on Custer's Wolverines. "This regiment was engaged the entire day, fighting both mounted and dismounted, charging and counter-charging," Kidd reported. "Not less than one hundred prisoners were captured by the regiment, but being surrounded for several hours, many men were necessarily lost."[99] The Seventh Michigan lost everything, including the horses of the dismounted men, rations, cooking equipment, and the regiment's black servants.[100] One member of the Seventh Michigan Cavalry was captured east of the station. When his captors led him away, they found on him a ring and brace of pistols belonging to James W. O'Hear, one of Fitz Lee's staff officers, killed at Haw's Shop on May 28.[101] Pvt. Dewitt C. Gallagher of Company E, First Virginia Cavalry, liberated from one of Custer's Wolverines "a fine Yankee Carbine, discarding my old one."[102]

Following Lomax's brigade westward down the road from Louisa, Wickham's brigade engaged the encircled Wolverines. "Had a considerable fight," one of Wickham's men noted in his diary that night, with great understatement. "Our company had 1 man mortally wounded and 3 severely. We lost in Regt. Heavy."[103] Lt. John D. Holtzman, a schoolteacher who served in Company D of the Fourth Virginia Cavalry, also known as the Little Fork Rangers, observed, "we . . . had a severe engagement with [Custer's brigade]. The Fourth Regt. bore a conspicuous part and came near being captured."[104]

Lt. Col. William R. Carter of the Third Virginia Cavalry was a thirty-one-year-old lawyer from Richmond and an honors graduate of Hampden-Sydney College. After enlisting in Company G of the Third Virginia Cavalry in May 1861, Carter rose through the ranks from private. He was a highly promising officer "of large intelligence and fine courage, and greatly endeared to the whole command." Leading his regiment in a charge on Custer's position, a Spencer carbine bullet knocked Carter from his saddle. Reeling, the mortally wounded colonel fell into Northern hands. Taken to a Union field hospital, Carter suffered until July 8 before succumbing to his wound.[105]

Sgt. Robert C. Towles, son of Rev. John and Sephronia Towles, was a member of Company A of the Fourth Virginia Cavalry. Along with his two brothers, J. Vivian Towles and James H. Towles, seventeen-year-old Robert enlisted in the Prince William Cavalry, as it was known, in April 1861. Two of the boys, James and Robert, were captured in 1862 and spent a brief time in Washington D.C.'s notorious Old Capitol Prison. They were exchanged in October 1862 and rejoined their regiment. The three brothers served together until J. Vivian, the oldest of the three brothers, was killed in action at Stevensburg, Virginia, on October 11, 1863. He was laid to rest on the battlefield. On April 9, 1864, his brother, James, was killed in action along the picket lines. Reverend Towles's already heavy burden was made all the worse on June 11, 1864, as his third son, Robert, of Wickham's command, was shot through the abdomen in the fighting along the Gordonsville Road. Robert lingered until June 16, when he too died. Later, the bodies of James and Vivian Towles were disinterred and transferred to Oakwood Cemetery in Louisa, where the three brothers were reunited in death.[106]

Another member of Company A of the Fourth Virginia, Pvt. Thomas P. Ellicott, age twenty-eight, was a Northerner by birth. Born in 1836 in Warren County, New Jersey, Ellicott enlisted in the Fourth Virginia Cavalry from his adopted home in Prince William County, Virginia. He had safely navigated the dangers of the war until the morning of June 11, when a good deed cost him his life. A comrade of Company A was wounded in the melee along the Gordonsville road, and Ellicott stopped to bear his injured comrade from the field. Ellicott too was hit by a Yankee carbine ball. After suffering for nearly two weeks, he finally died on June 23, 1864, and was buried just a few feet away from the Towles brothers. Not even death could separate the comrades of the Prince William Cavalry, as Company A of the Fourth Virginia was also known.[107]

Capt. R. C. Conrad, regimental chaplain of the Third Virginia, was scouting along the Gordonsville Road when he discovered a Yankee sheltering in the edge of the woods. The Northerner surrendered to Conrad and indicated that "quite a number of non-combatants were scattered through the woods and were ready to give themselves up if protected; that they had been cut off from their command and were without a guide." Conrad rode a short distance and found a regimental chaplain. He asked the chaplain to accompany him. Capt. James Thomson joined the two officers and the three men returned to the woods. Arriving there, Thomson rose in his stirrups and said, in a commanding voice, "If you Yankees will come forward and surrender like men you shall be treated as prisoners of war. But if not we will blow you to hell in five minutes."

In short order, Wolverines trickled out of the woods until a whole squad of twenty men and forty horses and mules had surrendered. "They embraced commissary sergeants, quartermaster sergeants, blacksmiths, teamsters and stragglers, and a chaplain." Conrad sent them to Hampton's provost marshal with a note that read, "I herewith forward twenty Yankees and forty horses and mules captured by two chaplains and a major of artillery after a bold bluff and a bloodless battle. Accept same with our comments." Conrad then told the other chaplain, if asked how three men could capture twenty, "Faith and be Jesus, I surrounded them."[108]

After galloping to the sound of the guns, the Sixth Virginia Cavalry of Lomax's brigade halted at the edge of dense woods bordering Custer's position. Although somewhat sheltered by the woods, the men of Company D of the Sixth Virginia, known as the Clarke County Troop, came under fire from Pennington's guns, six hundred yards distant. Along with the Rappahannock Troop, these men made up the regiment's first squadron, consisting of approximately eighty officers and men. While trying to find whatever meager shelter the woods offered from artillery shells whistling overhead, the first squadron received orders to charge the Federal guns. Led by Capt. Daniel A. Grimsley, the first squadron moved out rapidly, drew sabres, and charged across the open field directly at Pennington's guns, which belched grape and cannister at them.[109]

Their target was a lone gun of Lt. William Egan's section of Pennington's battery, "placed in a somewhat dangerous position." Egan, seeing the rebels bearing down on him, ordered his men to retreat, leaving the gun behind; as its limber had already been withdrawn, it would have been impossible to remove the gun if captured. Pvts. John Kennedy and Charles O'Neil, whose line of retreat was cut off by the onrushing Confederates, remained at their piece, fending off the Virginians with hand spike and sponge staff. Grimsley's troopers crashed into them, sabres flashing in the bright morning sun. The brief stand by the two lone artillerists allowed Lieutenant Egan and the other crewmen to escape to a small knoll nearby. Kennedy recalled, "things looked blue, the battery losing 4 caissons with their horses, harness and contents. The gun, a 12-pound brass, which I was gunner of, was detached a little ways in front of the rifle platoons. Well, a little before relief came, they charged the gun. In the confusion the limber managed to escape, leaving me and 4 men at the gun. With our ammunition gone, in the tussle, we used our pistols." He continued, "When we emptied them we took the sponge staves and handspikes and used them freely until overpowered, by their actually riding us down. I was fencing with the handspike with a cavalryman when another came in rear of me and knocked me down."[110]

Kennedy's and O'Neil's sacrifice bought time for their fellow gunners to flee. The two privates soon began their journey to Andersonville, where O'Neil died in captivity. Private Kennedy received the Medal of Honor in 1893, "for distinguished bravery in the battle of Trevilian Station . . . remaining at his gun, and resisting with its implements the advancing cavalry and thus securing the retreat of his detachment."[111]

After brushing off the two Federal gunners, the men of the Sixth Virginia thundered past their prize toward Custer's triangular formation, taking fire all the way. Yankee Spencer fire emptied saddles. The accurate artillery fire of Pennington's other section, commanded by Lt. Carle Woodruff, also took its toll on the Rebels. Before retreating, Lieutenant Egan sent his bugler, James J. Reilly, to Woodruff to ask Woodruff to cover Egan's lone gun. Woodruff obliged, firing several rounds toward the gray-clad troopers, some

700 yards distant. Because of the highly fluid nature of the fighting that day, Woodruff recalled that, even though his two guns were only eighteen yards apart, they were firing in opposite directions.[112]

Seeing the rebel troopers take Egan's gun, Maj. Melvin Brewer of the Seventh Michigan Cavalry ordered sixty men of his regiment to charge. Bursting from the woods, the Wolverines gave the Virginians the sabre, emptying many Southern saddles in the resulting melee. Major Brewer was wounded in the fighting, but the Wolverines retook Egan's gun, driving the Confederates back.[113] Reflecting years later, Lt. Eustis Wallace of the Sixth Virginia, who was desperately wounded in this melee, believed that Custer had set a trap for the Virginians, writing, "we saw at once that 'some one had blundered.'" Wallace, shot through the lungs and left for dead, heard Custer order that the recaptured gun be turned on the retreating Virginians.[114] Rebuffed by Brewer's countercharge, Grimsley's Virginians fell back, taking a caisson or two with them, but without their glittering prize. Writing long after the war, Captain Grimsley noted, "In this charge Co. D of the Clarke Cavalry suffered severely."[115]

Although impetuosity had gotten him into trouble in the first place, Custer was seemingly everywhere at Trevilian Station once the crisis began. Tireless, fearless, and personally taking command wherever needed, his legendary good luck held fast in spite of the frenzy eddying about him. Hard, determined fighting by his Wolverines saved them from certain destruction that morning. Custer had expected support from the rest of Torbert's division and pitched in when he undoubtedly heard the violent fight raging on the Fredericksburg Road. Rosser later praised his rival: "[H]e made a gallant and manly effort to resist me. Sitting on his horse in the midst of his advanced platoons, and near enough to be easily recognized by me, he encouraged and inspired his men by appeal as well as by example."[116]

Custer was hit twice in the arm and shoulder by spent bullets, causing bruises but no real harm. Spotting Custer standing in the road, directing the fighting, one of his staff officers ran up and said, "General, you ought not to stand in the road, the sharpshooters have too good a range." The Boy General stood his ground, saying that he was "all right" until he completed his observations. Turning to go to another part of the field, he was hit on the shoulder by a bullet. "The sound of the ball was plainly heard by those around him, and none can understand the feelings of those around for a moment. By the same good fortune which had always attended him, the bullet had struck some obstacle, and was partially spent before it hit him, and inflicted but a bruise." A moment later, Custer's assistant inspector general, Maj. George A. Drew of the Sixth Michigan, was hit in the hand by a Rebel bullet, "but this wound too was very slight."[117]

Custer spotted a wounded trooper of the Fifth Michigan, who had been shot in the chest by one of the Virginians. Still exposed to galling fire, Custer "could not bear the thought of his being struck again," even though it was clear that the wound was mortal. Impulsively, the general "rushed forward, and picking him up, bore him to a place of safety. As I turned a sharpshooter fired at me—the ball glanced, stunning me for a few moments."[118] Seemingly impervious to either pain or danger, Custer inspired his beleaguered Wolverines to hang on until support arrived.

The Rebels took one of Pennington's guns and seemed determined to capture the Northern artillery pieces at almost any price. As the desperate fighting unfolded, Lt. Harman Smith of the Seventh Michigan Cavalry and the nineteen men of his Company F fended off five separate charges on a single piece of Pennington's artillery. When one of those determined attacks seized one of the guns, the distraught battery commander rode up to Custer and cried out, "General, they have taken one of my guns!"

His blood up, Custer bellowed, "No! I'll be damned if they have! Come on!"[119] Gathering thirty troopers and running toward the mob of Confederates trying to pull away their prize, Custer pitched in, but the enemy quickly repulsed his little force. Adding his loyal staff officers, some nearby horse holders and Lieutenant Smith's company of the Seventh Michigan to his hodgepodge force, the Boy General made a second, more determined attack. Lieutenant Smith recounted,

In one of these charges a large part of the Rebel Cavalry got one of our pieces in their control and tried to disable it, but a force of seventy-five to one hundred of our boys made a saber charge, one of the sharpest hand to hand contests I ever witnessed and recaptured it. The Commander of the Battery stood gallantly with his gun. One of the Johnnies stunned him by a saber stroke. It was my privilege to take after this chap, a Johnnie took after me, Lieutenant [Charles] Lyon [of the Seventh Michigan Cavalry] after the Johnnie, another Johnnie after Lyon, and another Yankee after him. This all happened in a moment's time, but we held the gun, and as the Rebels got out the Artillery boys sallied into them, letting the Johnnies have three shots, Boom. Bang. Bang. As the smoke cleared away there were five of our men and fifteen Johnnies lying dead. I never knew as to what became of all in the race farther than the fellow ahead of me went down, and Lyon said the one after me followed suit. He was no good with the saber, as he gave me five blows on the back, any of which with a well directed point would have run me through.[120]

The Boy General's satisfaction with saving the gun from capture was short lived, however.

Seeing that Chew's guns were vulnerable, George Custer called for the men of the First and Seventh Michigan Cavalry to make a charge on the Rebel battery, intending to capture it. These two regiments were to be supported by a section of Pennington's battery. The First Michigan was to charge Chew's flank, while the Seventh Michigan was to charge straight up the road, right for the guns. Custer called for Maj. Alexander Walker, now commanding the Seventh Michigan, pointed at Chew's guns, proclaimed that he had the "Johnnies surrounded," and pointing to the right, exclaimed, "Torbert is over there on the next road and we will soon make a charge!" Walker rode off to prepare for the charge under the protection of Pennington's guns.[121]

Two important members of Custer's entourage were lost in the successful attempt to recover the lost gun. Lt. Richard Baylis fell, badly wounded in the shoulder while leading a charge against a detachment of the enemy. Although painfully wounded, he "continued to fight and encourage the men until compelled to leave the field from loss of blood."

Custer also lost his color bearer, Sgt. Mitchell Beloir, of the First Michigan Cavalry, a man Custer described as "one of the 'bravest of the brave.' " That morning, not long after Rosser pitched into the fray, Beloir was riding alongside Custer, carrying the brigade flag at the head of one of the attempts to retrieve Pennington's lost gun, loudly urging his fellow Wolverines forward. Maj. Holmes Conrad, of Rosser's staff, drew a bead on Beloir, mortally wounding him with his revolver; the shot may have struck Beloir in error, as it is quite possible that Custer, riding only a few feet away, was Conrad's true target. The color sergeant reeled. Custer lamented to Libbie, "When shot he remained in his saddle till our lines began to waver, when he made his way to me, saying, 'General, they have killed me. Take the flag!' To save it I was compelled to tear it from his staff and place it in my bosom."[122]

Custer realized his peril. Encouraging his weary Wolverines, he rode the lines, cursing like a sailor. The Boy General, already legendary for his extraordinary command of profanity, was in rare form that long, hot, dry Saturday as he waited for support to arrive. His Michigan men had fought a hard and tiring engagement and were completely encircled by the enemy. Kidd later wrote that "Custer's bulldog courage alone" prevented the destruction of the Michigan Brigade that day.[123] On June 11, the Michigan Brigade suffered 11 killed, 51 wounded, and 299 captured, for total casualties of 361, including nearly half of the Fifth Michigan Cavalry.[124] One of Davies's men observed, "The Rebels did just slay them."[125] Having made a lonely stand for almost three hours, Custer was impatient for Merritt and Devin to join him. He "now began to rave some and look around for reprisals."[126] One of the Wolverines proudly wrote, "During the last five hours this brigade, or three regiments, had held at bay and repulsed seven different assaults of the following brigades, from all of which we had taken prisoners: Wickham's, Rosser's, [Wright's], and [Lomax's]; yet we had actually less than 800 men fighting." He continued, "A rebel lieutenant colonel told us that they thought they were fighting 3,000 men, and when told of our actual numbers, said, 'They were most splendidly handled.' "[127]

As the noon hour approached, Hampton recognized dangerous signs of activity along Torbert's front. The Federals appeared ready to mount another attack toward the station to cut their way to the surrounded Michigan men and to drive Hampton's hard-pressed troopers back against Custer, a potentially dangerous situation. Hampton recognized that with pressure on two fronts, the long defensive lines north of the train station could no longer be held. Accordingly, Hampton ordered Butler and Wright to withdraw to a low ridge to the west of the railroad, while Sheridan's blue-clad troopers readied themselves to assault.

A brief lull fell across the battlefield, as the players steeled themselves for the next act of the bloody drama unfolding in the fields and dense woods surrounding Trevilian Station.[128]

Notes

1. Jay Monahan, "Custer's 'First Last Stand'—Trevilian Station, 1864", included in ed. Paul Andrew Hutton, *The Custer Reader* (Lincoln: University of Nebraska Press, 1992), 53.

2. Carle Woodruff to Adjutant General, U.S. Army, July 3, 1892, John Kennedy

Medal of Honor File, RG 94, File No. 18184PRD1891, the National Archives, Washington, D. C.

3. O.R., vol. 36, part 1, 823 and 832.

4. Wallace, A *Few Memories of a Long Life*, 37.

5. Ferguson Itinerary, entry for June 11, 1864.

6. James L. Rock, "Foraging around Trevilian's Station," included in Lee, *Personal and Historical Sketches*, 149.

7. *Detroit Advertiser & Tribune*, July 6, 1864.

8. Robert Sproul, "Battle of Trevilian's Station, Va.," included Lee, *Personal and Historical Sketches*, 53.

9. Harmon Smith, "Company F at the Battle of Trevilian's Station," included in Lee, *Personal and Historical Sketches*, 230.

10. Fitch diary, entry for June 11, 1864. The intensity and duration of the skirmish that morning are subjects for interesting debate. There are few available accounts describing this opening engagement, so much of it remains open to speculation.

11. Nelson, *"If I Am Killed,"* 16.

12. Diary of Dexter Macomber, entry for June 11, 1864, Clarke Historical Library, Central Michigan University, Mount Pleasant, Michigan.

13. O.R., vol. 36, part 1, 823 and 832.

14. Fitch diary, entry for June 11, 1864.

15. O.R., vol. 36, part 1, 823.

16. George A. Custer to Elizabeth B. Custer, June 21, 1864, included in Merington, *The Custer Story*, 104.

17. *Detroit Advertiser & Tribune*, July 6, 1864.

18. *Ibid.*

19. O.R., vol. 36, part 1, 823.

20. Kidd, *Personal Recollections*, 351–52.

21. Husby and Wittenberg, *Under Custer's Command*, 87.

22. O.R., vol. 36, part 1, 823.

23. Hunt and Brown, *Brevet Brigadier Generals in Blue*, 10. Alger resigned his commission in September 1864, when Sheridan accused him of being away without leave and preferred court-martial charges against Alger. The taint of this unfortunate incident haunted Alger for the rest of his life. Alger also did not perform well as Secretary of War, garnering the blame for the explosion and sinking of the U.S.S. *Maine*.

24. O.R., vol. 36, part 1, 830. Alger appears to have exaggerated the distance covered by his charge, as a charge of this distance would have carried his men far beyond the intersection of the Gordonsville and Charlottesville Roads.

25. *Ibid.* This number also appears exaggerated.

26. *Detroit Advertiser & Tribune*, July 6, 1864.

27. Conrad, *The Rebel Scout*, 110.

28. Butler, "The Cavalry Fight at Trevilian Station," 237.

29. Hansell memoirs, entry for June 11, 1864.

30. Kidd, *Personal Recollections*, 352–53.

31. *Ibid.*, 354–55.

32. *Ibid.*, 356–57.

33. James H. Stevenson, *"Boots and Saddles": A History of the First Volunteer Cavalry of War, Known as the First New York (Lincoln) Cavalry, and also as the Sabre Regiment, Its Organization, Campaigns and Battles* (Harrisburg, Pa.: Patriot Publishing Co., 1879), 202, and William H. Beach, *The First New York (Lincoln) Cavalry, from April 19, 1861 to July 7, 1865* (New York: The Lincoln Cavalry Association, 1902), 269–270.

34. John Hertz service records, Memorandum from Prisoner of War Records, the National Archives, Washington, D.C.; John Hertz pension file, the National Archives, Washington, D.C. Hertz's pension application indicates that as a result of his confinement at Andersonville, "he contracted a disease of the head which affected his hearing and leaving him also deaf; he also contracted rheumatism from which he greatly suffers." John Hertz Declaration for Original Invalid Pension, April 19, 1876, Hertz pension file. Despite these impairments, Hertz lived until October 1915, and was buried in the National Cemetery in Baltimore, Maryland.

35. McVicar diary, entry for June 11, 1864.

36. Kidd, *Personal Recollections*, 358.

37. McDonald, *History of the Laurel Brigade*, 253.

38. Waring diary, entry for June 11, 1864.

39. Milledgeville, Georgia, *Southern Recorder*, July 26, 1864.

40. O.R., vol. 36, part 1, 1095.

41. Fitzhugh Lee to Dear General, December 20, 1866.

42. Rosser, *Riding with Rosser*, 38.

43. McDonald, *History of the Laurel Brigade*, 253.

44. Petersburg *Daily Register*, June 29, 1864.

45. Report of Thomas L. Rosser, June 30, 1864, included in Swank, *Battle of Trevilian Station*, 59.

46. James F. Wood diary, entry for June 11, 1864.

47. Chew, "The Battle of Trevilians," 5–6.

48. Roger P. Chew to Capt. Dudley D. Pendleton, November 16, 1864, included in *Supplement to the Official Records of the Union and Confederate Armies, Reports, Addendum*, series 1, vol. 6 (Wilmington, N.C.: Broadfoot Publishing Co., 1997), 821. This position is probably across the Gordonsville Road from the train station, site of some modern-day apartments.

49. McVicar diary, entry for June 11, 1864.

50. Waring diary, entry for June 11, 1864.

51. Petersburg *Daily Reporter*, June 29, 1864.

52. Waring diary, entry for June 11, 1864.

53. McDonald, *History of the Laurel Brigade*, 253.

54. Neese, *Three Years in the Confederate Horse Artillery*, 285.

55. Petersburg *Daily Register*, June 29, 1864.

56. Hansell memoir.

57. Myers, *The Comanches*, 297.

58. *Ibid*.

59. *Detroit Advertiser & Tribune*, July 6, 1864.

60. McDonald, *History of the Laurel Brigade*, 254; Myers, *The Comanches*, 300.

61. Avery memoir, 76.

62. O.R., vol. 36, part 1, 830–31; Russell A. Alger to T. S. Bouris, September 18, 1865, Simon Gratz Collection, Civil War Generals, Case 4, Box 39, Historical Society of Pennsylvania, Philadelphia.

63. O.R., vol. 36, part 1, 831. Sgt. James Henry Avery was one of the twenty-eight left behind. Avery left an outstanding account of the trials and tribulations faced by these men as they made their way back to safety. That account can be found in Husby and Wittenberg, *Under Custer's Command*, 83–96.

64. *Ibid*.

65. Alger to Bouris, September 18, 1865.

66. J. K. Lowden, "A Gallant Record: Michigan's 5th Cavalry in the Latter Period of the War," *The National Tribune*, July 30, 1896.

67. Hansell memoir.

68. Myers, *The Comanches*, 297–98.

69. Woodruff to Adjutant General United States Army, July 3, 1892, Kennedy Medal of Honor file.

70. O.R., vol. 36, part 1, 823.

71. Myers, *The Comanches*, 299.

72. Lee, *History of the Seventh Cavalry*, 230.

73. O.R., vol. 36, part 1, 824.

74. John Patrick Kelly to Patrick Kelly, May 26, 1876, Wyles Collection, University of California at Santa Barbara.

75. John Fortier, *Fifteenth Virginia Cavalry* (Lynchburg, Va.: H. E. Howard Co., 1993), 75. Critcher, a lawyer and former state legislator, scathingly wrote, "Having enlisted & mustered into the service nearly half the Regt., & having commanded it for nearly twelve months, I was informed yesterday on the battlefield in the presence of my Regt. That it was placed under the command of another. Under such circumstances, my honor & self respect require that I promptly & unconditionally, but respectfully, resign my commission, which I do accordingly to take effect from this date." Lomax forwarded the resignation and endorsed it, writing, "I consider Lt. Col. Critcher a gallant officer & regret to lose his services entirely

from the command." *Ibid.* After the war, Critcher resumed his political career, serving in the postwar U.S. Congress. Krick, *Lee's Colonels*, 105.

76. Fitzhugh Lee to Dear General, December 20, 1866.

77. *Richmond Examiner*, July 1, 1864.

78. James F. Wood diary, entry for June 11, 1864.

79. Merington, *The Custer Story*, 104–05. In December 1876, Wade Hampton, then a United States senator from South Carolina, encountered Custer's old friend Isaac P. Christiancy. That day, Hampton gave to Christiancy Custer's field glasses, captured at Trevilian Station on June 11, 1864. Christiancy wrote that Hampton "had thought of presenting it to you, but hesitated, lest it be misconstrued, and instead of being kindly received as a tribute of respect for your deceased husband and yourself, you might think it inconsiderate or unfeeling on his part." Christiancy disabused the courtly South Carolinian of his notion, telling Hampton that Libbie Custer "would appreciate it as a token of respect from one gallant man to the memory of another." (I. P. Christiancy to Elizabeth Bacon Custer, December 17, 1876, Dr. Lawrence A. Frost Collection of Custeriana, Monroe County Historical Museum Archives, Monroe, Michigan). Many of Custer's other personal items also were eventually returned to Libbie Custer by Thomas T. Munford long after Custer met his destiny at the Little Big Horn. A grateful Libbie wrote to Munford, "I feel that I can say very little with the cold medium of pen and paper to express my gratitude to you for giving back to me the precious souvenirs of my husband. Though I am not a spiritualist, I live so in the past that I find myself unconsciously telling my husband of what I know and ignore time. The day I hung the old cap and sash in my room I could hear him say 'how good of Munford,' his manner of speaking is so oral to me even now and living to commemorate him as I try to do intensifies this feeling of comradeship." (Elizabeth Bacon Custer to Thomas T. Munford, August 1, 1901, Munford-Ellis Family Papers, Thomas T. Munford Division, Duke University, Special Collections Library, Durham, North Carolina).

80. Merington, *The Custer Story*, 105–06.

81. *Ibid.*, 104.

82. *Detroit Advertiser & Tribune*, July 6, 1864.

83. Jacob L. Greene to George A. Custer, September 29, 1864, Alderman Library, Special Collections Department, University of Virginia, Charlottesville, Virginia; Merington, *The Custer Story*, 104.

84. Fitzhugh Lee to Dear General, December 20, 1866.

85. Merington, *The Custer Story*, 104.

86. *Richmond Examiner*, July 1, 1864.

87. Robert J. Driver Jr., *Second Virginia Cavalry* (Lynchburg, Va.: H. E. Howard Co., 1995), 124–25.

88. Robert J. Driver Jr., *Fifth Virginia Cavalry* (Lynchburg, Va.: H. E. Howard Co., 1997), 82.

89. O.R., vol. 36, part 1, 823–24.

90. Kidd, *Personal Recollections*, 360.

91. Grommon diary, entry for June 11, 1864.

92. James F. Wood diary, entry for June 11, 1864.

93. Asa B. Isham, *Historical Sketch of the Seventh Regiment Michigan Volunteer Cavalry* (New York: Town Topics Publishing Co., 1893), 59–60.

94. James H. Kidd to John Robertson, Adjutant General of Michigan, December 17, 1864, the National Archives, Washington, D.C.

95. William Onweller Service Records, the National Archives, Washington, D.C. Onweller's voluminous pension file paints a sad story indeed. The boy's father was a heavy drinker who could not support his family's needs, and the burden of support fell on the teenager's shoulders, and "was all the help [his mother] had at the time of his enlistment." While in the service, all of Onweller's pay was sent home to help the family make ends meet. His mother's application for a pension indicates that William, her older son, "worked for me and others in the house and in the field and worked for others to support the family" on its sixty acre farm in Michigan. Her other son "makes a very poor living." One sister was "deaf and dumb" and the other sister "married a shiftless vagabond that is not worth one cent." After a protracted battle, the pension application was rejected because the family farm of eighty acres had substantial value and could have been liquidated instead. William Onweller Pension File, the National Archives, Washington, D.C.

96. John C. Fitzgerald Service Records, the National Archives, Washington, D.C. Interestingly, on March 20, 1865, Fitzgerald's brother, then recovering from a disabling combat wound in a hospital in Buffalo, New York, wrote to the commissary general of prisons, inquiring as to his brother's whereabouts and well-being. Frustrated by being unable to locate his missing brother, Fitzgerald was hoping for information, stating "I feel very uneasy about him as he is an only brother and we are orphans at that—If you could give me any word of him, You will be conferring a favour on a crippled soldier." A small notation of "No Record" appears on the letter. It is not known whether the commissary general responded. Fortunately, the brothers were reunited only weeks later when the end of the war freed John Fitzgerald from captivity. James Fitzgerald to commissary general of prisons, March 20, 1865, John C. Fitzgerald Service Records.

97. Oscar Wood diary, entry for June 11, 1864, Jim Wood Collection, Howell, Michigan.

98. Macomber diary, entry for June 11, 1864.

99. Kidd to Robertson, December 17, 1864.

100. Lee, *Seventh Michigan*, 53–4.

101. Ferguson Itinerary, entry for June 11, 1864.

102. DeWitt C. Gallagher, *A Diary Depicting the Experience of DeWitt Clinton Gallagher in the War between the States while Serving in the Confederate Army* (Reorganized Company E, First Virginia Cavalry, 1945), 6.

103. Nelson, *If I Am Killed*, 16.

104. Kenneth C. Stiles, *Fourth Virginia Cavalry* (Lynchburg, Va.: H. E. Howard Co., 1985), 53.

105. Fitzhugh Lee to Dear General, December 20, 1866. When Sheridan withdrew after the conclusion of the fighting at Trevilian, Col. Carter was left behind. On June 13, Capt. Zimmerman Davis of the Fifth South Carolina Cavalry was sent to scour the field for casualties left behind. Davis found Carter in an abandoned aid station, and Carter was taken to the Confederate hospital at Gordonsville, where he was cared for until his death nearly a month later. See Krick, *Lee's Colonels*, 86. Carter's diary, which unfortunately ends about a month before the Trevilian Raid, was recently published and contains some interesting insights for those interested in additional information. See William R. Carter, *Sabres, Saddles and Spurs: Lieutenant Colonel William R. Carter, CSA*, ed. Walbrook D. Swank (Shippensburg, Pa.: Burd Street Press, 1998).

106. Stiles, *Fourth Virginia Cavalry*, 139–40; Towles family grave markers, Oakland Cemetery, Louisa Court House, Virginia; Sallie Conner to Mrs. Towles, June 13, 1864, Towles Family Papers, Keith Kehlbeck Collection, Marshall, Michigan; Keith Kehlbeck to the author, February 7, 2000.

107. Stiles, *Fourth Virginia Cavalry*, 109; Thomas P. Ellicott grave marker, Oakland Cemetery, Louisa Court House, Virginia.

108. Conrad, *The Rebel Scout*, 113–14.

109. L. Eustis Williams, "Charge of the Clarke Cavalry at Trevelyan Station," *Southern Bivouac*, vol. 3 (September 1884–May 1885), p. 218. A slightly different account by the same author also appears in John N. Opie, *A Rebel Cavalryman with Lee, Stuart and Jackson* (Chicago: W. B. Conkey Co., 1889), 299–302.

110. John Kennedy Medal of Honor file, RG 94, File No. 18184PRD1891, the National Archives, Washington, D.C.

111. Kennedy Medal of Honor file. Kennedy survived Andersonville and returned to Regular Army service at the conclusion of the Civil War, finally retiring as an ordnance sergeant in 1891. The application for Kennedy's Medal of Honor was submitted by Lt. Carle A. Woodruff without Kennedy's knowledge. His battery commander, Lt. Alexander C. M. Pennington, by 1892 a major in the Regular Army, heartily endorsed the application, writing, "I would be exceedingly glad to have [Kennedy's] service recognized by the presentation of a medal of honor which he deserves not only for his gallantry but for long and faithful service."

112. Woodruff to Adjutant General, United States Army, July 3, 1892, Kennedy Medal of Honor file.

113. O.R., vol. 36, part 1, 824 and 832.

114. Opie, *A Rebel Cavalryman*, 300.

115. Daniel A. Grimsley, "Battle of Trevillian's Station," *Battles in Culpeper County, Virginia, 1861–1865 and Other Articles Written by Major Daniel A. Grimsley of the Sixth Virginia Cavalry* (Culpeper, Va.: Raleigh Travers Green, 1900), 34.

116. Thomas L. Rosser, report of fighting at Trevilian Station, June 30, 1864, included in Swank, *The Battle of Trevilian Station*, 59.

117. *Detroit Advertiser & Tribune*, July 6, 1864.

118. Merington, *The Custer Story*, 105.

119. Lee, *Seventh Michigan*, 230; *New York Herald*, June 21, 1864.

120. Lee, *Seventh Michigan*, 230–31.

121. Account of Pvt. Daniel Eldridge, contained in Isham, *Seventh Michigan*, 59.

122. *Ibid.*; O.R., vol. 36, part 1, 824. There are many accounts of this story, including one by Rosser, who witnessed the incident and recounted it later that month. See Thomas L. Rosser, report of fighting at Trevilian Station, June 30, 1864, included in Swank, *The Battle of Trevilian Station*, 60. See also *New York Herald*, June 21, 1864, and John Kelly, "Trevilian Station: How Custer Saved the Flag and How His Brigade was Helped out of a Tight Place," *The National Tribune*, August 12, 1886.

123. James H. Kidd, "Historical Sketch of General Custer", included in Eric J. Wittenberg, ed., *At Custer's Side: The Civil War Writings of James H. Kidd* (Kent, Ohio: Kent State University Press, 2001), 92.

124. Kidd, *Personal Recollections*, 364–66; O.R., vol. 36, part 1, 832.

125. Benjamin W. Crowninshield, *A History of the First Regiment of Massachusetts Volunteer Cavalry* (Boston: Houghton-Mifflin, 1891), 223.

126. *New York Herald*, June 21, 1864.

127. *Detroit Advertiser & Tribune*, July 6, 1864.

128. Rosser, *Riding with Rosser*, 38.

5

Union Breakthrough
along the Railroad

*The result of this engagement was that we gained possession
of the railroad at Trevilian Station.*

Alfred Torbert fretted as the sounds of the maelstrom engulfing Custer's Brigade increased in volume. He consulted with Sheridan, and the two generals decided to try to communicate with the Boy General and his brigade. At one point during the morning, a squadron of the Sixth New York Cavalry was sent to find Custer. The New Yorkers "found him and found more—they were cut off and surrounded by the enemy, and in cutting their way out a number were captured." Rebuffed, the New Yorkers fell back, reporting their findings.[1]

As the noon hour approached, desperate to obtain news of the plight of his subordinate, Torbert sent staff officers to Custer, who bore orders to bring back situation reports. For nearly two hours, all attempts to reach Custer failed. Nathaniel Davidson, a correspondent from the *New York Herald*, watched as the drama unfolded: "Each time the officer would run into the enemy's fire and up to his lines; thinking it possible they might be Custer's, at the imminent risk of capture, only to find that he must race back again for dear life."[2]

Lt. Robert C. Wallace, usually a member of Custer's Fifth Michigan Cavalry, was serving as one of Torbert's staff officers during the campaign. He joined Capt. Theodore H. Bean of Torbert's staff, and Sgt. Joseph C. Jones of the Seventeenth Pennsylvania Cavalry, on one of these forays. The three men climbed into their saddles and spurred off toward the sounds of the fighting. Wallace recalled, "We started off at a good pace and had gone some two miles or more, when, coming to a sharp turn in the road, leading down into a little valley, we saw a party of cavalry at the foot of the grade, dismounted and standing to horse, about a hundred yards away." Thinking that a light-colored horse in the party looked like that of Capt. Robert Judson of the Fifth Michigan, Wallace happily reported to Bean that "we were in luck to find our friends so soon." Their joy, unfortunately, did not last long. While Wallace told Bean of their good fortune, "bang, came a volley in our faces and several of the mounted came for us with a yell. It did not take us long to about face and light out at our best gait. Both of us being mounted, they soon gave up the chase after half a mile or more."[3] Most of Torbert's other attempts to reach Custer met similar fates. Bean recalled that Torbert "was now convinced that Custer's situation must be critical."[4]

Merritt's Regulars itched to pitch into the fray. Trooper John Kelly and the other men of the Second U.S. Cavalry watched the maelstrom whirling around the Wolverines. Saddled up, the Regulars watched "Custer's men charge wildly against the rebel lines, which had formed in his rear, and failing there wheel and charge to the right; baffled again, they would reform and dash to the left, in the vain endeavor to break through the lines or beat them back." Kelly noted, "As these movements were repeated, our boys began to fidget in their saddles and look anxiously in the direction of Sheridan's headquarters for the expected order to go to their assistance." No such orders came, and as the smoke of battle thickened, the Regulars caught only fleeting glimpses of the Wolverines. The Regulars relied on the familiar guidon of the Michigan Cavalry Brigade to track the progress of the Wolverines.

Kelly continued, "At last the flag went down, and every eye again turned in the direction of headquarters. Still no messenger came; a few moments, and the flag was raised again." Nevertheless, the Regulars grew increasingly restless watching the plight of their fellow blue-clad troopers. Unable to resist, and in violation of the code of strict discipline that marked Regular Army soldiers, the men of the Second U.S. vented their frustration, blurting out remarks like, "Why don't we go in and win?" "Awaiting orders be damned!" "It's a damned shame!" "They'll all be gobbled up in a few minutes!" "Headquarters be damned!" When the brigade guidon dropped again, as Custer tore it from its standard, the tension increased markedly: "With set, determined features, our men look at each other,—a suppressed exclamation seems to tremble on every lip. They are silent now, watching intently; the flag does not appear; the combatants are enveloped in a cloud of dust and smoke, and we realize the crisis has come. Short, sharp and decisive must be our action or we will be too late."[5] Still no orders came.

Finally, about noon, Capt. Amasa G. Dana of the Eighth Illinois Cavalry, Torbert's assistant adjutant general, received permission to try to reach Custer. Dana fell in with the Sixth Pennsylvania Cavalry of Merritt's brigade and advanced with them, driving the enemy out of a ravine. Hearing Pennington's guns, the captain split off from the Pennsylvanians and rode up a small hill, where he could see Custer's predicament through his field glasses. He rode to the battery. A distressed Pennington described the plight of the Wolverines. Dana watched as Custer tried to recapture his headquarters wagon. Dana finally made his way to the Boy General, who cried out, "For God's sake, Dana, tell Torbert to send me some men. I have saved Pennington's guns, but I've lost my teams and ambulances." Dana noted, "I never before saw Custer so tired and weary. He was literally exhausted by physical effort."[6]

Dana reported all of the efforts made by Torbert to make contact with the missing Wolverines. The first portion of Custer's line he came to "was facing in one direction, and their seven shooters were going crack, crack, crack, in the most lively manner. Reaching the centre he found that, facing in an exactly opposite course, the same weapons discoursing the same music there. Again the other wing was facing in a third front and just as fiercely engaged as the rest."[7] Dana drew the same conclusion as the men of the Second U.S. Cavalry—the situation was desperate and decisive action was needed or the Wolverines would be annihilated. Leaving Custer, Dana sped off to Torbert's headquarters, where he found the distraught division commander preparing a general advance to cut its way through to Custer's position.

Brig. Gen. Wesley Merritt also watched events unfold. Although he and the Boy General were rivals, Merritt was not about to sit idly by and watch the fine Michigan Cavalry Brigade destroyed without at least making an effort to rescue it. Finally, he could take it no more, and "took his brandy flask from his saddle bags and took a good long pull at it, and who would have blamed him, for there was a fair prospect of it being the last he would ever take." Merritt handed the flask to one of his staff officers, and "turning a troubled, anxious look in the direction of headquarters and seeing no messenger in sight, thus addressed his command: 'Men, we must cut open a way to let Custer out of that scrape!' "

His proud Regulars did not need to be told twice. Immediately, the command, "Trot, march, gallop!" issued, and the bugles rang out the stirring notes of the charge. The Regulars galloped toward Rosser's and Lee's troopers, looking for a weak spot. Trooper Kelly recalled, "our lines bounded forward in a sweeping charge before we were upon them, when they broke to the right and left and fled precipitously for the timber, hurrying off a few of Custer's men with them. Some of these we recaptured, together with the guns which they had got temporary possession of."[8] When Merritt finally found the Boy General, a relieved Custer exclaimed, "Merritt, they had me in a tight place that time; and look here (taking the flag from his bosom), it was the only way I could save it!"[9] A few minutes later, Sheridan rode up and inquired, "Did they get your headquarters flag, General?" The triumphant Boy General held the flag up and exclaimed, "Not by a damned sight! There it is!"[10]

The men of the First U.S. withdrew to resupply. They were then sent to the flank to defend against Butler. The Regulars moved down a steep hill and across a little valley, through which the South Fork of Hickory Creek ran. On the other side of the little stream, the ground rose again into higher ground. On the crest stood a brick farmhouse, several outbuildings, and an orchard and a stout stone wall held by the enemy. As the Regulars approached, Confederate troopers popped up and poured a heavy fire into the ranks of the dragoons. Capt. George B. Sanford remembered, "It was a very ugly position. They were well protected, and we had nothing bigger than a blade of grass. The hill was very steep and the grass slippery, and it looked exceedingly doubtful whether we could carry the crest."[11]

Sanford's battalion held the far right of the regiment's position. As he advanced, his friend Lt. Frederick C. Ogden, the regimental adjutant, accompanied him. When the enemy opened fire, Ogden remarked, "Well, I must join Sweitzer," jumped the creek, and ran back toward the center of the regiment's position. Sanford's battalion then pushed straight up the hill, carrying the stone wall, and penetrating the orchard. After regrouping, the Regulars advanced across the enemy's flank to the brick house, forcing the Southern horse soldiers to withdraw from the stone wall. Sanford noticed that his battalion was separated from the rest of the regiment, which was holding the stone wall. Although the position was strong, it was untenable because of its isolation. The captain ordered his men to fall back to the stone wall, which they reached "with considerable loss, as the enemy made it very hot for us in crossing the open ground between us and it." When Sanford reached safety and paused to catch his breath, another officer informed him, "Ogden is killed." Sanford recalled, "Altogether it could not have been ten minutes since we had separated at the stream and it seemed impossible that my closest friend was gone. A bullet had struck him directly between the eyes and he fell dead without a word, within three minutes of the time I last saw him."[12]

Ogden was a good soldier. "Frederick Callender Ogden was one of the most brilliant young men of his time and in all respects one of the most promising," lamented Sanford. The young officer, a graduate of Yale University, was commissioned immediately into the Regular service in 1861. Without formal military training, Ogden demonstrated great natural talent and was soon promoted to first lieutenant and appointed regimental adjutant. Sanford continued, "It is with no intention of saying anything to the disparagement of the many gallant officers who have held that position during my term of service of nearly thirty years in that regiment that I say I never saw his equal. All who knew him would willingly say the same."[13] Merritt concurred, "The modest, unaffected, generous Lieutenant Ogden, of the First, whom to see was to respect, and to know was to admire, poured out his life's blood at Trevilian."[14] That night, Sanford and another man carried Ogden's body to the Trevilian house and gently laid it there.

In the meantime, Sheridan "directed Torbert to press the line in front of Merritt and Devin, aided by one brigade of Gregg's division on their left."[15] As the two Yankee brigades moved forward in a general assault, looking to connect with Custer's flank, some of Butler's and Wright's men "came out of the woods in our front and opened on us with artillery and musketry." Colonel Devin ordered up Heaton's guns, which quickly opened on the Rebels, driving them back to the shelter of the woods. The historian of the Sixth New York Cavalry recalled, "When we were not fighting, we were in line of battle."[16]

"The men were deployed only a few feet apart, and as far as possible kept in line as we advanced. But we had some rough ground to go over, creeks to cross, and woods with thick underbrush to pass through. Then bear in mind there were a lot of ugly rebels in our front inclined to dispute our way by shooting in our faces, charging, and taking every possible advantage to discomfit us. Thus you will understand it was often a difficult thing to keep our alignment," described the regimental chaplain of the First New York Dragoons, James R. Bowen. "Both hostile lines were ablaze, and bullets flew like hailstones, cannon on either side were throwing their missiles of death, and the air was sulphurous with smoke, our artillery often shooting over our heads and dropping their shells in the ranks of the enemy." Then came the order all awaited: "Forward, double-quick, charge!" As Bowen recalled, "the bugles sounded the charge, and at once our boys set up a yell, like so many devils, rushing forward regardless of shot or shell; and the scene became terrific beyond description as both sides contended for the mastery in the sanguinary struggle."[17]

Adding to the intensity of the fighting, the day was hot and dry, with dust and clouds of acrid gray smoke swirling everywhere. Without time for food or drink, the men of the Reserve Brigade, fighting for nearly eight hours, were parched. The hot sun was taking its toll. Portly Col. Alfred Gibbs of the First New York Dragoons was overcome by sunstroke and left the field. With his second in command, Lieutenant Colonel Thorp, already a prisoner of war, command of his regiment fell upon Maj. Howard M. Smith. Smith, hit by three bullets that day, was only slightly injured. He noted, "A little after noon, the Reb. line began to wane and we were soon chasing them. . . . Many of our best and bravest men are killed or badly wounded."[18]

"The rapid advance of our forces cut off a portion of the rebel cavalry which had been attacking Custer. . . . (Rosser's Laurel Brigade) and at one time the rebels seemed to be perfectly panic stricken," wrote Lt. Louis H. Carpenter of the Sixth U.S. Cavalry.[19] With a concerted effort by the Union cavalry, it looked more and more like Sheridan's plan would work after all, opening the way to Gordonsville.

In the meantime, Hampton was consolidating his division in the area around the train station. Although Butler had orders to withdraw, his troopers were being heavily pressed by Torbert's steady advance. Hearing that he had been ordered to fall back, Butler responded, "Say to General Hampton it is hell to hold on and hell to let go! If I withdraw my entire line at once the blue coats will run over us, and that the best I can do is to mount one regiment at a time and gradually retire." By employing these tactics, the South Carolinians retreated to Poindexter's Orchard in good order. "If his troops had not been the finest in the world they would have become demoralized and precipitated confusion that might have led to a serious disaster," bragged Butler.[20] Butler pulled back to a field aid station, where he briefly consulted with a concerned Wade Hampton.

As Butler slowly withdrew, the pressure along his front intensified, and Hart's section of horse artillery, posted to the north of the station along the Fredericksburg Road, was in imminent danger of being captured. Wade Hampton recognized this threat and reacted quickly. First, he told the Fifth South Carolina, "Dismount and protect that battery!" The order was obeyed instantly by Butler's men.[21] Then, dashing to the right of the Sixth South Carolina Cavalry, Hampton ordered Maj. Thomas B. Ferguson, commanding the regiment after Colonel Hugh Aiken's early-morning wounding, to mount his men and charge to save the battery. The only troopers available were Company F, also known as the Cadet Rangers, consisting of cadets from The Citadel, South Carolina's state-run military academy.

Capt. Moses B. Humphrey commanded the Cadet Rangers. Humphrey, who was in his penultimate year at The Citadel when war came in 1861, was a cool customer and bravely led the former cadets into battle. Butler praised the young captain, saying, "I have never seen a man of more fortitude than Capt. Humphrey," high praise indeed from the likes of the one-legged general.[22] His two lieutenants, Alfred Aldrich and William J. Nettles, aligned the cadets. When they were ready to advance, Wade Hampton, mounted on his magnificent charger "Butler," dashed to their front and led the cadets forward in a fierce saber charge that blunted the Federal attack and covered the withdrawal of Hart's endangered guns.[23]

Characteristically, Hampton pitched into the fray, emptying two Federal saddles with his revolver. Long after the war, the aged Hampton was asked how many Yankees he had killed during the war. The general replied, "Eleven, two with my sword and nine with my pistol." His interviewer asked, "How about the two at Trevilian?" Hampton responded, "Oh, I did not count them, they were running."[24] Hampton and a Yankee lieutenant emptied their revolvers at each other at close range, neither hitting the other, proving how hard it is to strike a moving target from horseback.[25]

Lt. John Bauskett of the Sixth South Carolina, "a brave and skillful officer," joined Hampton's charge and spotted a Yankee drawing a bead on William G. Simms Jr. of the Cadet Rangers. Bauskett "shot the officer leading the charge and the man next to him," shattering the momentum of the Federal attack.[26]

One of the South Carolinians recalled, "Seeing a body of cavalry coming down the road, we were ordered to draw sabre and charge which was done in fine style, charging under and between the two fires of artillery." The charge of the South Carolinians shattered the Yankee charge, and "every Yankee was killed, wounded or taken prisoner, don't think one escaped as all of our men did their duty with pistol and sabre, some bringing out two and three wounded prisoners."[27]

Sgt. W. H. Dowling of Company B, Fifth South Carolina Cavalry, also helped repulse the Federal efforts to capture Hart's guns. His company commander warned Dowling and his friend Wiley Thomas about a Federal sharpshooter perched in a nearby tree, picking off the South Carolinians at his leisure. Dowling and Thomas raised their Enfields, and "we paid him our best compliments for that occasion and saw him hurry down." Having chased away the sniper, Dowling and Lt. A. J. Harrison were sent to watch the left flank, where they again came under fire from Northern sharpshooters, Spencer bullets hissing angrily by their ears. Dowling recalled, "The Rebel yell ... dust and cyclone noise of small arms told us that the chivalrous cavaliers were measuring arms, but the Yankee flanks were too strong." An officer informed Harrison and Dowling, "Boys, the brigade has fallen back. Morris (one of your company) is killed." As the three beleaguered Confederates made their way back toward Netherland Tavern and safety, "every gun of every battery seemed to pour on us three, but we got back to our regiment all the same."[28]

Butler saw that the Federals were about to capture his ambulances and wounded. Desperate to save them, Butler ordered his provost marshal, Lieutenant Long of the Sixth South Carolina, to charge the enemy with his headquarters escort of thirty men. Long promptly obeyed the order and charged with his small detachment, their sabres flashing in the bright afternoon sun. The South Carolinians cut and slashed "right into the enemy and evidently surprised them by the audacity" of their charge, although the melee emptied several of Long's saddles. The ambulances successfully withdrew in the face of a galling fire.[29]

Butler then rode up to one of Hart's guns, now redeployed near the tavern. At one point, Butler and Lt. Col. William Stokes of the Fourth South Carolina, who rode with him, were nearly captured while protecting the Confederate rear. The two officers were cut off and had to slash their way through the Federals to escape.[30] As they rode toward the tavern, one of Wright's staff officers spotted Butler and spurred up yelling, "General, for God's sake get away from here, that is the enemy," pointing toward a line of advancing Union horse soldiers not far away. Unconcerned, Butler replied that the gun must be saved and ordered the sergeant in charge to move it up a hill toward Rosser's position to the southwest. The gunners concentrated a sharp fire on the advancing Federals.[31] Hart's gun was again saved from capture.

Butler sent the Sixth South Carolina and the Phillips Legion of Wright's brigade to reinforce the position near the station. The two regiments charged, driving Custer's men back toward Louisa. The South Carolinians formed a new line of battle on the crest of a low rise, nearly at right angles to his original position. They linked with Rosser's position. Butler later praised his men, writing, "but for their stubborn and invincible courage [we] must have been annihilated."[32]

After the fighting passed the Netherland Tavern, an unusual incident briefly interrupted the fierce combat. Mrs. Lucy Dettor Hughson lived in a house a couple of hundred yards west of the train station. All morning, she listened to the crescendo of firing and realized that her home lay directly in the path of the fighting. A Yankee trooper spotted her watching nervously from an upstairs window and demanded that she pull her head back inside to safety. "Where shall I go?" asked the frightened woman. The Union soldier replied, "Get in the cellar!" "But we don't have a cellar," responded Mrs. Hughson, prompting the Northerner to say, "Well, then, one place is as good as another!" A few moments later, an errant artillery shell passed through the house. Mrs. Hughson then recognized the wisdom of the advice. She gathered her infant child, dashed out of the house, into the yard and ran toward her sister-in-law's house, several hundred yards to the southwest. As she ran, her hair streaming and dress billowing, shells crashed around her, and bullets whizzed by her ears. By this time, the young woman was frantic with fright and nearly out of breath.

Seeing her plight, Capt. C. H. Orme, a Federal officer, spurred forward and lifted the baby from her arms. After a brief argument, Mrs. Hughson caught her breath and Orme carried the child half a mile or so to the rear. As the Federal officer rode slowly, Mrs. Hughson clutched his stirrup the whole way, struggling to keep pace with the mounted man. Orme heard shouted orders for his company to fall in, brought his steed to a halt, and returned the baby to its mother, now both safely out of the line of fire. He recalled, "she was a very pretty lady and had a very pretty baby." That night, while Mrs. Hughson rested safely at her sister-in-law's house, her child clutched to her breast, her house was ransacked by Northern horse soldiers who carried her tables into the yard and used them as troughs. Her food supplies were confiscated, and her bedding was impressed for use at field hospitals. However, both mother and child were safe.[33]

The situation was now untenable for the Confederates. Torbert's determined attack split Butler's brigade from Wright's brigade and Fitz Lee's position, creating a potentially disastrous gap. Wade Hampton grimly hung on, seemingly everywhere at once, dashing about, personally giving orders, and directing staff officers and couriers. Hampton steadied his beleaguered command by his calm, cool presence and courage. However, his division was in danger of being flanked and facing increasing pressure. He was separated from Fitz Lee, who was being pushed steadily back toward Louisa Court House by the determined Federal attack.[34] Sheridan saw a chance to destroy Hampton's isolated division.

J. Irvin Gregg's brigade delivered the decisive blow. As the guns from Custer's fight boomed, a staff officer approached Maj. M. Henry Avery, now commanding the Tenth New York. Hailing the staff officer, Avery inquired, "What's the matter?" "Custer has stirred up a hornet's nest in front. You are to move your regiment into the open space and guard the trains as they come up," replied the staff officer. Although the Tenth New York was actually part of Davies's brigade, an aide rode up to Major Avery and ordered him to report to Irvin Gregg "for duty with his brigade." When the New Yorkers reported to Gregg, the Pennsylvanian positioned the regiment near the tavern.[35] Gregg intended to drive away a battery of dogged Confederate artillerists and dismounted cavalry, posted near the Netherland Tavern, whose fire greatly annoyed Sheridan's men.

About 3:00 P.M., with support from Randol's battery, the Tenth New York dismounted and formed line of battle in a small clump of trees. With a yell, the New Yorkers went forward, Major Avery leading the way across an open field toward the meager shelter of a rail fence while Rebel bullets whistled by. An officer of the regiment recalled, "Reaching the fence each man went to the ground and through the lower rails of the fence gave the enemy his compliments. The muzzles of the cannon we wanted were just visible over the knoll in our front."[36] Capt. John Ordner of Company A was killed outright in this charge. Cpl. Kimball Persons of Company L was mortally wounded, shot through by a Rebel bullet. Sinking to the ground next to Capt. George Vanderbilt, the dying corporal turned and said, "Captain, here is my diary; send it to my sister, and tell her that I am not sorry that I enlisted," prompting Vanderbilt to write of the young man, "Noble boy."[37]

Going to ground, an officer of the Tenth New York called out to the regimental adjutant, George W. Kennedy, "For God's sake, Adjutant, what are you going to do? We can't lie here much longer!" Kennedy sought out Avery. After learning that the initial charge had caused heavy casualties among the ranks of the Tenth New York, Avery ordered a second charge.[38] "After giving them one volley and taking a long breath, as if by a common impulse each man went over the fence and for the guns." The Southern artillerists, not eager to make the acquaintance of the advancing New Yorkers, limbered up and withdrew, no longer annoying the Yankees in their front.[39] The New Yorkers jumped down into the railroad cut, capturing a rich harvest of prisoners.

Seventeen-year-old Pvt. Azil M. Pendil, of Company D, a new recruit, stood nearly six feet tall. Pendil endured a lot of teasing from the veterans in his company. He responded by saying that once he got into his first fight, he would show them some "tall fighting." The charge at Trevilian was the boy's first combat, and he proved his prediction correct. Spotting a nearby house, Pendil made for it, "chasing a reb, even taller than himself, both bareheaded. It was as even a race as I ever saw. Pendil ran the reb around the house and into it, and, when the rest of the company came up, they found Pendil standing in the doorway, holding eight rebs prisoner with an empty revolver!"[40]

Two members of the Tenth New York distinguished themselves in this assault. Lt. Noble D. Preston, the "fighting commissary," was the brigade commissary that day. However, when he heard Irvin Gregg order the Tenth New York forward, he requested and obtained permission to "go in" with his regiment as it advanced. Shouting as he ran, Preston called out, "All ready for a charge, boys!"[41] Leading the way across the open field, a Southern ball hit Preston in the right hip, causing "a very dangerous wound." He was carried back to the shade of some trees, where the wound was examined. Accompanied only by his black manservant Aaron, the injured man was left until evening, the loss of blood causing Preston to lose consciousness for a time. The regimental surgeon, believing that Preston was mortally wounded, left the commissary officer behind, telling Preston that he would not survive a day's march. The hurt man responded, "I had rather die with the boys than live with the rebs!", and they took him with them.[42] As a reward for his courage, Preston received the Medal of Honor in 1889, his application supported by enthusiastic endorsements from Generals Davies, D. M. Gregg, and Sheridan, and by Major Avery. The citation read, "for bravery in battle, especially in the action of Trevilian Station, Va. June 11, 1864."[43]

Twenty-nine-year-old Sgt. Maj. Herbert Farnsworth of the Tenth New York, a farmer from Cataraugas, had risen from bugler to sergeant, and eventually was commissioned an officer. Maj. Theodore H. Weed of the Tenth New York recalled that Farnsworth's "gentlemanly conduct and bravery was known to every one in the regiment." After the charge across the field to the fence, the exposed New Yorkers came under friendly artillery fire. Weed, who commanded the regiment's Third Battalion that day, realized that "it became necessary for a man of nerve to carry orders to the rear and across an open field," for the artillery fire from Randol's guns to be redirected, a duty "which seemed instant death for any man to attempt."[44] Weed called for volunteers, and Farnsworth readily volunteered.

Sgt. Llewellyn Norton recalled, "It was a perilous task as he had to pass over a crest which was swept by the artillery of both armies, and a cross fire from the Rebel artillery." Norton continued, "Sergeant Farnsworth walked rapidly over the open space to the cover of the woods, where he found his horse and informed Gen. [David M.] Gregg of the state of affairs and the firing was stopped. Sergeant Farnsworth was highly complimented by Avery for his bravery and soon afterward was promoted to a lieutenancy."[45] Gregg recalled, "A message was brought to me on another part of the field from the Brigade Commander to the effect that the shells from our Battery were falling on his line and behind it, the Battery Commander not being aware

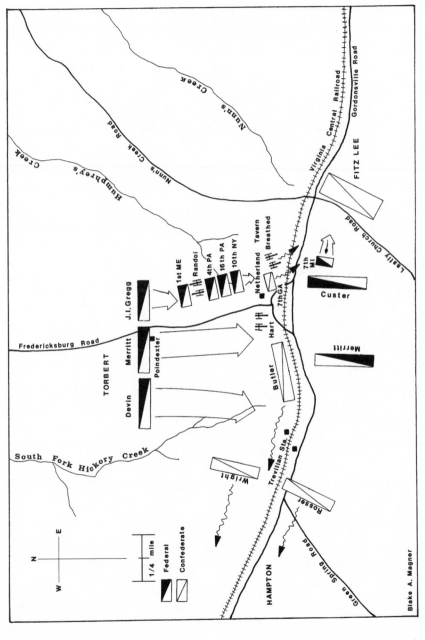

Tobert Captures Trevilian Station, Late Afternoon, June 11, 1864

Blake A. Magner

of this, because of an intervening woods. The fire of the Battery was ordered to cease." Gregg endorsed a Medal of Honor for Farnsworth.[46] In March 1898, Farnsworth was issued a Medal.[47]

The Sixteenth Pennsylvania Cavalry also charged. Lt. Samuel Cormany, in his first full day as a commissioned officer, recorded in his diary, "The whole line charges with splendid results—Capturing 750 prisoners—Our regiment lost 4 killed and 10 wounded—the Brigade's loss was very small comparatively." He continued, "We had a very responsible position, and on our wild and dashing, mounted charge upon the enemy's right, getting almost in rear of their artillery—we caused them to concentrate on the center—and put up a hot resistance—which gave our dismounted line a rather confused and demoralized mass to charge into." The mounted Pennsylvanians, providing larger targets than their dismounted comrades, naturally drew the attention of the Confederate riflemen. Cormany's mare "Gayety Gray" made an especially attractive target, "which was somewhat annoying to my sensitive ears."[48]

Capt. Isaac Ressler of Company L of the Sixteenth Pennsylvania struck a similar note in his diary that night, writing, "Fighting early in A.M. and all day at . . . Trevilian Station. 1st Div. on right cut the Rebs line in two. Our Brig. on left charged up to houses and tavern across top station. Charged two miles. *Dreadful times.* . . . 16th charged ahead of our two lines and took advance." Ressler noted that his company suffered one man killed and another five enlisted men and one officer wounded in the day's fighting.[49] Another Pennsylvanian wrote that Gregg's brigade "had a splendid fight with Fitz Hugh Lee's cavalry. They had a good position and we had to charge them out, and our loss was considerable."[50] The triumphant troopers of Col. Pennock Huey's Eighth Pennsylvania captured the Netherland Tavern.[51]

R. H. Ferguson, a bandsman of Davies's brigade, was severely wounded during the fighting and had his horse shot out from under him. When the animal fell, it pinned Ferguson's leg, and he was captured. The injured man was carried to a nearby house, where he hid his cornet under his uniform blouse. When the enemy troopers left him there, he asked Richard Bibb, the owner of the house, to guard the horn for him. The Confederates soon learned that the instrument was there and sent a detachment to seize it. Instead, Ferguson gave the horn to Bibb, who offered to sell it in Richmond instead of having it captured. Bibb sold the horn.[52]

The Fourth Pennsylvania Cavalry, another of Irvin Gregg's regiments, also joined the grand assault. Capt. William Hyndman of Company A recalled that the Confederates tried to make a stand along the railroad bed. He wrote, "Our brigade here made a gallant dismounted charge, driving the rebels in confusion from that position, and completely routing them. We took possession of the railroad and station, destroying several miles of track." His company took several casualties from Chew's guns. Hyndman saw the devastating effect of artillery shells on horses: "I witnessed here the striking of two of our horses by a solid shot, which tore out the intestines of these poor animals, and scattered their contents among the troops. It was a horrible spectacle."[53]

After withdrawing from the Fredericksburg Road, the men of the Seventh Georgia fought on near the Netherland Tavern. Maj. Ned Anderson went looking for the commander of the Seventh Georgia, Lt. Col. Joseph McAllister, a forty-three-year-old lawyer who had attended Amherst College. Although he had little military training, McAllister had natural ability to command men; his grandfather, Col. Richard McAllister, commanded a regiment of Pennsylvania infantry in George Washington's Continental Army.[54] Joseph McAllister, a wealthy and well-respected rice planter, was "an upright, useful citizen, charitable to the poor and kind to all, a sagacious and dashing soldier, and a true patriot."[55] He led troops in combat for the first time at Trevilian Station. Anderson found McAllister around noon, recalling that "both were well, in good spirits, but very tired—they parted in about fifteen minutes not meeting again."[56] Anderson led a small detachment of Georgia men and left McAllister to his devices.

McAllister directed the final counterattack of the Georgians along the Fredericksburg Road, just north of the tavern. Pitching into the fray, "shot and shell, cannister and grape, mingled with the booming of artillery, made war's grand chorus jeeringly sublime. But on, on, through the missiles of death, he bore himself as though he courted death in defense of his country's liberties." The Georgians retreated into the railroad cut at the East Crossing, and many of them were captured by Gregg's onslaught. Yankee troopers completely surrounded McAllister. He cried out to his men, "Strike for God and our native land!" A Yankee bullet struck him in the arm, and he reeled in his saddle. Despite the pain, he emptied his revolver at the attacking Northerners, who demanded his surrender. The defiant McAllister threw the empty pistol at his attackers. A Yankee bullet in his chest and another to his throat killed him instantly, "without his uttering one word."[57] The Federals took McAllister's boots and hat and cut his stars and the buttons on his coat from his uniform. Fortunately, the Georgian's loyal manservant Jack recovered his horses, sabre, spurs, and other personal effects, which were returned to his family in Georgia. McAllister's body lay on the battlefield for nearly two days.[58]

Maj. Ned Anderson, McAllister's second in command, received a wound to the hip while leading a charge of his small detachment and was captured. Anderson hid his pocket watch and feigned that he could not walk as a result of the wounded hip. Later that day, he escaped. Anderson made his way back to the regiment the next day. The Seventh Georgia lost three company commanders early in the day on June 11. Capts. John P. Hines, A. R. Millar, and William D. Russell were killed.[59] Capt. Frank W. Hopkins, commander of Company G, was captured. Hopkins spent ten months at Fort Delaware and then joined the "Immortal 600," a group of Confederate officers placed on a list for retaliation. These men, housed on Federal gunboats known as "torture ships," were exposed to the friendly fire of Confederate guns at Charleston, South Carolina. Hopkins survived his stint on the torture ships and eventually was freed from prison at Fort Pulaski at the end of the war.[60]

The Federals captured twenty-five-year-old second sergeant Adam J. Iler of the Seventh Georgia that morning. A farmer from rural Georgia, Iler joined McAllister's company, the Hardwick Mounted Rifles, a local militia unit that became Company H of the Seventh Georgia. Iler, who later served for two years in the postwar Georgia legislature, fell into the hands of Torbert's troopers during the fighting on the Fredericksburg Road. Iler's war ended that day. He spent the duration as a prisoner of war in the infamous Northern prisoner of war camp at Elmira, New York.[61]

Pvt. John McClatchey served in Company I of the Seventh Georgia. A close friend stated "a better, more noble generous hearted man" than the popular McClatchey never "lived, a truer soldier never breathed a breath of life." As the action commenced, McClatchey stooped to pick up his cartridge box. A Spencer ball tore into the upper part of his collarbone, shattering it. The bullet then passed out below his shoulder blade, leaving an ugly exit wound. The horribly wounded young man fell and was left behind when the Seventh Georgia pulled out. He lay on the battlefield for the rest of the day as fighting raged around him. Finally, one of the local residents carried him to safety. After the battle, McClatchey lingered for a month in the large Confederate hospital at Gordonsville, before he finally died. His first battle was also his last.[62]

The green men of the Seventh Georgia fought long and hard that day, earning the respect of the veterans of both sides. Hampton rode by their position and praised McAllister's men for their lonely but tenacious fight. "For four hours we fought alone, against fearful odds," claimed a proud Georgian, "and I regret to state that the 7th suffered in killed, wounded and prisoners. . . . You may judge how desperately we fought by our thin and decimated ranks. We carried six hundred men into the fight and brought out three hundred only."[63] "Every field officer of the regiment was killed or wounded, and many of the men," reported Major Anderson, "Our troops were badly handled by [Col. Wright]."[64]

The men of the First Maine Cavalry were still supporting Randol's guns as the general assault swung forward. The Maine men grew a bit careless. They lolled on the ground in front of their horses, writing letters and relaxing. Suddenly, though, they came under fire from Chew's guns, which had the range of the position held by Randol's guns. The first shot was a shrapnel shell that landed amidst Randol's gunners, wounded an officer, disabled horses, and scattered pieces of shell and iron balls into the position held by the men of the First Maine. Others caused the dismounted troopers to scatter as Randol returned the fire. Sgt. Nathan Webb of the First Maine remembered, "our Battery . . . furiously shelled the line of the railroad." The dismounted Webb spotted a "staunch hardwood board fence . . . in our front and I lay flat in the twinkling of a cat's tail."[65]

Col. Charles H. Smith coolly rode his lines, calling out, "At-TEN-tion! Fours LEFT! FORWARD!" The Maine men obeyed the order and moved out of range while the brief artillery duel raged. When it ended, Smith again rode his lines, asking each company commander how many men from his company had been hurt. To Smith's great surprise, only a handful of men were hurt, and only five horses killed, prompting him to say, "I cannot understand it; I cannot understand it. I cannot understand how they could throw so much of that stuff in amongst us and not hurt more of us."[66]

Pvt. Thomas A. Trask of Company B suffered a serious arm wound. When Trask was taken to a field hospital, the surgeons decided to amputate, but Trask refused to allow them to do so. He ran out of the field hospital and returned to his company until he could find a real medical facility. After six weeks, Trask returned to the regiment, his arm fully healed.[67]

The First New Jersey Cavalry of Davies's brigade did not participate in the general assault. Instead, it scouted and picketed a road leading off to the right that may have been the Nunns Creek Road, the same route taken by Custer. Col. John W. Kester, the regiment's commanding officer, advanced his main body around Hampton's left flank toward Louisa as far as he judged advisable. Kester ordered Maj. Hugh Janeway and the regiment's third battalion to examine the country in front. Janeway and his small force rode off through the woods, which at length curved to the left and intersected with the railroad. There, a few Southern pickets, shocked by the sudden appearance of the Jerseymen, scattered in all directions. Spotting the main body of the Rebel cavalry along the line of the railroad, Janeway ordered his men to attack. He deployed one squadron as skirmishers, who quickly ran into the pickets of Wright's brigade, one of Butler's regiments, and some of Chew's guns. Janeway ordered the Jerseymen to charge.

The Union troopers struck Wright's men, who broke and fled. The regimental historian of the First New Jersey recalled that Chew's guns "were well served, though not well aimed, firing rapidly and steadily, but without doing any damage; and the Carolinians, unable to run away, covering themselves by some houses and fences, opened with small arms upon our line. Had there been no obstructions, or had there been another battalion to follow up the charge, the guns and the dismounted men would have been taken." There was no support for the charge, and Maj. Janeway called it off, content to rout the enemy's resistance along the railroad. The Jerseymen suffered only one man killed and a handful of men wounded. The regimental historian noted, "With only these casualties, this force of a hundred men had engaged two regiments and a section of artillery, and had so surprised the rebels in our front that Custer got through with no more fighting, and the whole rebel line withdrew from their positions."[68]

Things grew desperate for those Confederates still holding the area near the station. A Rebel ball grazed Colonel Gregg's cheek and lodged in his whiskers. The men of the Eighth Pennsylvania Cavalry overlapped the Confederate right flank, exposing the end of the Southern line. Unless they were relieved, the dogged Confederates would not be able to hold on much longer.[69]

Torbert ordered Custer to advance with his brigade. The Wolverines held a position only a couple of hundred yards west of Fitz Lee's lines. The moment the Michigan men stepped forward, they came under a heavy fire and fell back. Torbert again ordered the advance. He sent a third order, this time carried by the intrepid Captain Bean. Bean hastened to find the Boy General. He spotted Custer, alone and mounted just behind the line of battle, sitting under the drooping branches of a chestnut tree that shielded him from the eyes of the enemy. After hearing the order, Custer told Bean, "Give my compliments to General Torbert and tell him if he wants my whole line advanced he must do it, for I will not." Bean noted, "From this point of observation it was clear that General Custer was right in his judgment and to advance that portion of the line would have resulted in the fruitless sacrifice of life." Bean rode back to Torbert and reported Custer's message. The division commander agreed that Custer's position on the right should be maintained while the rest of the First Division bore the burden of the primary attack.[70]

Around this time, Custer saw an opportunity to redeem his performance. Spotting Lee's withdrawal, Custer led a charge of the Seventh Michigan Cavalry in an attempt to recapture the wagons. "We came upon the rear of them, and recaptured two caissons, three ambulances, and several wagons. The enemy's force being so much greater than mine, I did not deem it advisable to follow them. I then ordered this regiment back to its position on the line," reported Custer.[71] The charge covered more than a mile without success, and "seeing little chance for it returned to the command." The men of the Seventh Michigan spent the rest of the day picketing.[72] Custer's long day of fighting ended after he recovered some of the losses sustained that morning.

Although Custer did not know it, the two caissons recovered in the charge of the Seventh Michigan were empty. As Capt. John J. Shoemaker, commander of one of Breathed's batteries, said, with tongue planted firmly in cheek, "During the first day's battle our cavalry captured four of the enemy's caissons filled with the most perfect ammunition, and we calmly appropriated what we wanted of it, as ours was anything but good. We were very glad to get it, and the next day returned some of it to them properly warmed up to suit the occasion."[73] Shoemaker also bragged that his battery "fairly whipped" the Federals "from every position they took. We were exposed during the whole time to the fire of dismounted men, but fortunately I had only one man wounded . . . in the body."[74]

Pvt. Samuel B. Rucker of Company F, Sixth Virginia Cavalry, of Lomax's brigade, was captured. Along with his lieutenant, George Vetch, and most of his company, Rucker sat dismounted near an old frame house situated alongside the railroad. Hastily building a temporary breastwork of railroad ties, the Virginians occupied some nearby cabins, knocking out slats to create firing portals. Several of the men sat eating cherries in an old orchard when a sudden enemy charge struck them. Rucker was sitting on one side of the house's chimney, his gun between his legs. "The first thing I knew minnie balls were knocking dust all over. I saw one of the Yankees come out of the orchard and shoot his gun, which made such a puff of smoke that I could not see him, so I fired at the center of the smoke. I do not know whether I hit him or not; but before I got my gun loaded the Yankees had me. . . . They just swarmed around us." Rucker quickly lost his new hat to an "old Dutchman," who left Rucker with his battered old hat. The prisoners were soon marched off. Rucker heard the laughter of the men of his company when they spotted his "new" headgear. He hastily scribbled a letter to his mother, letting her know that he had been captured, but not hurt. Along with twenty-five other men of his regiment, Rucker marched off toward the Union prison camp at Point Lookout, Maryland, where he spent the rest of the war.[75]

Lt. D. E. Gordon of Company I, Fourth South Carolina Cavalry, captured during Sheridan's general assault, reported to his wife that he was unhurt. He told her that eight other men of his company had also been captured, that they were unhurt, and that his wife should notify their families of the men's plight. He concluded by writing, "You must not give yourself any uneasiness for I hope to get on well & will write by every opportunity. I am well—May God bless you and the children." The lieutenant asked a Federal sergeant if he would leave the letter somewhere where it would fall into Confederate hands. The sergeant did so, and the letter reached Gordon's wife a few days later. Gordon marched off to captivity.[76]

Charles Calhoun of the Sixth South Carolina complained bitterly, "It seems that Fitzhugh [Lee] by some means, did not occupy the position Hampton had assigned him and was not in the fight at all." Blaming Lee's failure to move promptly to the sound of the guns for the Confederate failure that day, Calhoun wrote, "Not receiving any support from General Lee we were compelled to fall back and reform another line. It was getting late and everything looked gloomy indeed."[77]

Lt. Wiley Howard of Cobb's Legion had escaped from his pinch that morning and turned the tables, capturing a fine mount from a Union officer. After pausing for a moment to dress his bleeding hand, he rode toward the sound of firing, hoping to find his own lost horse and saddle bags, which contained new clothing from home. Along with a couple of other refugees, Howard found his way back into friendly lines. Hampton stopped Howard and asked the surprised lieutenant about his morning experiences. After hearing Howard's tale, Hampton asked the young Georgian to remain with him, as all of his couriers were off delivering orders to various parts of the battlefield. Howard accompanied the general to the front and held Hampton's horse while the general issued orders. Finally, Hampton turned to Howard and asked him to deliver a message to Rosser, who was still heavily engaged along the Gordonsville Road to the west of the station, which was in imminent danger of being taken by the Yankees. Howard swung into the saddle of his captured mount, and rode off to find Rosser. After a time, Howard "came upon the brigade hotly engaged dismounted. It was powerful uncomfortable where I found Rosser, but I was bound to go to him unless bullets stopped me."

Howard found the Texan, and delivered his message. Rosser responded, "Give the general my compliments and tell him we are giving 'em hell." Howard hastily rode off to find Hampton, who had moved forward again. When Howard found the general, he saluted and reported Rosser's message. Hampton "snapped his eyes, smiled, and said to his staff, 'General Rosser is a magnificent fighter and has done much to turn the tide in our favor today.' "[78]

Rosser was indeed giving the Union troopers hell, but his force was also being slowly encircled. His Laurels watched the spirited artillery duel, prompting Capt. James Thomson to exclaim, "Oh! But don't that sound wicked!"[79] Rosser still believed that a determined attack would drive Custer from the train station that would allow the Laurels to link up with the rest of Hampton's beleaguered division. Riding out to reconnoiter with Chew and his staff, Rosser drew heavy fire. Chew's handsome mare was badly wounded, but continued on, her front covered with blood. Around 4:00, the mounted Rosser led his dismounted brigade in a determined attack against the natural breastwork of the railroad bed. While leading the assault, a carbine ball struck Rosser just below his knee, breaking both bones. Reeling in the saddle, the wounded general made his way to safety.[80]

Sgt. Charles McVicar, of Thomson's battery, watched Rosser sway. Several of the artillerists ran forward and helped the wounded general off his horse, laying him down on the grass. A quick examination showed that Rosser had been hit in the leg and that his boot was quickly filling with blood. The alarmed gunners quickly applied a tourniquet, but Rosser was still trying to direct the fighting. McVicar overheard him say, "that he could whip Sheridan with his gallant brigade, that God never placed better men on earth."[81]

Rosser's personal surgeon, Dr. Burton, tended to his wounded general and removed the Texan to safety. As the doctor ministered to him, Rosser called for his senior regimental commander, Col. Richard H. Dulany of the Seventh Virginia Cavalry. When Dulany rode up, Rosser, who detested fighting dismounted in heavy woods, directed, "Col. fight with the men mounted. Let the other cavalry fight as infantry!" The injured brigadier remained within earshot of the heavy fighting still raging near Trevilian Station.[82] When he penned his after-action report, Hampton lamented, "In the list of wounded [was] Brigadier-General Rosser, who received a painful wound . . . while charging the enemy at the head of his brigade."[83]

As Rosser was carried from the field, McVicar and another of the artillerists sat on top of a split rail fence, watching the action unfold. Their stay did not last long, as a Northern artillery shell cut the fence stakes between the two men. The two gunners fell on either side of the fence, "both shaken and stunned but not hurt." Quickly gaining his composure, McVicar spotted a beautiful horse running between the lines. He recalled, "Like all lovers of fine horses, temptation was too much. Mounted and after it, just as he leaped the fence about one length ahead, a shell passed through him. I got down and took saddle, martingale, breast strap, crupper and a fine leather saddle valise, swung them on my mare." Although a mere 100 yards away, the enemy did not open on McVicar while he tended to the poor beast, but when he started back with his prizes, "My, didn't they send a hornets nest of bullets after me. Can hear them zipping by yet."[84]

Colonel Dulany ordered the Laurels to fall back. Capt. George Baylor of the Twelfth Virginia recalled, "we were ordered back, much to our gratification, as the work ahead appeared to me a task of no easy accomplishment."[85] General Butler sent his brother, Capt. "Pick" Butler, to ask if Hampton could spare a piece of artillery, as Butler still believed he could destroy Custer's brigade. However, Butler received orders to fall back in the face of Torbert's determined attack.[86] Edward L. Wells of the Sixth South Carolina later wrote, "The situation was very grave; indeed, in view of the original disparity of numbers and the present position of his command, it might well have been that Hampton should have utterly despaired of success, and only hoped at best to save a part of his troops by a hasty retreat."[87] Hampton continued resisting, riding the lines and exerting a steadying influence over his shaken troopers. Gradually his Confederates, flanked and outnumbered, fell back several miles to a position along the Gordonsville Road, still blocking Sheridan's route to the important rail junction at Gordonsville. Lee's division retreated toward Louisa, and "Night ended the conflict and found the relative positions of both sides about the same."[88]

About 6 P.M., Torbert made a final attempt to dislodge Hampton's dogged Confederates. Devin sent the Fourth New York and First New York Dragoons forward to feel out the strength of the Confederate position. Devin led the Fourth New York and personally reconnoitered the ground. He discovered that the Confederates had withdrawn beyond the fork of the Gordonsville and Charlottesville roads and called off the pursuit. A squadron of the Fourth New York made "several splendid charges" that brought in eighty-five prisoners, thirty-two horses, and possession of the train station "before any other regts were even in sight of it," announced Col. Luigi Palma Di Cessnola, the commanding officer of the Fourth New York.[89] Torbert instructed Devin to hold the critical road junction, prompting the Old Warhorse to send the Sixth New York Cavalry to the crossroads. The colonel then withdrew his remaining regiments to the station, where he connected with Custer and Merritt. The troopers of the Fourth and Ninth New York spent the balance of the afternoon tearing up the tracks of the Virginia Central near Trevilian Station. As dusk fell, Col. Di Cessnola found two squadrons of the Fourth New York sprawled about the yard of the train station, "reading a large captured mail, in drinking two large barrels of Sherry wine captured there and looking at a large number of rebel Richmond papers of the previous day." In spite of the day's triumphs, gained at the cost of seven men killed and wounded, including one of his company commanders, who had to have both legs amputated, the colonel was unhappy. He claimed that his men had captured the train station, "yet Genl. Torbert in his report suppressed everything concerning it, He or some body else attributed to him and to Genl Custer's men the honor of capturing Trevilian's Station, when the fact is they were thousands of yards from the Station when my regiment captured and held it."[90]

Soon afterward, the Seventeenth Pennsylvania, which had been sent nearly twenty miles away to locate wounded Union soldiers left behind after the brutal fighting at the Wilderness, returned after a grueling day's march. The Pennsylvanians captured and paroled sixty-four Confederate prisoners that day, and brought in another thirty-six men as they made their way back to the regiment.[91]

Sheridan's men expected a counterattack, and "every preparation was made to receive them, but in this we were agreeably disappointed. Some lively skirmishing closed the day's operations."[92] Lieutenant Carpenter of the Sixth U.S. noted, "We captured 400 prisoners, killed rebel colonels, wounded Brigadier General Rosser and killed and wounded a good number of inferior officers and men. About 30 of their officers were among our prisoners. The result of this engagement was that we gained possession of the railroad at Trevilian Station."[93] Torbert reported, "On account of the exhausted condition of the men, it was not deemed expedient to advance farther that day, and I made dispositions to hold the railroad."[94] The firing petered out, the long day's combat finally over, with Sheridan's tired horse soldiers in control of the battlefield.

Sheridan's troopers held a position between Lee's division to the east, and Hampton's to the west. The Reserve Brigade occupied a position to the left of the point of the angle, and Devin's brigade held a spot to the west of the station, with Gregg's division held in reserve north of the station.[95] That night, more soldiers occupied a two-mile square area around Trevilian Station than the entire population of Louisa County. The opposing lines were less than half a mile apart.[96] The last shots sputtered out as night gathered around the exhausted horse soldiers.[97]

As dusk fell, Torbert and his entire division staff stood along the railroad tracks about 100 yards west of the train station, surveying the day's battlefield. The victorious Northerners had just realized that there would be no further counterattacks. Although they were exhausted, the Federals basked in the day's successes. Just then, a final Confederate artillery shell burst in the midst of the group, prompting Captain Bean to note, "If it had dropped from the clouds as thunderbolts do it could not have been more amazing."

One of Torbert's staff officers, Capt. John J. Coppinger, a thirty-year-old Irish immigrant described as a "model soldier," dropped to the ground. Before the smoke cleared, Coppinger was on his feet, explaining in his soft Irish brogue, "that he saw the cussed thing coming and concluded to dodge it, you know." Fortunately, none of the Northern officers were injured by the shell, and many of them gathered up pieces of it for souvenirs.[98]

That night Sheridan assessed his situation. Hampton's bold decision to stand and fight had stymied Sheridan's march. From talking to some of the prisoners, Sheridan learned that Hunter's command, instead of advancing on Charlottesville, had turned instead toward Lynchburg on the south side of the James River. Sheridan further learned that Breckinridge's infantry command was somewhere near Waynesboro, effectively blocking Sheridan from reaching his objective. Although Hampton had been forced to retreat, his veterans were still full of pluck and ready to resume the fight. Well after the fact, Little Phil also claimed that his men had expended so much ammunition that day that they had an insufficient supply to continue the expedition. Sheridan decided to retire.[99]

Sheridan issued orders for the wounded of both sides be collected and put in hospitals and instructed that arrangements be made for their transportation in ammunition wagons and other vehicles gathered from the surrounding countryside. He also had more than 500 new prisoners of war to attend to and was worried about his ability to guard them and tend to their needs.[100] The accuracy of Sheridan's accounts may be questioned, which may have been written with the benefit of clear hindsight. The next day's actions suggest that Sheridan might have penned these words later to justify his conduct during the raid and the battle at Trevilian Station.

In fact, both sides had suffered that day. Of the approximately 9,300 Union troopers engaged on June 11, Sheridan's command suffered 699 casualties, including 53 killed, 274 wounded, and 372 captured, of whom nearly half of the captured came from Alger's Fifth Michigan. Its heavy losses rendered Custer's brigade hors de combat. Sheridan's casualties amounted to nearly eight percent of his total force, heavy losses for cavalry, including two of his regimental commanders, Rodenbough and Sackett. Capt. Craig Wadsworth of Torbert's staff had two horses shot out from under him. Dr. Wilson, the Reserve Brigade's chief surgeon, also had his horse killed. A Southern ball tore the coat sleeve of Lt. Eugene Bertrand, Merritt's adjutant general, but the lieutenant was uninjured.[101] The Confederates likewise suffered, sustaining approximately 530 casualties out of 6,512 men engaged; the Southern officer corps in particular suffered, losing three regimental colonels in the day's engagement.[102] The fighting on the first day "was mostly at close quarters, and the wounds in consequence were generally severe."[103]

Sheridan's horse soldiers won a tactical victory on June 11. They drove Hampton's troopers from the station and held the day's battlefield as the sun set that night. His men had fought long and hard, with Torbert's command doing the bulk of the day's work. Merritt's Regulars and Custer's Wolverines had borne the brunt of the combat and suffered the largest number of casualties. Torbert effectively managed his troopers, fighting them more as infantry than as cavalry, using the difficult terrain to his advantage. Gallant charges and hard fighting by Devin's men, especially the Ninth New York, helped Torbert carry the day. Although Custer's impetuosity nearly destroyed his brigade, Torbert nevertheless praised his subordinate: "Much credit is due to General Custer for saving his command under such trying circumstances." He continued, "This day General Merritt and Colonel Devin particularly distinguished themselves for bravery and coolness in action."[104] Likewise, Irvin Gregg's brigade, and especially the gallant troopers of the Tenth New York, tipped the balance with their bold and determined attack south of Netherland Tavern.

Only a portion of Gregg's division engaged. Only three of Davies's regiments participated in the fighting that day. The First Pennsylvania Cavalry, a solid, veteran unit, spent the day guarding wagon trains and did not fire a shot in anger. "It was our duty to picket the rear and protect our wagon train, a very delicate post to occupy, too, but fortunately were not molested during the day, the enemy having considerable more than he could attend to in the front," wrote Lt. Thomas Lucas of the First Pennsylvania.[105] Although Davies's regiments were not fully engaged, they made a difference, fighting hard during the afternoon's engagement.

Even the Confederates recognized that they had not carried the day. Lt. Alan Edens of the Fourth South Carolina Cavalry told his wife that his regiment "had a severe battle lasting all day without decision on either side."[106] Butler stated, "This day's operations ended disastrously for our arms."[107] "The operations of the day were evidently against the Confederates," complained Capt. Frank Myers of White's Comanches, "and the men

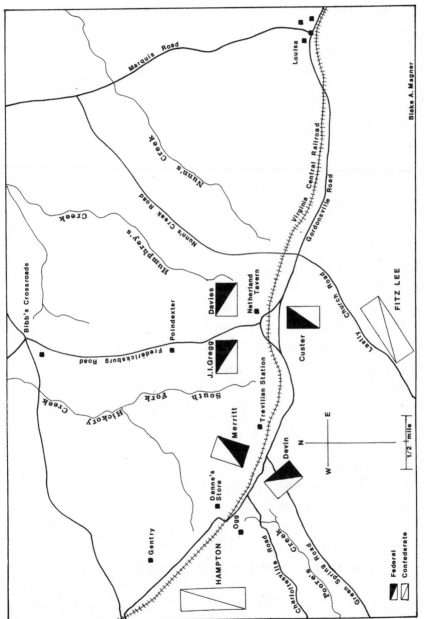

Positions of the Opposing Forces, Night, June 11, 1864

were blaming Hampton for allowing his men to be beaten in that way, by brigades, but he was working out his problem and baiting his trap for tomorrow."[108]

Merritt claimed, "The enemy's retreat finally became a rout, led horses, mounted men, and artillery all fled together in the wildest confusion," their retreat hastened by shells of Williston's battery lobbed into their midst for good measure.[109] The correspondent from the *New York Herald* crowed, "The grand charge . . . resulted in driving the enemy some two miles from the station, and ended the fighting for the day in one of the most brilliant victories ever achieved for the Union arms."[110] The pugnacious Hampton refused to acknowledge defeat at Sheridan's hands, writing simply, "My new line being established I directed General Lee to join me with his command as soon as possible. The enemy tried to dislodge me from my new position but failed, and the relative positions of the opposing forces remained the same during the night."[111]

Despite the tactical victory, Sheridan nevertheless failed to achieve his strategic objective of driving Hampton out of the way in order to make a junction with Hunter. Hampton's troopers, although tired and beaten, still sat firmly astride Little Phil's line of march to Mechanicsville.

Butler's men carried the burden of the fighting that day, and they performed magnificently. He proudly wrote, "I venture to believe that I am not claiming too much for the gallant troops under my immediate command when I say that they bore the brunt of the fight, and but for their stubborn and invincible courage must have been annihilated."[112] They got little help from Fitz Lee's division, which did not fulfill Hampton's plan for the day and failed to reach the field in a timely fashion. Lee never explained his reasons for not pushing Custer's position south of Clayton's Store early on the morning of June 11, or why his men took so long to join the fighting just three miles to the west of Louisa that day.

One of Butler's troopers wrote, "Fitzhugh Lee certainly failed to execute General Hampton's orders on the morning of the first day's fighting at Trevilian, thereby permitting Custer to pass between the two divisions . . . which Hampton was commanding, whereby the prearranged plan of battle was frustrated and a terrible disaster to our arms only averted by the brilliant generalship of Hampton, and the heroic fighting of his men."[113] Hampton's words are perhaps more telling: "Lee returned to Louisa C. H. just after

Rosser's charge, & he did not join me until 2 P.M. the next day!" Ever the politician, Hampton continued, "Of course, I shall not say anything about this matter unless forced to do so."[114]

Sheridan attempted to justify his actions by claiming that he broke off the engagement and withdrew after the fighting of June 11. However, his actions betrayed his words. Instead of withdrawing to the north and east, Sheridan camped on the ground surrounding Trevilian Station that night and made preparations to continue west the following morning. Sgt. George M. Neese of Thomson's battery was an especially prescient observer. That night, he wrote in his diary:

> I am no prophet, nor the son of a prophet, but if General Sheridan fights tomorrow on the same plan that he did today, by tomorrow evening he will be a defeated general. I do not know what forces or strength the enemy has,—it may be far superior to ours in numbers,—but if General Sheridan attacks tomorrow without some extensive flanking General Hampton will repulse and defeat him in bulk. The probability is that there will not be much flanking done by the enemy, as this makes twice that we have been on the flank-watching business today, and we have found no game yet, and, judging from today's operations, we may expect nothing but sledge-hammer blows from the front tomorrow, as flanking in an actual battle does not seem to belong to General Sheridan's tactics.[115]

It would be a long night for the soldiers on both sides, especially those wounded in the day's fighting. There would also be more fighting and Neese would make a major contribution to long-forgotten history.

Notes

1. Hall, *History of the Sixth New York Cavalry*, 198.
2. *New York Herald*, June 21, 1864.
3. Wallace, *A Few Memories of a Long Life*, 37.
4. Bean, "Sheridan at Trevilian."
5. Kelly, "How Custer Saved the Flag," *National Tribune*, August 12, 1886.
6. Amasa G. Dana to Theodore H. Bean, February 28, 1886, quoted in Bean, "Sheridan at Trevilian." Throughout his letter, Dana repeatedly and mistakenly refers to Pennington's battery as Alanson Randol's and also confuses Randol for Pennington. The author has taken the liberty of correcting this error.
7. Dana to Bean; *New York Herald*, June 21, 1864.
8. Kelly, "How Custer Saved the Flag."

9. Kelly to Kelly, May 26, 1876; Kelly, "How Custer Saved the Flag."

10. N. D. Preston, "Trevilian Station: The Most Stubborn Cavalry Fight of the War," *The National Tribune*, January 5, 1888.

11. Hagemann, *Fighting Rebels and Redskins*, 242–43.

12. *Ibid.*, 243–44.

13. *Ibid.*, 244.

14. O.R., vol. 36, part 1, 851.

15. Sheridan, *Personal Memoirs*, 1:421.

16. Hall, *History of the Sixth New York Cavalry*, 197.

17. Bowen, *History of the First New York Dragoons*, 188.

18. Howard M. Smith diary, entry for June 11, 1864.

19. Carpenter to his father, June 22, 1864.

20. Brooks, *Butler and His Cavalry*, 245.

21. Mulligan, *"My Dear Mother and Sister,"* 183.

22. Holmes, "The Fighting Qualities." In fact, Humphrey received a mortal wound in August 1864 while leading a mounted charge into a battery of Federal artillery at Gravelly Run. Humphrey declined having an arm amputated, saying he preferred death to dismemberment, again prompting Butler to praise the young man's courage.

23. Brooks, *Butler and His Cavalry*, 195; Gary R. Baker, *Cadets In Gray: The Story of the Cadets of the South Carolina Military Academy and the Cadet Rangers in the Civil War* (Columbia, S.C.: Palmetto Bookworks, 1989), 100–01.

24. Brooks, *Butler and His Cavalry*, 548.

25. Isham, *Seventh Michigan Cavalry*, 57.

26. Brooks, *Butler and His Cavalry*, 548; Bauskett memoir, 21.

27. Calhoun, *Liberty Dethroned*, 125.

28. Mulligan, *"Dear Mother and Sisters,"* 184.

29. Brooks, *Butler and His Cavalry*, 246.

30. Halliburton, *Saddle Soldiers*, 146.

31. Brooks, *Butler and His Cavalry*, 246–47.

32. Butler, "Trevilian Station," 238.

33. H. C. Orme, "Who is the Lady," *Richmond Times-Dispatch*, August 1, 1915; Pat Jones, "Mother's Race across Battlefield is Recalled: Mrs. Lucy Hughson Carried Baby in Arms across Field at Trevilians in 1864 during Bitter Engagement," *Richmond Times-Dispatch Sunday Magazine Section*, date unknown, copy in files at Louisa County Historical Society, Louisa, Virginia.

34. Wells, *Hampton and His Cavalry*, 200–01.

35. Preston, "Trevilian Station: The Most Stubborn Cavalry Fight of the War," *National Tribune*, January 5, 1888.

36. C. W. Wiles, "On Horseback: Leaves from the Record of the 10th N.Y. Cavalry," *National Tribune*, November 4, 1886.

37. Preston, *History of the Tenth Regiment*, 199.

38. *Ibid.*, 198.

39. Wiles, "On Horseback."

40. Preston, *History of the Tenth Regiment*, 205.

41. Preston, "The Most Stubborn Cavalry Fight."

42. Preston, *History of the Tenth Regiment*, 200.

43. Noble D. Preston Medal of Honor File, RG 94, File No.4466VS1882, the National Archives, Washington, D.C.

44. Theodore H. Weed to Russell A. Alger, December 17, 1897, Herbert E. Farnsworth Medal of Honor File, RG 94, File No. RHP316795, the National Archives, Washington, D.C.

45. Llewellyn P. Norton to Russell A. Alger, December 4, 1897, Farnsworth Medal of Honor File.

46. David M. Gregg to Russell A. Alger, January 10, 1898, Farnsworth Medal of Honor File.

47. Russell A. Alger to Herbert E. Farnsworth, March 22, 1898, Farnsworth Medal of Honor File.

48. Mohr and Winslow, *The Cormany Diaries*, 434.

49. Ressler diary, entry for June 11, 1864.

50. William S. Keller to his sister, June 22, 1864, *Civil War Times Illustrated* Collection, United States Army Military History Institute, Carlisle, Pennsylvania.

51. O.R., vol. 36, part 1, 867.

52. R. H. Ferguson, "Seeks Lost Cornet," *Richmond Times-Dispatch*, August 23, 1914.

53. Hyndman, *History of a Cavalry Company*, 126.

54. *Savannah Morning News*, October 5, 1930.

55. *Savannah Republican*, June 20, 1864.

56. Swiggart, *Shades of Gray*, 73.

57. *Ibid.*

58. "From the Seventh Ga. Cavalry"; Burroughs to his mother, June 16, 1864; *Savannah Morning News*, October 5, 1930.

59. "From the Seventh Ga. Cavalry."

60. Obituary of Frank Hopkins, Thomasville, Georgia, January 25, 1892.

61. Muster rolls of the Seventh Georgia Cavalry, and prisoner of war rolls, Elmira, New York prison camp; Family records provided by Ernie Iler.

62. J. Bolan Glover to Mr. McClatchie, September 3, 1864; George W. Sites to Respected Madam, September 28, 1864; JRB to Friend Pam, August 6, 1864, McClatchie Family Papers, Atlanta History Center, Atlanta, Georgia.

63. "The Seventh Georgia Cavalry at the Battle of Trevilian's Station," *Savannah Republican*, June 27, 1864.

64. Swiggart, *Shades of Gray*, 74.

65. Webb diary, entry for June 11, 1864.

66. Tobie, *First Maine Cavalry*, 285–86.

67. *Ibid.*, 286.

68. Pyne, *Ride to War*, 220–21.

69. Carpenter to his father, June 22, 1864; *New York Herald*, June 21, 1864.

70. Bean, "Sheridan at Trevilian."

71. O.R., vol. 36, part 1, 824.

72. *Ibid.*, 832.

73. John J. Shoemaker, *Shoemaker's Battery: Stuart Horse Artillery, Pelham's Battalion, Army of Northern Virginia* (Memphis, Tenn.: S. C. Toof & Co., 1908), 74.

74. The wounded soldier was Pvt. Abner D. Ford. See John J. Shoemaker to Maj. Robert Breathed, September 1, 1864, included in William Johnson Black diary, Virginia Military Institute Archives, Lexington, Virginia.

75. Samuel Burns Rucker, Sr., "My War Record during the Confederacy," Jones Memorial Library, Lynchburg, Virginia, 5.

76. D. E. Gordon to his wife, June 12, 1864, Elinor S. Brockenbrough Library, Museum of the Confederacy, Richmond, Virginia.

77. Calhoun, *Liberty Dethroned*, 125–26.

78. Howard, *Sketch of Cobb Legion Cavalry*, 16.

79. Myers, *The Comanches*, 302.

80. Rosser, *Riding with Rosser*, 38.

81. McVicar diary, entry for June 11, 1864.

82. Rosser, *Riding with Rosser*, 38; Vogtsberger, *The Dulanys of Welbourne*, 219.

83. O.R., vol. 36, part 1, 1096.

84. McVicar diary, entry for June 11, 1864.

85. George Baylor, *Bull Run to Bull Run: Four Years in the Army of Northern Virginia Containing a Detailed Account of the Career and Adventures of the Baylor Light Horse, Company B, Twelfth Virginia Cavalry C.S.A.* (Washington, D.C.: Zenger, 1983), 224.

86. Brooks, *Butler and His Cavalry*, 245–46.

87. Wells, *Hampton and His Cavalry*, 200.

88. Fitzhugh Lee to Dear General, December 20, 1866.

89. Luigi Palma Di Cessnola to Judge W. Woods, July 7, 1864, Luigi Palma Di Cessnola letters, Jonathan Dayton Papers, Schoff Civil War Collection, William L. Clements Library, University of Michigan, Ann Arbor, Michigan.

90. Di Cessnola to Wood, July 7, 1864.

91. O.R., vol. 36, part 1, 841–42.

92. Bean, "Sheridan at Trevilian."

93. Carpenter to his father, June 22, 1864.

94. O.R., vol. 36, part 1, 808.

95. *Ibid.*, 850.

96. Meyers, "Trevilians!," 37. According to Meyers, the local population was 16,701 inclusive of soldiers and escaped or kidnapped slaves as opposed to 16,700 soldiers plus servants and camp followers. See note 32.

97. King, *To Horse*, 12.

98. Bean, "Sheridan at Trevilian." Coppinger received a brevet for valor at Trevilian Station, probably for his efforts to locate Custer. Coppinger led an interesting life. He had fought in the Papal War with Myles W. Keogh before immigrating to the United States and was decorated for valor in both the Papal and United States Armies. By the end of the war, he was a colonel commanding the Fifteenth New York Cavalry, and was wounded at the critical battle of Five Forks. Coppinger remained in the army for many years after the end of the Civil War and achieved the rank of brigadier general in the Regular Army and major general of volunteers in the Spanish-American War. He married the much younger daughter of prominent Maine senator James G. Blaine and is buried in Arlington National Cemetery. He was a fine, daring soldier. For more information, see John P. Langellier, Kurt Hamilton Cox and Brian C. Pohanka, eds., *Myles Keogh: The Life and Legend of an "Irish Dragoon" in the Seventh Cavalry* (El Segundo, Ca.: Upton and Sons, 1998), 64–5.

99. O.R., vol. 36, part 1, 796.

100. *Ibid.*, 797.

101. *New York Herald*, June 21, 1864.

102. See Appendices B, C, and D to this book. Aiken of the Sixth South Carolina, badly wounded, as well as McAllister of the Seventh Georgia and Carter of the Third Virginia, both mortally wounded.

103. *Charleston Daily Courier*, June 17, 1864.

104. O.R., vol. 36, part 1, 803.

105. Thomas Lucas to his wife, June 13, 1864, Thomas Lucas letters, Dona Sauerburger collection, Gambrills, Maryland.

106. Walbrook D. Swank, ed., *Confederate Letters and Diaries 1861–1865* (Mineral, Va.: privately published, 1988), 142.

107. Butler, "Cavalry Fight at Trevilian Station," 238.

108. Myers, *The Comanches*, 301.

109. O.R., vol. 36, part 1, 850.

110. *New York Herald*, June 21, 1864.

111. O.R., vol. 36, part 1, 1095.

112. Butler, "Cavalry Fight at Trevilian Station," 238.

113. Edward L. Wells to Frank Dorsey, January 8, 1904, Wells Correspondence.

114. Wade Hampton to Edward L. Wells, January 18, 1900, Wells Correspondence.

115. Neese, *Three Years*, 287. Neese accurately continued, "In these latter days it seems that Uncle Sam is depending on, and putting his trust in, the might of numbers to grind the armies and the rebellious Southland down by sheer attrition and brute force; consequently the powers that be at Washington select the commanders for their butting qualities instead of strategical capabilities."

6

A Long Night on the Battlefield and a Morning of Destruction along the Virginia Central Railroad

It was horrible, the dead and wounded, the groans of the suffering.

As night fell, Custer's exhausted Wolverines scattered in the fields near Trevilian Station. Many of them fell asleep within minutes, near the spot where they had struggled for six long, hard hours that day.[1] Others spent a long, unpleasant night standing to horse, waiting for the day's brutal combat to resume.[2] However, some of them ransacked Mrs. Hughson's house. The Federals liberated several barrels of flour from her attic and fed the contraband to the Yankee cavalry horses. They also appropriated her bedding and bedclothes for use in field hospitals.[3]

The burden of caring for the many wounded men fell on the shoulders of the local civilians. Pattie Ann Carter, a young woman from the area, recalled, "The Southern ladies from all around went down after the battle and carried food and water to the wounded friend and foe alike. I went myself to one mortally wounded Yankee soldier, lying on the ground. I went to give him water but the doctor said there was no chance."[4]

Martha Harper, another local, had several brothers serving in the Confederate army. Worried for their safety, she and her family spent the day barricaded in their home, the walls lined with feather beds intended to prevent bullets from entering their house. Yankee troopers filled her outside yard. She went to her neighbor's house, where she found several of the neighborhood ladies. The women moved closer to the action to determine who was winning the battle. As the firing sputtered out, they had a clear view of the day's carnage: "It was horrible, the dead and wounded, the groans of the suffering." Still terrified, the women retreated. Mrs. Harper and her family spent a seemingly interminable night, waiting and hoping "to get some news or to get word who was dead or wounded. We could not hear anything." As the night dragged on, Sheridan's hungry men plundered most of the family's livestock.[5]

Both prisoners and wounded men had a difficult night on June 11. Pvt. Samuel B. Rucker of the Sixth Virginia Cavalry had been captured during the morning's fighting. The Southern prisoners camped near Sheridan's headquarters. It rained very hard, and Rucker spent a long, cold, wet, miserable night trying to steal a few moments of sleep in a soggy corn furrow. Rucker considered himself fortunate that he did not catch his death of cold from that hideous time in Northern hands.[6]

Typhoid fever continued to hinder William Ball of the Eleventh Virginia Cavalry. His horse was mortally wounded in the fighting near the train station that morning. Too ill to remain in the ranks, Ball, dazed and almost delirious with fever, set out on foot alone for Gordonsville and the large Confederate hospital there. Somehow, he made it there early the next morning and encountered his uncle. The uncle quickly realized that his nephew was ill and took him home to rest and recuperate. Ball's expedition was over, cut short by the fever that had plagued him for days.[7]

The third squadron of the Seventh Virginia Cavalry spent the night on picket. Pvt. James F. Wood manned one of the vidette posts. Union scouts found Wood's picket post and tried to capture him. Wood shot both men and escaped capture. Near dawn, word arrived that the Federals were active, and the third squadron came in from picket duty and rejoined the rest of the Seventh Virginia on the Charlottesville Road. Poor Wood had had a rough night, and the call for his squadron to mount up came at a bad time— he had just started cooking his breakfast, and the hasty orders meant another day without food.[8]

Sgt. W. H. Dowling of the Fifth South Carolina recalled that the area was desolate because the local citizens had fled. Dowling and his friends tried to sleep that night, but the lack of rations left their stomachs growling painfully. They slept fitfully, disturbed by "phantomed scenes of ghastly dead and groans of wounded, and reverberations and echoes of eleven hours of bursting shells and zipping bullets." He recalled, "the morning of the 12th was Sabbath, beautiful and bright. There was no breakfast nor dinner for us and not a thing for our horses. As our custom was, we held our divine services and as we thought of congregations far away . . . and saw many around us slain the day before, 'sleeping the sleep that knows no waking.' "[9]

Pvt. Noble Brooks of the Sixth South Carolina recalled that the fighting of June 11 was "not very satisfactory I imagine on either side." His regiment pulled back to Green Spring, about three miles from Trevilian Station, and bivouacked in a pleasant spot. "There we fortunately found an abundance of water for man and beast. We slept on our arms," recalled Brooks.[10] Despite the rain, the exhausted South Carolinians slept soundly. Another member of the Sixth South Carolina recalled, "Sunday morning opened quiet and apparently peaceful, but the boys knew what to expect and were preparing all through the night in making improvised entrenchments for the coming conflict."[11]

Capt. James M. Loeser of the Second U.S. Cavalry had a similarly miserable night. After being marched to a field filled with other Union prisoners, Loeser searched the crowd for a familiar face, but failed to spot one. He waited patiently for rations to be distributed, but they never were. The hungry and dispirited Loeser had not eaten anything since four o'clock that morning. His misery was compounded "in the shape of an exceedingly severe rain-storm, which, as [I] had no overcoat, set [me] to wondering why General Butler had not sent the other poncho. Finally, having given up both the poncho and the supper, [I] sought out a comfortable furrow, and being very wet and very hungry, and having no further business on hand, went to bed."

As the first tendrils of daylight crept across the morning sky early on June 12, Loeser stirred and took stock of his companions. There were only a few: an unidentified lieutenant colonel of cavalry, a chaplain, several company officers, and a sprinkling of men from various regiments who had shared Loeser's same terrible accommodations. The lieutenant colonel, stirring in the morning light, said, "I am sorry for my regiment." The chaplain responded, "I am in favor of squatter sovereignty; but this is running the thing into the ground." Loeser recalled that "this assertion was received with general and continued applause, and we put in on record here, not so much on account of its intrinsic merits—which would not, perhaps, make it immortal—as to note the sort of wit which makes up the stock in trade of the gentlemen who give themselves up to it in prison; and we deliberately assert that, barring the physical inconvenience of hunger, the greatest suffering to which one is subjected under such circumstances is the inability to escape from these drivelling witticisms."[12]

One battalion of the First Maine Cavalry picketed the road to Louisa Court House, and the rest of the regiment bivouacked on the field with Randol's guns near Netherland Tavern. The pickets spent a long night along the lines, but those assigned to support the battery would have had a comfortable night's sleep but for the rain. Luckily, they drew rations.[13] Two men at a time went back and ate their supper. Sgt. Nathan Webb's turn finally came about 1:00 that morning, and he ate a hearty meal. He noted in his diary, "All the time it was raining like great guns and we sat on the ground under a 'shelter' eating as if our lives depended upon disposing of the food before us in so long a time."

Webb and his companions returned to their post near the guns, and they found as comfortable positions as possible against the rough breastworks thrown up to protect the guns. They pulled their caps down over their faces to get some protection from the rains while they tried to steal a few minutes' sleep. About three o'clock in the morning, two shots rang out, and the troopers awoke instantly, making sure their cartridges were dry. Fortunately, nothing came of it, and the men settled back in for the night. Webb noted, "I got sound asleep and did not awake till broad daylight."[14]

As the morning sky brightened, an exhausted Custer searched for a good spot to establish his headquarters. The reconnaissance by the men of the First Maine Cavalry had determined that there were no Confederates in the vicinity of the train station. Charles Goodall Trevilian, who owned a handsome plantation house located near the station that bore his name, had a young daughter who was very ill with typhoid fever. The anxious Mr. Trevilian went to Custer and asked him to keep it as quiet as possible. Custer replied, "I can only do so by making the house my headquarters on the front porch." Trevilian later recalled that the Boy General treated his family very considerately. Custer instructed his surgeon to leave medicines for the sick child when he departed later that day.[15]

Lt. John Bauskett of the Sixth South Carolina Cavalry led his men to a position along the Charlottesville Road, north of where it intersected with the Gordonsville Road. A wooden fence lined the road there. Bauskett dismounted his men, sent their horses to the rear, and manned the fence. Late on Saturday, after exchanging shots with some of Devin's men, the South Carolinians settled in. Soon, General Hampton rode by, inspecting his line. The Palmetto men cheered their commander, who told them to pull down the fence and pile the rails together for breastworks. Bauskett and his men obeyed the order, using their crude breastwork for shelter. Bauskett and two other men spent the night huddled together for warmth as the rain and cool breezes from the mountains chilled them to the bone.[16]

The wounded suffered from their peculiar horrors that night. James Bowen, regimental chaplain of the First New York Dragoons, spent the night ministering to the wounded. Watching the surgeons working on mangled bodies, Bowen felt deep compassion for their patients, regardless of whether they wore blue or gray. One poor boy's plight left an indelible mark. The young man had been shot through both cheeks, nearly severing his tongue. The same bullet also shattered the young man's shoulder. Another trooper had his chin and lower jaw torn away by a piece of shell. Bowen continued, "some with shocking wounds were stretched upon the ground in the last stages of life, while swarms of flies reveled upon their gashes. Some were shot through the lungs or bowels, and were groaning in their agony of suffering. But such things are too horrible to dwell upon."[17]

Lt. Noble D. Preston of the Tenth New York Cavalry had been badly wounded while leading the decisive charge near the train station, suffering a shattered leg. Carried to a field hospital, Preston joined other wounded men of both sides. In the flickering light of a wood fire, Preston rested next to a "handsome young Confederate major" from the Seventh Georgia Cavalry named Whiteford D. Russell. Russell had been shot through the spine and "was very weak and pale." Preston recalled that Russell was "a bright, intelligent looking man, who bore his sufferings with soldierly fortitude. He made mention of his family, and also spoke of the disastrous result of the day's fighting to his regiment." Major Russell lingered for three agonizing days, finally dying on June 14.

Early on the morning of June 12, Union soldiers roused Preston, carried him to the door, and threw him into a waiting ambulance. An officer supervising the activity urged the orderlies, "Hurry up; get these wounded out, quick!" As soon as Preston was loaded into the ambulance, the driver cracked his whip, and the ambulance moved rapidly off, bouncing over rough roads. The jolting opened Preston's wound, which began bleeding afresh. Despite his suffering, Preston was no longer at the mercy of the enemy.[18]

Tremors of fear rippled toward Gordonsville, six miles away. Maj. Edward

McDonald of the Eleventh Virginia Cavalry commanded Hampton's contingent of dismounted men at Gordonsville. Arriving there on the morning of June 11, he received a telegram announcing Sheridan's attack at Trevilian Station. McDonald took active measures to repel any attacks by Sheridan. He later recalled, "I remember my anxiety for two days at Gordonsville with my force of 400 dismounted men to fight 10,000 cavalry under Sheridan. I moved out of the town on the road to Trevilian Station in a thick woods, and made my preparations for a fight there where his cavalry could not charge me, and in case I had to run, we could scatter in the woods." McDonald and his small force spent three days hiding in the woods waiting for an attack that never came.[19]

Hampton showed great foresight and good planning by sending a regiment-sized force forward to hold a blocking position on the night of June 10. His actions further demonstrate the South Carolinian's concerns about being flanked. Finally, sending a regiment-sized force of dismounted men to hold a blocking position indicates his intent to take the offensive on the morning of June 11th.

The battle's outcome had not been decided the day before. While Sheridan claimed that he wanted to disengage and withdraw, his actions belied this intent. Instead of withdrawing, Sheridan extended his picket lines and set about destroying the Virginia Central Railroad. Sunday, June 12, dawned clear and beautiful, and his blue-clad troopers knew that a day of hard work lay ahead. The men of the Sixteenth Pennsylvania Cavalry of Irvin Gregg's brigade had an especially pleasant repast. Lieutenant Cormany found some commissary whiskey for his men, who had a restful morning, watering and grazing their horses.[20] Some of Davies's men skirmished with the enemy for a time, and then settled in for a quiet morning of making coffee and caring for their horses.[21]

Sergeant Webb of the First Maine Cavalry slept soundly until the sun was well up in the sky. Webb woke with a start, several members of his company standing over him, laughing at his appearance. He wrote, "I certainly was a laughable character. I lay there flat on my back and foot in a puddle, my other over a small log, my rubber blanket in a wad across my neck, my cap between my legs, my face all mud and my carbine across my body." Webb had slept so soundly that he was entirely unaware of his plight. After stretching and waking up, Webb shared in the morning's bounty, a

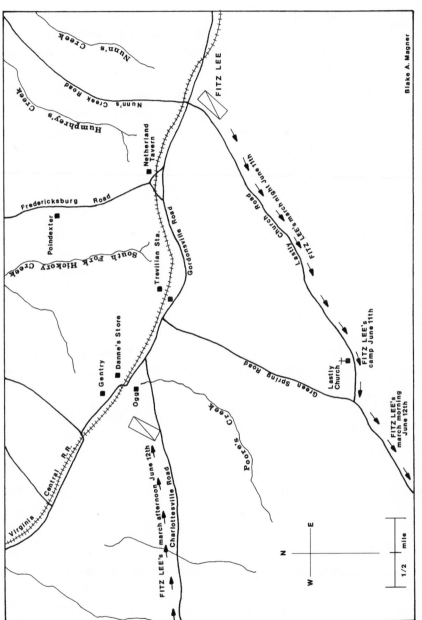

Route of March, Maj. Gen. Fitzhugh Lee's Division, June 12, 1864

Blake A. Magner

Confederate pig impressed into the Federal service. After breakfast, Webb and his company reconnoitered to find out whether there were any enemy troops in the vicinity of the station.[22]

As Gregg's men enjoyed their morning repast, Fitz Lee's division also had a fine time. They camped near the Lastly Church. Striking their camp early, they "moved out quite easy this morning in the direction of the Green Spring." Setting out around 9:30, Lee's line of march swung wide to the south, passing around Sheridan's far left flank close to the South Anna River. After a leisurely march, the Virginians arrived near Green Spring around noon where they "halted . . . and grazed for some time after which we drew rations and corn." Fitz Lee and his troopers did not join the rest of Hampton's command until nearly two o'clock that afternoon.[23]

Not everyone had such a pleasant morning. A number of Federal troopers buried the dead of both sides. Capt. George B. Sanford of the First U.S. Cavalry faced an especially unpleasant task, burying his best friend, Lieutenant Ogden. Sanford and some of the men of his company buried Ogden in a nearby front yard and placed a board at the head of the grave. The chaplain of the Tenth New York performed an Episcopalian funeral, with all the men of the regiment that could be spared from picket duty in attendance. Sanford noted, "the regiment never seemed quite the same afterward to me." Around 11:00, as the funeral wrapped up, the Regulars received orders to move out to the front.[24]

His fellow Regular, Captain Loeser, suffering through his first full day in captivity, did not enjoy his situation either. As the morning wore on, the provost marshal in charge of Loeser and the other prisoners found him, bearing the news that Loeser's close friend and West Point classmate, General Thomas L. Rosser, wanted to see him at Rosser's quarters. Loeser recalled that "after the usual ante-chamber affectation," he was ushered into Rosser's presence, the wounded general lying on his back in the middle of the floor, surrounded by several other wounded men. Rosser greeted his old friend cordially, and immediately began teasing the unhappy captain mercilessly, such that Loeser recalled that the "bantering was so sharp that [I] was not sorry when the pain of his wound caused him to desist, with a wound, from talking."

Rosser called his personal physician into the room, and at the general's behest, offered Loeser some brandy. Rosser apologized for not joining in the imbibing, "saying that his surgeons would not permit him to endanger the healing of his wound by drinking spirits." Not long after, Loeser rejoined his fellow prisoners, all of them lamenting their plight. Later that morning, they watched Fitz Lee's veterans pass by, affording them "a fair opportunity to take a good look at the men who had given them so much trouble the day before." The new prisoners of war spent a long and unhappy day, left with nothing to do but contemplate the captivity that lay ahead of them.[25]

Pvt. Dexter Macomber and his fellow Wolverines of the First Michigan Cavalry spent their first full day as prisoners of war behind the Confederate lines, quietly waiting and listening to the action. In addition to the misery of being a prisoner, Macomber was also ill. He and his comrades finally got some rations, mostly raw bacon, late in the afternoon, but this meager fare did little to ease the growling of their stomachs. The reality of their plight gradually settled in. For many, the day began a journey into hell from which they would never return.[26]

The Confederate prisoners faced interrogation by their Union captors. Stanton P. Allen of the First Massachusetts Cavalry recalled that the interrogations, typically conducted by staff officers, followed this pattern:

"What brigade do you belong to?"

"Lomax's brigade of Fitzhugh Lee's division."

"Where is Lee's division?"

"Don't know."

"When did you leave it?"

" 'Bout sun up."

"Where was it then?"

"On the Gordonsville Road, near Louisa Court House, just south of the railroad."

"Which way was Lee going?"

"He was headed this way. We were sent ahead to feel the Yankees, and your men gobbled us down there by the railroad."

"Was Hampton with Lee?"

"No."

In this fashion, the Union staff officers gained useful intelligence from their new prisoners of war. They quickly transmitted this intelligence up the chain of command.[27]

Their captors busily prepared their new defensive position. Bauskett and his company assumed positions along the Gordonsville Road. They took a position near a two-story house farmhouse owned by the Ogg family, to the left of the road and located in a grove of oak trees. Seeing that the gray-clad troopers meant business, the Oggs, their young son, and a woman slave wisely took refuge in their basement. A thicket of bushes nearly a thousand yards long to the rear of the house extended in both directions, leaving an open field between the Confederate position and the thicket.[28]

The Confederates held an L-shaped position on the road behind the Ogg house, the point of which rested along the Gordonsville Road and was anchored along the railroad cut. The railroad crossing fronting this position became a focal point as the day's action unfolded. While the Confederate line had no rifle pits, the men holding it used the fence rails and a few hastily constructed trenches for protection. Butler's South Carolinians held this strong defensive position. The line was formed as follows: the Fourth South Carolina on the left, the Sixth South Carolina in the center at the angle in the line, and the Fifth South Carolina on the right. Wright's and Rosser's brigades stretched out to the right of the South Carolinians, guarding the flank. Two Napoleons of Thomson's battery were posted to the right of center of the line, and the guns of Hart's battery, as well as the other two guns of Thomson's battery, were placed at intervals along the line.[29] Butler, commanding Hampton's division, was "always calm and cool when in action, his handsome, clear-cut face showed on this occasion no emotion as he scanned the details of the field." Col. B. Huger Rutledge of the Fifth South Carolina, the brigade's senior colonel after Aiken's wound, assumed command of Butler's brigade.

It was an excellent defensive position. The crude breastworks, the railroad cut, and the long-range Enfield rifles of Butler's men made for a formidable position. Chew, Hampton's horse artillery battalion commander, recalled that the position near the Ogg farm "was the finest position you ever saw."[30] It became the focus of the day's action.[31]

Directly across the Gordonsville Road from Butler's position, on the east side of the railroad tracks, sat two structures that became significant as the day's fighting unfolded. At the southern end of the line sat a store owned by Charles F. Danne, a Prussian immigrant who was a successful merchant. The store occupied the first floor, and the Danne family's quarters were upstairs. The Gentry family's farmhouse and outbuildings anchored the other end of the line. A rather steep declivity that sheltered those Federal troops moving along the line lay at the back of the ridge.

Sgt. Charles Hansell of the Twentieth Georgia and his companions rose early. They pulled their shoes out from under their heads and put them on their feet, and finally put on their coats. After rolling their blankets and strapping them to their horses, they rode back to the intersection of the Gordonsville and Charlottesville roads. They dismounted near a house. Hansell and nine other men held a position in the yard of the house, facing the road. They built a three-foot tall breastwork of rails with scattered openings cut into the rails for the firing of their weapons. They chose a good spot; the ground in front of the rude barricade sloped gently downward for several hundred yards, and thick woods backed the position. There, Hansell and his men waited to see whether Sheridan would test their little stronghold.[32]

As the sun rose, Hampton sent White's Comanches to reinforce Butler's line. Not much happened. "Without any hurry at all," White's men "fed their horses, got breakfast, and prepared for the business of this bright and beautiful Sunday morning in June. A shower of rain had fallen during the night, and the stifling dust was nicely laid, so that with the exception of fighting, whatever they had to do, could be performed in comfort." The Virginians held a position alongside the South Carolinians and enjoyed a pleasant morning on picket duty, protecting Butler's flank. One of White's officers recalled, "Sheridan did not seem to be in any hurry to break the glad Sunday quiet of the Valley, and hardly any firing was heard until 12 o'clock." Periodic bursts of sniper fire shattered the early afternoon calm.[33]

While the Southerners waited for the day's fighting to resume, most of Gregg's Union division spent the day tearing up the Virginia Central Railroad. Gregg himself was "under severe indisposition all day," but remained with the division's wagon trains and a portion of his command.[34] While Gregg rested, Lieutenant Cormany and his Pennsylvanians took particular pleasure in the destruction of the railroad tracks, a task he described as "rather simple." First, they broke a joint in the tracks on one side. The men stood shoulder-to-shoulder along the rail, a few with fence rails and chunks, prying up the rail and ties for 100 feet or more, underpinning the one side, at the height of several feet. When ready, the appropriate command sounded, and each man lifted harder and harder until the ties were perpendicular to their original position. They pushed the heavy rails and ties beyond perpendicular until they finally lay upside down on the ground, the spikes sticking straight up in the air. Cormany noted, "when once fairly started the R.R. track is turned upside down with considerable speed and the extreme strain and twist, of the turning over mass, twists and otherwise damages nearly every rail."[35]

The rails were then ruined. The Union troopers piled the ties and laid the rails across them. They then fired the piles. As they became heated in the center, the cool ends drooped from gravity, and they bent the rails to render them "utterly worthless without rerolling."[36] Still others wrapped the superheated rails around trees and telegraph poles.[37] In this fashion, the Federals claimed they destroyed somewhere between one and five miles of the railroad tracks, from near Louisa to nearly a mile to the west of Trevilian Station. One Pennsylvanian of Gregg's division observed that the destruction of the tracks "was done to keep the Rebs from whipping Hunter with men from Richmond."[38] Elements of Devin's brigade destroyed the station as well as the water tower. These festivities occupied the morning and stretched into the early afternoon. As a result, few of Gregg's men saw combat on June 12.[39]

Other elements of Gregg's division went on various reconnaissances toward the left flank of Sheridan's position. Led by Gregg's commissary officer, Capt. Charles Treichel of the Third Pennsylvania Cavalry, the First Maine Cavalry sortied toward Louisa in two columns, traveling via different roads.[40] Along the way, the Northerners encountered scattered pockets of Fitz Lee's men, meaning that the Maine men had to skirmish nearly the length of their advance. Brushing small contingents of the enemy out of the way, the First Maine clattered into the town of Louisa. The troopers of the First Maine had visited Louisa in May 1863 during the Stoneman raid, and a number of them had spent time there as prisoners of war after the Battle of Brandy Station. Their first visit had not been a friendly one, and the Federals did not harbor fond memories of the townspeople. Scouring the town, they found a number of wounded men left in the care of locals, including Col. Hugh Aiken of the Sixth South Carolina Cavalry. Aiken had been seriously wounded in the battle's opening moments. The Maine men also found a number of badly hurt Wolverines.[41]

Before leaving, the men of the First Maine foraged, "securing goodly quantities of forage, bacon, and tobacco, and some government stores had been destroyed." The Maine men never forgot the appearance the head of the column made as it left the town. Some of the men had found several jars of preserves, and were enjoying them, dipping their hardtack into the sweet jam. While they enjoyed their treat, the unhappy residents jeered the Maine horse soldiers. Others seized honey from local hives, using the sweet delicacy to make their hardtack more appetizing. About 1:00, the First Maine returned to the primary Federal position near the train station, finding the demolition of the railroad in full swing. The Maine men had a delightful morning excursion.[42]

Arrangements for the care of the many seriously wounded men on both sides had to be made. Sheridan's doctors had their work cut out for them. The regimental surgeon of the Sixth U.S. Cavalry had established "a splendid corps hospital at the station in the railway warehouse," located on the south side of the railroad tracks, east of Charles Trevilian's house. While the surgeons prepared the field hospital, Lt. Myron Hickey of the Fifth Michigan, Sheridan's acting ambulance officer, along with the officers of both divisions, undertook the Herculean task of locating and transporting the hundreds of injured troopers of both sides. They transported all but thirty-six of the most seriously wounded men to the large field hospital at Trevilian Station. They laid the injured men on fresh straw mats, and "every possible attention given them." Dr. Roger W. Pease, Sheridan's chief surgeon, assisted by the division surgeons, Rulison and Phillips, and by the various brigade and regimental surgeons, did superb work "in preparing hospitals and making arrangements for dressing wounds."[43]

While the men of the First Maine enjoyed their frolic and his surgeons went about their grisly work, Sheridan planned a final effort at reaching Gordonsville. He ordered Torbert to reconnoiter up the Gordonsville Road with his entire division. While Sheridan later claimed that he intended for Torbert to locate an alternate route to Mallory's Ford on the North Anna, this reconnaissance also carried his troopers right into the teeth of the nearly impregnable position occupied by Hampton's division along the Gordonsville Road. It appears that Sheridan still intended to reach Gordonsville. Otherwise, he would not have sent an entire division on a reconnaissance. General Gregg, who was unwell, would not be called upon to fight that day.[44]

In the interim, Butler, gazing out over the wide fields of fire created by his line along the railroad, sent scouts well out to the front to watch for Sheridan's expected movements.[45] He would not have long to wait. The second bloody day of the Battle of Trevilian Station was about to begin, and once again Butler's South Carolinians would bear the brunt of the fighting.

Notes

1. Fitch diary, entry for June 11, 1864.
2. King, *To Horse*, 12.
3. Jones, "Mother's Race."
4. Diary of Pattie Ann Carter Detter, copy in the files, Louisa County Historical Society, Louisa, Virginia.
5. Martha A. Harper, "Trevilian Station: Remembrances of an Aged Virginia Woman of the Battle," *The National Tribune*, March 15, 1917.
6. Samuel Burns Rucker Recollections, 4.
7. Ball memoir, 38.
8. James F. Wood diary, entry for June 12, 1864.
9. Mulligan, "*My Dear Mother and Sisters*," 184.
10. Brooks, *Butler and His Cavalry*, 247.
11. Calhoun, *Liberty Dethroned*, 126.
12. Loeser, "Personal Recollections," 313.
13. Tobie, *First Maine Cavalry*, 286.
14. Webb diary, entry for June 11, 1864.
15. Interview with Mrs. Charles Danne, transcript in the files, Louisa County Historical Society, Louisa, Virginia, date unknown.
16. Bauskett memoir, 14.
17. Bowen, *History of the First New York Dragoons*, 189.
18. Preston, *History of the Tenth Regiment*, 201–203. Preston recounted this tale in several newspaper articles also.
19. Edward McDonald Reminiscences, Southern Historical Collection, University of North Carolina, Chapel Hill, 109.
20. Mohr and Winslow, *The Cormany Diaries*, 434.
21. King, *To Horse*, 12.
22. Webb diary, entry for June 12, 1864.
23. Stiles, *Fourth Virginia Cavalry*, 53. The precise time of Lee's arrival is open to some debate. The accounts suggest a variety of times.
24. Hagemann, *Fighting Rebels and Redskins*, 244–45.
25. Loeser, "Personal Recollections", 318–19.
26. Dexter Macomber diary, entry for June 12, 1864; Oscar Wood diary, entry for June 12, 1864.

27. Stanton P. Allen, *Down in Dixie: Life In a Cavalry Regiment in Civil War Days* (Boston: D. Lothrop & Co., 1888), 363–64.

28. Bauskett memoir, 15.

29. Brooks, *Butler and His Cavalry*, 247.

30. Chew, "The Battle of Trevilians," 8.

31. Wells, *Hampton and His Cavalry in '64*, 202–03.

32. Hansell papers, 9.

33. Myers, *The Comanches*, 303.

34. *New York Herald*, June 22, 1864.

35. Mohr and Winslow, *The Cormany Diaries*, 434–35.

36. *New York Herald*, June 21, 1864; Keller to his sister, June 22, 1864 ("We took up the rails, piled the ties and some dry fence rails in piles 3 feet high, put the rails on them, and burned them, bending and destroying the rails. We tore up seven miles this way.")

37. Allen, *Down in Dixie*, 365.

38. Keller to his sister, June 22, 1864.

39. O. R., vol. 36, part 1, 842.

40. William Brooke-Rawle, ed., *History of the Third Pennsylvania Cavalry, Sixtieth Regiment Pennsylvania Volunteers, In the American Civil War, 1861–1865* (Philadelphia: Franklin Printing Co., 1905), 398; *New York Herald*, June 22, 1864. Capt. Treichel's brother, Maj. William P. C. Treichel, should have been the commanding officer of the Sixth Pennsylvania Cavalry during most of the Trevilian raid, since he was the regiment's senior officer. However, he was on sick leave, recuperating from acute malarial fever, for much of it, and only rejoined the regiment on June 21, when it arrived at White House Landing. However, Major Treichel's health was shattered, suffering from chronic hepatitis, and he was forced to reluctantly resign his commission on July 12, 1864. See William P. C. Treichel service records; Gracey, *Annals of the Sixth Pennsylvania Cavalry*, 265 and 268.

41. *New York Herald*, June 22, 1864.

42. Tobie, *First Maine Cavalry*, 287–88.

43. *New York Herald*, June 22, 1864; Report of Chief Surgeon Roger W. Pease, *Supplement to the Official Records of the War of the Rebellion*, vol. 6, 549–50. The role of these dedicated ambulance drivers and surgeons cannot be understated. There were a large number of seriously wounded men who needed care, and arrangements had to be made for attending their needs in short order. These men would be even more sorely tested in the days following the Battle of Trevilian Station.

44. O.R., vol. 36, part 1, 797. Sheridan wrote, "[I]n the afternoon I directed Torbert to make a reconnaissance up the Gordonsville Road to secure a by-road leading over Mallory's Ford, on the North Anna, to the Catharpin road, as I proposed taking that route in returning, and proceeding to Spotsylvania Court House, thence, via Bowling Green and Dunkirk, to the White House." This version of events, written in 1866, does not appear to be an accurate version of the facts,

given the severe fight that would rage for most of the afternoon. It is one of three different accounts penned by Sheridan, and, because of the deviations in them, it is difficult to lend credence to any of them.

45. Butler, "The Cavalry Fight at Trevilian Station," 238.

7

Sheridan Is Repulsed at the Bloody Angle: The Second Day of the Battle of Trevilian Station

Tell General Butler that we will hold . . . until hell freezes over!

Sheridan was worried. He suspected that the Confederate cavalry still hovered on his flanks, but he had not seen or heard anything of them since sundown on June 11. He decided to send part of his command out to feel for the enemy's position. According to Lt. Louis H. Carpenter of the Sixth U.S. Cavalry, Sheridan was "anxious to determine their real strength." Around 3:00 P.M. on Sunday, June 12, Little Phil ordered General Torbert to take his three brigades on a reconnaissance along the Gordonsville and Charlottesville Roads, to the west of the train station. Davies's brigade of the Second Division would support Torbert.[1]

Torbert found no Confederates holding the Green Spring Road and left a regiment and a section of artillery to secure it. The Federals continued on in the direction of Gordonsville. Custer's Wolverines, who had fought so long and hard the day before, and who were in no condition for more severe combat, advanced along the Gordonsville Road. Merritt's Reserve Brigade held the extreme right, with orders to support Custer. The Regulars moved along a local road to the north of the railroad tracks.[2]

Roving scouts dispatched by Butler detected the flanking movement.[3] Butler's scouts gave him ample notice that the Federals were about to attack his stout defensive position from two different angles. The one-legged, twenty-eight-year-old brigadier general awaited the Yankee approach.

Maj. James H. Kidd led Custer's column up the Gordonsville Road, his Sixth Michigan Cavalry at the head of the Michigan Brigade's advance. No more than half a mile from the train station, Kidd's skirmishers spotted

Butler's stout defenses. The mounted Wolverines exchanged shots with the South Carolinians at long range. Kidd deployed a squadron and sent Sgt. Marvin Avery forward to reconnoiter the enemy position, probably moving into the swale of Poore's Creek. Avery came back a few minutes later and reported that the breastworks were thoroughly manned. Avery also said that he had seen another thousand men moving into entrenchments on the enemy's right.[4]

Col. B. Huger Rutledge of the Fourth South Carolina Cavalry sat atop a pile of wood by the railroad track as the first shots by Kidd's troopers rang out. After a few seconds, a bullet struck one of the logs with a dull thud. Butler, standing nearby, calmly remarked, "That is the opening of the ball." Indeed it was, and a long and violent ball it would be.[5]

Butler's men reacted quickly to the advancing Wolverines. Capt. John C. Calhoun of the Fourth South Carolina, whose squadron had performed so gallantly during the previous day's fighting, was in bad shape that afternoon. Exhausted from the prior day's heroics, and weak from not having eaten anything for two days, the intrepid captain tried to lead his men into battle once again. However, the lack of food and rest proved too much for him. Moving toward the breastworks at the double-quick, Calhoun passed out after about fifty yards. He had to be carried to the rear, where he missed the day's brutal fighting.[6]

Hearing Sergeant Avery's report, Major Kidd dispatched the sergeant to relate his report to Custer. The Boy General dismounted the Sixth Michigan to fight on foot. The Sixth Michigan formed line of battle on the left side of the railroad, with the Seventh Michigan on their left. The two regiments drove in Butler's pickets. They moved on Butler's left flank, probably unaware that the line had its flank refused and that Butler awaited an attack. Kidd recalled, "I encountered and drove the Rebel pickets upon their main reserves, which was nothing less than their whole force posted in formidable entrenched positions."[7] A member of the Seventh Michigan stated, "We advanced up to the edge of the field, in front of the rebel works, and then began one of the hottest battles I saw during the Rebellion."[8]

Butler recalled that this first, tentative assault was "repulsed without much effort" by the brisk fire of his men's Enfield rifles. Reacting, the reluctant Custer put in his other two regiments, the First and Fifth Michigan, which joined the attack as Wesley Merritt's Regulars trotted into position alongside the Wolverines, linking the two commands. Col. Peter Stagg's First Michigan went up the railroad tracks, advancing alongside the Sixth and Seventh Michigan, while Col. Russell A. Alger's Fifth Michigan stayed back in reserve. Charging across the open fields, at a point about 500 yards from Butler's main line of battle, Stagg's Wolverines came under a deadly fire from behind the enemy breastworks. The men of the First Michigan made it only halfway across the field before being repulsed. Stagg lost eleven men killed and sixteen wounded in just a few minutes of fighting, prompting Kidd to write, "When the First Michigan could not stand before a storm of bullets, no other regiment of the cavalry corps need try. That is a certainty."[9]

The men of the Seventh Michigan crawled up the slope in front of Merritt's position on their hands and knees, looking for shelter behind a rail fence that ran along the edge of the woods. They went to ground there, "every man to suit himself." Able to reload without exposing themselves to enemy bullets, the Wolverines exchanged shots until Butler directed artillery fire at them. Although Confederate artillery shells dropped branches and tree limbs on the Michigan men, they did not curtail the barking of their carbines. A member of the Seventh recounted, "We lay in this position for several hours, firing all the time until our cartridges were gone. Some of the men had used eighty or one hundred rounds apiece."[10]

Kidd suffered a loss during the fighting that day. In one of the opening assaults on Butler's breastworks, a Confederate cannon ball killed Sergeant Avery. Kidd lamented Avery as "one of the bravest of the brave" and wrote, "I must pay to him the tribute of admiration due to every soldier who is always found at his post, bravely and conscientiously discharging his duty." He continued, "Had his life been spared, a commission would have . . . rewarded him for his conspicuous gallantry." In spite of this loss, Kidd proudly observed, "In the bloody work of that day we were the first regiment engaged and one of the three last to leave the field."[11]

The men of the Seventh Michigan attacked an old log house at the edge of the Confederate works. A Frenchman of the Seventh Michigan chased some of the Rebels into the log house, muttering oaths in French the whole time. He shot two of the Johnnies, prompting the others to wildly throw up their hands in surrender. Pvt. Daniel Eldridge had followed the Frenchman, and said, "those men have surrendered." Oblivious, his blood up, the Frenchman clubbed his musket and started jumping up and down like a wild man, muttering, "me not take prizone! Me no take prizone!" The terrified Southerners, unable to understand the French oaths, huddled and blanched. The Frenchman did not shoot his terrified captives.

The heavy enemy fire drove the Michigan men back to the edge of the woods. They left the relieved Rebels behind. The men of the Seventh Michigan resumed their position along the edge of the woods and began firing on the main enemy line of battle once again. They held this position until dark.[12]

Custer recognized the strength of Butler's position and realized that his command, which had been rendered largely combat ineffective as a result of their heavy losses from the previous day, faced the severe fire of Wright's brigade. Custer received orders to carry the strong Confederate position. However, with most of his staff officers already out of action, Custer elected not to make an all-out assault on Butler's lines. Instead, the Wolverines stayed in line of battle about 500 yards east of Wright's position, protected by the swale enclosing Poore's Creek. There, they supported the assaults of the Reserve Brigade for most of the afternoon. Late in the afternoon, the Boy General was told that he need not attack if he deemed it impractical. "Too late," he said, his face clouding as he spoke.[13] Although the Michigan Brigade did not fully engage in the heaviest part of the fighting, it nevertheless lost four captains killed or wounded, and another four lieutenants killed or wounded. Considering that, aside from the First Michigan's single sortie, the Wolverines did not directly participate in the primary assaults on Butler's line, their losses of thirteen men killed, twenty-eight wounded, and five captured that day were heavy.[14]

Wright's men also took casualties. Lt. Wiley C. Howard of the Cobb Legion recalled that he and the regiment's popular adjutant, Lt. Frank Jones, had enjoyed a hearty breakfast that morning. As they ate, Jones laughingly said, "Eat, drink, and be merry, for tomorrow you may die." Later, the two officers went on an uncomfortable reconnaissance, narrowly dodging the shots of Custer's marksmen, who had advanced to a position in range of Wright's line. Jones's luck ran out, though. As he went over the top of the Confederate works, leading the Georgians forward, a piece of a Federal artillery shell tore away his side, exposing his lungs and heart. The hideously wounded officer suffered for two days before finally dying.[15]

The men of the Twentieth Georgia Cavalry took deliberate aim, firing their rifles at the smoke of the Federal guns. They exhausted their forty rounds per man before long. Sgt. Charles P. Hansell sent Cpl. Billie Lee for ammunition. As Lee returned, he was in plain view of the Union troopers, who trained their carbines on him. Lee pulled down the brim of his hat and pressed on, bringing the much-needed ammunition to the men of the firing line. Resupplied, the Georgians resumed firing. Not long after, a Spencer ball to the knee shook up forty-five-year-old trooper William Baggs. Hansell told the injured man to go to the rear, and as Baggs started off, he received a mortal wound.

The regimental adjutant, Thomas G. Pond, came to see how the men were doing. The adjutant was armed only with a pistol, and Hansell suggested that the officer stay off the firing line. Disregarding Hansell's advice, the adjutant rested his head against the top rail and looked through the opening for a moment. A sharpshooter's ball cut a piece off the top rail, spraying the adjutant with splinters. He beat a hasty retreat. Pvt. Leonard Sims then assumed the same exposed position along the barricade, and was mortally wounded in the neck a few moments later. Not long after, an officer of the Jeff Davis Legion told Hansell to pull his men back off the line. They took up the unhappy task of burying the dead.[16]

In the meantime, Devin's brigade, held in reserve, had massed in the rear of Custer's brigade.[17] Around 3:30, Sheridan and his staff rode to the sound of the guns, but Little Phil did not take personal command of the fighting, preferring to leave tactical command to Torbert.[18] At Torbert's command, Merritt formed a line of battle on the north side of the railroad tracks on the reverse slope of the ridge connecting Danne's store and the Gentry house.

Capt. Isaac Rothermel Dunkelberger of Pennsylvania commanded a squadron of the First U.S. Cavalry. Dunkelberger was not a West Pointer. He enlisted in the First Pennsylvania Infantry in April 1861 and was quickly elected first sergeant of his company. The following month, he was commissioned second lieutenant in the First U.S. Cavalry, and promoted to first lieutenant in June. In recognition of his fine service at the Battle of Brandy Station, June 9, 1863, Dunkelberger was promoted to captain and commanded his regiment at the Battle of Gettysburg. A year later, Dunkelberger was a capable veteran field officer, well regarded by both officers and men.[19]

As the captain formed his men into line of battle, he observed, "The enemy was lying behind an old railroad bank. The country was thickly wooded with heavy underbrush." He spotted Sgt. John Navy, who had been badly wounded in the neck the day before. Navy had no weapon, and his stiff injured neck largely incapacitated him. In a sharp tone, Dunkelberger ordered Navy to the rear. The sergeant obeyed the order, responding, "All right, sir." Enemy bullets fired from some slave huts to the left of the First U.S. position buzzed by. Dunkelberger directed Lt. John H. Nichols, the regimental commissary of subsistence of the First U.S., a man described by Wesley Merritt as "frank and impulsive," to take a squadron and try to dislodge the riflemen from the slave huts and to burn them. Nichols spurred ahead. An Enfield ball killed him instantly. The two companies fell back with their task unfulfilled. A detail of the Sixth U.S. Cavalry carried Nichols's body back to the Trevilian house, where they buried him under some trees in the yard. Lieutenant Carpenter, who led the detail, left a sheet of paper stating Nichols's name and regiment in case any of his relatives tried to reclaim his body later.[20]

Lt. Charles H. Veil of the First U.S. recalled, "They occupied a railroad cut in our advance, which was on foot through thick brush. As we neared the cut, they opened upon us. As soon as we saw them, we dropped to the ground and their volley went over our heads, but to this day I can hardly see how we got away with our lives." Even though the Regulars were at close range, the railroad cut shielded the South Carolinians almost completely. The Regulars "did not have much of a mark to shoot at."[21]

Dunkelberger realized that his position was untenable as long as the enemy held the slave huts. He decided to move and came within the sights of the Sixth South Carolina's rifles. Lt. John Bauskett, commanding a company of the Sixth South Carolina, correctly guessed the range and aimed his Enfield at an officer on a white horse. Bauskett squeezed off a shot.[22] As Dunkelberger wheeled his regiment to the left to dislodge Butler's men, Bauskett's shot passed under Dunkelberger's left shoulder blade and crushed it. The captain reeled senseless in his saddle, and his demoralized Regulars fell back to their original position.

When Dunkelberger came to, Sergeant Navy was carrying him from the field. He later learned that the faithful sergeant reached his side first, and with the help of another man, carried the unconscious captain to safety. Dunkelberger recalled, "His only object on the line of battle appeared to be to watch me and help me should I require assistance. I had previously noticed his fine soldierly qualities and bravery, and with the aid of General Sheridan secured him a commission from the War Department as Ordnance Sergeant. But he declined it, saying: 'I would rather be a private in the Captain's company.' "[23]

The Federals held a strong position. One of Thomson's gunners noted, "A portion of the enemy's line was in a brush woods with an open field in front, but the strongest point of their line and the key of their position was a railroad cut which was full of dismounted riflemen."[24] Less than 500 yards away from the apex of Butler's line, the two sides stared tensely at each other as Merritt prepared to commit the entire Reserve Brigade to the fight. He wrote, "The brigade went in on an open field to its right and attacked the enemy's left flank vigorously. It was slow work, however, and as the enemy was not pressed on the left [by Custer] he concentrated his force on [my] brigade, and by large number and fresh troops, gave the command as much as it could attend to."

One of Merritt's opening volleys, directed at the Second Squadron of the Sixth South Carolina Cavalry in the angle, parted the hair of one trooper, leaving him unharmed but poorly coiffed.[25] Pvt. Whitfield "Fieldy" Brooks, a member of Bauskett's company, grabbed a rifle, climbed the parapet of Butler's breastworks, and was killed when a Spencer bullet hit him squarely in the temple. Bauskett recalled that "I heard the bones crunching as the ball passed through and out the left." Brooks stood up straight and fell over backwards. Bauskett caught the boy as he fell, kissing him on the cheek and laying him gently on the ground. His commanding officer recalled that Fieldy Brooks was "brave and utterly fearless, and promptest to obey an order—a true Christian Southern boy."[26] Years later, his brother, Ulysses, who chronicled the exploits of Butler's brigade, dedicated his history to the memory of his deceased brother and the brave stand of the South Carolinians.[27]

Colonel Devin had received orders to hold the road to Mumford's Ford across the South Anna River, covering Torbert's rear. He picketed the road heavily, and sent the Ninth New York Cavalry to support the pickets while the Confederates demonstrated along the road. The New Yorkers repulsed the enemy probe. Torbert ordered Devin to commit one dismounted regiment on the right of the railroad bed, and to send two mounted regiments to report to Merritt. He dismounted the Seventeenth Pennsylvania Cavalry, which had not been engaged in the first day's fighting, and sent it forward with one of his staff officers, and dispatched the Fourth and Sixth New York to Merritt. Devin remained with the Ninth New York and Heaton's battery on the Green Spring Road, west of the intersection of the Gordonsville and Charlottesville Roads. Devin faced his two regiments and the guns south, covering the division's rear.[28]

Merritt's men, joined by elements of Devin's brigade, launched a concerted attack against Butler's position. Col. Luigi Palma Di Cessnola of the Fourth New York Cavalry bitterly observed that "my regiment was sent to help General Merritt, who was hardly pressed by an enemy who was allowed stupidly the day before (after being defeated) to concentrate himself and throw up any amount of breastwork." The New Yorkers dismounted and formed line of battle in full view of Butler's Enfields. "The enemy could pick out man by man of my command, while I could scarcely see them behind the breastwork," wrote Di Cessnola. In the face of Butler's severe fire, the men of the Fourth New York had to lay down flat on the ground "and from that reclining position to fire and advance like snakes." The Fourth New York went into battle with one hundred eighty-one men that day, and in less than two hours took fifty-one casualties in the face of Butler's fusillade.[29]

Lt. O. L. Wood of the Fourth New York was on the left of Di Cessnola's line. The lieutenant slightly raised his head to see, and Di Cessnola "saw him falling on the ground in a hurried way, and at the moment I thought nothing about it as the falls were coming as thick as hail and it was natural enough and beside, my orders, to avail themselves of any stumps on the ground to cover themselves to any advantage." However, Wood had been shot in the head, and had been killed instantly.[30]

Butler noted, "The second attack was made with more vigor, and was directed sharply upon the angle above described, where the Sixth South Carolina was stationed. This, too, was repulsed." Butler also brought Thomson's two guns to bear, directing their fire on the angle. Even in their exposed position, the gunners blasted away at Merritt's advancing line with shrapnel and canister at close range.[31] However, the gunners suffered severe losses there in the open, exposed to the sharp fire of the Union carbineers. Thomson's color bearer, John "Jap" Pierce, sat on his horse behind the guns, waving his flag in the face of the enemy until six Yankee bullets brought him down. Lt. Col. J. Fred Waring wrote, "A terrible fire was poured into the gunners, but they repaid the Yankees with canister, & ran all back except a few sharpshooters."[32] Cpl. Frank Riely, a cousin of Thomson, was shot through the breast. "He mechanically inserted the cartridge, it was rammed, then the shell and he fell dead without a groan." Chew noted that nearly every man tending Thomson's guns was wounded or killed, and that every horse attached to the battery was killed but Chew's.[33]

Finally, the gunners abandoned one of the guns and took shelter behind the Ogg house. Sgt. George Neese ran back from the front line, reaching a rail fence behind the other section of Rebel guns. As Neese climbed the fence at the edge of the woods, one of Williston's cannonballs whizzed through the fence, snapping the third rail from the ground in two as the fortunate artillerist sat astride the top of the fence. He noted, "If I had been a second later or a few moments earlier I might have lost a leg or two; but once more a miss was as good as a mile."[34] With his gunners driven off by the combination of Torbert's Spencers and Williston's rifled guns, Butler relied upon the fire of Thomson's other section and Hart's guns, stationed farther to the right.[35]

Sergeant McVicar of Thomson's battery was hiding behind the Ogg house when an orderly arrived, looking for three volunteers to replace fallen gunners. Along with two other men, McVicar volunteered. When he reached the front line, Thomson told him to take five men and carry the abandoned gun off by hand. Under a galling fire, McVicar led the men forward. As McVicar raised the trail handle with his left hand, the soldier next to him, Anthony Beale Burgess, was killed when a Spencer ball passed through his skull over the right eye and exited above his left ear. Burgess "quivered and fell forward on my breast and some of his brains and blood were on my jacket. As I raised the trail higher his body fell backward."

With no time to mourn the fallen cannoneer, another man came forward to take his place and was also shot down. Cpl. Carthage Kendall "was struck and crazed, he was holding the trail hand spike. We had trouble to keep him out of the way." Cal Miller was shot in the back, and John Hare was shot through the thigh. McVicar noted, "I was the only one with no loss of blood and a whole hide, but my clothes had three bullet holes. We fought in desperation and all who helped came out but poor" Burgess. Along with three other men, and under the cover of heavy fire from the Southern artillery, McVicar retrieved Burgess two hours later. The desperately wounded artillerist lingered until nine o'clock that night, although McVicar noted, "I do not think he was at any time conscious of misery or anything that was going on around him."[36]

The Sixth Pennsylvania Cavalry, holding the end of Merritt's line among the house and buildings of the Gentry farmstead, received flanking fire from the Confederates. Seeing this threat, Merritt committed the Second U.S. Cavalry to support the Sixth Pennsylvania. The Second U.S. "charged gallantly, and, though few in numbers, by the impetuosity of their onslaught drove the enemy back and protected the right until they were relieved" by two of Devin's regiments, brought forward to reinforce Merritt's position.[37]

Merritt also brought up Battery D, Second U.S. Artillery, commanded by a Vermont man, Lt. Edward B. Williston. Williston, a fine soldier, was a member of the class of 1856 of Vermont's military academy, Norwich University.[38] When the war began, he was living in San Francisco but felt duty-bound to serve his country and came east to join the army. Arriving too late to participate in the First Battle of Bull Run in June 1861, he fought in every major campaign of the Army of the Potomac. Commissioned into the Second Artillery in August 1861, he received a promotion to first lieutenant a month later. By the end of the war, he was a captain, and he eventually achieved the rank of colonel in the Regular Army and brigadier general of volunteers during the Spanish-American War. His veteran battery of horse artillery did good service during the war, but none better than on June 12, 1864.

Under heavy musketry fire, Williston's gunners came up "right gallantly" and deployed three guns to blast away at Butler's position. Merritt wrote, "Lieutenant Williston moved one of his brass 12-pounders onto the skirmish line. In fact, the line was moved to the front to allow him to get an eligible position, where he remained with his gun, in the face of the strengthened enemy (who advanced to its very muzzle), dealing death and destruction with double loads of canister."[39] He praised Williston and his men lavishly: "I cannot speak too highly of the battery on this occasion. The light 12's were magnificent." Torbert concurred, commenting, "Great credit is due to Lieutenant Williston, of the artillery, for the gallant manner in which he used his guns, part of the time upon the front line of our men."[40]

The gunners even impressed the enemy; Ulysses Brooks overheard Butler remark that the firing of Williston's guns was the most accurate and effective he had ever known.[41] Years later, Butler wrote, "At one time during the progress of the fight, one or two of Sheridan's guns . . . got in a position to enfilade my line along the railroad embankment and were playing havoc with my men." "Six guns had been brought into position, and were partially enfilading the entire brigade line," noted one of the South Carolinians. "These pieces were capitally served, and were doing severe execution, the shrapnel killing men lying down behind the rail-fence breastwork as if they were in a completely open field, a very hard thing for any troops to endure steadily, without the prospect of relief."[42]

Responding, Butler ordered Hart to concentrate the fire of his six guns in an effort to silence Williston's barking cannons. Butler recorded, "This was done with great promptness and efficacy, and the enemy's guns were silenced."[43]

Years later, Merritt submitted Williston's name for a Medal of Honor. Merritt claimed, "In the crisis of the action at Trevilian, when my lines were being pressed by an overwhelming force of the enemy, Lieutenant Williston planted three guns of his battery in an exposed but favorable position for effective work; and then personally moved the fourth gun onto the skirmish line." The general continued, "Using double charges of canister he, by his individual efforts, greatly aided in resisting successfully the charges of the enemy on our front. . . . I have the honor to recommend that Major E. B. Williston, 3rd U.S. Artillery, be awarded . . . a Medal of Honor for having especially distinguished himself at the action of Trevilian Station, Virginia, June 12, 1864." In April 1892, Williston received a Medal of Honor for "distinguished gallantry."[44]

Thus reinforced, Merritt continued attacking Butler's line. Devin's New Yorkers took the extreme right and dismounted, with orders to flank the enemy position if possible.[45] After galloping nearly half a mile, the Sixth New York Cavalry hastily advanced through a thick wood to meet the enemy advance. Their skirmish line engaged with the enemy, and soon the entire regiment came under a severe fire. The New Yorkers pushed Butler's troopers back across the open field and to their main line of battle. As the Sixth New York advanced across the open field, they "were greeted with a perfect shower of bullets, the air seemed to be alive with them." This galling fire pinned them down for nearly half an hour. The New Yorkers returned fire to the best of their ability. Sgt. Alonzo Foster believed that the Confederates outnumbered them by at least two-to-one, and "I have always wondered why they did not charge our line and sweep us from the field." He knelt by a stump and fired his carbine so quickly that the barrel grew dangerously hot. An Enfield ball passed through the top of his kepi, cutting the hair from his scalp. His company commander remarked, "A close call, my boy." Foster kept the hat as a good luck souvenir for the rest of his life.[46]

In the meantime, the Fourth New York joined the Sixth New York in the advance. However, the Fourth New York soon gave way under the flurry of Rebel bullets, and took up a position some distance to the rear of that held by the Sixth New York. The Sixth New York was alone in front, both of its flanks threatened. The Sixth New York receive orders to retreat. They slowly fell back as the dusk gathered. Mistaking them for the enemy, the Fourth New York opened as they fell back, "and it was with much difficulty that we made them understand that we wore blue jackets instead of gray coats. From this point we fell back some distance and took up a second position on a rise of ground skirting a small stream. Our dead and wounded were placed beneath some trees a little to the rear of our line."[47] Eventually, the New Yorkers ran out of ammunition and had to hope for a fresh supply. It never came.[48]

By nightfall, Butler had repulsed six separate attacks along the railroad, prompting the veterans to dub its apex "The Bloody Angle," in honor of the desperate struggle at Spotsylvania Court House a few weeks earlier. Major Chew, the talented Southern horse artillerist, recalled, with some exaggeration, that the Bloody Angle "was a terrible spot, and men were killed there by the thousands. Trees twelve and fourteen inches around were shot down, not by shells, but by bullets."[49] With each unsuccessful attack, the Yankee troopers held positions closer and closer to Butler's line, so that by the sixth attack, the two lines were only a few yards apart.[50] Butler barked stern orders to the men of the Sixth South Carolina to hold the Bloody Angle at all costs. Bauskett, holding the apex of the angle, reported that his men could hold the angle if they received a resupply of ammunition. Another trooper said, "Tell General Butler that we will hold it until hell freezes over!"[51]

The heavy fighting took a toll on the men of the Sixth South Carolina.

As the fighting commenced, Sgt. Andrew Giles and a squad of men received orders to do some sharpshooting from the Ogg house, but Giles was mortally wounded before reaching the house. Four other men of the squad were killed within minutes; the courage of one of the Carolinians, young Eddie Padgett, so impressed the Federals that they got a pillow from the house and placed it under his head to alleviate his pain. The mortally wounded trooper died while the fighting raged around him. Company B of the Sixth South Carolina had thirty-seven of its sixty-four men killed or wounded in the intense struggle for possession of the Bloody Angle.[52] Another trooper, his spine shattered by a Spencer bullet, lay "there in the hot sun all day, without a drop of water, which he was crying for." Bauskett asked Sgt. Hill Winn for his canteen to take water to the wounded man, but the canteen was empty because Winn "had just poured the last of the water into his gun to cool it, since it had become too hot to load."[53]

Capt. John C. Calhoun of the Sixth South Carolina was very worried. Realizing that they were low on ammunition and that their line was in danger of being broken, Calhoun looked for Lee's men to reinforce the South Carolinians. Calhoun noted, "it's well known that Gen. Lee could not have been many miles off during the Saturday fight which commenced early in the day, he certainly heard our guns, our force was so small, we were enveloped by the enemy, and yet he did not reach us, until evening of the second day." Hearing the thunder of hoof beats, he looked back and saw Lee's men riding toward the battle lines. He saw Lee's "horses were in a foam of sweat with nostrils extended, coming with lightning speed." Calhoun watched Lee's men coming to the rescue of Butler's hard-pressed brigade.[54]

The fire laid down by the Enfield rifles of the South Carolinians convinced many of the Union troopers that they either faced enemy infantry, or that the Confederates had concentrated their entire force there.[55] Colonel Waring of the Jeff Davis Legion recalled that for more than five hours, "a perfect fusillade was kept up."[56] One Federal trooper recalled, "At sunset the battle became doubly furious, we having driven the enemy until he was strongly reinforced, which gave us a sudden check. For a short time after sunset the fighting was fierce, their larger numbers giving us volley after volley."[57]

The Confederates had a strong defensive position and a disregard for secrecy on behalf of the enemy. "The attacking forces would spread out, and at times open fire along our entire front, but whoever was in command of the attacking column, with the eye of a good soldier, selected this angle for his most determined assaults." With the Federal bugle calls echoing in the woods, preparations were clearly in evidence for each attack. Butler's South Carolinians grimly steeled themselves to meet the next one. Butler observed, "between then and dark, five distinct and determined assaults were made upon us, making seven in all." His men performed magnificently that day.[58]

Chew's gunners were also brilliant on June 12. Lieutenant Carpenter observed, "On the second day's fight, I was exposed to some of the hottest artillery fire that I have ever been in." Only 200 yards away from Hart's and Thomson's guns, Carpenter recalled that "the shells and round shot dropped around lively for a time." Lt. Lawrence Kip of the Third U.S. Artillery, one of Sheridan's aides-de-camp, sat his horse just behind Carpenter as the Southern guns belched fire. A shell fragment severely wounded Kip in the back of the head, and a large fragment of the same shell passed within three inches of Carpenter's head.[59]

At one point during the fighting, some of Merritt's men took a position facing the Bloody Angle between the Danne and Gentry houses on the north side of the railroad. Their effective fire, sheltered by the houses, took a toll on the South Carolinians who manned the Southern line of battle, prompting one of the Confederate artillerists to write, "The yanks . . . shot from the openings down into the rail barricades at our men who filled them. You could hear the bullets strike the men."[60] Realizing that these Federal troopers had to be driven out of their sheltered positions, Butler ordered two of Hart's guns turned toward the houses, "and in a short time they set fire to the [Danne] house . . . , and it was consumed by fire."[61] Orderly Wade Hampton Manning of Company K, Fourth South Carolina Cavalry searched for Butler to deliver a message from Hampton. Manning found Butler on his horse behind Hart's guns, calmly watching the action as Federal bullets whistled by "unpleasantly near—so near, in fact, that though the general would not dodge, Hampton's courier would." Manning recalled that Butler's "face was as quiet, as if he was facing a party of ladies in a parlor, or at a picnic, instead of hostile Yankees. . . . He seemed to me at the moment a picture of absolute indifference to either fear or danger—and it was bravery not recklessness."[62]

As the fighting raged on that afternoon, the Sixth Pennsylvania Cavalry held the end of Merritt's line, anchored in the woods near the Danne house. Capt. Frank H. Furness of Company F of the Sixth Pennsylvania Cavalry commanded the squadron at the end of Union line. The twenty-five-year-old Furness, son of a prominent clergyman and abolitionist, was not a professional soldier. Rather, at the outbreak of the Civil War, the gifted young architect was studying his art in New York under his mentor, the famous architect Richard Morris Hunt.[63] Furness enlisted in 1861 and was commissioned lieutenant in Company I of the Sixth Pennsylvania. When the Army of the Potomac's Cavalry Corps was formed in the winter of 1863, Stoneman appointed Furness to his staff. The young architect served in that capacity until after the Battle of Gettysburg. In January 1864 he was promoted to captain and commanded a company. Furness had a long and highly successful architectural career after the Civil War ended. This day, though, would be his best day.[64]

Furness and Capt. Robert Walsh Mitchell of the Sixth Pennsylvania learned from a noncommissioned officer that an outpost of Pennsylvanians located among some outbuildings of the Danne farmstead was nearly out of ammunition. Butler's men occupied the house itself and poured fire into the isolated contingent, which was in imminent danger of being captured by the enemy. An open grass field separated the house and the outbuildings. The sergeant crawled on his hands and knees through high grass to carry this message to Furness. Reacting quickly, Furness took two boxes of ammunition from his already scanty supply, and placing one on his head, asked for another officer to volunteer to help carry the ammunition. Mitchell volunteered, and the two men ran across the killing field between the isolated Pennsylvanians and the main line of battle. They deposited the ammunition there. The fresh supply of ammunition allowed the Pennsylvanians to hold their ground and the Reserve Brigade's exposed flank until the day's fighting finally ended.

Their return trip was even more dangerous. Butler's men sent swarms of lead buzzing by their heads like so many angry bees. Mitchell remarked to Furness, "For God's sake, run zig-zag so they can't draw a bead on you!" No sooner did Mitchell speak these words that one bullet passed through the top of his cap and another through the skirt of his coat. The two officers made it back to the main line. For this feat, with the endorsement of Merritt, Furness received the Medal of Honor in 1899. The citation read:

On this occasion, a detachment holding an exposed and isolated outpost having expended its ammunition, Captain Furness, carrying a box of ammunition on his head, ran to the outpost across an open space that was swept by a fierce fire of the enemy. This ammunition together with that carried by another officer who had responded to Captain Furness's call for volunteers, enabled the detachment to hold its position until nightfall, thus saving the main line from severe loss.[65]

Furness was the only architect of note to earn the Medal of Honor in the American Civil War.

Pvt. John Thistlethwaite Baynes of the Sixth Pennsylvania Cavalry received his second combat wound during these attacks. Baynes, with tongue planted firmly in his cheek, wrote to his sister, "I have been lucky enough to get wounded again at *Trevilian Station* near Gordonsville on the 12th of this month. The rebels seem to have a great spite at my legs as the other time I was wounded it was in the right leg this time was in the left, but I shall not grumble if they do not hit me in the head."[66] The Sixth Pennsylvania suffered six killed, twenty-six wounded, and four men captured on June 12, which later prompted the regimental historian to write, "the fighting on the 12th, was, if possible, more desperate than that of the day previous."[67]

George Stockweather of Company F of the First New York Dragoons, which held the position next to that of the Sixth Pennsylvania, was badly wounded during the fighting on June 12. While he was on the front line during the day's hottest fighting, an Enfield ball knocked out Stockweather's teeth, destroyed his left ear, and passed out the back of his neck, leaving a gruesome wound. The other men of his company thought Stockweather had been killed, but, as the Dragoons fell back, they heard him yell, "Boys! Boys! Don't leave me!" However, the New Yorkers could not retrieve him, and the wounded man fell into the hands of the advancing enemy when Merritt's brigade fell back later that evening. Despite the horrible wound, Stockweather survived and was later paroled from Libby Prison.[68] The Dragoons lost two officers. Their commanding officer, Maj. Howard M. Smith, had a very close call, a bullet passing through his coat sleeve but somehow missing him. A few days later, he reported to his mother that the fire from the Bloody Angle was "the severest the Regiment was ever under."[69]

The men of the Fifth South Carolina confronted a daunting task. They had only a few rails for protection and a wide-open field in front of them.

A portion of the regiment faced the railroad cut, where Union artillery fire and sharpshooters enfiladed it. The other portion held the fence corner in the road, exposed to the fire of the sharpshooters in the Gentry house.[70] Sergeant Dowling of the Fifth South Carolina Cavalry held the very end of Butler's line near the Ogg house. Dowling saw the Union right flank stretched out in front of him, ready to sweep around Butler's own flank. Butler sent Wickham's brigade and the independent First Maryland Cavalry to link up with the Palmetto men, the Marylanders holding the extreme left of Butler's line of battle.[71] Forming a compact column to Dowling's elbow, a Rebel yell quavering from their lips, the Virginians drove the Federal flank back.

However, the Yankee troopers quickly regrouped and pressed forward again, charging the Southern line with bugles blaring. "To add to the trying nature of the situation ammunition had run short," recalled a member of the Fourth South Carolina Cavalry. "It had been necessary to collect car-tridges from the bodies of the dead and wounded, and now a very insufficient number remained with any of the regiments with which to resist further assaults, and the Fourth had nearly empty boxes."[72] "We poured a hail storm of bullets into their raging lines, and again they give back," remembered Dowling. "Just then our ammunition gave out, and Lieut. Foster from our company and others were sent for cartridges. The ordnance wagon was dashing up and in a few minutes all were resupplied . . . we will never forget [Foster's] countenance as a bee swarm of bullets flew around his head as he got back to us and inspired us with his heroic spirit."

Company B of the Sixth South Carolina was also nearly out of ammuni-tion. Torbert clearly was not ready to give up the attack. A young private, Bill Turner, volunteered to go for ammunition and was wounded immedi-ately. Two others, Wash Allen and Tom Sego, took Turner's place. With shot and shell raging around them, the two troopers braved a hail of lead "and got as much [ammunition] as they could carry and returned in time for us to repulse another charge. This daring deed of these boys was one of the bravest of the war."[73]

As the men of the Sixth South Carolina fought on, Pvt. Ned Holder of Bauskett's company pitched over onto his back after receiving a wound in the left breast. Bauskett ran to his side, and felt his pulse. The lieutenant noticed that Holder's heart was still beating, and the young man told

Bauskett in a whisper that he was shot through the heart. Bauskett reacted quickly, opening the young man's jacket and shirt, finding the Spencer bullet flattened against Holder's skin. It passed through a prayer book and bible in the young man's pocket before striking him. Bauskett grabbed the bullet and held it up for Holder to see, telling him that it had not broken the skin. Holder "came to life immediately; in another minute or two he would have been dead from shock and imagination. He felt that bullet go through as plain as if it had been a bayonet thrust."[74]

Butler's men struggled to repulse the seventh Union assault of the afternoon. Dowling described the action: "On our right they were fighting 'hand to hand,' and somehow they got possession of the railroad and were enfilading us. The situation seemed awful, but the Stonewall Brigade at Manassas did not stand more impregnable." He continued, "we shot off the corners of the houses, strewed the grounds with their dead until we are sick to think about it and again they gave back, but again and again they charged us, but again and again they were repulsed." During a brief lull, Dowling's company commander, Capt. Abner B. Mulligan, ordered Dowling and another sergeant named Richardson to climb over the breastworks and see what Sheridan was doing. The two men went over the top, seeing "both of our batteries . . . shelling the enemy with incessant thunder bolts of death and their batteries were sending over our heads and among us bursting missiles at the rate of twenty-four per minute."

The weary Confederates girded themselves for the seventh and final assault by Torbert's horse soldiers while the artillery exchanged thunderbolts. One young officer of Butler's brigade, oblivious to the danger, strode his company line, encouraging his men to fortitude. He reminded them "of mothers and wives, sisters and sweet-hearts, who at their homes in the 'far South,' in their venerable much loved churches, were at that very moment sending up to the Most High prayers for their safety." Capt. Moses Humphrey, commander of the Cadet Ranger company of the Sixth South Carolina, also paced his line, telling his troopers, "Now, boys, you will have a chance to show your training; I want you to fire fast and aim straight, but wait for the command to commence firing."[75]

These tactics worked. The South Carolinians responded by saying, "Let the beggars come on, and be damned." Others watched the nearby Federals doling out drams of whiskey, "which was very tantalizing under the circum-

Maj. Gen. Philip H. Sheridan, commander of the Union Cavalry Corps.

Cathy Marinacci

Brig. Gen. Alfred T. A. Torbert, commander of the First Cavalry Division. Torbert, a native of Delaware, spent most of his career in the Civil War commanding infantry in the Army of the Potomac.

Brig. Gen. David M. Gregg of Pennsylvania, commander of the Army of the Potomac's Second Cavalry Division.

Brig. Gen. Wesley Merritt, commander of the Reserve Brigade of the First Division, Cavalry Corps, Army of the Potomac. Merritt had a forty-three-year career in the United States Army and commanded the American expedition that captured Manila during the Spanish-American War.
United States Army Military History Institute

Brig. Gen. George A. Custer of Michigan, commander of the Army of the Potomac's proud Michigan Cavalry Brigade.
Cathy Marinacci

Col. Thomas C. Devin of New York, known as the "Old War Horse," commanded the Army of the Potomac's Second Brigade, First Cavalry Division.
United States Army Military History Institute

Brig. Gen. Henry E. Davies of New York, commanded the Army of the Potomac's First Brigade, Second Cavalry Division. Davies was a lawyer who became a fine commander of cavalry.
Library of Congress

Col. J. Irvin Gregg of Pennsylvania commanded the Army of
the Potomac's Second Brigade, Second Cavalry Division.
Colonel Gregg and Brig. Gen. David M. Gregg were first
cousins.

Lt. Alexander C. M. Pennington, commander of
Battery M, 2d U.S. Artillery.

Capt. Alanson Randol, commander of combined Batteries H & I, 1st U.S. Artillery.
Library of Congress

Col. William Sackett, commander of the 9th New York Cavalry, mortally wounded on June 11, 1864.
United States Army Military History Institute

Capt. Isaac R. Dunkelberger, of the 1st U.S. Cavalry, wounded on June 12, 1864.
United States Army Military History Institute

Lt. Col. George H. Covode, commander of the 4th Pennsylvania Cavalry, mortally wounded at Samaria Church, June 24, 1864.
Library of Congress

Col. Pennock Huey, commander of the 8th Pennsylvania Cavalry, captured at Samaria Church, June 24, 1864.

Lt. Col. Peter Stagg, commander of the 1st Michigan Cavalry. Stagg was a carpenter by training. He would be the last commander of the famed Michigan Cavalry Brigade.
Library of Congress

Maj. James H. Kidd, commander of the 6th Michigan Cavalry. Kidd succeeded Custer as commander of the Michigan Cavalry Brigade in the fall of 1864.
Bentley Historical Library, University of Michigan

Maj. Melvin Brewer,
commander of the 7th
Michigan Cavalry.
Brewer was wounded in
action on June 11, 1864.

Col. Russell A. Alger, commander of the 5th Michigan
Cavalry. A prominent lawyer
from Detroit, Alger served as
secretary of war during the
McKinley Administration.

Col. Alfred Gibbs, commander of the 1st New York Dragoons.

Lt. Noble D. Preston, 10th New York Cavalry, awarded the Medal of Honor for gallantry on June 11, 1864.

From Noble D. Preston, *History of the Tenth Regiment of Cavalry, New York State Volunteers, August 1861 to August 1865*. New York: D. Appleton, 1892

Sgt. Maj. Herbert E. Farnsworth, 10th New York Cavalry, awarded the Medal of Honor for gallantry on June 11, 1864.

From Noble D. Preston, *History of the Tenth Regiment of Cavalry, New York State Volunteers, August 1861 to August 1865*. New York: D. Appleton, 1892

Capt. Theophilus F. Rodenbough, commander of the 2d U.S. Cavalry, badly wounded in the opening moments of the Battle of Trevilian Station on June 11, 1864, and awarded the Medal of Honor for gallantry that day.
Library of Congress

Capt. Frank Furness of the 6th Pennsylvania Cavalry, awarded the Medal of Honor for gallantry on June 12, 1864.
Jay Townsend

Lt. Edward B. Williston, commander of Battery D, 2d U.S. Artillery, awarded the Medal of Honor for gallantry on June 12, 1864.

Col. Charles H. Smith, commander of the 1st Maine Cavalry, awarded the Medal of Honor for gallantry at Samaria Church, June 24, 1864.

Capt. Henry C. Weir, staff officer to Brig. Gen. David M. Gregg, awarded the Medal of Honor for gallantry at Samaria Church, June 24, 1864.

Sgt. Nathan B. Webb, Co. D, 1st Maine Cavalry. Webb's diary is one of the finest sources available on the Trevilian raid.

From Edward P. Tobie, *History of the First Maine Cavalry, 1861-1865.* Boston: Press of Emory & Hughes, 1887

Pvt. William Onweller, 6th Michigan Cavalry, wounded on June 11, 1864.

John Sickles

Bugler John Fitzgerald of the 6th Michigan Cavalry, captured on June 11, 1864.

The Netherland Tavern, which served as Wade Hampton's headquarters during the battle. It became a focal point of the first day's fighting at Trevilian Station.

The Battle of Trevilian Station, by James E. Taylor.
Little Big Horn Battlefield National Monument

The Charge of the Cadet Rangers at Louisa Court House, June 11, 1864, by David Humphreys Miller. Wade Hampton leads the charge at center, with drawn sabre.
The Citadel Archives and Museum

Maj. Gen. Wade Hampton, commander of the Confederate
cavalry forces in the Trevilian Raid.

Maj. Gen. Fitzhugh Lee of Virginia, commander of Lee's Division. Lee was the nephew of General Robert E. Lee.

Brig. Gen. Matthew C. Butler of South Carolina, commander of Butler's Brigade of Hampton's Division. Butler, a lawyer, had lost a foot in combat in 1863. He became one of the finest of the Confederate cavalry commanders.

Brig. Gen. Thomas L. Rosser of Texas, commander of the Laurel Brigade. Rosser and George A. Custer were close friends. Rosser was wounded on June 11, 1864.

Col. Gilbert J. Wright of Georgia, commander of Young's Brigade of Hampton's Division.

Brig. Gen. Williams C. Wickham of Virginia, commander of Wickham's Brigade of Lee's Division. Wickham was a prominent lawyer from one of Virginia's oldest families. In the fall of 1864, he resigned his commission to take a seat in the Confederate Congress.

Brig. Gen. Lunsford L. Lomax of Virginia, commander of Lomax's Brigade of Lee's Division. Lomax, a West Pointer, came from one of Virginia's oldest and best-known families.

Brig. Gen. John Chambliss of Virginia, commander of Chambliss's Brigade of W. H. F. Lee's Division. Chambliss was killed in action in August 1864.

Brig. Gen. Martin W. Gary of South Carolina, commander of Gary's Independent Brigade of cavalry. Known as the "Bald Eagle," "Mart" Gary was one of Hampton's protégés.

Maj. Roger Preston Chew of Virginia, commander of Hampton's horse artillery battalion.

Maj. James Breathed of
Virginia, commander of Lee's
horse artillery battalion.

Lt. Col. J. Fred Waring of Mississippi,
commander of the Jeff Davis Legion
Cavalry.

Col. Thomas T. Munford of Virginia, commander of the 2d Virginia Cavalry. Munford was a fine soldier. His inability to get along with Thomas L. Rosser prevented him from receiving a well-deserved promotion to brigadier general.

United States Army Military History Institute

Col. Richard Dulany, commander of the 7th Virginia Cavalry. Dulany assumed command of the Laurel Brigade when Rosser was wounded on June 11, 1864.

Nathaniel Morison

Lt. Col. William Stokes, 4th
South Carolina Cavalry.
Stokes's letters home provided
great insight into the plight of
Matthew C. Butler's South
Carolina troopers.
Marcia French

Lt. Col. Joseph L. McAllister,
commander of the 7th Georgia Cavalry, in a photograph
taken in 1859. McAllister
was killed in action on June
11, 1864.
Carolyn Clay Swiggart

Col. Richard L. T. Beale of Virginia, commander of the 9th Virginia Cavalry. Beale would receive a promotion to brigadier general after Chambliss was killed in battle.

National Archives

Lt. Col. Elijah V. White, commander of the 35th Battalion of Virginia Cavalry of the Laurel Brigade, also known as the "Comanches." White and his men led Rosser's charge into Custer's Wolverines on the morning of June 11, 1864.

Horace Mewborn

Capt. Moses B. Humphrey, commander of the Cadet Rangers Company of the 6th South Carolina Cavalry. Humphrey was killed in action.

Sgt. Robert C. Towles, Co. A, 4th Virginia Cavalry, mortally wounded on June 11, 1864.

Captured at Trevilian Station on June 11, 1864, Sgt. Adam J. Iler, Co. H, 7th Georgia Cavalry, spent the rest of the war in a prisoner-of-war camp in Elmira, New York. This photo was taken shortly after his release.
Ernest A. Iler, Jr.

Cpl. Washington Proctor of the 7th Georgia Cavalry, who fought at Trevilian Station.
Dusty Eisenburg

stances, it must be confessed, even by teetotalers."[76] Just in the nick of time, as the blue-clad troopers prepared their final assault, Butler's ammunition wagon "came rattling down the road with the mules on a full run, the driver lashing and cracking his whip. He continued at the same furious pace along the line in plain view of the enemy, a man in the rear of the wagon throwing out the packages, which were instantly caught up, and the contents quickly found their way into the hungry cartridge-boxes."[77]

Colonel Rutledge of the Fourth South Carolina, standing at the outside of his regimental line, had the shoulder and upper part of the sleeve of his coat cut by a Federal bullet. The colonel disregarded this missile, but moments later a second bullet furrowed the breast of his uniform coat. Again, the colonel played the incident down until one of the regiment's officers approached to consult with Rutledge. As the two officers conferred, yet another bullet scratched the colonel's cheek, and soon afterward another plowed through his beard, carrying away a clump of hair. Finally, the colonel realized that he made a prominent target. The men of the Fourth South Carolina desperately searched for the origin of these sniper shots. They spotted a big red-headed Yankee sharpshooter perched in a nearby tree, waiting for another opportunity to shoot Rutledge down. Two soldiers of the Fourth South Carolina "promptly served their protest, doing this simultaneously so as to leave an agreeable doubt as to which gave the settler, and down he sank all in a heap." The next day, the Confederates found the man "stiff and stark, with rifle full-cocked lying between his legs."[78]

Lt. Col. William Stokes, Rutledge's second in command, likewise had a close call that day. In a letter to his wife, he reported, "My escape on Sunday was very narrow indeed. A cannon ball struck some rails about twelve feet from me and passed only a few inches over my back. Had the rails not been there it would have cut me in two."[79] A company commander of the Fourth South Carolina recalled, "I fired all my pistol cartrages away— had three men wounded in the same jam in the fence by the balls—we was exposed to a galling fire from cannon and small arms but God was our help in trouble."[80]

A Yankee artillery shell horribly wounded John Moss of the Sixth South Carolina, laying bare the bone in his leg but somehow not breaking the leg. His brother, Matt, spotted the hideous wound and ran to his brother, throwing his arms around him. As he held his brother, a Yankee bullet pierced Matt's heart, and he fell dead lying across his brother's chest. John died a short while later. Ulysses Brooks, who served in the same company with the brothers, remembered them as "splendid soldiers—splendid in physique and splendid in courage."[81]

The combination of the gathering dusk and the billowing clouds of black smoke engulfing the battlefield persuaded Butler that the darkness would protect the gunners from the Federals' effective fire. Accordingly, Butler ordered Major Chew to reman Thomson's two howitzers and load them with double charges of canister. Butler expected the final assault to emerge from the woods just a few yards from the Bloody Angle, cross the fence, and charge the line. "They did just as I had anticipated, and came charging out of the woods in the open field and into the railroad cut immediately in our front," recalled Butler. "Before the canister and still steady fire of our carbines and rifles the enemy fell back for the last time before the deadly aim of our troops."[82]

Sgts. Dowling and Richardson found a position where they could overlook the length of Merritt's line of battle. They watched the Federal officers rallying their men for another attack. With bugles blaring, the dauntless Northerners charged the Bloody Angle again. One of Butler's men described the final Union attack: "One body marched straight for the cut in the embankment; it moved with beautiful precision, in close order, shoulder to shoulder, the rifles . . . held horizontally at the ho, and shooting continuously." Undaunted, the Federals came on, an officer leading their advance. The officer, probably one of the Regulars, held his "right arm bent, holding his cocked revolver pointing perpendicularly upwards at the 'Ready!' and he counted time to keep his troopers in regular step. He presented a fine mark, but somehow no bullets, it seemed, could hit him, and when any of his men dropped, the rest closed-up beautifully and marched straight on. It was a handsome sight, always to be remembered."

Finally, at the parapet of the breastworks, the brave Federal fell, and his men broke and ran.[83] The South Carolinians tenaciously resisted the attack. One officer of the Sixth South Carolina threw his empty pistol at the approaching Yankees.[84] Dowling noted, "We sent several bullets, now one of their caissons had been burst by one of our shells, and volley after volley of our bullets brought them to a halt and recoil. The sun, red with the smoke of battle, was down."[85]

While Wickham's men fell into line, Lomax's brigade of Virginians waited for an opportunity to strike a blow. They hid in "some dense shrubbery on the enemy's right flank," waiting for the order to attack.[86] Late in the day, Hampton saw the chance to turn Sheridan's right flank. He sent Lomax's brigade and part of Breathed's horse artillery battalion around the exposed flank on a narrow wood road, through two ravines and across the South Fork of Hickory Creek. The dense undergrowth made the march tedious.[87] The Virginians held a position on the extreme left flank of the Confederate line along the railroad bed, their horses safely ensconced on a dirt road that led to Bibb's Crossroads.[88]

Lomax's men finally got into position to attack just before dark. They formed lines of battle at right angles to the railroad, about 200 yards away. Capt. John Shoemaker's guns prepared to fire at point-blank range. As the Virginians finished aligning for the attack, Hampton made efforts to coordinate an attack by the entire Confederate force. Capt. Daniel Grimsley, commander of the Sixth Virginia Cavalry, received the following orders: "as we uncovered and relieved the front of our line from the pressure of the enemy, it would move forward, and joining on to the right of the charging column, would make the movement connected and continuous along the whole front."[89]

The gray-clad horse soldiers sprang to their feet, with both divisions moving forward. Charging with a ringing Rebel yell, the Confederates crashed into Merritt's right flank, surprising the Yankees with their on-slaught. Supported by the accurate fire of Shoemaker's guns, the attack first doubled the Union line of battle back on itself, and then broke it. The Federals fell back in confusion.[90] Dowling wrote, "the moment was awful, the scene sublime, the rebel yell and exultant shouts of victory all along our line, lasting ten to twenty minutes, will never be forgotten while one of those brave men stay this side of the Jordan of death."[91]

Pvt. Thomas M. Fowler of Company G of the Third Virginia Cavalry of Wickham's brigade sprang forward with the main assault. The Virginians had received orders to "do or die," and Fowler was determined to fulfill the orders. Leading the way, they bore down on Williston's guns. As Fowler and his comrades approached, the guns belched cannister. The blast knocked Fowler from his horse and carried away the lower third of his left arm. Sgt. John T. Foster, riding with Fowler, reined in, jumped from his horse, and went to Fowler's aid. He tied Fowler's tattered shirt over what was left of the arm in a crude tourniquet and helped Fowler to remount. The intrepid Fowler, still determined to do or die, took the reins between his teeth and continued to fight until he finally passed out from loss of blood. Fowler recovered, eventually becoming state librarian in Virginia and an attorney in Richmond.[92]

A member of the Sixth Virginia Cavalry recorded that the assault was "one of those sublime spectacles sometimes witnessed on a battlefield. Amid the surrounding gloom could be seen a constant stream of fire from our lines as we advanced with victorious shouts upon the bewildered foe." He continued, "Again the air was illuminated by the flash of opposing batteries as they belched forth their terrible thunders at each other while screaming shells traced fiery arches through the air and bursting, scattered fire and death around."[93] Grimsley noted, "as Lomax moved forward, driving the enemy before him, the fire was kept up from some portions of our own line, and his brigade suffered more from its friends than it did from the enemy."[94]

The Yankee troopers broke and ran. The regimental historian of the Sixth New York Cavalry of Devin's brigade noted, "a heavy movement on our right, and an enfilading fire from one of their batteries, caused us to fall back, placing our whole division in a critical position, being followed by a heavy force. But a longer stand was impossible against such odds, and a general retreat of the whole line was necessary."[95] "The whole of the rebel line then advanced, their artillery throwing grape and Canister into our led horses," recounted Col. Di Cessnola of the Fourth New York of Devin's brigade, "creating a great stampede and the horses belonging to the Regulars to the 6th N.Y. and to my regiment were all running over the country."[96] Fitz Lee boasted, "The enemy, surprised, offered but some slight resistance—their right flank gave way, and they were driven back in confusion. Night and the thickness of the country put an end to the pursuit."[97] Horatio Nelson of the Fourth Virginia recorded in his diary, "Attacked the enemy and gave him a lesson that he'll long remember. Our loss slight. The enemy lost very heavily."[98]

A member of the Third Virginia Cavalry, of Wickham's brigade, proudly announced, " 'Our Riding Infantry'—as we now call ourselves, for we have been in eight engagements during this campaign and have fought only one on horseback—hold a line of battle as our veteran infantry, and Jackson's

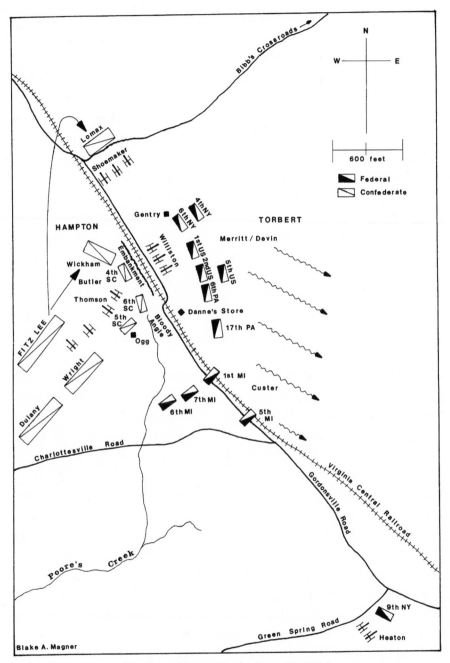

The Second Day's Battle, June 12, 1864

'foot cavalry' never fought greater odds nor lost more than we have this campaign."[99] Hampton reported, "This movement was successful and the enemy, who had been heavily punished in front, when attacked on his flank fell back in confusion, leaving his dead and a portion of his wounded on the field."[100] Lt. Allen Edens of the Fourth South Carolina Cavalry colorfully described the scene: "the batle . . . raged with great fury until dark when the Yanks gave way and fled like wild goats leaving the ground strewed with dead and dying—our loss was heavy but half that of the enemy. . . . One thing I know the Yankees was severely punished."[101]

One of Chew's gunners, writing with the benefit of hindsight, noted, "Had we known the extent of their panic, and had we not been broken down ourselves and pursued that night, we would most certainly have started a rout which would have broken up Sheridan's raids for some time." However, Hampton's exhausted command could not press its advantage because it was as fought-out as the Northern horse soldiers.[102]

As night fell, the Federals fled toward the train station. They had to leave their dead and wounded behind; Col. Di Cessnola noted "it was wholesale murder to try to approach one another."[103] Saddler Edgar Strang of the Sixth Pennsylvania Cavalry recalled that his regiment "had a rather unpleasant experience for about an hour, having to pass through a low piece of swampy ground where our progress was necessarily very slow." Their slow progress made the Lancers an attractive target for the Confederate gunners, who "opened on us with one of their batteries, but their range being a little too high, the shells went screaming over our heads, which made our position anything but pleasant." After struggling their way along, their march plagued both by the swampy ground and the Southern artillery, Strang recalled, "at last we gained the road and all hands drew a long breath of relief."[104] One of Devin's men, relieved at reaching a safe position, wryly commented, "At eight o'clock we got a good position on a hill a mile back from our battleline, and held it until eleven o'clock, during which time the enemy amused us by throwing numerous shells along our line—appearing like a celebration with sky rockets, but doing us no damage."[105]

While the First Division fell back, Davies posted pickets to guard the front and flanks, blueclad videttes holding positions dangerously close to the enemy's.[106] Dr. Alphonzo D. Rockwell, regimental surgeon of the Sixth Ohio Cavalry, recalled that his regiment, which had not been engaged during the day's fighting, went out to do picket duty around twilight, relieving the men of the First Maine Cavalry. Rockwell noted, "The dust raised must have been seen by our watchful foe, for a storm of shell was opened upon us, which for a few moments was as fearful as anything we had experienced." Shells fell on the exposed position of the Ohioans, their explosions lighting up the night sky. Fragments of shrapnel and pieces of bark hit many of the men. The exploding shells shook loose branches of trees. "The fact that not a man was injured illustrates how out of all proportions to the damage inflicted may be the noise and demoralizing effect of an artillery fire," stated an astonished Rockwell.[107] The First Massachusetts Cavalry of Davies's brigade was the last Union unit to leave the field. An officer recounted, "We held them there until dark, and then you ought to have seen us get out, part at a trot and part at a gallop. My squadron was the last on the field, and you can bet we got out lively when our turn came."[108] The great battle of Trevilian Station was over.

The South Carolinians conducted a brilliant fight. At one point, Hampton offered Butler the services of the Laurel Brigade, but the confident Butler declined the offer, preferring to man the line with his own men.[109] They held their own against the best that Torbert's troopers had to offer. Many of the Union horse soldiers believed that they had faced Breckinridge's infantry instead of dismounted cavalry.[110] Colonel Waring simply wrote, "The Carolinians fought well."[111] Years later, Hampton said, "Butler's defense at Trevilian was never surpassed. He was as good a soldier as we had."[112] Capt. John Shoemaker, whose men were all natives of Lynchburg, proudly said, "I don't think I ever saw the boys fight with as much dogged determination before as they did then. . . . They . . . knew they were fighting for home and homefolks—father, mother, and sisters."[113] Indeed, as Lieutenant Bauskett remembered, "Fighting all day as hard as we could, without food or drink, the men were worn to frazzles, and could not have successfully coped with troops in a fresh charge; and had they come on, we would have been wiped out. Had they known our weakening of line, and bodily and physical weakenings—they would have overrun us and swept our field."[114]

Bauskett's men had been at the vortex of the climactic fight, and they had suffered accordingly. At roll call the next morning, the lieutenant had less than half the men available for duty than he had three days earlier. Bauskett was brilliant that day. General P. G. T. Beauregard offered him a lucrative staff position as a reward for his service on June 12. Bauskett rejected the offer, preferring to remain with his beloved men.

Sergeant McVicar of Thomson's battery praised the Confederate cavalry, saying, "Large bodies of our Cavalry are dismounted and fighting with more stubborn determination than I have ever seen."[115] Federal prisoners reported that they were surprised to find that they faced only Butler's dismounted cavalrymen and not infantry reinforcements.[116] One of the South Carolinians reported that a diary, taken from one of Sheridan's troopers a few days later, stated, "Sunday, June 12th. Fought on the same ground. Got whipped like the devil. Lost more men than the rebs did the day before."[117]

Without committing their entire force, they had repulsed Torbert's determined assaults in some of the most severe cavalry fighting of the war. Sheridan incorrectly stated, "The cavalry engagement of the 12th was by far the most brilliant one of the present campaign."[118] Torbert reported, "From this position on the Gordonsville Road it was impossible to drive him, except by having a large force, and then with heavy loss, for the enemy had been reinforced by one or two regiments of infantry from Gordonsville."[119] The First Division suffered 38 men killed, 169 men wounded, and another 37 captured, for total losses of 244 out of just over 4,000 men engaged. These losses are a tribute to the firepower of the South Carolinians given the task of defending the Bloody Angle.

For some reason, Torbert never committed Davies's brigade to the fighting that day. Perhaps the addition of another brigade might have helped; there has never been a satisfactory explanation of the reasons why Davies's troops, less than two miles distant, stayed out of the combat. The division commander stated only that "A portion of the command had severe fighting with the enemy. The rest were on picket duty guarding the flanks; lost 2 officers and 24 men; did not unsaddle or lie down."[120] "We remained on picket duty . . . until noon of the 12th, when we moved to the front just in time to take part in a reconnaissance that was being made up the railroad," reported a member of the First Pennsylvania Cavalry. "Here we witnessed another hard fight and lay on the skirmish lines nearly all the afternoon, right under the fire of our artillery and the rebels too and did not fire a shot nor have a man hurt."[121] J. Irvin Gregg's brigade did not fire a shot in anger that afternoon, comfortably remaining in camp while the guns boomed less than a mile away.[122]

While the two sides disagreed as to the outcome of the battle, all agreed that the intense, bloody, and protracted fighting had been even more intense than the previous day's.[123] Writing years after the war, Sheridan quite correctly observed, "This engagement, like that of the day before around Trevilian, was mostly fought dismounted by both sides. . . . Indeed, they could hardly have been fought otherwise than on foot, as there was little chance for mounted fighting in eastern Virginia, the dense woods, the armament of both parties, and the practice of barricading making it impracticable to use the sabre with anything like a large force."[124] Chew recalled, "This was a terrible fight. Indeed, I think it was as severe and destructive a fight as I ever saw."[125] A Georgia newspaper grudgingly admitted, "The Yankees fought with a courage and determination worthy of a better cause. They charged our line again and again, but were repulsed every time, leaving their dead and wounded in a few steps of our line."[126]

The severe fire of the South Carolinians' Enfield rifles completely cut down the dense thicket surrounding the smoldering ruins of Danne store.[127] One of Butler's troopers, writing long after the war, noted, "The Yankees displayed pluck and splendid courage that bloody day in their attempt to drive us away, but were sadly in need of a good cavalry leader. Sheridan was no match for Butler."[128]

Notes

1. Carpenter to his father, June 22, 1864. This explanation for sending an entire division down the Gordonsville Road makes far more sense in light of his later story that he was looking for an alternate route to Mallory's Ford. When the actions of the day are viewed in their full context, it is clear that Sheridan was not being entirely honest when he wrote in his official report that he intended to withdraw and not continue the fight.

2. O.R., vol. 36, part 1, 808–09.

3. Butler, "The Cavalry Fight at Trevilian Station," 238.

4. This was probably Wright's brigade coming into position along the Confederate line of battle, but it also might have been Lomax's brigade of Lee's division arriving after their long flank march around Sheridan's position.

5. Wells, *Charleston Light Dragoons*, 66.

6. Brooks, *Butler and His Cavalry*, 191.

7. Kidd to Robertson, December 17, 1864.

8. Isham, *Seventh Michigan*, 60.

9. Kidd, *Personal Recollections*, 363.

10. *Ibid.*, 60–61.

11. Kidd to Robertson, December 17, 1864.

12. Isham, *Seventh Michigan*, 62.

13. *Detroit Advertiser & Tribune*, July 6, 1864.

14. O.R., vol. 36, part 1, 824–25.

15. Howard, *Sketch of Cobb Legion Cavalry*, 17.

16. Hansell, *Reminiscences*, 8.

17. Kidd, *Personal Recollections*, 361–62; O.R., vol. 36, part 1, 824 and 842; Butler, "The Cavalry Fight at Trevilian Station," 238.

18. Hall, *History of the Sixth New York Cavalry*, p. 198.

19. Heitman, *Historical Register*, 1:388.

20. Reminiscences of Isaac Rothermel Dunkelberger, Michael Winey Collection, United States Military History Institute, Carlisle, Pennsylvania; O.R., vol. 36, part 1, 851; Carpenter to his father, June 22, 1864. The night before, Nichols had carried the watch and some trinkets from Lt. Frederick Ogden to Ogden's best friend, Capt. George B. Sanford. Sanford noted, "This evening I performed the same duty for poor Nichols himself." Hagemann, *Fighting Rebels and Redskins*, 245.

21. Veil, *Personal Recollections*, 45.

22. Bauskett memoir, 15.

23. Dunkelberger, "Reminiscences." The loyal sergeant was killed in action at the Battle of Fisher's Hill, September 22, 1864. Returning to duty in September, Dunkelberger later received a brevet to major for his gallantry at the Battle of Trevilian Station. See Heitman, *Historical Register*, 1:388.

24. Neese, *Three Years*, 288.

25. Bauskett memoir, 15.

26. *Ibid.*, 17.

27. Brooks, *Butler and His Cavalry*, 248.

28. O.R., vol. 36, part 1, 842.

29. Di Cessnola to Wood, July 7, 1864.

30. *Ibid.*

31. Neese, *Three Years*, 288.

32. Waring diary, entry for June 12, 1864.

33. Chew, "The Battle of Trevilians," 9.

34. Neese, *Three Years*, 289–90.

35. McVicar diary, entry for June 12, 1864; Butler, "The Cavalry Fight at Trevilian Station," 238.

36. McVicar diary, entry for June 12, 1864.

37. O.R., vol. 36, part 1, 850.

38. Robert G. Poirer, *"By the Blood of our Alumni": Norwich University Citizen Soldiers in the Army of the Potomac* (Mason City, Iowa: Savas Publishing, 1999), 209. Years later, Williston's exploits were brought to the attention of another

famous American artillerist, President Harry S. Truman, who once said that he would rather have won the Medal of Honor than be president of the United States.

39. When Merritt submitted Williston's name for a Medal of Honor, he wrote, "Lieutenant Williston . . . then personally moved the fourth gun on to the skirmish line where, using double charges of canister, he, by his individual efforts, greatly aided in resisting successfully the charge of the enemy on our front." Wesley Merritt to Adjutant General, United States Army, November 19, 1891, Edward B. Williston Medal of Honor file, RG 94, File No. 20120PRD1891, the National Archives, Washington, D.C. Given the abundant praise for Williston's performance in the Official Records, the medal was quickly issued with little investigation or question.

40. O.R., vol. 36, part 1, 850 and 809.

41. Brooks, *Butler and His Cavalry*, 251.

42. Wells, *Charleston Light Dragoons*, 67.

43. Butler, "The Cavalry Fight at Trevilian Station," 239.

44. Merritt to Adjutant General, November 19, 1891 and citation, Williston Medal of Honor file, RG 94, File No. 20120PRD1891.

45. Hall, *History of the Sixth New York Cavalry*, 198.

46. Alonzo Foster, *Reminiscences and Record of the 6th New York V. V. Cavalry* (Brooklyn, N.Y.: privately published, 1892), 60–1.

47. *Ibid.*, 61–2.

48. Di Cessnola to Wood, July 7, 1864.

49. Chew, "The Battle of Trevilians," 9.

50. Wells, *Charleston Light Dragoons*, 67.

51. Brooks, *Butler and His Cavalry*, 249.

52. *Ibid.*

53. Bauskett memoir, 19–20.

54. Calhoun, *Liberty Dethroned*, 127–28.

55. Howard Smith diary, entry for June 12, 1864.

56. Waring diary, entry for June 12, 1864.

57. Hall, *History of the Sixth New York Cavalry*, 198.

58. Butler, "The Cavalry Fight at Trevilian Station," 238.

59. Carpenter to his father, June 22, 1864.

60. McVicar diary, entry for June 12, 1864.

61. Butler, "The Cavalry Fight at Trevilian Station," 238–39.

62. Brooks, *Butler and His Cavalry*, 265.

63. Blake A. Magner, ed., *At Peace with Honor: The Civil War Burials of Laurel Hill Cemetery, Philadelphia, Pennsylvania* (Collingswood, N.J.: C. W. Historicals, 1997), 72.

64. See Gracey, *Annals of the Sixth Pennsylvania Cavalry*, 310. In fact, Furness became the leading American architect of the nineteenth century, designing and

building many of the most significant and handsome buildings in Philadelphia. Today, although most of his work has been largely forgotten, he is considered to be the first great American architect, having built more than 650 buildings, and commanding a high price for doing so. Furness's most famous student was Louis Henry Sullivan, who designed much of downtown Chicago after the Chicago Fire. Sullivan, of course, was the teacher of the most famous American architect, Frank Lloyd Wright. For examples of Furness's work, see, James F. O'Gorman, *Architecture of Frank Furness* (Philadelphia: Philadelphia Museum of Art, 1987), or George E. Thomas, Michael J. Lewis, and Jeffrey A. Cohen, *Frank Furness: The Complete Works* (New York: Princeton Architectural Press, 1991). For a detailed biographical sketch of Frank Furness that places his career as an architect in its proper context, see Michael J. Lewis, *Frank Furness: Architecture and the Violent Mind* (New York: W. W. Norton, 2001).

65. Frank Furness Medal of Honor File, RG 94, File No. F164VS1862, the National Archives, Washington, D.C. Furness's application for the Medal of Honor was also endorsed by Col. Albert P. Morrow. Morrow was one of those great natural soldiers who emerged during the Civil War. A sergeant in 1861, Morrow, who was not a professionally educated soldier, was a twice wounded lieutenant colonel in 1865. Remaining in the Regular Army after the Civil War, he served with various cavalry regiments, including the Seventh Cavalry, until the turn of the century, when he finally retired as a full colonel with a nearly forty-year career. Brig. Gen. St. Clair A. Mulholland, a former commander of the legendary Irish Brigade, who held a position of great political power and influence in Philadelphia after the Civil War, further endorsed the application.

66. Richard C. Baynes, ed., *The Life and Ancestry of John Thistlethwaite Baynes (1833–1891)* (Irvine, Calif.: privately published, 1987), 40–41.

67. Gracey, *Annals of the Sixth Pennsylvania Cavalry*, 262–63.

68. Bowen, *First New York Dragoons*, 193–94.

69. Howard M. Smith diary, entry for June 12, 1864.

70. Brooks, *Butler and His Cavalry*, 251–52.

71. Again, the precise role played by the First Maryland Cavalry remains very much a mystery. There are no specific surviving accounts of participation by the Maryland men during the fighting on June 12, other than Bradley Johnson's statement that "In the battle of Trevilian's I had, during the second day, been made to do pretty much the duty of a brigade, for which my force was utterly inadequate." Bradley T. Johnson, "My Ride around Baltimore in Eighteen Hundred and Sixty-Four," *Journal of the United States Cavalry Association* 2 (1889), 250. There are also a couple of vague statements by other members of the regiment indicating that they participated in the fighting on both days. A recent regimental history of the unit indicates that it was engaged on the second day, holding the end of the Confederate line, to the left of Wickham's command. As there are no other contradictory accounts, the author accepts this premise. Robert J. Driver, Jr., *First and*

Second Maryland Cavalry, C.S.A. (Lexington, Va.: Rockbridge Publishing, 1999), 84.

72. Wells, *Charleston Light Dragoons*, 67.

73. Brooks, *Butler and His Cavalry*, 250.

74. Bauskett memoir, 26.

75. Baker, *Cadets in Gray*, 107.

76. Wells, *Hampton and His Cavalry*, 204–05.

77. Wells, *Charleston Light Dragoons*, 68–69.

78. *Ibid.*, 71.

79. Halliburton, *Saddle Soldiers*, 147–48.

80. Swank, *Confederate Letters and Diaries*, 142.

81. Brooks, *Butler and His Cavalry*, 253.

82. Butler, "The Cavalry Fight at Trevilian Station," 238–39.

83. Wells, *Charleston Light Dragoons*, 69.

84. Bauskett memoir, 27.

85. Mulligan, "My Dear Mother and Sisters," 184–85.

86. Shoemaker, *Shoemaker's Battery*, 74.

87. Fitzhugh Lee to Robert E. Lee, December 20, 1866.

88. Grimsley, "Battle of Trevilian's Station," 34.

89. *Ibid.*, 34–5.

90. Shoemaker, *Shoemaker's Battery*, 74.

91. James D. Ferguson diary, entry for June 12, 1864; Mulligan, "My Dear Mother and Sisters," 185.

92. Stephen V. Donahue to the author, August 24, 2000. Mr. Donahue is the great-great-great grandson of Sergeant Foster. See also Thomas P. Nanzig, *Third Virginia Cavalry* (Lynchburg, Va.: H. E. Howard Co., 1989), 108.

93. John C. Donohoe diary, entry for June 12, 1864, Virginia State Archives, Richmond, Virginia.

94. Grimsley, "Battle of Trevilian Station," 35.

95. Hall, *History of the Sixth New York Cavalry*, 198–99.

96. Di Cessnola to Wood, July 7, 1864.

97. Fitzhugh Lee to Robert E. Lee, December 20, 1866.

98. Nelson diary, entry for June 12, 1864.

99. Nanzig, *Third Virginia Cavalry*, 54.

100. O.R., vol. 36, part 1, 1096.

101. Swank, *Confederate Letters and Diaries*, 142.

102. Petersburg *Daily Register*, June 29, 1864.

103. Di Cessnola to Wood, July 7, 1864.

104. Strang, *Sunshine and Shadows*, 51.

105. Hall, *History of the Sixth New York Cavalry*, 199.

106. See, e.g., Carlos McDonald diary, entry for June 12, 1864, *Proceedings of the Sixth Ohio Cavalry*, 55.

107. A. D. Rockwell, M.D., *Rambling Recollections: An Autobiography* (New York: Paul B. Hoeber, 1920), 150; King, *To Horse*, 12.

108. Benjamin W. Crowninshield, *A History of the First Regiment of Massachusetts Cavalry Volunteers* (Boston: Houghton-Mifflin, 1891), p. 223.

109. Petersburg *Daily Register*, June 29, 1864.

110. See, e.g., Gracey, *Annals of the Sixth Pennsylvania Cavalry*, 262 ("our whole cavalry force fought all day dismounted, being opposed by infantry behind earthworks and barricades.").

111. Waring diary, entry for June 12, 1864.

112. Brooks, *Butler and His Cavalry*, 254–55.

113. Shoemaker, *Shoemaker's Battery*, 74.

114. Bauskett memoir, 27.

115. McVicar diary, entry for June 12, 1864.

116. Brooks, *Butler and His Cavalry*, 252.

117. Wells, *Hampton and His Cavalry*, 212.

118. O.R., vol. 36, part 1, 785.

119. *Ibid.*, 809.

120. *Ibid.*, 858.

121. Lucas to his wife, June 13, 1864.

122. O.R., vol. 36, part 1, 863.

123. See, e.g., Gracey, *Annals of the Sixth Pennsylvania Cavalry*, 262.

124. Sheridan, *Personal Memoirs*, 1:424–25.

125. Chew, "The Battle of Trevilians," 9.

126. Athens, Georgia, *Southern Banner*, July 13, 1864.

127. Bauskett memoir, 33. Interestingly, and perhaps as a consequence of the destruction of the family business and home, young Charles F. Danne Jr., son of the proprietor, enlisted in Company F of the Forty-third Battalion of Virginia Cavalry, otherwise known as Col. John S. Mosby's Rangers, on September 15, 1864, just over ninety days after the battle destroyed the family home. Young Danne served out the balance of the war with Mosby's command, and was active in veterans' activities with the Rangers. See Williamson, *Mosby's Rangers*, 483; Keen and Mewborn, *43rd Battalion Virginia Cavalry*, 311. In the meantime, the store was rebuilt a few yards from its original location and the Danne family resumed their role in the community. A few years later, Danne married one of Charles Trevilian's daughters, and moved into the Trevilian home along the railroad tracks in 1873.

128. Brooks, *Butler and His Cavalry*, 252–53.

══ 8 ══

Sheridan's Retreat to White House Landing from Trevilian Station

I regret my inability to carry out your instructions.

As his troopers precipitously retreated from the Bloody Angle, Sheridan realized that he had to break off the engagement. His exhausted men, nearly out of ammunition and rations, and with a large number of wounded men and prisoners to tend to, were not going to reach Charlottesville. Furthermore, he had no idea where to find Hunter's army and concluded that it would be impossible for him to make a junction with Black Dave Hunter and his command. There was no choice. He had to withdraw.[1]

Sheridan mounted his horse and rode back to Trevilian Station. There, he ordered supper and invited David Gregg to join him. When the quiet Pennsylvanian, one of Sheridan's favorite campfire companions, arrived, the two men had tea and toast and made plans for the Union troops' withdrawal.[2] Many details needed to be worked out. They had hundreds of seriously wounded men to transport, details of surgeons had to be selected to stay behind to tend to those too badly hurt to travel, the order of march had be determined, and the route mapped. Correspondent Nathaniel Davidson of the *New York Herald*, traveling with Sheridan's headquarters, observed that the Federal commander acted "with as much coolness and absence of excitement as though he were about to pursue an enemy instead of withdrawing from his front." As the necessary arrangements were carried out, Little Phil "took his tea and quietly smoked his cigar."[3]

The decision to withdraw was a bitter pill for Sheridan to swallow. None of the objectives of the raid had been met. He had not made a junction with Hunter, he had not rendered the Virginia Central Railroad unusable, and Hunter was not going to be able to reinforce the Army of the Potomac.

The march back would be no lark, either. The area had been largely stripped of forage, the citizenry was hostile, and Sheridan had a large contingent of wounded men, prisoners, and runaway slaves, called "contrabands," in his care that would slow the march. Not surprisingly, Sheridan apologized to Grant: "I regret my inability to carry out your instructions."[4]

Sheridan's biggest obstacles were the wounded men and the prisoners, of which there were nearly 500. About 100 Union wounded, along with a large number of the enemy's, who had to be left behind in the charge of brave Federal surgeons. These brave surgeons received a trip to Libby Prison for their troubles. Lt. Samuel M. Powell, the thirty-six-year-old assistant surgeon of the First New Jersey Cavalry, volunteered to stay behind, prompting an officer of the regiment to recall, "he nobly remained with [the wounded men], preferring rather to brave the horror and misery of Libby Prison than desert his wounded comrades." Powell was a hero—Hampton's troopers quickly captured him, and the doctor was imprisoned in Libby for a time. Powell was then transferred to Andersonville, where he contracted dysentery and died on August 8, 1864, less than sixty days after his selfless decision to stay behind and care for the wounded.[5]

Sheridan left three hospitals behind, along with medicines, liquor, and food, including bread, sugar, and coffee. Dr. Robert Rae, the surgeon of the First New York Dragoons, also stayed behind, in charge of the field hospital at the train station. He recorded, "No sooner had Sheridan departed than the rebels, regardless of all rules of civilized warfare, looted the hospital. They at once removed most of my clothing, even to my boots; took the blankets, rubber ponchos, and the clothing from the wounded, acting so like savages that two Confederate officers . . . who were under my care, were disgusted." The two wounded Southerners freely expressed their disapproval of the conduct of their comrades, to no avail. The looting continued.[6] Other soldiers, too badly injured to be moved, were left in various houses in the care of the local populace. An enlisted man volunteered to stay and care for the dying Col. William Sackett, whose suffering finally ended on June 13. The enlisted angel of mercy earned a trip to Andersonville for his loyalty.[7]

Ambulances and wagons, gathered in the surrounding countryside, carried those wounded men who could travel. "There were antiquated family carriages and buggies, old stage coaches, carts, and in fact, everything obtainable on wheels."[8] Sheridan's dead, sadly, had to be left unburied as a result of the hasty withdrawal. The Federals left their dead to the tender mercies of the hostile local population and the benevolence of the enemy.

Those Confederates captured during the fighting further swelled the ranks of the column. Nearly 2,000 contrabands also joined the line of march.[9] The return route would be quite lengthy, and Sheridan's column had to move slowly in order to accommodate the dismounted prisoners following along behind. The march had to be slow out of consideration for the wounded men, for whom each rut in the road or bump could cause agony. Sheridan knew that the return march would not be the frolic that the march to Trevilian Station had been.

As Sheridan contemplated the options, he ordered his troopers to make campfires as if they intended to remain in place, masking the wagon train's head start.[10] Some of the Federals searched for wounded or missing friends, or took a few minutes to say good-bye to their dead companions.[11] The First Pennsylvania Cavalry of Davies's brigade had not been involved in the fighting on either day, although it had accompanied Davies's command to the front on the twelfth. That evening, the First Pennsylvania guarded the extreme right flank and came under heavy artillery fire while the rest of the division prepared to march.[12] Just before pulling out, Williston took one of his twelve pounders up to the skirmish line and "poured forty rounds of canister into the ranks of the enemy, causing them to howl most bitterly." A Confederate dash nearly captured the gun, but Merritt's Regulars and "the canister were too much for them, and they slunk back to their holes."[13] The Confederate gunners, of course, responded in kind, and for a brief time, the guns of both sides blazed in the gathering darkness.

One of Devin's men recalled that "the enemy amused us by throwing numerous shells along our line—appearing like a celebration with sky-rockets, but doing us no damage."[14] Lt. Robert C. Wallace of the Fifth Michigan Cavalry, serving on Torbert's staff, recalled standing among a group of officers behind the railroad embankment near Trevilian Station as enemy artillery shells arced overhead. A shell dropped nearby, striking a rail directly in front of Wallace and exploding. Ducking to avoid the rain of shell fragments, Wallace and his companions escaped unharmed. "Only for the protection of that rail, some of us would have been wiped out," wrote the Michigander.[15]

Around midnight, Sheridan's primary column moved out, with the First

Maine Cavalry leading the way. The Federals marched up the Marquis Road to Clayton's Store and on to Carpenter's Ford.[16] An Ohioan of Davies's brigade noted, "After midnight the withdrawal was skillfully accomplished and with entire secrecy, and a retrograde march commenced, which in some respects was more painful than anything we had before or would hereafter experience."[17] "Oh what a tiresome job it is to march all night. It is a job that is not craved every day," complained Sgt. Lewis Fitch.[18]

The First New Jersey Cavalry brought up the rear of the column, moving as quietly as possible. As the rear guard, the Jerseymen moved out near dawn.[19] A member of the Ninth New York Cavalry noted in his diary, "Commenced moving the train back, march all night, some of the enemy follow."[20] Sheridan's rear guard did some minor skirmishing; trooper James F. Wood of the Seventh Virginia Cavalry recorded in his diary that "Today was fought the fight of Nelson's Bridge across the N. Anna River. Had my spur shot out of shape." Three members of the 7th Virginia were slightly wounded in the fracas.[21]

Most of the Northern horse soldiers camped on the south side of the North Anna River, four to six miles from the June 11 battlefield. They had stolen a few hours' march on the enemy. Elements of Devin's brigade continued on all the way to the North Branch of the North Anna, with the rest of the vast Federal force following early the next morning, filling the area between the two branches of the river.

Some of Sheridan's men fanned out, picketing the long lines surrounding his wagon train and guarding the foraging parties spread out along the Federal front. A detachment of the First Maine Cavalry, advancing to take up position along the picket lines, was "furiously attacked by a party of guerrillas." The Confederates wounded the man commanding the vidette post, and several men lost their horses to the stinging assault. However, the remainder of the First Maine fled to the safety of the regiment's main camp and brought in a large haul of forage.[22]

Another trooper of the First Maine, sent out on picket duty, fell victim to sheer exhaustion. His sergeant woke the sleeping sentinel. Pickets who fell asleep on picket duty committed serious breaches of discipline that normally warranted severe punishment. However, the picket "was a good soldier, and the sergeant, knowing he had been without sleep for two nights, felt like excusing him, and as none but the two knew of it, the secret was locked into their own breasts, where it remains to this day. And it may be said that the sergeant never regretted that action."[23] Lt. Samuel Cormany of the Sixteenth Pennsylvania wrote that he and his men were "a pretty tired lot of Boys."[24] Sheridan recognized that after two days of long, hard, bloody fighting, his exhausted men needed rest.[25] Their mounts, which had not had food or forage for nearly forty-eight hours, were unsaddled and turned out to graze. They had a pleasant respite.

The Northerners resumed their foraging. Cormany noted that he and his men had a sumptuous turkey dinner that evening, after he and his men spent the day laying "around resting."[26] "The violence & brutality which characterized the greater part of both Officers and men made a most painful impression on my mind," commented a distressed officer of the Fourth New York Cavalry, "which created a feeling akin to disgust for the discipline of the Cavalry Corps."[27] The unhappy citizenry took potshots at the marauding Federal foragers, causing discomfort among the Northerners. An officer of the First Massachusetts Cavalry reported home that "the foraging had to be done by squadrons, the bushwhackers were so thick."[28] Late that afternoon, the long, slow-moving column advanced through the dry heat for about twelve miles to Twyman's Store.[29] One of the Yankee troopers noted that "our prospects were not very bright, and as our men and horses were completely played out, we went into camp and remained there for the night."[30]

After going into camp for the night, the troopers got their first chance to relax in two days. "Having stopped to rest and eat the first meal in twenty four hours, and having finished the meal and found a nice shade tree with a beautiful grassy plot under it and a bird warbling sweet cadences over my head," wrote an officer of the First Pennsylvania, "my trusty old war horse a few feet off satisfying his hunger on the tender young grass—my mind being at ease, naturally enough, reverted to an anxious wife and two dear children in my far off northern home."[31] The Yankee horse soldiers spent a quiet night.

As the column slowly marched, billows of dust made both men and animals miserable. Edgar Strang of the Sixth Pennsylvania Cavalry recalled, "It was hard to tell what color we were or whether our uniforms were blue or grey, for we were covered with about a week's accumulation of the sacred soil of Virginia, and it was hard for a man to recognize his tent-mate."[32] The clouds of dust, towering high into the sky, made tracking Sheridan's retreat easy. The long wagon train offered an attractive target for Hampton's horse soldiers, and constantly Sheridan had to be on his guard.

Word of Sheridan's repulse reached Hunter on the 13th. Although "Sheridan had met with a reverse at Louisa Court House," Hunter decided to continue his advance because "he had assurances there was no considerable force of the enemy in or near Lynchburg."[33] Even though Hampton had prevented the junction of the two forces, Hunter intended to continue his mission to destroy the massive supply depot at the crucial railroad junction town.

Hampton's exhausted men also suffered greatly throughout the raid. Although they learned of Sheridan's withdrawal soon after daylight, they did not pursue the Northern horse soldiers aggressively.[34] Butler summed up the plight of his soldiers succinctly: "Pursuit by my command was out of the question. We had been engaged in this bloody encounter from the beginning without food or rest for either men or horses, in the broiling sun of a hot June day, and recuperation was absolutely necessary. As it was, I was not relieved and did not withdraw from my lines until 2 o'clock on the morning of the 13th, and in the meantime had to care for the wounded and bury the dead."[35] They left their wounded to the tender mercies of the local women, who were left in the Green Spring area, "where there is plenty of everything besides the patriotic attention of the ladies who had already crowded our hospitals with good things before we left."[36]

One Federal trooper wrote, "The rebels were so badly used up that they did not venture outside of their breastworks when Sheridan withdrew toward the North Anna."[37] Another observed that Hampton didn't "wish to send their cavalry after us in force."[38] "The enemy did not attempt to follow or to annoy us in any way, having been so badly cut up and beaten during the last engagement," reported one of Merritt's Regulars.[39] That night, the Confederates drew three double handfuls of corn per horse, the first grain their horses had eaten since June 8.[40]

On the morning of Monday June 13, a Richmond newspaper proudly reported the success of the battle at Trevilian Station: "A dispatch just received from Gen. Hampton, states that he defeated the enemy's cavalry near Trevilians with heavy loss, capturing 500 prisoners besides their wounded. The enemy retreated in confusion, apparently by the same route he came, leaving his dead and wounded on the field."[41] Fitz Lee also checked in, writing, "Sheridan was defeated yesterday afternoon at Trevilian Depot by our two divisions, and retreated during the night, abandoning his dead and wounded, in the direction he came." Fitz continued, "I am moving along railroad toward Hanover Junction, which place I will reach tomorrow morning. Hampton is moving between me and the North Anna, and expects to intersect my line of march at Beaver Dam." Ominously, he concluded, "We hope to intercept the enemy as he crosses the Fredericksburg Railroad."[42]

A pleased Robert E. Lee sent a telegram congratulating Hampton for the hard-fought victory at Trevilian Station. Capt. Abner Mulligan of the Fifth South Carolina, whose squadron fired the first shots of the great two-day battle, claimed that Sheridan "left in the night, leaving his dead & wounded in the field. . . . I do not think we will be able to over take him as our horses are all tired down."[43]

Most of the Confederates spent the day ministering to the wounded, burying the dead, and tending to their horses. Hampton sent Col. Bradley T. Johnson and the 250 men of the First Maryland Cavalry and the four guns of the Baltimore Light Artillery on an extended raid toward Baltimore in an attempt to try to capture Lincoln.[44] While the Marylanders set off on their ride, a few of the gray-clad horse soldiers rode over the battlefield near Trevilian Station. One commented that "the Trevilian battlefield . . . resembled a hard fought infantry battle."[45] The Ogg family's handsome home served as a field hospital. The dining room table, covered with a blanket, served as an operating table. Weary surgeons toiled by the light of dim oil lamps, their primitive instruments working on the torn bodies of the men carried there. Straw placed on the floor soaked up some of the blood spilled, but the floor remains stained to this day.[46]

Pvt. Noble Brooks of Cobb's Legion visited the battlefield, writing, "as I rode over the field saw a great many dead—mostly all shot in the head and breast and been stript by our men a very barbarous act. Saw Col. McAllister of the Seventh Ga. Cav. lying by the road dead and squad of men digging his grave."[47] The colonel was buried in his uniform alongside the Gordonsville Road, about a mile to the east of Netherland Tavern. The spot was marked, so that the fallen officer's body could be recovered later.[48] Sgt. Charles Hansell of the Twentieth Battalion Georgia Cavalry drew grave-digging duty for the first time. He wrote, "The tools we had were very poor and the ground very hard and rocky; so the grave was not very deep and it was hard to shovel the dirt right back on them with nothing like a coffin to keep it off their bodies."[49]

Many wounded Southerners who fell into Federal hands the day before were recovered after Sheridan pulled out. Pvt. Edward Wells of the Charleston Light Dragoons was one such trooper. When Sheridan withdrew "during the night after the second day, they were compelled to leave me & most of their own wounded behind. After a time I managed to reach the Jackson Hospital at Richmond."[50] Maj. Ned Anderson of the Seventh Georgia Cavalry had a similar experience. Wounded in battle on June 11, Anderson escaped during the confusion of the Federal withdrawal and made his way back to his regiment. The Seventh Georgia fought hard at Trevilian Station, losing 179 men captured during the two days of the engagement.[51] Other Confederates scoured the dense woods for booty, finding a large haul of Spencer carbines, which they adopted as their own.[52]

A wounded officer of the Cobb Legion, lying in a private home near Green Springs, noted, "while I saw much of war and human suffering there, I also witnessed the devotion and heroism of those angels of mercy and loving kindness, the lovely women—mothers and daughters of that far famed Green Spring neighborhood—to our boys and our holy cause." He continued, "their sacrifice of themselves, their time and all they possessed was complete, lavishly and charmingly bestowed, while they wept because they had no more to give and could not do more to alleviate pain and suffering."[53]

Late in the day, the Southern horse soldiers finally pursued Sheridan. Hampton's division, its strength reduced by the loss of Johnson's First Maryland, followed Sheridan's route. Hampton remained on the south bank of the North Anna River, closely shadowing the Federals across the river and protecting the Virginia Central Railroad from further threat. Hampton kept his force interposed between Sheridan and the bulk of the Army of the Potomac.[54] Fitz Lee's division marched to Freedrickshall Station on the Virginia Central and encamped about two miles from the train station.[55] "As [Sheridan] had a pontoon train with him which enabled him to cross the river at any point, I was forced to keep on the south of the rivers, so as to interpose my command between him and Grant's army, which he was seeking to rejoin," wrote Hampton in his official report of the Trevilian raid. He continued, "During several days while we marched on parallel lines I constantly offered battle, which he studiously declined."[56]

The lack of fodder and supplies plagued the Confederates just as badly as it did their Northern foes. A frustrated Colonel Waring recorded in his diary on the 14th, "Our horses came in last night to find nothing to eat. This morning we sent out & got plenty of clover but no corn. Mr. Sheridan gets away from us without further fight by reason of the exhausted condition of our horses."[57]

As the two forces moved slowly back toward the main lines of their parent armies, Lee and Grant set their major strategic gambits into motion. Grant decided to act and followed his strategic plan. He recognized that supplies were growing scarce in Richmond and that the sources for additional supplies lay either in Union hands or were cut off by Union forces. Sheridan's raid had successfully drawn off Hampton's and Fitz Lee's cavalry from his front. On June 11, Grant ordered Meade's army to move toward a crossing of the James River. On June 13, the Army of the Potomac moved out. Its lead elements crossed the James River on the 14th.

A New Jersey infantry brigade commander reported home, "Before morning our Corps had slipped from under the noses of the enemy and were on our way to [Windmill Point, on the James River]." The same officer continued, "I have no doubt that as soon as we are all across and ready we will move up this side of the river. . . . We know nothing of our intended movements. But on looking at the map, we can, like yourselves, made a pretty good guess. Genl. Grant is good at swinging round."[58] The Confederates discovered the Army of the Potomac's empty trenches on the morning of the 13th. The Northern army had vanished.[59]

After safely crossing the river, the Army of the Potomac linked with Maj. Gen. Benjamin F. Butler's Army of the James. The combined force began moving toward the critical railroad junction town of Petersburg, twenty-five miles southwest of Richmond. Petersburg was only lightly held by a small but tenacious Confederate force under command of Gen. P. G. T. Beauregard. If Grant could win the race to Petersburg, he would cut off Lee's army from its railroad lines of supply and force the evacuation of Richmond. The brilliant plan was foiled only by poor execution by Grant's subordinate commanders and the adroit tactics of Beauregard, whose stubborn defense bought time for the rest of the Confederate army to reach the defenses of Petersburg. Although Sheridan had lost the Battle of Trevilian Station, the long and brutal raid drew off the two best divisions of Lee's cavalry. Grant stole a march across the James River.[60]

Likewise, Robert E. Lee was not quiet. Hunter's army inched toward the crucial railroad junction and supply depot at Lynchburg. If Hunter captured Lynchburg and its supplies, he would cut off Lee's primary source of supplies. In response, Lee dispatched Lt. Gen. Jubal A. Early's Second Corps of the Army of Northern Virginia, the veterans of Stonewall Jackson's Army of the Valley, to bolster Breckinridge's small garrison at Lynchburg. Setting out before dawn on June 13, Early's men followed a portion of the route of the Virginia Central. The bold gamble stripped the Army of Northern Virginia of an entire infantry corps. Lee's reputation as a bold gambler would be enhanced if it succeeded. If it failed, the war might end disastrously. Hampton's victory at Trevilian Station had saved the Virginia Central from demolition and left it available for use by Lee's army. Early's men reached Lynchburg just in time to repulse Hunter's assaults on the beleaguered garrison at the railroad junction.[61]

The retreat was sheer misery for Sheridan's weary horse soldiers. One of Davies's men stated, "From sunrise to sunset the long cavalcade of canvas-covered vehicles toiled along with jar and jolt, enveloped in clouds of dust and eliciting from the wretched sufferers a continuous succession of groans and heart-rending outcries." He continued, "The excitement and dangers of the battle is over, the resultant suffering is quickly removed and left to proper care. Our brave and humane old Colonel had occasion to ride forward along the line of the moving ambulances. He returned actually pale with suppressed excitement, and exclaimed, 'My God! No consideration would tempt me to go over that course again and see the sights and hear the groans that I have this day seen and heard.' "[62]

With Devin's brigade leading, Sheridan's column marched ten miles before camping on the 14th. After a tense but undisturbed day, Sheridan bivouacked at Shady Grove Church, three miles from Todd's Tavern. One Federal trooper wrote, "Hampton was reported as making for us, but was careful not to disturb us." An exhausted member of the Sixth Pennsylvania Cavalry recalled that after dismounting at the church, "as I laid down under those fine old trees I wondered if such a congregation had ever gathered under their shade before."[63] "Drew one and one-half days rations," complained an Ohio trooper in his diary, "and ordered to make them last four days."[64] Roving Northern pickets found Maj. William B. Darlington of the Eighteenth Pennsylvania Cavalry in a local house recuperating from the amputation of a leg. Darlington was horribly wounded at the Battle of Todd's Tavern on May 7, 1864. The Yankee troopers were surprised to find him, as he had been left for dead on the battlefield. They bundled Darlington into an ambulance and carried him away.[65]

That same day, near Frederickshall Station, Hampton reported to army headquarters. He noted, "Enemy camped last night near Twyman's Store. Route this morning not yet ascertained. Portions of railroad near Trevilian destroyed. You shall hear regularly." The South Carolinian concluded with the critical portion of his dispatch: "We need supplies"; shortages were plaguing his march and limiting the effectiveness of his pursuit.[66]

He also scribbled a letter to his sister Mary Fisher Hampton, known as Fisher. Writing on the captured stationery of a trooper of the Sixth Pennsylvania Cavalry, Hampton reported, "As you may well imagine I have had no time of late to write to you. I have not even changed my clothes for a week, nor have I had them off during much of that time. But though I am not very clean, I am well, in spite of dirt. And again have to thank God for his merciful protection of me and mine." He continued, "I am deeply thankful that he was pleased to give me success, for I was greatly concerned at the responsibility of my position." Praising the performance of Butler's South Carolinians, he stated, "The cavalry has never had harder fights or achieved greater success than on this expedition & I am very much gratified that they have done so well under me. But I do not seek the command of this corps & will not have it unless I can have full command of it." He concluded, "The Yankees are retreating very much cut up & down. I have lost heavily but my men are in fine spirits. If they had rations I would push on."[67]

Pausing near Garrett's Store, Hampton fired off the day's second report to Robert E. Lee. He informed Lee that the "Enemy retreating toward Fredericksburg, reported in very bad condition, wagons and ambulances full of wounded. I am forced to pause for supplies. Will move as soon as possible."[68] Shortly after noon, while still at Garrett's Store, he sent a third telegram, noting, "It is a great regret to me that I am forced to halt, because the men are out of rations. They have borne this cheerfully, in some instances for forty-eight hours, but I cannot follow up the pursuit of the enemy when it carries me from all supplies. If he had kept down the river I would have attacked him again." He concluded, "I am borrowing some rations in the country, and if enough can be had for one day's supply I shall push on tonight in the hope of striking the enemy in flank. My men are jaded but in fine spirits."[69]

The next day, Lt. Col. William Stokes reported to his family, "We are all completely worn out by hard fighting and forced marches both day and night, but all are in fine spirits and willing to keep on. Our rations gave out and we were forty-eight hours without any."[70] Likewise, Fitz Lee noted, "We followed as fast as our jaded condition would allow but could not bring [Sheridan] to bay. His trail was strewn with dead horses, which, as fast as they gave out, were shot."[71]

Col. Richard Dulany, commanding the Laurel Brigade in Rosser's absence, recounted, "There is scarcely a family along [Sheridan's] line of march left one pound of meal or meat—a chicken, cow, or hog. In many instances after taking all they could carry away, they destroyed every particle of clothing in the house. I think orders will be given to take no prisoners, hereafter, when found plundering defenseless women and children." Some of Dulany's scouts, shadowing Sheridan's line of march, found several Yankee troopers plundering a house. The scouts killed three of them and carried the others away as prisoners. A fourth Federal would have been shot, too, but for his quick thought to grab a child to use as a shield. Instead, the quick-thinking trooper started on his long journey to Andersonville.[72]

The grateful residents, whose houses had been plundered by the blue-clad foragers, often opened their pantries to the hungry Southerners, offering what little bread and milk they could spare. "God bless them and their descendants," wrote a grateful member of the Sixth South Carolina Cavalry.[73] The regimental chaplain of the First New York Dragoons noted, "we . . . have lived like kings for fifteen days. In fact, the boys prefer being their own commissaries on such expeditions. We have had flour and meal for pancakes, ham and bacon in any quantity, chickens, pigs, and sheep, together with various knicknacks in the shape of honey, apple-butter, preserves, butter, and cheese. Our greatest lack was time to cook, being rushed through as fast as the condition of our wounded would permit."[74] The foraging was systematic, with parties of fifty to a hundred men sent out to call on the people along the route of march and "politely invite them to exemplify their wonted 'Southern Hospitality' by ministering to our wants. Of course they could not resist so polite an invitation, and our forage sacks were always filled with hams, bacon, poultry, potatoes, and the like."[75]

The bounty for the Federals, however, often made it difficult for the Confederates to find food for themselves and horses. A trooper of the Laurel Brigade scrawled in his diary: "Drew two crackers and a little meat; nothing for the horses. Marched all day on the county roads; borrowed a few rations from another command for us. No corn tonight and not a particle of grass."[76]

Owing to the intense heat and unrelenting thick dust, which nearly suffocated the men, Sheridan's men suffered. "At times we could not see ten feet ahead, or even distinguish our file leader. It is also true that as the men perspire the dust adheres so freely that except for the dissimilarity of features, we can scarcely tell a white man from a negro." "Dust, dust, dust, nothing but dust," groused one of Davies's men, "The air is full of it all the time. The direction of the column is seen a mile ahead by the dust in the air. Our ears, eyes, noses and mouths are full. We are coated with it. It lays in winnows in all wrinkles and cracks."[77]

The men were also realistic: "But then we should not complain when we think of what our poor wounded boys have to endure on such a journey."[78] When he wrote his full report of 1864's campaigns nearly two years later, Sheridan recalled, "On my march from Trevilian . . . we halted at intervals during each day to dress the wounded and refresh them as much as possible. Nothing could exceed the cheerfulness exhibited by them, hauled as they were in old buggies, carts, ammunition wagons, &c., no word of complaint was heard. I saw on the line of march men with wounded legs driving, while those with one disabled arm were using the other to whip up the animals."[79]

Sheridan marched slowly across the countryside toward the supply depot at White House Landing on the Pamunkey River. One sight left an especially strong impression on the minds of the retreating Federal troopers. On June 15 they passed through the ravaged battlefield at Spotsylvania Court House and bivouacked near Guiney's Station. Observing the tremendous destruction wrought by the lengthy battle, Sanford vividly remembered, "In many places trees of ten or twelve inches in diameter had been cut in two by the hailstorm of bullets, and the smaller growth looked as if it had swept by a cyclone. Fire had also broken out in the timber and we saw many instances where the seriously wounded had been burned to death in the flames."[80]

As they marched, the men of the Reserve Brigade saw many unburied bodies strewn about the Spotsylvania battlefield.[81] An officer of the Fourth Pennsylvania Cavalry recorded, "here were myriad graves of soldiers, so shallow that it seemed the sod had just been lifted to receive them. Thirty or forty bodies had been consigned to this hasty sepulchre at one time and in one place. Hands, feet and portions of the head sometimes protruded from the ground. Locks of hair were seen exposed, the winds tossing them at their own reckless caprice." He continued, "Sometimes a portion of the tattered uniform was seen, through openings in the ground. A hand now and then was clearly visible, from which the flesh had been devoured or decomposed—a skeleton hand without, attached still to the bloated and decaying flesh of the body within the tomb." One of J. I. Gregg's soldiers, bold and curious all at the same time, probed one of the partially uncovered skulls with the point of his sabre. The man raised the sabre above his head. "The decomposition not having been completed, "the brains in a dark stream of putrid corruption, ran down the glittering blade, over his hand, and into his coatsleeve." The horrified soldier "was at once prostrated with a deathly sickness, at the revolting and ghastly spectacle which he had evoked from the sepulchre."[82]

"We passed through the Spotsylvania Court House, and over the ground where a month previous thousands of the bravest men of North and South had laid down their lives in defense of the cause that was dear to their hearts," reflected Saddler Edgar Strang of the Sixth Pennsylvania Cavalry. "As we halted for an hour or more it gave us an opportunity to see the effect of the terrible conflict that had raged over that ground; behind the enemy's breastworks many trees, as large around as a man's body, could be seen that had been cut nearly in two by the bullets of our brave boys, as they made charge after charge upon the rebel works," he continued. Strang concluded, "As we passed out among the graves we could not help but think that truly it was an honor to rest in a grave on such a battlefield as that."[83] Not all had the same reaction, though. An officer of the First Massachusetts noted, "Everything had the gloom of death for miles, and everywhere were mounds, where men lay in their last resting-places. I tell you, it was a sad sight. Not one human being did we see all the time. I never want to go there again."[84]

Hampton's command left at sunrise on the clear, cool morning of June 15, crossing the North Anna at De Jarnette's Ford. The Southern horse soldiers marched through Chilesburg and Centreville to Cane's farm, finding a beautiful field of clover. They turned their horses out to graze. Finally

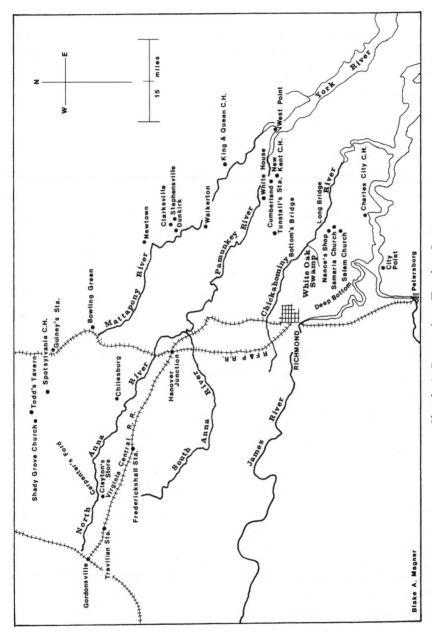

Sheridan's Retreat from Trevilian Station

Blake A. Magner

receiving rations, the Confederates ate their fill, their meals supplemented by the local populace. Colonel Waring bitterly noted in his diary, "The army, if the Yankees only knew it, is better fed & better clothed than ever. We get not only enough but can actually help with our rations the poor creatures whom the Yankees have robbed. Starving our women and children will not end the war."[85] The exertions of the campaign devastated Hampton's horses, too. With hundreds of newly dismounted troopers trudging along behind the body of the Confederate column, Lt. Robert Aldrich, adjutant of the Sixth South Carolina Cavalry, organized three companies of these dismounted men into what they facetiously named "The Stud Horse Battalion," which struggled to keep pace in the choking dust.[86]

Thursday, June 16, dawned cool and pleasant. Sheridan's column covered another nineteen miles that day, moving through Bowling Green and crossing the Mattapony River and camping near Mattacocy Creek. However, the campsite was "the worst camp that we ever had," grumped Sgt. Lewis Fitch of the Fifth Michigan.[87] "Everything is quiet," noted Michigander Frank Grommon in his diary.[88] Lt. Charles Veil of the First U.S. Cavalry recalled, "The enemy were desperate and saucy by this time. They followed and skirmished with us all day. We had to keep a strong rear guard and continual firing was going on. When we halted for the night we threw up barricades of fence rails, logs and such." He continued, "after we had halted for the night and my regiment was holding the road, I did not feel satisfied with the way things looked and rode to the right through a piece of woods where I discovered about a regiment of Rebel cavalry in a field."

Spurring back in great haste, Veil got too far out in front and was visible between the lines. The Federal troopers manning the barricades did not recognize the fleeing lieutenant in the gathering dusk and opened fire on him. Fortunately, they missed. Veil commented, "Why the Rebels didn't open too, I never could account for, but I got in all right and our right flank was looked after."[89]

Three Confederate scouts discovered Sheridan's rear guard grazing their horses in a field of clover. One of the scouts proposed that they dash into the field and capture a horse apiece. They made their dash successfully, but only one managed to lead out a horse. One had to be abandoned, and pursuing Yankee bullets shot another. Although the losses to the Rebel scouts buzzing around the rear and flanks of the long Federal column were light, the presence of these annoyances meant that the weary Yankees had to remain alert every moment of every day. The constant vigilance only added to their growing sense of weariness.[90]

Not all of the Northern horse soldiers had a bad day. "Lay 'round till 9 A.M.—got a fine mess of Cherries. So did lots of the boys," reported Cormany.[91] That day, the 16th Pennsylvania dismounted and gave their horses to the wretched Confederate prisoners stumbling along behind the Federal horsemen.[92]

Sheridan took pity on the Confederate prisoners accompanying his retreating column. Forced to follow both horses and wagons, and encased in billowing clouds of choking dust stirred up by thousands of hooves and wagon wheels, these poor wretches suffered mightily. On the 16th, the prisoners arrived at the plantation of a Dr. Butler along the Mattapony River. They were left under a strong guard. The prisoners, many of whom were "red with dust, weary, hungry and dry," were assured that they could have all of the privileges and hospitality their accommodating host could bestow. Capt. Theodore Bean of Torbert's staff noticed that the grateful Southerners were soon "a thoroughly washed and jolly set of fellows who were making the best possible use of all they could avail themselves of, and it was evident that the doctor's family were doing all they could for their Confederate friends."[93]

That day, Sheridan finally decided to communicate with Meade in an effort to locate the body of the Army of the Potomac. He scrawled an initial account of the expedition on the 16th, reporting his failure to comply with Grant's orders and asking for rations.[94] Sheridan detailed twenty-two men of the Sixth U.S. Cavalry under command of Lt. Daniel Madden to cross the river. Lt. Col. John B. Howard, the chief quartermaster, Capt. Thomas W. Moore, of Sheridan's staff, and Nathaniel Davidson, the correspondent for the *New York Herald*, accompanied them.

The little party set off as the first streaks of dawn crept across the morning sky on the 16th. The small force arrived at the town of Bowling Green, five miles south of Guinea's Station. The small force charged through the town at a gallop and stopped just outside to secure a local guide. After a short period of adjustment to their new guide, the column marched another ten miles. They spotted a saddled cavalry horse alongside the road and saw two Rebel troopers scurrying toward the woods. The advance guard opened fire on the fleeing graybacks and confiscated the horse. Another shot rang out near Newtown, about halfway to West Point and southwest of Bowling Green. The whole Northern party charged, raising such clouds of dust that they could not see where they were going.

Arriving in the town, the Federals captured Capt. A. Garnett, brother of the late Confederate Brig. Gen. Richard Garnett, killed during Pickett's Charge at the Battle of Gettysburg nearly a year earlier. Captain Garnett, a quartermaster, bled profusely from a pistol ball wound to his arm. He told his captors that he had been trying to reach Richmond, and informed the Yankee troopers that Meade's army had crossed the James. They brought Garnett along after they bound up his wounds. The captain reported that the bridges and ferryboats across the Pamunkey at Dunkirk had been destroyed. He also reported that Meade had abandoned White House Landing as his principal supply depot. The blue-clad troopers went a few miles farther, capturing additional prisoners, who confirmed Garnett's intelligence. Thus rebuffed, Lieutenant Madden decided that Sheridan needed this information. The little command backtracked until it found the main body of the Federal column near Newtown.[95]

That night, Sheridan dispatched the entire Sixth U.S. Cavalry on a similar expedition. The regimental commander, Capt. Ira W. Claflin, led the excursion. Maj. George "Sandy" Forsyth, another of Sheridan's staff officers, accompanied them. The Regulars followed the north bank of the Mattapony River and marched through Newtown, Clarksville, and Walkerton. They followed the river through King and Queen County. At Walkerton, the fifty blue-clad troopers clashed with a small group of home guards, described by the correspondent of the New York Herald as "highwaymen." The guerrillas ambushed the Northern horse soldiers, opening fire on them as they crossed a narrow bridge. One Regular was killed, and the rest fell back, with Captain Claflin commencing "some flanking that even Grant need not have been ashamed of." The column reached Stephensville, engaging in running skirmishing as it went.

When Claflin realized that the several hundred guerrillas outnumbered his force, he tried another dodge. Returning to Walkerton, he found the head of Custer's advance. Howard, Forsyth, and Davidson attempted a waterborne journey. Accompanied by two enlisted Regulars, they started for West Point, thirty miles away. Forsyth and Howard periodically spelled the hard-rowing troopers, but the tide was against them, and their progress was slow. Their skiff finally reached its destination at noon on Saturday, June 18. The happy Northerners opened telegraphic communications with General Meade, who finally got his first intimations of the whereabouts of Sheridan's columns.[96]

On the 17th, Sheridan's command marched to Walkerton on the Pamunkey and camped on a large plantation along the river. Lieutenant Cormany had a thoroughly unpleasant day. That morning, he took command of the dismounted contingent of his regiment, the 16th Pennsylvania, with orders to march them on the flanks of the artillery. "Is a Bore! Indescribably hot and dusty," he complained.[97]

The First Maine Cavalry stopped at a local house for corn. While feeding, the Maine men spotted a mounted force approaching quickly across the field. Since the approaching force was between the Maine men and the rest of the column, they "could only make preparations to do the best we could." The approaching force stopped and deployed into line of battle, advancing at the trot. The two mounted forces maneuvered for position a bit before "we discovered we were friends, and upon a closer acquaintance, members of the same Brigade." The thick dust had made it impossible to tell friend from foe.[98]

On the night of the 17th, the Ninth New York Cavalry had picket duty. Confederate troopers harassing Sheridan's rear mortally wounded Charles H. Williams of Company D of the Ninth New York while he manned the picket lines. He died on July 5.[99] Other elements foraged. A young woman greeted a group of foragers by drawing a revolver. She tried to shoot the Yankee troopers raiding her farm but was unable to cock the gun. The laughing blue-clad horse soldiers quickly disarmed her and helped themselves to "all of the forage both for our selves & horses that we wanted."[100]

Also on June 17, Robert E. Lee informed Hampton that Grant's army had crossed the James River. He instructed Brig. Gen. John Chambliss and his brigade of Rooney Lee's division as well as the independent cavalry brigade of Col. Martin W. Gary to report to Hampton and cooperate in crushing Sheridan. The next day, Lee told the South Carolinian, "If Sheridan escapes you and gets to his transports at the White House you must lose no time in moving your entire command to our right near Petersburg. Keep yourself thoroughly advised of his movements and intentions as far as practicable."[101]

On the 18th, Sheridan's slow but steady march continued to West Point in King and Queen County, near the spot where Col. Ulric Dahlgren had been killed that spring. A member of the Ninth New York Cavalry noted in his diary, "passed where Col. Dahlgren was killed, saw the grave in which he was buried."[102] An officer commented, "King and Queen Court House is now one mass of ruins, burned by Kilpatrick in retaliation for Colonel Dahlgren's murder. The people of the South are beginning to understand that such wanton acts of barbarism will not go unnoticed."[103]

Confederate scouts continued to buzz around the fringes of the vast blue horde as it snaked its way through King and Queen County. Along with three other scouts, Capt. Thomas N. Conrad "was hanging on the flanks of Sheridan's column capturing and killing the stragglers who left the main line for the purpose of plundering defenseless citizens." Upon entering the back yard of a gorgeous brick plantation house, Conrad spotted several horses tied to the fence. He asked an old black man if the horses belonged to friend or foe. Even though the old man said "Our people," Conrad knew Yankee horses and accoutrements when he saw them.

Two of the Southerners dismounted and ran through the back door of the house, while the other two took position at the front door. Soon a pistol shot rang out, and two Federals rushed out the front door. Conrad drew a bead with his pistol and killed one of the Yankees. "Instantly we dismounted and rushed through the front entrance, and as fast as a Yankee showed himself one of us shot him, until of the seven all but one were killed or mortally wounded. It was all done within five minutes." The lady of the house threw her arms around Conrad and thanked him for delivering her household from the "vile Yankees" and asked who the deliverer was. Conrad meekly responded that he was the chaplain of the Third Virginia Cavalry.

The next day, Conrad met another Yankee forager along the road. The blue-clad soldier's horse "was strung with chickens, hams, ducks and turkeys from its head to its tail. I shot him, took his feet out of the stirrups and dropped him on the road, led his horse far into the thicket and secured him until I could return and get him after nightfall." Conrad traded that horse for his played-out mount.[104]

That evening, only fifteen miles from White House Landing, Sheridan made contact with army headquarters. He reported to Meade that "I have been marching with my command down the north bank of the Mattapony

River. My advance is tonight at Walkerton." Sheridan justified his route of march: "I have taken this route, as my command was entirely out of rations and forage, and had to be subsisted off the country and I knew that by crossing the river and moving down between the Pamunkey and Mattapony Rivers I could not supply myself." After indicating his intention to march to White House Landing, he concluded, "I am doing very well at present in the way of supplies and think that I'll do better as I move on. I have sent forward to West Point to make arrangements for rations, &c., for my troops and to send off my wounded and prisoners of war." The missing horse soldiers had finally surfaced.[105]

Hampton shadowed Sheridan's line of march. On the 16th, the gray-clad cavalry left camp soon after sunrise and marched to Burrow's farm on Pole Cat Creek, near Chesterfield Station. They established their camp in Boot Swamp. Hampton also learned that Sheridan had sent his prisoners forward and was moving southwest toward Newtown. Once again receiving rations for both men and beasts, the Confederates rested several hours before moving off, noting that the surrounding country had been "left desolate by the Yankees, on their route to Hanover Town & on Sheridan's route to Trevellyan's." However, Hampton's men found ripe, sweet, juicy cherries along the way, stopping to enjoy the rare treat. "Had we been able to get corn two days ago, we should have crossed the Rapidan," complained a frustrated Waring.[106]

Captain Mulligan of the Fifth South Carolina reported, "Today finds me quite well. We are about 35 mile N.W. from Richmond having thoroughly whipped the great yankee Genl. Sheridan & driven him some 50 mile into the yankee lines ... we are still pursuing him but I do not think we will be able to over take him as our horses are all tired down. Sheridan remounts his men on fresh horses as fast as their horses break down by taking them from citizens."[107]

The next day, the Southern horsemen swung into their saddles early, marching to the Berkley plantation on the Mattapony. They stopped at 6 P.M. to graze and water their horses, preparatory for further marching. At 2 A.M., they finally went into camp, but the gray-clad troopers were not permitted to unsaddle their horses. Waring observed that "Hampton seems determined to dispute [Sheridan's] crossing to the Peninsula." Continuing the theme he started the previous day, Waring observed, "Scarcely a negro, horse or cow is to be seen anywhere along the road. The Yankees have ravaged the country & laid waste every farm. The poor fools, not to know that by rendering our people poor they prepare them for more desperate enterprises."[108]

"All quiett & no prospects for a fight," reported Mulligan. "Sheridan has stopped. He has killed over 3000 horses. We pushed him so closely that his horses, many of them, broak down & rather than leave them for us he would have their throats cut," he continued.[109] That day, Colonel Stokes wrote home, "We are away off here still, in pursuit of the enemy, who are only a few miles on the north side of the river moving down, I think, to join Grant and I think General H. is trying to prevent it." He continued, "All this country has recently been occupied by the enemy and the people are certainly in a destitute and distressing condition. They seem so glad to see a Confederate again."[110]

In the interim, Fitz Lee sent his staff officer, Maj. Robert Mason, to hold a position near Dunkirk with a detachment of 150 troopers and a piece of artillery. Lomax's brigade followed, supported by the horse artillery and Wickham's brigade. The division camped near Dunkirk late that afternoon. That night, Lee ascertained that "the enemy were moving still further down the river and that pursuit was useless." An officer of the Fourth Virginia complained, "We have given up following Sheridan."[111] Fitz pulled back after sending out scouts to watch Sheridan's movements. Word of heavy fighting near Petersburg reached Lee's camp, a direct result of Grant's uncontested crossing of the James River.[112]

On the 18th, Sheridan's dispatches reached the War Department. Little Phil claimed a great victory over the Rebel cavalry at Trevilian Station, an exaggeration at best.[113] Sheridan ordered Gregg's division to march to White House Landing the next morning, detailing two regiments as an escort for the wagon train of wounded men and the prisoners. His arrival at White House Landing promised welcome supplies. More than 795,000 pounds of grain and 370,000 pounds of hay awaited the horse soldiers there. Gregg received further instructions to arrest all male citizens capable of bearing arms that happened to cross his path.[114] As they foraged, a superior force from the Fourth Virginia Cavalry attacked Sgt. Maj. Herbert Farnsworth and eight men of the Tenth New York Cavalry. The New Yorkers lost five men, including two men killed in the skirmish.[115]

Frustrated blue-clad horse soldiers complained about Sheridan's seeming lack of decisiveness. "It was nothing but damn, damn, all the time, all tired out, and half starved, the horses playing out every minute, and men getting sick; it was rough indeed. A thousand fresh cavalry could have knocked us all to pieces easy," groused an officer of the First Massachusetts Cavalry.[116] Three squadrons of the Sixth Pennsylvania Cavalry picketed while the rest of the regiment set up their camp.[117] The duty was unpleasant; the regimental historian recalled that because the Lancers drew the unfortunate task of bringing up the rear of Sheridan's column, "we became unpleasantly familiar with the 'sacred soil' " of the Old Dominion.[118] A member of the Ninth New York recalled, "I never saw it so dry before it is enough to kill a man."[119]

That night, his weary troopers found time to pen letters home. "We have had no trouble with the rebels but have had hard marching through the sun and dust and short rations," reported Lt. Thomas Lucas of the First Pennsylvania. "We . . . cannot complain as we have had plenty all the time, luckily. The men of our company have done very well but the Corps generally has been short of rations. Out of twelve (12) days that we have been out we have drawn six days, the balance we have been compelled to take out of the country. . . . Nevertheless, I am tired and pretty well worn down."[120]

The fires blazed in Sheridan's bivouacs, presenting "a wonder to behold. Everybody was tired, hungry and sleepy. Yet it was long after taps before the groups around the campfires began to disperse." Sgt. Stanton P. Allen of the First Massachusetts Cavalry toured the camp with another member of the regiment. They spotted the ambulance train, parked in a field near headquarters. While making the rounds of the ambulance train, Allen heard a wounded trooper ask the surgeon tending to his shattered leg whether the column would resume the march the next day. The surgeon replied, "I understand so."

"When will we get to a hospital?"

"In a day or two, I think."

"Well, doctor, I don't want to complain, but I'm afraid that two days more of this sort of thing will bring my final statements."

The doctor paused. "No, no, my man; you've got too much backbone to be talking about final statements," he encouraged. "You'll pull through all right and be ready for another charge on the rebels in a few months." Fortunately, the doctor was correct about the trooper's survival, but he lost the leg a few days later at a hospital at White House Landing.[121]

Sheridan marched at 7 A.M. on June 19 and advanced to Dunkirk. The enlistment of Samuel J. Marks of Williston's battery expired that morning, and the artillerist was eager to return home to his wife, Carrie. He reported to her that "we have defeated the rebel cavalry in every battle." However, instead of going home that day, Marks was requested to take a contingent of twenty-one dismounted men to White House Landing, where they were to catch transports to City Point in order to remount the men and await the arrival of the balance of the Cavalry Corps. Worried about the safety of the men entrusted to his care, Marks refused to leave them, as "they are eternaly coaxing me not to have them remounted but give them a rest, and exclaiming in their Irish brogue to let the bloody horses to the divil." The lure of home proved too strong, though, and, a week later, Marks made arrangements for transportation home, ending his military service and sending him toward a reunion with Carrie.[122]

Sheridan's horses, worn out from overwork and insufficient fodder, dropped by the wayside in masses. Dead Federal horses lined the road "at a rate of about fifteen horses to ever mile. . . . We passed down a portion of the road that he retreated on and I never saw the like of dead horses in my life."[123] As Torbert's division advanced, Devin sent two squadrons of the Sixth New York Cavalry to swim their horses across the Mattapony and hold the opposite front until the pontoons could be laid. Heaton's guns covering the crossing, securing the passage.[124]

Sheridan directed David Gregg to destroy the mill at Walkerton. Gregg burned the mill and then brought up the rear of the Federal column. Sheridan also detached the Eighth Pennsylvania Cavalry and the Sixth Ohio Cavalry. Col. Pennock Huey, commander of the Eighth Pennsylvania, was to take the two regiments and the dismounted men of the corps to escort the long wagon train headed to the supply depot at West Point on the York River. There, the dismounted men, contrabands, and wounded would be transported to Fortress Monroe via boat, or ferried across the York River and sent to White House Landing. Sheridan sent the Sixth Ohio Cavalry to West Point on the James River with the prisoners and wired word to headquarters that he was bringing in 375 captives who would be sent to Point Lookout in Maryland.[125]

On the night of the 19th, Grant instructed Sheridan to remain at White House Landing to await further orders. Grant wrote, "His horses require rest, which they can get as well at White House as here. His stock of

ammunition ought to be replenished at the same time his orders go to him."
On the 18th, Grant had dispatched two naval gunboats to patrol the river
between West Point and White House Landing.[126] Sheridan backtracked
to Dunkirk, waiting to cross over to White House Landing on the morning
of the 20th. The column marched up the river to Dunkirk Bar. The Federals
crossed the river to the south side at a place where the pontoon train still
traveling with the command could bridge the narrow stream.[127]

On the morning of the 20th, the Yankee horse soldiers found the corps
wagon train, "which gave the cheerful promise of something to eat." They
stopped long enough to draw rations and forage for the first time in two
weeks and received mail. However, orders to march arrived before the rations
were fully issued. The disappointed Federals had been looking forward to a
decent meal. Sheridan had received word that the Union garrison at West
Point Landing was under enemy fire. He rode out to the front of the column
faster than usual that day. Sheridan's haste prompted his troopers to suspect
that something was up, "a suspicion that was soon verified by the sounds
of cannon in the distant front." They trotted off toward the sound of the
guns.[128] Sheridan and his staff arrived in the vicinity of White House Landing
to learn that a Confederate attack had been repulsed by the combination
of the gunboats, invalids, and U.S. Colored Troops stationed at the supply depot.[129]

As the Yankee column advanced, Butler's South Carolinians led Hampton's advance on White House Landing. Captain Mulligan wrote, "I have
only time to say that I am up & going notwithstanding I have been subjected
to the severest exposure. We have not had any fighting since today week
ago." He continued, "We have been following Sheridan & are still watching
him but he keeps out of our way. Our Regt is reduced to less than one
hundred men from killed, wounded, sick, broak down horses, &c., &c. No
cavalry has now under gone as much as we have. We have done more hard
fighting & endured more hardships any way since we arrived in Va. than
most troops under go in a year."[130]

Sergeant Charles McVicar was tired. "We have been in the saddle daily
and almost hourly since the 8th. Have slept in old infantry camps, our
clothes full of vermin as our wagons are back near Richmond. No change
of clothes for two weeks past, officers and men scratching and not a few
cuss words. We have never been filled with creepers for this long before,"

he groused. He noted, "General Sheridan and his men are under protection of their gunboats. The ball has opened. We have run him 120 miles since the 12th from Trevilian, skirmishing and fighting daily."[131]

At dawn on June 20th, Butler's men surprised a picket post of Federal infantry. After capturing the pickets, Butler decided to charge the garrison with the Fifth South Carolina Cavalry. As the Carolinians formed for the charge, one of Hampton's couriers rode up and directed Butler not to attack. Trooper Ulysses Brooks commented, "I verily believe but for this restraining order we would have taken the place and everybody in it." Instead, Butler's men did some desultory skirmishing for a while, "but all efforts to make an assault on the fort were abandoned and we withdrew to the adjoining hills." Sitting atop the ridge, the Confederates plainly saw Sheridan's line of march, marked by great billowing clouds of dust.[132]

Hampton's men held a strong position on slightly higher ground nearly a mile from White House Landing. Chew deployed his horse artillery atop the low ridge. McVicar noted in his diary, "We have an excellent position on the high ground, three of our guns are for the first time firing on full uniformed negroes backed by whites. They are replying to our little six pound rifle guns with twelve pound Parrotts." Sgt. George Neese poetically described the scene below: "The silvery water was marred by the darker track of the pontoon, crowded from shore to shore with fleeing wagons jammed close together, and all covered with white canvas, presenting the striking appearance of white water fowl gliding swifly across the shimmering water."[133] Soon, the tempting sight caused the Confederates to open fire on the concentration of wagons and the pontoon bridge across the Pamunkey. Alexander Newburger, a farrier for the Fourth New York, awoke with a start "to the unpleasant noise of some shell and shot bursting in the vicinity of my tent." Not long after, Newburger "was politely notified to move my habitation to another situation by a special messenger from the Johnny Rebs in the shape of a shell & round shot."[134]

The Federal gunboats responded, opening on them with 150-pound shells, "crashing the trees over us, limbs falling, it looks like an angry devil as she vomits forth her firey hail."[135] The garrison evacuated the wagons as the shelling increased in intensity.[136] The exchange continued for nearly two hours. A Federal artillery shell exploded a Confederate caisson. It was "a terrible sight, two men up in the air, one as he hit ran hollering fearfully, eyes burnt, clothes on fire."[137] One Federal observed, "One of his batteries was seen to move into position in an open field on the bluffs where a gunboat threw a big shell which appeared to explode in the midst of the battery, and men, horses and guns flew in every direction. When the smoke and dust cleared away there was no battery in sight."[138] That single destructive shell killed John Lewis and Samuel Jay of Hart's battery, and mortally wounded another gunner.[139] Hampton, although reinforced with some infantry, broke off the engagement and assumed a position that covered the approaches to Richmond.[140]

On the 20th, while Hampton shelled White House Landing, Fitz Lee's division crossed the Pamunkey at Norman's Ferry and sent its wagons around Wickham's plantation, crossing the Pamunkey at Wickham's Ford. When Lee's troopers camped that night, Chambliss's brigade joined them. Lee learned that Sheridan had received supplies and that 3,000 to 5,000 Federals held White House Landing. He consulted with Hampton, and the two generals decided that their reinforced command would attack again the next morning.[141] The combined force set out for White House Landing, finally camping for a few hours at 11:30 P.M. The command received orders to move out at 2 A.M., prompting Waring to complain, "We are pretty well fagged down."[142]

The exhausted horse of trooper James F. Wood of the Seventh Virginia finally gave out that morning. As the poor beast hemorrhaged, Wood trudged off "on foot to fight a gunboat in the Pamunkey." Failing to find a remount, Wood returned "after an eventful day to wagons some 6 miles off. Very tired at night." Now a reluctant member of Company Q, Wood spent the balance of the Trevilian Raid tending to the Confederate wagon train and dreaming of finding a new mount.[143]

On the morning of the 20th, the Union horse soldiers moved out, crossed the river at Dunkirk, and proceeded to White House Landing. The Fourth New York of Devin's brigade lagged behind as rear guard. One member of the Fourth Pennsylvania Cavalry noted, " 'Twas 18 miles and our horses had been out 13 days on 5 days forage, and the men had been out 14 days on 7 days rations except what we could pick up in the country. It was noon and very hot but we went the 18 miles at a right smart rate."[144] Arriving on the brow of a hill overlooking White House Landing about 6:00 P.M., the Yankee horse soldiers saw the most welcome sight they had seen in days—

the Stars and Stripes waving from a flagpole at the Landing, surrounded by ranks of tents and an enormous wagon train.[145]

The two gunboats, anchored in the river, supported the Federal garrison at the White House. This garrison received a new commander on June 20, when Brig. Gen. George W. Getty took over for the prior commander, Brig. Gen. John J. Abercrombie. Getty had been badly wounded at the Battle of the Wilderness and commanded the supply depot at White House Landing while he recuperated. The cavalry arrived just in time. Hampton shelled the Cavalry Corps wagon train, parked there to await Sheridan's arrival, and threatened Getty's beleaguered garrison of invalids and a brigade of U.S. Colored Troops.[146] "When we arrived here, instead of the short respite we had anticipated after the long and exhausting services of this memorable raid, we found the enemy again in our front, whose force must be met, forced back and held at bay until our trains could be moved to the south side of the James River, where the army had gone a week before," noted one member of the First Pennsylvania Cavalry.[147]

Hampton retreated, and the Yankee troopers entered the fortifications at White House Landing, enjoying friendly surroundings for the first time in two full weeks. One trooper observed, "The two following days were passed in camp near the White House, in the enjoyment of rest, not at all ungrateful to the men. The exhausting effect of such a campaign can hardly be conceived by one who has not felt it, nor can it well be described by one who has."[148] "Soon we shall be home again and I guess shall stay for I don't see where we can go on another raid," wrote Sgt. Nathan Webb of the First Maine, viewing the welcome sight of the friendly confines of White House Landing.[149]

Torbert and his staff traded in their tattered, filthy clothing for naval uniforms, leaving them looking "like a lot of sailors on horseback."[150] Others did some horse trading. Looking to trade in their played-out mounts, some of the Yankee troopers haggled with the garrison soldiers to swap their fresh horses for played-out steeds of the cavalrymen. Unfortunately, some of these new mounts were not well suited to service under saddle or to the needs of the cavalry. However, an ill-suited horse was still better than membership in Company Q.[151]

After escorting the prisoners to West Point on the York River, the men of the Sixth Ohio got a well-earned rest. Matthew King, a young Ohio trooper, led a squad on a foraging expedition. "Had poor luck," he complained. "Always some other party had been there first and cleaned up." The frustrated Buckeye finally gave up at noon and returned to camp. Finding himself with little to do, King "took a much needed swim in the York River." They remained in there in camp until late the next afternoon, when the Sixth Ohio crossed the York on ferries, dismounted, and stood to horse all night, waiting for a fight that never came.[152]

The arrival of the two weary divisions of Federal cavalry did not spell and end to their tribulations. More fighting and more severe tests remained.

Notes

1. O.R., vol. 36, part 1, 785.

2. The relationship between Sheridan and Gregg has been the subject of a great deal of speculation by historians. When Gregg resigned his commission without explanation in the spring of 1865, just before the end of the war, many speculated that he was bitter about having been passed over for command of the Army of the Potomac's Cavalry Corps. Others theorize that Gregg came to distrust Sheridan for his conduct of the Trevilian raid, and especially for leaving Gregg's division alone and unsupported and subject to attack by nearly the entire Confederate cavalry force at Samaria Church on June 24, 1864. However, Sheridan's assistant adjutant general, Maj. Frederick C. Newhall, recounted that Sheridan "seems to care most for the company of the placid and easygoing, and is fond of a quiet chat about old times on the frontier with such boon companions as General D. McM. Gregg." Newhall, With General Sheridan, 16.

3. New York Herald, June 22, 1864.

4. O.R., vol. 36, part 1, 785.

5. James N. Stratton, "Assistant Surgeon Samuel M. Powell, 1st New Jersey Cavalry Regiment," Department of Defense, Civil War Memorials of Officers, Box No. 2, Memorial No. 116, New Jersey State Archives, Trenton, New Jersey.

6. Bowen, First New York Dragoons, 192–93.

7. Cheney, History of the Ninth Regiment, 187.

8. Bowen, First New York Dragoons, 190.

9. O.R., vol. 36, part 1, 797. One member of the First New York Dragoons wrote, "there were negroes like the locusts of Egypt for number; where on earth they came from no one could tell. I judge there were from two thousand to three thousand of these poor fugitives, of all ages, both sexes, and every shade of complexion, all having unbounded confidence in 'Massa Linkum's sogers.' There were old men and women, bent nearly double with infirmities of years. I saw several mothers with babes on one arm and leading little toddling youngsters with the other, yet

all plodded through, and were sent down the river from here." Bowen, *First New York Dragoons*, 190.

10. Wallace, *A Few Memories of a Long Life*, 38.

11. Foster, *Reminiscences and Record*, 62–3.

12. Lloyd, *History of the First Regiment Pennsylvania Reserve Cavalry*, 98.

13. *New York Herald*, June 22, 1864.

14. Hall, *History of the Sixth New York*, 199.

15. Wallace, *A Few Memories of a Long Life*, 38.

16. Tobie, *First Maine Cavalry*, 288.

17. Rockwell, *Rambling Recollections*, 150.

18. Fitch diary, entry for June 12, 1864.

19. Pyne, *Ride to War*, 222.

20. William G. Hills diary, entry for June 12, 1864.

21. Wood diary, entry for June 13, 1864.

22. Webb diary, entry for June 13, 1864.

23. Tobie, *First Maine Cavalry*, 288–89.

24. Mohr and Winslow, *The Cormany Diaries*, 435.

25. Ressler diary, entry for June 13, 1864.

26. Mohr and Winslow, *The Cormany Diaries*, 435.

27. Frank E. White Diary and Memoir, entry for June 14, 1864, Book, Manuscript and Special Collections, Dalton-Brand Research Room, Duke University, Durham, North Carolina.

28. Crowninshield, *History of the First Regiment*, 222.

29. Cheney, *Ninth New York Cavalry*, 188.

30. Strang, *Sunshine and Shadows*, 52.

31. Thomas Lucas to his wife, June 13, 1864.

32. Strang, *Sunshine and Shadows*, 52.

33. O.R., vol. 37, part 1, 98–100.

34. Ferguson diary, entry for June 13, 1864.

35. Butler, "The Cavalry Fight at Trevilian Station," 239.

36. *Southern Banner*, July 13, 1864.

37. Allen, *Down in Dixie*, 367.

38. Hills diary, entry for June 12, 1864.

39. Carpenter to his father, June 22, 1864.

40. Myers, *The Comanches*, 306.

41. *The Camden Journal*, June 17, 1864.

42. O.R., vol. 51, part 2, 1009.

43. Mulligan, "My Dear Mother & Sisters," 124.

44. Johnson, "My Ride around Baltimore," 251. Johnson proposed taking the First Maryland along the base of the Blue Ridge; passing through Culpeper, Madison, and Loudoun Counties; crossing the Potomac at Muddy Branch; surprising the

Second Massachusetts Cavalry; speeding to the Soldier's Home, seizing Lincoln, and taking him south to Richmond. He would then split his small command and ride on both Baltimore and Washington. The plan was, at best, audacious. An adjunct to Early's raid on Washington, the Confederate invasion prompted Grant to commit two infantry corps and two cavalry divisions to the Shenandoah Valley under Sheridan's command.

45. Howard, *Sketch of Cobb Legion Cavalry*, 17.

46. Swank, *The War and Louisa County*, 92.

47. Noble Brooks diary, entry for June 13, 1864. McAllister was later reinterred in Oakland Cemetery in Louisa, along with approximately 100 of the Confederate battle dead from Trevilian. He and Capt. Hines rest under handsome markers a few yards from a number of unknown enlisted men.

48. Swiggart, *Shades of Gray*, 73.

49. Hansell reminiscences at 11.

50. Wells memoir, 23–4.

51. Waring diary, entry for June 13, 1864.

52. Ferguson diary, entry for June 13, 1864.

53. Howard, *Sketch of Cobb Legion Cavalry*, 17.

54. Vogtsberger, *The Dulanys of Welbourne*, 166.

55. Ferguson diary, entry for June 13, 1864.

56. O.R., vol. 36, part 1, 1096.

57. Waring diary, entry for June 14, 1864.

58. James I. Robertson Jr.,ed., *The Civil War Letters of General Robert McAllister* (New Brunswick, N.J.: Rutgers University Press, 1964), 440–41.

59. Waring diary, entry for June 13, 1864; Grant, *Personal Memoirs*, 594–98.

60. O.R., vol. 36, part 1, 25–27.

61. For a detailed discussion of Early's march and his victory over Hunter at Lynchburg, see Duncan, *Lee's Endangered Left*, 262–65.

62. Rockwell, *Rambling Recollections*, 150–51.

63. Strang, *Sunshine and Shadows*, 52.

64. King, *To Horse*, 12.

65. *New York Herald*, June 22, 1864; *History of the Eighteenth Regiment of Cavalry, Pennsylvania Volunteers, 1862–1865* (New York: Publication Committee, Eighteenth Pa. Cavalry Assn., 1909), p. 21. Interestingly, when Capt. Theophilus F. Rodenbough recovered from the severe wound he suffered in the opening moments of the Battle of Trevilian Station, he was commissioned a colonel of volunteers and assigned to command the Eighteenth Pennsylvania Cavalry. He would later head the editorial committee that produced the unit's regimental history in 1909.

66. O.R., vol. 51, part 2, 1013.

67. Wade Hampton to Mary Fisher Hampton, June 14, 1864, Wade Hampton Papers, Manuscripts Division, Library of Congress, Washington, D.C.

68. O.R., vol. 51, part 2, 1013.

69. *Ibid.*, 1013–14.

70. Halliburton, *Saddle Soldiers*, 147.

71. Fitzhugh Lee to Dear General, December 20, 1866.

72. Vogtsberger, *The Dulanys of Welbourne*, 166; James F. Wood diary, entry for June 16, 1864.

73. *Ibid.*

74. Bowen, *History of the First New York Dragoons*, 190.

75. Howard M. Smith to his mother, July 5, 1864, Smith papers.

76. McDonald, *History of the Laurel Brigade*, 257.

77. Webb diary, entry for June 16, 1864.

78. Bowen, *History of the First New York Dragoons*, 190.

79. O.R., vol. 36, part 1, 798.

80. Hagemann, *Fighting Rebels and Redskins*, 246.

81. Howard M. Smith diary, entry for June 15, 1864.

82. Hyndman, *History of a Cavalry Company*, 126–27.

83. Strang, *Sunshine and Shadows*, 52.

84. Crowninshield, *History of the First Regiment*, 223.

85. Waring diary, entry for June 15, 1864.

86. Wellman, *Giant in Gray*, 150.

87. Fitch diary, entry for June 16, 1864. Fortunately, Sergeant Fitch got called to division headquarters that evening and "there I had a good place to camp."

88. Frank Grommon diary, entry for June 16, 1864.

89. Veil, *Personal Recollections*, 46–7.

90. Moncure, *Reminiscences*, 17.

91. Mohr and Winslow, *The Cormany Diaries*, 435.

92. Ressler diary, entry for June 16, 1864.

93. Bean, "With Sheridan," June 11, 1887.

94. O.R., vol. 36, part 1, 785–86.

95. *New York Herald,* June 22, 1864.

96. *Ibid.* Sandy Forsyth's telegram to Maj. Gen. A. A. Humphreys, Meade's chief of staff, read:

As it may be difficult for me to get to Yorktown immediately I have concluded to telegraph my dispatches from this point. I will report to army headquarters at once. General Sheridan was within 5 miles of Walkerton last night. He will probably move toward White House as soon as he can hear from his chief quartermaster, who came through with me.

O.R., vol. 36, part 3, 777.

97. Mohr and Winslow, *The Cormany Diaries*, 435.

98. Webb diary, entry for June 17, 1864.

99. Cheney, *Ninth New York Cavalry*, 189.

100. Fitch diary, entry for June 17, 1864.

101. O.R., vol. 36, part 3, 901.

102. Hills diary, entry for June 18, 1864. Dahlgren's body had been removed from the shallow grave by men of the Ninth Virginia Cavalry and delivered to Richmond for positive identification. The body was reinterred outside Oakwood Cemetery in the Confederate capital. The body was then stolen by Union sympathizers and secreted until the end of the war.

103. Howard M. Smith to his mother, July 5, 1864.

104. Conrad, The Rebel Scout, 111–13. Conrad claimed that his former horse, "Old Whitie," was the same horse that John Wilkes Booth rode during his escape from the Lincoln assassination.

105. O.R., vol. 36, part 3, 778.

106. Waring diary, entry for June 16, 1864.

107. Mulligan, "My Dear Mother and Sisters," 124.

108. Waring diary, entry for June 17, 1864.

109. Mulligan, "My Dear Mother and Sisters," 124.

110. Halliburton, Saddle Soldiers, 148.

111. Stiles, Fourth Virginia Cavalry, 55.

112. Ferguson diary, entries for June 17 and 18, 1864.

113. New York Times, June 19, 1864.

114. O.R., vol. 36, part 3, 778.

115. Preston, History of the Tenth Regiment, 211.

116. Crowninshield, History of the Regiment, 224.

117. Diary of Charles H. Coller, entry for June 18, 1864, Wiley Sword Collection, United States Army Military History Institute, Carlisle, Pennsylvania.

118. Gracey, Annals of the Sixth Pennsylvania Cavalry, 263.

119. Taylor, Saddle and Saber, 160.

120. Lucas to his wife, June 19, 1864.

121. Allen, Down in Dixie, 374–75.

122. Samuel J. Marks to Dear Carrie, June 26, 1864, Civil War Miscellaneous Collection, United States Army Military History Institute, Carlisle, Pennsylvania.

123. Halliburton, Saddle Soldiers, 148–49.

124. O.R., vol. 36, part 1, 842–43.

125. Ibid., part 3, 779–80.

126. Ibid., 779.

127. Cheney, Ninth New York Cavalry, 189.

128. Tobie, First Maine Cavalry, 290. The regimental historian of the First Maine noted of Sheridan that day, "he seemed to make it a point to ride along the whole length of the column each day on the march, as if to let every man in the command see him daily, which calls to mind the same characteristic of Napoleon Bonaparte."

129. Pyne, Ride to War, 224.

130. Mulligan, "My Dear Mother & Sisters," 124–25.

131. McVicar diary, entry for June 19, 1864.

132. Brooks, *Butler and His Cavalry*, 267–68.

133. Neese, *Three Years*, 296–97.

134. Diary of Alexander Newburger, entry for June 20, 1864, Library of Congress, Washington, D.C.

135. McVicar diary, entry for June 19, 1864.

136. Newburger diary, entry for June 20, 1864.

137. McVicar diary, entry for June 19, 1864. Dewitt C. Gallagher of the First Virginia Cavalry recorded in his diary, "Fight with negro infantry," an event that obviously made a major impression on the minds of the Confederate troopers, unaccustomed to seeing black men in military uniforms. Gallagher, *A Diary*, 6.

138. Cheney, *Ninth New York Cavalry*, 190. U. R. Brooks, of the Sixth South Carolina Cavalry, commented that the fifteen-inch shells lobbed by the Federal gunboats were called "flour barrels" by the gray-clad cavalry, and that "Whenever they struck the ground and exploded they would shake the earth and make holes in the ground large and deep enough to hide a small-sized horse." Brooks, *Butler and His Cavalry*, 268.

139. *Charleston Daily Courier*, October 15, 1864.

140. McVicary diary, entry for June 19, 1864.

141. Ferguson diary, entry for June 19, 1864.

142. Waring diary, entry for June 19, 1864. Hampton's division moved off through Hanovertown, camping near the farm of Confederate firebrand Edmund Ruffin. Ruffin was one of the leading agronomists of his time, and his farm was known widely as a leading center of agricultural research. Waring noted, "Ruffin's farm must have been a superb one."

143. Wood diary, entry for June 20, 1864.

144. William S. Keller to his sister, June 22, 1864.

145. Allen, *Down in Dixie*, 379.

146. Brig. Gen. John J. Abercrombie, a member of the West Point class of 1822, and one of the oldest men in the Union service, was still technically in command of the garrison at West Point Landing. However, he was absent from the post. Getty assumed command on June 12 as the second day of the Battle of Trevilian Station raged.

147. Lloyd, *History of the First Regiment Pennsylvania Reserve Cavalry*, 99.

148. Samuel H. Merrill, *The Campaigns of the First Maine and First District of Columbia Cavalry* (Portland, Maine: Bailey & Noyes, 1866), 212–13.

149. Webb diary, entry for June 20, 1864.

150. Wallace, *A Few Memories of a Long Life*, 39.

151. Allen, *Down in Dixie*, 381.

152. King, *To Horse*, 13.

✧ 9 ✧

The March from White House
Landing to the James River

Another day passed, another engagement fought.

s Sheridan's men reinforced Getty, the army's high command contemplated its next moves. On the morning of the 20th, Meade wrote to Grant, inquiring as to the whereabouts of the Confederate cavalry. He asked whether Grant thought that Hampton's command would be drawn back into the defenses of Richmond to defend against any potential raiding parties. Meade noted, "It has occurred to me that with Hunter's position as known, Sheridan would be more likely to communicate with him and assist him by going from [Petersburg] up the south bank of the James, than from the White House." He suggested that Wilson's division join Sheridan there. The combined force would cross the river for further raiding.[1]

Later that day, Grant replied, "In view of the location of General Hunter, as reported in the rebel papers, and the fact that General Sheridan cannot carry supplies with him from the White House to make an effective raid against the enemy's communications north of the James, you may direct his immediate return to the Army of the Potomac." Grant also directed General Getty to break up the depot at the White House and send the garrison and the invalids stationed there back to Washington. Meade instructed Sheridan to march to Deep Bottom on the James River. The Federal engineers would throw a pontoon bridge across the river there for Sheridan's crossing, allowing him to move on to City Point. Sheridan's two divisions would then rejoin the Army of the Potomac.[2]

Even though Hampton withdrew on the 20th, Sheridan and his horse soldiers were still in danger. "Another day passed, another engagement fought," observed a war-weary man of Davies's brigade.[3] At 2:00 A.M. on the 21st, both Union divisions heard the shrill sounds of reveille. The Yankee troopers hastily grabbed their arms for a fight on foot, leaving their horses in the charge of a guard. The Northern horse soldiers crossed the Pamunkey on an old railroad bridge under the cover of a heavy fog. Gregg's dismounted division, supported by the Regulars, moved out toward Tunstall's Station. Custer's mounted brigade moved out toward Cumberland, and Devin's toward Baltimore Cross Roads. They found that the Confederates had fallen back to higher ground overlooking the river, nearly two miles away. Davies's brigade crossed back over, got their horses, and recrossed the river, moving forward to support J. I. Gregg's brigade, which had advanced on foot to probe the strength of Hampton's position.[4] Most of Davies's men spent the day standing to horse, waiting for orders to pitch in.[5]

The Confederates also got an early start that morning. Breaking camp about 6:00, the gray-clad horsemen moved toward White House Landing. They reached the same ground they had held the day before, and the opposing forces made contact about four miles from the landing. Soon, skirmish fire broke out along both lines.[6]

Devin's and Custer's brigades of the First Division engaged first. Torbert held the Regulars in reserve. They stood to horse all day.[7] On the night of the 21st, the Boy General fired off a lengthy letter to his new bride, Libbie, describing the Battle of Trevilian Station and his travails there. He reported, "Under a tree near . . . 'White House' on the Pamunkey . . . we crossed this morning, but have been unable to advance from it more than two miles, as the enemy have us completely hemmed in. We have been fighting all day." He continued, "The Michigan Brigade have discovered a gap by which we will probably move out to-morrow. The firing has almost ceased and quiet is almost restored along our lines."[8]

Devin's brigade engaged the Confederate right upon entering a wood line. Devin drove them back toward St. Peter's Church, where they made "a determined stand" in a strong defensive position fronted by deep ravines that separated the opposing forces.[9] The Seventeenth Pennsylvania of Devin's Brigade engaged first with the combined forces of Hampton and Fitz Lee. The Sixth and Ninth New York regiments supported the Pennsylvanians. The Sixth New York fought on the left for nearly three hours before the gray-clad horse soldiers withdrew toward St. Peter's Church. The old red brick church, built in 1723, had been the site of George Washington's wedding. A Confederate correspondent described it as "the ancient place of worship of the Lees and other 'F.F.V.'s' of this region."[10] After driving Hampton back, "we contented ourselves with holding the position already gained. The enemy opened upon us with shot, shell, and bullets, but soon the firing on both sides ceased, the enemy evacuated the church, and we took possession."[11] As Devin prepared to follow up the afternoon's success, he received orders not to attack. He ruefully noted, "on the right the enemy's rear guard could be seen withdrawing in haste."[12] Sheridan's five brigades were engaged nearly all day. Maj. Wilbur G. Bentley of the Ninth New York Cavalry was badly wounded, losing a leg.[13]

The First Pennsylvania Cavalry of Davies's brigade faced a severe test "in a bad position" that day.[14] Around 4:00 the Pennsylvanians attacked Hampton's flank, hoping to capture or compel the removal of an artillery piece harassing the Federal advance. Supported by only one mounted squadron of the First New Jersey Cavalry, the First Pennsylvania moved along a narrow strip of cleared land skirted on all sides by thick woods. Pursuant to their orders, but contrary to the judgment of the regiment's officers, the First Pennsylvania advanced rapidly without the protection of skirmishers on either flank. After nearly half a mile, the Confederates hit the Pennsylvanians on both flanks. One member of the regiment noted, "To retrace our steps, and precipitately, too, was the only course left." Nearly surrounded, the regiment suffered heavily, losing thirty-eight officers and men killed, wounded, or taken prisoner. The Pennsylvanians fought furiously as they held back Hampton's flanking columns until a new line could be formed in a safer position. The Pennsylvanians withdrew from the battlefield at dark after being hammered by Hampton's troopers.[15]

The First Maine Cavalry held the right of Gregg's line atop a ridge about 800 yards from Black Run. They remained mounted until afternoon, when they dismounted to fight on foot. Through an ill-conceived order by a staff officer, two companies of the First Maine withdrew from the line, leaving a gap in the Federal battle line. Hampton promptly capitalized on this error and punched through the Union line. Only a severe fight by the Maine men drove the stubborn enemy horse soldiers back. One wrote, "For a few minutes, we fought hand to hand, using our pistols, firing almost in one another's faces in the bushes."[16] The First Maine's regimental adjutant, Capt. A. H. Bibber, had found the gap and reported it to the regimental commander. Col. Charles H. Smith sent Bibber back to find out who was responsible for the breach. Looking for the end of the Maine line, Bibber rode along a wood line. Five Rebel troopers, their Enfields raised and at the ready, demanded his surrender. The quick-thinking adjutant raised his hand and inquired, "Hold on there! What in thunder are you going to shoot at?"

The Confederates lowered their guns. Bibber wore corduroy pants and a straw hat, sat on a civilian saddle, and did not present a very military appearance. The Confederates paused, but then spotted his shoulder straps, recognizing a Federal officer when they saw one. Bibber threw the reins around his horse's head and touched the animal's side with his spurs, prompting him to turn sideways. Bibber pulled his left foot from the stirrup and leapt from the saddle. He recounted, "I hardly touched the ground before they all fired, my horse falling where it stood. I jumped into the woods. There I saw a skirmish line of them moving to our rear and evidently getting into position to assault our flank." Possessed of a big, booming voice, the captain moved through the woods, calling for Colonel Smith, who heard his adjutant's voice and recognized it. Calling Smith's name, the captain ran to the colonel and warned him of the impending Confederate attack.

Unfortunately, Bibber interrupted Smith's dinner. The colonel had hoarded a box of sardines all throughout the long march to Trevilian and back and had finally decided to enjoy his delicacy. Dropping the box of sardines, the colonel and his officers rallied the men and repulsed the attack, losing the sardines in the process. The regimental historian of the First Maine observed that the colonel "never forgot or forgave the loss of that box of sardines." A Rebel ball struck Pvt. Charles W. Jordan, another member of the First Maine, in the chest. The bullet struck a small pair of scissors in the watch-pocket of his vest, leaving him shaken but unharmed.[17] "Altogether it was quite a spirited little affair and resulted in nothing particular," observed Sgt. Nathan Webb.[18] An account published in one of the Richmond newspapers called the engagement "unimportant skirmishing."[19]

As the fighting ended on the 21st, the Federals camped on the high ground, where they read mail from home for the first time in two weeks. "There many of us got the first good wash we had enjoyed in the same length of time. With the rest that we . . . enjoyed, the replenishing of our haversacks, and a good supply of ammunition we felt that we were able to perform" the task of escorting the wagons of wounded on to the main body of the Army of the Potomac.[20] Maj. William P. C. Treichel, who had been on extended sick leave with malarial fever and acute hepatitis, returned to take command of his regiment, the Sixth Pennsylvania Cavalry, that evening. Unfortunately, the illness forced him to resign his commission less than three weeks later.[21] Many of the Yankee horse soldiers wrote home, reporting on their whereabouts. Maj. James H. Kidd of the Sixth Michigan Cavalry was one of them. "For 14 days . . . we have been constantly in the saddle, often marching night and day," he recounted, "What the object sought to be accomplished may have been I am of course ignorant."[22]

After the fighting finally petered out, Sheridan reported to army headquarters, "I found on my arrival here yesterday two divisions of the enemy's cavalry in front of this place. This morning, I crossed the bridge. The enemy fell back behind Black Creek at a point near Tunstall's Station. This place is all right. The enemy shelled the trains yesterday before I arrived. They were yesterday evening all crossed over to the north side of the Pamunkey." While Sheridan planned his route to Deep Bottom, Meade wrote to Grant, "I don't think Sheridan will have much chance of getting to Deep Bottom bridge in the face of Hampton unless he is able to give him a severe and serious defeat."[23]

On the 21st, as the first shots echoed near White House Landing, the men of the Sixth Ohio finished their coffee and tended to their horses. They then mounted and rode to White House Landing, crossed the Pamunkey on pontoons, and rejoined the rest of Sheridan's column in time to go on picket duty for the entire night. The Buckeyes paid dearly for their two-day respite.[24]

While the fight raged near White House Landing, another Union cavalry raid commenced. On June 21, Grant ordered Meade to send Wilson to take the Army of the Potomac's Third Cavalry Division and destroy the principal supply arteries for Petersburg, the Weldon and South Side railroads on another diversionary raid. Brig. Gen. August V. Kautz's small cavalry division of the Army of the James augmented Wilson's division.[25] Departing on June 22, the Wilson–Kautz raid had no opposition for the first couple of days. Nearly the entire Confederate cavalry force was concentrating near White House Landing, looking to destroy Sheridan's command.[26] While planning his raid, Wilson predicted, "If Sheridan will look after Hampton, I apprehend no difficulty."[27]

On the night of the 21st, Hampton pulled back to try to round up some infantry support for a planned assault on the depot at White House Landing. He crossed the Chickahominy at Bottom's Bridge, leaving the Federal base alone. After taking more than thirty additional casualties in the fighting, his men were weary.[28] Fitz Lee's division fell back to a position near Bottom's Bridge, getting a much-needed day of rest on the 22d. However, when Lee learned that Sheridan was advancing from White House Landing toward Forge Bridge, Lee ordered his men to cross White Oak Swamp at 1:00 A.M. The Virginians then moved to Nance's Shop, just to the north of Samaria Church in Charles City County, a few miles north of the James River. Lee marched south toward Salem Church after learning that the Federals were again moving. He camped seven miles from Charles City Court House.[29]

On the 22d, Lt. Col. William Stokes, acting as commander of Butler's brigade since June 18, wrote home, "Where we will go from here I have no idea but think we will remain near here for several days to prevent Sheridan from joining Grant." Stokes felt that Hampton had missed an opportunity at White House Landing. "We dashed on the pickets at the White House on Sunday morning and captured 17 and had the whole command been up Genl. H could have dashed on the place and taken it, I think with little loss & captured a large wagon train of some one or two hundred in number."[30] The Confederate troopers rested along the Chickahominy River about ten miles from Richmond.[31]

The weary Union horse soldiers of Gregg's division rested for part of the day on June 22. Many dashed off letters home and caught up on the local newspapers. They washed their clothes and groomed their equally weary mounts. The respite, albeit brief, was a most welcome one.[32] Lieutenant Cormany scrawled in his diary, "Our pickets brought in one Reb—they caught napping—The 4th Pa. relieved our regiment at sun set, and we made ourselves comfortable."[33] The men of the Fourth Pennsylvania Cavalry skirmished with the Rebels, prompting Pvt. William Keller to note, "We had a nice little fight driving the Rebs 5 miles," before calling off the pursuit.[34] The First Pennsylvania Cavalry marched to Baltimore Cross Roads and took up a position that held "the roads for the protection of the wagon train, on its passage to the James River."[35] In the meantime, Torbert's division heard "boots and saddles" at 8:00 and reconnoitered to Jones's Bridge at 9:00, looking for a place to cross the Chickahominy.[36] The First

Division's arrival at Jones's Bridge was timely. They saved it from the Confederate rear guard, which was trying to burn it as the Federals trotted up.[37] After securing the bridge, Torbert's command encamped along the banks of the Chickahominy.

A delighted member of the Sixth Pennsylvania Cavalry noted, "For a wonder, we found this wretched stream quite clear, and enjoyed a bath in it, so delicious that it made us forgive the treacherous flood for many previous disappointments and labors."[38] Sgt. Lewis Fitch of the Fifth Michigan Cavalry celebrated his twentieth birthday on June 22. He did not have an extended raid in mind as a joyous birthday party, but the good campsite and clear water took some of the sting out of his lack of celebration.[39] As Torbert's men settled into their comfortable bivouac, Sheridan reported that he intended to start the trains toward Jones's Bridge that night. He planned to go through New Baltimore, down to Jones's Bridge and then south to Charles City Court House. There, he would head west along the northern bank of the James to Haxall's Landing. The march would be dangerous and harrowing. He hoped "to get everything off by tomorrow morning."[40]

On the morning of June 23, Sheridan learned that Torbert's division had secured the crossing at Jones's Bridge. Sheridan set out for Deep Bottom, followed by an immense, nine-hundred-wagon train. The White House garrison augmented his train, meaning that the column snaked along for more than four miles.[41] The regimental historian of the First New Jersey Cavalry commented, "It was a very serious matter for two divisions, worn down by such excessive labors to less than five thousand men, to escort nine hundred wagons across the Peninsula to the James River; but the necessity was urgent and had to be undertaken."[42] All knew that Hampton was headed for the river, looking to interdict the long wagon train and destroy Sheridan's force.

Maj. Frederic C. Newhall of the Sixth Pennsylvania Cavalry, Sheridan's assistant adjutant general, described the challenge facing the blue-clad horse soldiers. "It required considerable maneuvering to march this immense train of unwieldy transportation in such manner as should protect it from the rebellious cavalry of General Hampton, which was hanging upon our flank and hungrily regarding said wagons."[43] One member of the Sixth Pennsylvania Cavalry observed, "When strung out it made a line ten miles long and was a very tempting prize for . . . General Hampton with his cavalry corps, who were hovering on our flanks ready to swoop down on us at the first chance of success."[44] Sheridan commented that he knew "well that I would be attacked if the enemy had any spirit left in him."[45]

After poring over the maps, Sheridan decided to cross the Chickahominy at Providence Forge, and if they could find a road to that point by way of New Kent Court House, the trains would travel it securely. The Federal cavalry would cover the direct road to the Chickahominy. The cavalry screen would also prevent the enemy from invading the little peninsula between the Chickahominy and the Pamunkey, where New Kent Court House lies. Newhall continued, "The most diligent study of the maps failed to discover any indication of such a road, and no consecutive series of lines could be traced in that direction; equally diligent search failed to discover any one to the manor born who knew of any such outlet: but the interests of the service demanded that it should exist, and so, after mature deliberation and much pondering over maps, the commanding general decided that there was a road, must be a road."[46] A good portion of this route covered ground traversed by Sheridan during his May Richmond raid.

Sheridan sent General Getty and another staff officer to reconnoiter the roads. A route had to be found, and it had to be found quickly. The local populace would be little help; "at that time, the Court House was a deserted village; gaunt dogs were the only living beings for miles around, and they could give no geographical information." However, as Newhall noted, "perseverance was rewarded with success; a good wood-road was found, the trains reached the Chickahominy without delay, and the general's topographic bump was vindicated."[47] Departing at 5:00 A.M., J. Irvin Gregg's men tore up the bridge and wharf at White House Landing, an "awfully hot job, and dusty."[48] The brigade then followed a parallel road, protecting the wagon train's flank from attack while Davies's brigade brought up the rear of Sheridan's immense column.

The pursuing Confederates soon learned that the Federals had moved out. Breaking camp early, Hampton's division snaked along the Chickahominy toward White Oak Swamp, about twelve miles from the heart of Richmond. The Southern horse soldiers had crossed the Chickahominy on Bottom's Bridge and marched down the south side of the Chickahominy to prevent the Federals from crossing at Jones Bridge. A brigade of the First Division took possession of and held the bridge until the entire command had crossed. When the Confederates attacked the bridge, "the two regiments of colored troops and the 13th Ohio Dismounted Cavalry, under Brigadier General Getty, rendered valuable service here. They fought remarkably well, and drove the enemy half a mile from their breastworks" and took a number of prisoners.[49]

After a break, Hampton's horse soldiers marched off to the southeast toward Charles City Court House on the James River.[50] Members of the Laurel Brigade skirmished with some of Sheridan's videttes. Capt. Thomas H. Buck of the Seventh Virginia Cavalry engaged a Yankee trooper in a sabre fight. Both combatants were knocked from their horses and Buck's mount was killed during the brief but violent clash. Capt. Benjamin P. Crampton rescued Buck, putting a pistol ball through the Yankee's head and ending the duel.[51]

On the morning of the 23d, "a heavy force" of Chambliss's brigade, along with a section of horse artillery, attacked Devin's brigade, near Samaria (St. Mary's) Church, along the roads to Charles City Court House and Long Bridge on the Chickahominy. In a "spirited engagement near an old saw mill in the vicinity of Nance's Shop," the gray-clad troopers drove Devin's men back, flanking his hastily constructed barricades and coming to a point within 500 yards of the main road; if they succeeded in taking and holding the road, Sheridan's line of march would be severed. Torbert observed that Devin "held his ground with his usual stubbornness, and finally drove the enemy from his front," attacking vigorously with the Fourth New York and Seventeenth Pennsylvania regiments.[52]

Six companies of U.S. Colored Troops of Getty's force reinforced Devin's small brigade. They repulsed the Confederate attack, prompting the regimental historian of the Sixth New York to brag that "a fierce but short engagement ended in the entire rout of the enemy."[53] Col. Richard L. T. Beale, commander of the Ninth Virginia Cavalry of Chambliss's Brigade, recalled the outcome of the fight differently, noting that the fight "was growing very interesting when we were ordered back," breaking off the engagement. Beale reported that he lost one private killed in the skirmish, and several wounded, including one fatally. Lt. James Pollard of the Ninth Virginia lost a leg to a severe wound, and he never returned to duty with the regiment.[54] Pollard's wound was very ironic, because he was generally credited with having caught one-legged Union colonel Ulric Dahlgren during the March Kilpatrick–Dahlgren raid.

One of the Wolverines heard that even though "there was brisk fighting for a little while," the black soldiers had "more than made" the Confederates "gett."[55] A prisoner informed Sheridan that Chambliss's probe was the advance of the entire enemy cavalry corps, "and through it that Hampton had been advised of our having already secured the crossing of the Chickahominy." Devin's command lost six men killed, one officer and eight men wounded, and one man missing. Nearly all of those men killed were pickets of the Sixth New York, who, with "desperate tenacity . . . endeavored to hold their position." The crossing of the James apparently would not be uncontested.[56]

The long column crossed the Chickahominy on pontoons near Jones's Bridge. Gregg's division marched along a parallel road, covering the flank of the wagon train. Sheridan then ordered Gregg to hold fast near Samaria Church "without fail till all the transportation had passed Charles City Court House."[57] Gregg's division camped by the church, about eight miles north of Charles City Court House. One trooper recalled that their bivouac occupied "the driest country" he had "ever camped in, the boys getting water to cook with only after long search and patient, persevering exertion."[58] The men feasted on pancakes and applesauce.[59] A Pennsylvanian groused, "We are on our road to the James River now, and hope our communications will not be as much interrupted hereafter. I always had a desire to make a raid but that desire is completely satiated now. I have been on raids enough."[60] Cormany complained to his wife, "At 10:30 when all were soundly asleep we were ordered to pack—to march immediately. We marched 1½ to 2½ miles bivouacked."[61] The Sixth Ohio Cavalry of Davies's brigade spent a tense night on the picket lines, only a few yards from the Confederate videttes.[62]

Sheridan had managed the wagon train's progress carefully and prudently, prompting one Pennsylvanian to note, "In performing this duty General Sheridan displayed great generalship, preserving the trains and delivering them safely inside our lines."[63] On the afternoon of the 23d, Hampton sent Chambliss's brigade to attack the train. Sheridan's careful and well-planned dispositions repulsed Chambliss's thrust, and Gregg's troopers drove off Chambliss's men without any damage to the wagon train.[64]

The *Richmond Daily Dispatch* observed prophetically, "If Sheridan reached the James River and escaped, he has done so at a heavy sacrifice. His expedition has been a series of disasters from beginning to end, and the command which started out from Grant's army so fresh and lively, and with such high expectations, returns discomfited, broken down, and greatly depleted in men and horses."[65]

That night, Hampton, fearing that Sheridan might pass up the James River through Charles City Court House and Westover, took up a position that covered the roads from Long Bridge to Westover. Picketing all the roads, Hampton held a good blocking position about six miles from Charles City Court House. At one point, he seriously considered launching a night attack and made his dispositions around midnight. However, he soon changed his mind and called off the assault because his horses were in nearly as bad a condition as Sheridan's.[66] Col. Stokes wrote home that day, "A great number of our horses are used up and if we do not get some rest soon the whole Regiment will be used up."[67] Fitz Lee's division camped near Bottom's Bridge, occupying the same ground it held on the night of June 7.[68] In the process, Hampton's command could fall upon Gregg's lone and unsupported division near Samaria Church the next day.[69] The final acts of the long drama of the Trevilian Raid remained to be played out.

Notes

1. O.R., vol. 36, part 3, 781.
2. Ibid., 781–82 and 784. Meade's order to Sheridan provided:
    You will, as soon as practicable after receiving this, move your command and trains from the White House to City Point. There will be a bridge thrown across the James at Deep Bottom, above Malvern Hill, on which you will endeavor to cross your command. Should this be impracticable, you will proceed to Douthat's Landing, opposite Fort Powhatan, where ferry-boats will be provided for bringing you across. It will be well for you in passing up the James to communicate with Fort Powhatan the fact of your being in the vicinity.
O.R., vol. 36, part 3, 784.
3. Webb diary, entry for June 20, 1864.
4. Lloyd, History of the First Regiment Pennsylvania Reserve Cavalry, 99.
5. King, To Horse, 13.
6. W. H. Arehart, "Diary of W. H. Arehart," The Rockingham Recorder, vol. 1, no. 7 (1948), 224; Philadelphia Press, July 4, 1864.
7. Coller diary, entry for June 21, 1864.
8. Merington, The Custer Story, 103–04.
9. O.R., vol. 36, part 1, 843.

10. *The Cavalier*, July 7, 1863. The term "F.F.V." refers to the "First Families of Virginia," the social and economic elite of the state, including the Lee and Custis families. The correspondent colorfully continued, "It is a venerable brick structure, of the English style. On the top of the tower is a pair of huge keys, the emblem of its patron saint, to whom so many believe was given the custody of Heaven's gate."

11. Hall, *History of the Sixth New York Cavalry*, 201.

12. O.R., vol. 36, part 1, 843.

13. Cheney, *Ninth New York Cavalry*, 294. Major Bentley was discharged as a result of disability because of the amputation of his leg in October 1864, another victim of the war's brutality.

14. O.R., vol. 36, part 1, 859.

15. Lloyd, *History of the First Regiment Pennsylvania Reserve Cavalry*, 100–101.

16. Webb diary, entry for June 21, 1864.

17. Tobie, *First Maine Cavalry*, 290–92.

18. Webb diary, entry for June 21, 1864.

19. "Narrative of Cavalry Operations from Trevillian's to Ream's Station," *Richmond Sentinel*, July 13, 1864.

20. Strang, *Sunshine and Shadows*, 53.

21. Gracey, *Annals of the Sixth Pennsylvania Cavalry*, 265 and 269.

22. James H. Kidd to James M. Kidd, June 21, 1864, James H. Kidd Papers, Bentley Historical Library, University of Michigan, Ann Arbor.

23. O.R., vol. 36, part 3, 787.

24. King, *To Horse*, 13.

25. O.R., vol. 40, part 2, 285.

26. Grant, *Personal Memoirs*, 604.

27. O.R., vol. 40, part 2, 286. While the details of the Wilson–Kautz raid go far beyond the scope of this book, it is related to the Trevilian raid. For further information, see Wilson's report, found at O.R., vol. 40, part 1, 620.

28. In the fighting on June 21, in Butler's brigade, the Fifth S.C. Cavalry reported two men killed, eight men wounded and one man captured, for total losses of eleven. *Charleston Daily Courier*, July 11, 1864. In Lee's division, Wickham's Brigade reported losses in the Third Virginia Cavalry of six men wounded and in the Fourth Virginia Cavalry, two men killed and nine wounded, for losses of eleven. *Richmond Daily Dispatch*, July 1, 1864. Since these are only fractional reports, we can assume similar losses for those of Hampton's other regiments that were engaged.

29. Ferguson diary, entries for June 22 and 23, 1864.

30. Halliburton, *Saddle Soldiers*, 149.

31. Arehart, "Diary," 224.

32. Tobie, *First Maine Cavalry*, 292.

33. Mohr and Winslow, *The Cormany Diaries*, 437.

34. Keller to his sister, June 4, 1864.
35. Lloyd, *History of the First Regiment Pennsylvania Reserve Cavalry*, 102.
36. Grommon diary, entry for June 22, 1864.
37. O.R., vol. 36, part 1, 846.
38. Gracey, *Annals of the Sixth Pennsylvania Cavalry*, 266.
39. Fitch diary, entry for June 22, 1864.
40. O.R., vol. 36, part 3, 789.
41. *Philadelphia Inquirer*, July 5, 1864.
42. Pyne, *Ride to War*, 224.
43. Newhall, *With General Sheridan*, 21.
44. Strang, *Sunshine and Shadows*, 53.
45. O.R., vol. 36, part 1, 798.
46. Newhall, *With General Sheridan*, 22. Newhall's brother, Capt. Walter Newhall, who served with the Third Pennsylvania Cavalry prior to his death in December 1863, participated in extensive reconnaissances of this area during McClellan's Peninsula Campaign of 1862. Their commander, Col. (later Brig. Gen.) William W. Averell, a West Point classmate of Fitz Lee's, was quite proud of these extensive reconnaissances and the fact that their work had helped save the Army of the Potomac from being defeated in detail in 1862. Averell noted that his staff officers sketched the terrain between the James and the Chickahominy, which, when put together, created a map for McClellan "far better than any Confederate commander" could provide. See O.R., vol. 11, part 2, 234–35.
47. *Ibid.*
48. Mohr and Winslow, *The Cormany Diaries*, 437.
49. JTM to the Editor, *Pittsburgh Evening Chronicle*, July 9, 1864.
50. Arehart, "Diary," 224.
51. Wood diary, entry for June 23, 1864; Richard L. Armstrong, *Seventh Virginia Cavalry* (Lynchburg, Va.: H. E. Howard Co., 1992), 131.
52. O.R., vol. 36, part 1, 810 and 844.
53. Hall, *History of the Sixth New York Cavalry*, 202.
54. Richard L. T. Beale, *History of the Ninth Virginia Cavalry in the War between the States* (Richmond: B. F. Johnson, 1899), 129; Robert K. Krick, *Ninth Virginia Cavalry* (Lynchburg, Va.: H. E. Howard Co., 1982), 92.
55. Fitch diary, entry for June 23, 1864.
56. O.R., vol. 36, part 1, 798 and 844.
57. Sheridan, *Personal Memoirs*, 1:432–34.
58. Tobie, *First Maine Cavalry*, 292.
59. Fitch diary, entry for June 23, 1864.
60. Lucas to his wife, June 23, 1864.
61. Mohr and Winslow, *The Cormany Diaries*, 437.
62. King, *To Horse*, 13.

63. Hampton S. Thomas, *Personal Reminiscences of Service in the Cavalry of the Army of the Potomac* (Philadelphia: L. R. Hamersly & Co., 1889), 19.

64. O.R., vol. 36, part 3, 791.

65. *Richmond Dispatch*, June 25, 1864.

66. Waring diary, entry for June 23, 1864.

67. Halliburton, *Saddle Soldiers*, 150.

68. Fitzhugh Lee to Robert E. Lee, December 20, 1866.

69. O.R., vol. 36, part 1, 1096.

⇥ 10 ⇤

The Battle of Samaria Church and the End of the Trevilian Raid

We realized for the first time how it felt to get a good thrashing and then be chased for our lives.

Hampton received reinforcements on the morning of June 24, 1864. Brig. Gen. Martin W. Gary's independent cavalry brigade joined Hampton's force. "Mart" Gary was also known as the "Bald Eagle" because of his shiny pate. Like Butler, Gary was a Hampton protégé. A thirty-three-year-old Harvard-educated lawyer from South Carolina, Gary joined the Hampton Legion at the outset of the war. He assumed command of the legion when Hampton was wounded at First Manassas in July 1861. When the Hampton Legion was converted to a cavalry unit, Colonel Gary commanded it. He received a promotion to brigadier general in May 1864 and assumed command of a brigade consisting of the Hampton Legion, Seventh South Carolina Cavalry, and the Twenty-fourth Virginia Cavalry.

"Col. Gary . . . is a thoroughbred fighter, cool and deliberate, with great good sense. We need such a man . . . with his band of trained veterans—men who have often fought as infantry alone fight," raved Gen. Samuel Cooper, the Confederate adjutant general, in endorsing Gary's promotion in the spring of 1864.[1] A member of the Hampton Legion recalled that Gary "was a fearless officer with love for his old regiment, an officer who always studied the comforts and wants of his men and did not hesitate to show by promotion his high appreciation of gallantry on the part of an officer or the most humble private in his command."[2] His commanded an independent brigade assigned to the defenses of Richmond a month earlier. It became one of the most effective fighting forces attached to the Army of Northern Virginia's cavalry corps.[3] Hampton called the Bald Eagle's command a "splendid brigade and good fighters."[4]

The weary Confederates welcomed the reinforcements with open arms. Hampton's troopers had been marching and fighting for two solid weeks without rest for either men or animals. Food for both had been scarce, meaning that "their privations, consequently [were] severe." One of the South Carolinians recalled, "Often the hungry fellows, as they watched their animals browsing on grass, or, in its absence, on any green thing, could not avoid envy, wishing they, too, could graze." Both men and horses neared their breaking points. Further, "from casualties and exhaustion the number of effective troopers and horses was much reduced, and it should be remembered that, at the commencement of the expedition, the odds were two to one against them."[5] Fresh troopers not only invigorated Hampton's command, they also gave him additional offensive punch. He needed additional clout if he hoped to capture Sheridan's wagon train or destroy Sheridan's cavalry before it escaped to safety.

When Gary's independent brigade arrived, Hampton detached Lomax's brigade and sent it to hold the river road. Lomax made a final, unsuccessful effort to destroy the wagon train. The Ninth New York charged the Virginians and drove them for nearly a mile and a half. Lomax retreated across Herring Creek and assumed a position there. He frowned as he watched the opportunity to bag the vast Federal wagon train slip through his fingers.[6] A member of the Sixth Virginia complained, "The enemy declining to attack us well back a mile or more." Taking up position behind a crude breastwork, the Virginians held their position until the next morning.[7]

Hampton planned to go into battle with six full brigades of cavalry. Although the big South Carolinian did not know it, Sheridan's wagon train had arrived at Wilcox's Landing at dawn that morning, leaving Gregg's Second Division alone and unsupported. Davies's brigade, Sheridan's rear guard, was especially vulnerable. Sheridan reported to Gregg around 10:00 that morning, "There is some skirmishing in front of Charles City Court House, on road to Harrison's Landing. . . . I am now moving the infantry down, and will move Torbert's division. Look out for Davies. Support him if necessary."[8] Hampton had one chance to prevent the Federals from crossing the James River to safety, and he hoped to make the most of it. His force surrounded Gregg's division, maintaining its lonely vigil guarding Sheridan's flank near Samaria (St. Mary's) Church.[9]

The area surrounding Samaria Church is mostly flat, with gentle folds in the terrain. Samaria Church lay about three and one-half miles south of Long Bridge over the Chickahominy River and on, or very near, an imaginary line drawn between White House Landing on the Pamunkey and Harrison's Landing on the James River. The church was about twenty miles from Richmond. Salem Church sat about a mile and a half southwest of Samaria Church. Hampton established his headquarters at the Phillips house, near Salem Church, where he could keep an eye on both the river roads as well as Samaria Church. He held a blocking position along a low ridge, on a north-south axis, anchored at one end by Salem Church and by Nance's Shop on the other.[10] Hampton deployed his brigades from north to south. Chambliss's brigade held the northern end of the line, near Nance's Shop. Butler, Dulany, Wright, and Wickham held the southern end. The Twelfth Virginia, Twenty-fourth Virginia, Phillips Legion, and Jeff Davis Legion were held in reserve. Gary's brigade made flank march.

General Gregg, on the other side, knew that Hampton's force outnumbered his veteran Second Division. Several miles separated his two brigades and Torbert's division, camped near Charles City Court House. Gregg probably knew that Torbert could not support him if he got into trouble. The men of the Second Division were tired. "Since starting on the Trevilian Raid, June 7, we had been living chiefly on horse hair, dust and hotness, and while we didn't complain of it as food to fight upon, we did not consider it as composed of material which would produce corpulency," wrote one, "and most of the men had buttoned the front lapel of their pantaloons around onto their back suspender buttons, as a necessary precaution against falling through them when they dismounted."[11]

At 8:00 on the morning of June 24, obeying Sheridan's orders, and with the weather already uncomfortably hot and dry, Gregg advanced to Samaria Church. Gregg's division joined the Sixth Ohio Cavalry, whose pickets were already skirmishing with the enemy troopers in the fields to the west of the church.[12] Some of the Federals joked that they had flanked the Rebels and were going right into Richmond by the side door. Rather than riding into Richmond, these Yankee horse soldiers faced a rude surprise.[13] Arriving there, Gregg sent the Eighth Pennsylvania Cavalry to engage a small force of Hampton's pickets. They drove the Confederates for nearly a mile before breaking off.[14] Elements of the First Maine Cavalry also engaged the Confederate pickets, driving them off with a single volley. "Fight, to-day, boys, the

First Maine's got the advance," cried a jubilant trooper, his battle blood up. The Maine men pursued them as far as Samaria Church, where they halted and formed a defensive position.[15] They found Confederate campfires still burning and cooking utensils scattered in confusion by the fleeing Southerners.[16]

The First Massachusetts Cavalry had picket duty that morning. One officer, out riding the vidette lines with the regimental adjutant, had an unexpected encounter with several Confederate scouts. The Bay Stater wrote, "It was a surprise party to both, and I expected to go to Richmond; but they ran away, and we emptied our revolvers at them. While I was firing, my little horse suddenly threw up his head, and I shot him through the neck." Fortunately, the beast was not badly wounded and recovered quickly.[17] A member of the First Maine observed that the position held by his regiment was "directly across the road, the hardest place to defend if an attack should be made upon us."[18]

Gregg then deployed his cousin's brigade north of Samaria Church and Davies's brigade to the south of the church. His line faced west and parallel to Hampton's, although the southern end of his line may have been refused to protect the flank. He deployed the batteries of Randol and Dennison "in commanding positions."[19] His flank was in the air, with a wide, open field in front, and heavy woods behind. He detached the First New Jersey Cavalry to guard the division's train and to try to cover the exposed flank. Gregg's blue-clad troopers held the main road to Charles City Court House at a junction in front of the church critical to protecting Sheridan's flanks and the long wagon train. The deploying Yankees knew that the Confederates had not gone far. One wrote, "we could distinctly hear the Johnnies knocking about in the brush getting ready to make some of us fit subjects for a funeral."[20] As the occasional picket fire continued, orders reached the First Massachusetts Cavalry to go to Wilcox's Landing to look for signs of Sheridan's train there. Arriving, the First Massachusetts found the train. The regimental commander, Col. Samuel E. Chamberlain, reported to Sheridan. Sheridan informed Chamberlain that the wagon train had arrived safely and instructed him to return to Samaria Church with orders for Gregg to retire.[21]

Both sides deployed pickets several hundred yards ahead of their main lines of battle.[22] For several hours, Gregg's division traded potshots with Hampton's men all along the line. Davies's brigade held an open space on slightly rising ground. A shabby little house occupied by an invalid, his wife, and several children stood at the center of Davies's line. The regimental surgeon of the Sixth Ohio Cavalry recalled that the residents of the wretched hovel "were thoroughly alarmed at the threatening outlook, as well they might be." When picket fire broke out, the family sought shelter in their basement. They only emerged when the fighting finally ended well after dark.[23]

As the men exchanged skirmish fire, Butler reconnoitered Gregg's position. Noting that heavy woods and a fence line surrounded Gregg, Butler concluded that a direct assault would lead to heavy losses to his men. He suggested that Hampton launch a flanking attack on the end of Gregg's line, just to the north of Samaria Church. The attack would "strike Gregg a fatal blow without a great loss to our side." While Butler awaited a response from Hampton, Fitz Lee rode up to Butler's headquarters, posted at the base of a large tree, "where the bullets were flying uncomfortably close." When Butler informed Lee that Gregg had an exposed flank, Lee sent Maj. James D. Ferguson to ask Hampton for permission to take command of the field. Hampton granted the request and instructed Butler to take orders from Lee.[24]

That morning Sheridan had ordered Gregg to hold fast at the church until the entire wagon train finally arrived. Those orders arrived midafternoon. The courier also informed Gregg that Torbert had been fighting Lomax's brigade south of Charles City Court House and that the Confederates had been driven back. He reported that Sheridan had decided to park the huge wagon train at Wilcox's Landing until the road to Deep Bottom could be opened, or other arrangements could be made for crossing the James.[25] Gregg later wrote, "A large force of the enemy was known to have passed St. Mary's Church, moving in the direction of Haxall's on the evening before." Aware that he was unsupported, Gregg made "every disposition . . . to resist an attack of the enemy should it be made."[26]

Hampton later noted that "the enemy had . . . thrown up strong works along his whole line, and his position was a strong one."[27] One of Chambliss's officers recalled that "These regiments, numbering eleven, with three batteries, were placed in a strong position, which they at once proceeded to fortify with breastworks of logs, rails, and felled trees."[28] Gregg's outnumbered command faced a severe test that day. It remained to be seen just how severe that fight would be.

In fact, Hampton was preparing an all-out assault on Gregg's line. After receiving word that Gregg's flank was exposed, Hampton sent Gary's brigade on a flank march from Salem Church to Nance's Shop. Gary was to attack Gregg's flank as soon as the main assault began. Two regiments of Gary's brigade, the Hampton Legion and the Seventh South Carolina, marched to Smith's Store, turned northeast, and deployed in line of battle in the fields surrounding Nance's Shop. Gary's other regiment, the Twenty-fourth Virginia, remained in reserve, along with the Jeff Davis Legion, Phillips Legion, and the Twelfth Virginia. A significant swale separated the shop and Gregg's line, and Gary's horse soldiers moved into position to assault Irvin Gregg's flank without being detected. "Only the videttes and men in the skirmish line had as yet seen a blue coat, owing to the woods of pine that restricted the view," recalled Lt. George W. Beale of the Ninth Virginia Cavalry of Chambliss's Brigade.[29]

Rufus Peck of the Second Virginia Cavalry remarked that "a lot of pines about as high as a man's head" intervened between the two lines.[30] Around 3:00, as Gregg received the order to withdraw, Gary's men went forward on foot. The Rebel yell—a yell intended to make the blue-clad horse soldiers believe that the Confederates meant business—quavered. Gary's South Carolinians crashed into Irvin Gregg's exposed flank.[31] Lieutenant Beale noted, "Scarcely had the Confederate line begun to advance before the line of skirmishers in the woods before them became more and more rapid. Presently, the main body had reached the skirmish line, and only sixty or seventy paces in front of them stretched away on either side the formidable line of breastworks, which were partly concealed and partly revealed by the smoke and fire of carbines."[32]

Sgt. Nathan Webb of the First Maine Cavalry watched the solid gray line advancing toward his hastily constructed works. "Instantly all our men were on their feet and everybody alert. As for myself, I confess my heart was in my mouth," recorded Webb. Trying to keep from panicking, the young Maine trooper envisioned watching the enemy fall back, repulsed from the strong Northern position. His mind's eye chose success over the less attractive alternative. "But in spite of me," he admitted, "I thought of home and possible wounds."[33]

As Gary's men engaged, Fitz Lee also committed Wickham's brigade to the fight. Wickham's brigade connected with Gary's and the two brigades moved against the end of David Gregg's line to the north of Samaria Church.

Watching the two brigades smash into the Union flank, Lee ordered the rest of the line to join the attack against the hastily constructed Federal works. Obeying the shouted orders, Chambliss's brigade went forward. After advancing about two hundred yards across the open field, the Virginians "were met by a very severe fire from a log breastwork in the woods, which curved considerably to the left." Responding with a piercing Rebel yell, Chambliss's men engaged the enemy at close quarters, breaking the initial Federal line. The Confederates soon received flanking fire from the stout Union breastworks, breaking the momentum of their charge. The Virginians had to fall back and regroup.

The Confederates then charged across an open field into the murderous fire of Gregg's carbines. One Federal recalled, "only our frail breastwork separates us and we fight so near each other that we distinguish each other's features."[34] Undeterred, "with excellent alignment and orderly movement two hundred yards were passed at a double-quick," the Virginians came on, finally crashing into the Northern breastworks and driving the Federals from them. Munford's Second Virginia Cavalry also advanced rapidly across the open field toward Gregg's line.[35] Unleashing volley after volley, the Virginians shattered Gregg's initial position.[36]

Col. Richard Dulany sent his Laurel Brigade in on the extreme left of Gregg's works, losing eight men wounded. Dulany noted, "As we turned their flank Genl. Butler dislodged them in front."[37] One officer of the Twenty-fourth Virginia Cavalry remembered that "the entrenchments were scaled and the enemy driven out."[38] A severe firefight raged, with the Confederates charging "in the face of a very heavy fire of artillery and musketry, and it was most handsomely accomplished."[39] One of the Maine men described the massed Southern assault as falling on the Federals "like a thunderbolt."[40]

In a matter of moments, Gregg's bugles sounded, "To horse! Double-quick!" and the orders "Mount! Mount!" rang through the woods.[41] Soon the entire Second Division faced severe pressure. The First Massachusetts arrived just as Hampton's attack jumped off. The Bay Staters "were sent at a gallop into the line, and found every regiment but ours fighting, dismounted, and heavily engaged."[42] Pvt. Giles Taylor of the First Massachusetts turned to his friend Sgt. Stanton P. Allen and said, "I wish I had enlisted in the infantry."

"Why so?" inquired Allen.

"Because the doughboys don't have to stay up all night doctoring sick horses, and then fight on foot, and have their horses led off so far that if they get whipped they can't use them to run away with. Here's the whole Southern Confederacy coming down on our one little division, and the general has had our horses taken so far to the rear that we never can reach them if we are obliged to get out of this. This is going to be a worse place than the Wilderness," predicted Taylor.

"Well," replied a resigned Allen, "they can't kill us but once."

As he watched the Rebel advance bearing down on their position, Taylor groaned, "But I'd rather be killed in an open field, on horseback, than to be sabred to death behind a fence."[43]

Lt. Samuel Cormany recalled that "our lines were charged many times, but we repulsed them and held our ground, or line handsomely."[44] "The rebel troopers needed but one volley at close range to convince them that they had a bigger job on hand than they had bargained for," observed Allen, "The first assault was repulsed all along our front, and the attack on our left flank by the brigades of Chambliss and Gary did not succeed in breaking Gregg's lines. The Federal troopers cheered as the rebels withdrew to prepare for a renewal of the onslaught."[45] It soon came and Gregg's proud veterans again repulsed the Confederates. The gray-clad troopers fell back to regroup again. The Yankee troopers knew that they would not have long to wait for a third assault. One of Davies's men reflected, "We were hoping that the strife was over and soon those of us alive would pursue our enemy towards the river. But again, as if the Devil possessed them, they are seen forming for another attack."[46]

Col. Charles H. Smith of the First Maine, a thirty-seven-year-old school-teacher, was shot in the leg. The same ball also killed his horse.[47] His men became demoralized and started falling back. Despite the pain of his wound, Smith refused to leave the field. Instead, he rallied his troopers, who in spite of the din of battle, called out three cheers for their injured commander. The Maine men turned on the enemy and made a stand, the tide of battle flowing back and forth. One of the Maine men wrote, "Up close to our works they come and after a few rounds are fired, muskets are clubbed, and savagely the conflict rages."[48] They repulsed three attacks before finally being driven from the field by the ferocity of the Southern attack.[49] In the closing moments of the fight, the colonel lost a second horse shot out from under him. Mounting an orderly's horse, the injured colonel rallied his troopers, preventing them from breaking and running. Smith was the last member of the First Maine to leave the field, and he received a brevet to brigadier general of volunteers for his gallantry that day. When Smith returned to duty, he received command of a brigade of cavalry that was specifically assembled for him.[50]

Years after the war, Gregg submitted Smith's name for a Medal of Honor. In nominating Smith for the Medal, Gregg wrote that the injured colonel "did not relinquish command as he might very properly have done, but resolutely held on, and by his presence encouraged his men to resist to the last." Gregg continued, "The gallantry of Col. Smith was conspicuous, and was mentioned in the report of his Brigade Commander, it contributed in a marked degree to our successful resistance of the enemy's fierce attacks." On April 6, 1895, Smith received the Medal of Honor "for gallantry at St. Mary's Church, Va., June 24, 1864."[51]

Gregg noted, not entirely accurately, "It was very soon evident that the force of the enemy was largely superior to ours, and that they were supported by infantry, but nothing daunted by the display of strong lines of an overconfident enemy, our men fell upon them and held them in check. The strife was in earnest now; there were no disengaged men on our side." Years later, he described the ordeal as an enemy "onslaught" that "necessitated unusually hard fighting to prevent the enemy from crushing us."[52] "Savagely the Rebels fight, clubbing their muskets and closely in their rear can be seen Wade Hampton and Fitz Hugh Lee, Gen. Chambliss and Gen. Butler driving their men on. The train! The train! is their rallying cry," observed Webb.[53] Capt. Hampton Thomas of the First Pennsylvania Cavalry had an apt description for the action: "We came together like two battering rams, then backed off for vantage-ground, and went at each other again and again."[54]

Sheridan praised Gregg in his memoirs: "For two hours [Hampton] continued to attack, but made little impression on Gregg—gain at one point being counterbalanced by failure at another."[55] The First Massachusetts, supporting the batteries, spent the balance of the fight with them, watching the eight guns belch flame.[56] The regimental historian of the First New Jersey Cavalry, watching the action, recorded, "Owing to the formation of the ground . . . the rebels could not bring their artillery into position, while we had two splendid four-gun batteries, which opened with great effect."[57] One of Wickham's Virginians recalled that the Federals "had a good deal of artillery, which did so much harm" that day.[58]

While the fighting raged, Lieutenant Cormany dismounted and sat on a stump, writing notes of his company's doings. A Confederate rifleman got his range. The Rebel sharpshooter's bullets kicked up little puffs of dust close in front of Cormany, causing one of his men to call out, "Lieut! That Johnny has pretty close range of you!" Cormany replied that he had noticed that fact when another bullet struck the stump, between his feet, "taking with it a bit of my boot and barely grazed my ankle—inside—slightly removing a little cuticle—but doing me no harm save what a boot-mender can repair." The lucky lieutenant moved to a safer place to finish writing his notes.[59]

With Munford leading the way, the Second Virginia Cavalry attacked dismounted. The determined Virginians drove a group of Federals from their breastworks. The Union men supported a battery perched atop a nearby knoll. Pursuing them, the Virginians saw their blue-clad quarries headed for refuge among some nearby farm buildings. The Northerners sheltered in a log home, shooting at their pursuers through cracks. Their fire caused no casualties among the pursuers. The Virginians flanked the position, swinging around the barn. When the Northerners saw that they had been flanked, about twenty-five of them ran out and tried to escape through a solid plank gate. However, the gate opened in instead of out, and a bottleneck developed. The surging Confederates demanded the surrender of the desperate Yankee troopers, but Gregg's men responded by opening fire. One member of the Second Virginia noted, "we had to fire at them. We killed or wounded every man." The Confederates then charged the artillery position, but the guns had already limbered up and withdrawn. The only loss sustained by the Virginians was Capt. Willoughby W. Tebbs of Company K, Second Virginia Cavalry. An unexploded artillery shell fell from a tree and burst, decapitating Tebbs.[60]

Pvt. Dewitt C. Gallagher of the First Virginia Cavalry described the day's action in his diary: "Fight—a sharp one, with Gregg's cavalry." As Gallagher and his comrades waited to move out, a Federal artillery shell exploded near him, striking the private's left boot. Staggered, Gallagher nearly fell. Some of his friends, believing that his ankle had been broken, tried to carry him from the field. Gallagher refused and joined the attack, hobbling across the open fields. He noted, "I got close up to a General, or a bunch of officers, trying to rally their fleeing men and took deliberate aim at him and can never understand why he did not fall as he galloped away. He may have been only wounded."[61]

Col. Pennock Huey mounted the Eighth Pennsylvania Cavalry and charged, driving the Confederates back toward the woods behind Nance's Shop. Huey's foray saved Randol's guns from capture by the onrushing Southern horsemen. The Pennsylvanians then dismounted and fought on foot. A Confederate rally forced them to fall back.[62] The rapid fire of the Federal carbines took a heavy toll on the onrushing Southerners, many of whom fell within a few feet of the Union breastworks. Some fell on them. With the fight raging, Gregg's two batteries "pitched load after load of canister into the staggering lines of the enemy."[63] Pvt. Horatio Nelson of the Fourth Virginia Cavalry fell mortally wounded. Nelson lingered in great agony for two days before dying in Richmond.[64] The gray-clad horse soldiers pressed on, looking to break Gregg's line.

The men of the Tenth New York were enjoying a meal half a mile behind the main line when the firing began. They moved forward into position alongside the Sixth Ohio, which was already engaged. The ferocity of Hampton's attack drove the Tenth New York from its initial position. They fell back to a second position and hastily threw up crude breastworks along the edge of a field. They soon abandoned this position and retreated another 150 yards to a natural entrenchment along a ditch. They tore down a fence and placed the planks across the top of the trench, creating a strong position.

Capt. George Vanderbilt recounted, "The rebs kept up a heavy fire from the woods for a few minutes, then out came a cloud of skirmishers, followed by a heavy line of battle; the skirmishers were soon absorbed by the main line; then with their peculiar yell they charged." He continued, "We held our fire until they were within fifty feet, then gave them such a terrific fire with our carbines and revolvers they could not stand it; they broke and fled pell-mell for the cover of the woods, our men dropping many of them on the way." Back in the shelter of the woods, the Confederates resumed firing at the New Yorkers. They came under both enemy fire and the fire of their own artillery bursting overhead. The beleaguered Tenth New York repulsed a second attack, gray-clad casualties piling up in front of the trench.

Soon, the New Yorkers ran low on ammunition. Captain Vanderbilt sent back for more, but none could be spared. Sgt. L. P. Norton of Company L asked for permission to try again. Vanderbilt tried to discourage the sergeant, telling him that he did not believe that the sergeant would come back alive. Norton replied, "Captain, I know it's risky, but I'll chance it." Soon, he returned with a small supply of ammunition, which he quickly distributed. A Rebel bullet had ruined his hat, another had passed through his coat sleeve and then between the coat and his arm, a third had cut holes in his clothing, and a fourth had punched a hole in his canteen.[65]

Another member of the Tenth New York, Pvt. Edmund M. Tuton of Company E, watched the Confederate wave crash into the flimsy rail barricade. An enemy ball struck Tuton in the left breast, hitting just to the left of the buttons on his tunic. The fierce fighting left Tuton no time to investigate the extent of the harm caused. Instead, he emptied his carbine at the attacking Rebels. At one point, his carbine grew so hot that the weapon discharged when he drew the lever block up to its place in the breech. Tuton recalled that "On casting my eye along the fence that extended through the woods to our left, I was almost paralyzed to see about a dozen rebs on the left, and on our side of the fence, some four or five rods away, while as far as I could see along the fence to our left in the woods they were coming over like so many sheep." Discharging his carbine randomly and beating a hasty retreat, Tuton made it to safety. He and his comrades fell back to a tree line and eventually retreated toward Charles City Court House.[66]

Although the Northern horse soldiers fended off the fierce attacks of Hampton and Lee, the Confederates badly outnumbered them. They realized that it was only a matter of time until they had to withdraw. Despite the heavy odds, the Federals resisted vigorously, artillery and carbines ringing. "As fast as one line fell back before the carbines of the cavalry and the terrible canister of Denison and Randol, a fresh line pushed forward to take their place," observed the regimental historian of the First New Jersey Cavalry, "and slowly, with unbroken formation, our men began to retire across the open ground." Through the fusillade of enemy fire, the men of the Sixth Ohio Cavalry sat their horses, sabres drawn. They protected the guns of Randol's battery from the mad dashes of the Confederates.[67] However, "it was no use; it did not stop them."[68] One Virginian noted, "When at a few points men in the attacking line began to leap over the piled logs, and the Federals were forced to beat a hasty retreat, receiving volleys as they ran."[69] David Gregg's beleaguered men held on for two long hours, before "it became evident that the contest was too unequal to maintain it longer."[70]

The men of the First Pennsylvania Cavalry, supporting Denison's battery, dismounted and advanced to a nearby hill that covered both the battery and the flank. They got there just before the Confederates. A well-timed volley dampened the Southerners' enthusiasm. The Sixth Ohio joined them there. Capt. J. H. Leeman, commander of Company C of the Sixth Ohio, sat to the right of the roaring guns, "showing no indication of fear or alarm as to the result, but directed us to fire by volley, as he gave the necessary orders in a clear, steady voice, 'Load—ready—aim—fire!'" Holding a position atop a low ridge, the two regiments opened a withering fire on the advancing Confederates.[71] The Pennsylvanians and Ohioans held them off with accurate fire until they saw that the bulk of Davies's brigade and Randol's battery had passed safely to the rear. Then they abandoned their strongpoint atop the knoll. The men of the First Pennsylvania and Sixth Ohio safely detoured through the woods and joined the rest of Gregg's division.[72]

With the First Pennsylvania withdrawing, Denison's guns also withdrew. The departure of the Pennsylvanians left the battery's right flank uncovered. The Confederate advance threatened their position. One of Gregg's aides-de-camp rode up to Lieutenant Denison and said, "Take care! They will get your guns!"

"Take my battery!" cried the artillerist. "They cannot take my battery. No rebels on that field can take my battery!" he exclaimed, still blasting away at the advancing gray-clad troopers. Denison would not pull out until he depleted all of his ammunition and the men of the First Pennsylvania withdrew.[73]

Gregg realized that he faced disaster unless he withdrew. Maj. Jonathan P. Cilley of the First Maine summed up the plight of Gregg's command: "the urge to run was almost irresistible at times."[74] Gregg sent his horses, wounded men who had transportation, and caissons down the road to Charles City Court House. Gregg's division broke off the engagement, one unit at a time, prompting one Confederate to brag, "we . . . drove them from every position in confusion, with but little loss to our ourselves."[75] The Sixteenth Pennsylvania Cavalry fought a delaying action as it fell back.[76]

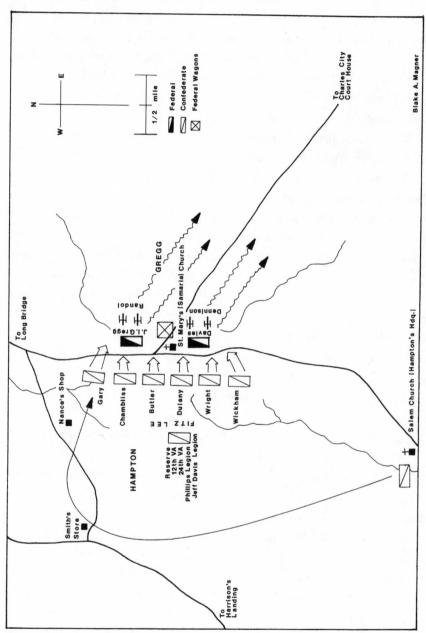

Battle of Samaria Church, June 24, 1864

Blake A. Magner

"As we came out of a wood, the Col. . . . with the First Squadron faces the charging enemy and they pour volleys into them—thus retarding them," recounted Lieutenant Cormany, "and while I rallied my squadron some distance in the rear or rearward on the opposite side of the road—on an elevation." As Cormany's men rallied, they lustily sang a popular marching song "We'll Rally Round the Flag, Boys." Others, routed and without leadership or organization, fell in with Cormany's squadron, forming a solid front. Cormany told his motley command that they could expect the rest of the regiment to come flying back at any moment, and that they should await his orders before opening fire. Once he gave the order to fire, the men were to "pour it in with precision—and continuously, until the Reg't had time to form further back on our right and rear."

He did not have long to wait. Soon, the balance of the regiment fell back. Lt. Col. John K. Robison called for them to remain steady as they passed Cormany's position. The heavy dust and smoke from the black powder of the carbines and rifles blinded Cormany's men, who could not see the enemy's advance until it was within 100 yards of his position. Cormany ordered his men to fire, and "such a volley greeted them as checked them all and dismounted many—and the same was repeated several times, when an effort to flank us made it necessary for us to 'By fours, right about face' and move to the rear steadily, firing occasionally to the rear or 'rear-right-oblique.'" Soon, they had reached the next position held by the rest of the regiment, and Cormany's men dropped back. He concluded, "Thus by 'echelon' we held the enemy back—until night relieved us from further pressure."[77] Similarly, a member of the Sixth Ohio Cavalry remembered that "it was a series of stands and retreats, for the foe greatly outnumbered our forces. At every position lost by us, the enemy planted his artillery, and vigorously bombarded our retreating troops, inflicting some damage, but the main effect was to increase the speed of the retreating trains and non-combatants."[78]

Commissary Sgt. James C. Boice of the Sixth Ohio Cavalry learned that his friend John S. Fulk had been shot through the left lung, just below the collarbone. Boice attempted to get Fulk to his horse, but the wounded man was in too much pain to ride. As Boice slowly led his friend's horse away, the gray-clad pursuers closed in. Soon, the enemy was so close that Boice heard their calls for his surrender. Lt. M. H. Cryer's horse, which was just behind Fulk, had been seriously wounded and struggled to keep up. Recognizing the danger, Boice gave Fulk his canteen and left him behind, recalling, "I did hate to leave him, and to this day I feel badly when I think of it." Following, Cryer said, "Go, and I will follow you." Reaching the safety of the woods, they found an unattended horse tied to a tree. Cryer mounted and went only a short distance when this horse, too, was shot. However, the two Buckeyes escaped.[79]

Fortunately, the heavy woods provided some degree of protection from the pursuing Rebels. "Our men continued fighting on foot, but were mounted from time to time," wrote Gregg.[80] Not all of the Federals remembered it as an orderly withdrawal. "Our men on the line were out of ammunition, and in ten minutes the whole line was on the skedaddle. The batteries' ammunition soon gave out, too, and we were seven miles from our trains, and there was nothing to do but run for it. We saved the guns with difficulty. . . . We were the last off the field, and I think it was as hot a place as I ever got into," recalled an officer of the First Massachusetts. More than thirty of the Bay Staters were captured.[81] Likewise, one of the Pennsylvanians recalled that "a general falling back takes place—with some regiments amounting to almost a stampede and panic."[82]

The mounted Lieutenant Beale chased a dismounted Yankee down a path alongside the road to Charles City Court House. Seeing his quarry fall, Beale assumed that the man had stumbled. However, on reaching the man, Beale noticed that a pursuing bullet had killed the man instantly. Beale paused for a moment to examine the body, taking "a fine pistol" and "a few letters, which proved to be tender missives from his New England lady love."[83]

Beale's father, Col. Richard L. T. Beale, commanded the Ninth Virginia Cavalry. The elder Beale, swept up in the pursuit of the fleeing Yankees, ran as far as he could. However, he soon collapsed beside the road, "overcome with heat and thirst, but he was making a tremendous noise yelling to the men *to go ahead!*" Colonel Beale recuperated quickly and resumed command of his regiment that evening. He greatly lamented the lack of a general pursuit.[84]

The extreme heat prostrated a number of Gregg's men and even produced some deaths as the Northerners fled toward the safety of the large Union bases along the James River. "The movement toward Charles City Court

House was made in the best possible order, without confusion or disorder," wrote Gregg. "The enemy pressed hard upon the rear of the command, but without advantage. A final stand made by mounted regiments at Hopewell Church on open ground determined the enemy to make no farther advance."[85] In fact, a strong second Union line of battle met the pursuing Southerners "with such a furious fusillade as made it necessary to pause and reform their line." Hampton's command paused to reform its lines, and their return fire quickly exhausted the ammunition of some of the Southern regiments. However, "some of Hampton's regiments were advancing under more favorable conditions, having the shelter of woods. Their advance soon caused the men under Gregg to withdraw from their barricade and remount in order to escape."[86]

The gray-clad tidal wave swept the dismounted Northerners from the field, meaning that the skirmishers had to no time to mount. The historian of the Tenth New York Cavalry remembered, "we came to a line the staff officers had formed. We passed through this . . . then formed another line. Soon the line we had passed came running through us; and so the retreat was kept up, running and fighting, a distance of about six miles, when the Johnnies stopped chasing us."[87] Gregg's steely veterans made numerous stands along the route of the retreat, buying time for their comrades to make it to safety.

The road to Charles City Court House, jammed by led horses and artillery mixed up with pack mules and panicked mounted and dismounted men, was a cacophony of shouting and cursing. Gregg and his staff officers and orderlies joined the rear guard, controlling the pace of the retreat as well as possible. At one point, Gregg dismounted beside a downed Union officer, who lay on the ground mortally wounded. The advancing enemy nearly captured the inattentive division commander. Gregg's assistant adjutant general, Capt. Henry C. Weir, had gotten separated from the division commander and his other staff officers. Riding back, Weir alerted Gregg to the imminent danger, getting Gregg to mount and ride off just in time to avoid capture.

Weir, whose father was an instructor at West Point, wheeled and faced the enemy armed only with his revolver. He opened fire, blunting the Confederate pursuit. Weir mounted his horse and escaped.[88] The staff officer was known as "intensely patriotic, high-toned in character, and one of the bravest men" in the Second Division.[89] Gregg later praised Weir's "great daring and love of fighting . . . he was always seeking opportunity to be in the midst of the severest fighting." He also commented that when Weir was caught up in the maelstrom of the rout on June 24 and did not turn up at divisional headquarters immediately, "I concluded that he had been killed or captured."[90]

Weir joined the fray as the retreat milled back. One of his fellow staff officers fell beside him in the melee. "Who did that?" asked Weir, pulling up his horse and wheeling around. An orderly pointed out the Rebel officer who had fired the shot. "The next moment Weir was among the enemy, and had blown out the rebel's brains. Then, with the same suddenness, he dashed back to our line." Weir gave his horse to the wounded officer and rallied some of the dismounted troopers. Armed with only his revolver, the heroic captain helped fend off the last charges of Hampton's men before they called off the pursuit. Col. John P. Taylor of the First Pennsylvania Cavalry, Weir's former regiment, wrote, "I feel sir if there is a soldier in the Army of the Potomac worthy of a Medal it is . . . H. C. Weir."[91] Weir received a brevet to major for conspicuous gallantry and meritorious service in August 1864, and got the Medal of Honor in May 1899 as a reward for his actions at Samaria Church.[92]

One Northerner observed, "It was the most disorderly retreat I ever have seen since I have been in the service. If the rebels had pushed hard just then they would have gobbled the whole thing." Many of Gregg's mounts were killed during the retreat, meaning more men joined the swelling ranks of Company Q, and also meaning that there were more stragglers to be snapped up by an aggressive pursuit.[93] The retreat was so chaotic that much of the fighting had to be done by ear. In one charge, a Southern horse soldier, "imagining that he was followed by his comrades, rode through the thickest dust, and suddenly came out in the presence of General Davies, and a crowd of our officers." When Davies inquired, "Who are you?" the man could respond with only one response, "I surrender."[94]

"Ambulances were in motion, and litters carried by four men each were noticeable bearing away the dead and wounded. A few sharpshooters were still in line, giving occasional shots, and shells continued to be thrown to check pursuit, but the order to retreat had been given, and the move had begun. Never, perhaps, had the Confederate cavalry a more inviting or promising occasion for a bold and rapid dash," keenly observed Lieutenant Beale.

The heat that day rendered many of Hampton's men combat ineffective. Hampton committed his reserve, the Twelfth and Twenty-fourth Virginia and the Phillips and Jeff Davis legions, to the fight. Crying, "The wagons! The wagons!," these units drew sabres and charged, chasing the fugitives for nearly five miles.[95] "This was done in fine style, men and horses seeming to have quite forgotten fatigue and hunger, and for three miles the pursuit was continued," stated an exhausted South Carolinian.[96]

Lt. George Baylor of the Twelfth Virginia Cavalry led his company, the Baylor Light Horse, after the fleeing Yankee troopers. Riding alongside his commanding officer, Col. Thomas B. Massie, Baylor saw the colonel receive a serious wound. Baylor continued on, leading his troopers as they chased Gregg's men. Suddenly, a spent ball struck Baylor in the chest. Fortunately, Baylor wore a badge of the Union Philosophical Society of his alma mater, Dickinson College, on his breast. The badge was a Maltese cross, surmounted with a shield. The spent ball tore off the shield and bent the cross into a distorted shape. Baylor's imagination played havoc with him and he believed himself mortally wounded. He thought that he could feel daylight passing through him and that blood ran down his front, leaving him gasping for breath.

One of his men, trooper John Terrill, riding near the lieutenant, noticed Baylor's pallor and peculiar behavior and jumped to the conclusion that his company commander had been mortally wounded. Leading Baylor's horse back over a small declivity, out of the range of more flying missiles, Terrill pulled open the captain's jacket and shirt and proclaimed, "Lieutenant, you are not much hurt, the ball hasn't gone in!" Terrill pulled the ball free with his finger and held it up for Baylor to see. Baylor remembered, "My spirits revived immediately, blood ceased to trickle, internal daylight disappeared, I breathed freely, vigor and strength returned, and, gathering up my reins, I was soon back in the fight."[97]

Lt. Col. William Stokes also chased the fleeing Federals. "I continued the pursuit some two or three miles where I finally broke down as did most of the Regiment (the horses were exhausted) and the mounted cavalry came up," he recounted, "so we stopped for our horses and . . . returned and slept on the battlefield."[98] Colonel Dulany, the commander of the Laurel Brigade, stated, "If we could have run our horses we would have captured many more, but we had nearly all broken down and had to stop and rest."[99] Trooper Gallagher of the First Virginia Cavalry, who had chased the fleeing Yankees on foot for three or four miles, collapsed with exhaustion. He noted in his diary, "I was never so tired in my life carrying my carbine pistol and ammunition, but the excitement kept me up. . . . Oh How glad I was to again mount my faithful horse and go into camp for the night!"[100]

Many of the exhausted Federal troopers, who had had no water all day, and who had fought for hours, collapsed by the wayside in the intense heat. The surging Rebels captured many of the dismounted men in the lines. The Federals were simply too tired to escape. "They were so completely used up that they could not run. They would go a few rods, and then, if their feet touched the least obstacle, they would pitch head over heels and just lie there. We told them the rebels were right after them, then they would get up with great effort and try again, but it was no use; they had not the strength, poor fellows."[101] Arriving at the court house, Gregg's division rallied, camping just outside the town.[102] The Federals established a rallying point at a crossroads near the town.

Northern officers cobbled together a line of battle, and all around could be heard cries like, "This way, First Maine," "Here you are, Eighth Pennsylvania," or "First New Jersey here."[103] An officer of the First Massachusetts Cavalry recalled, "Hampton drove us until it got dark, when he stopped, and we tried to get some order into the division. In the confusion the men had got away from their regiments and in the darkness everybody camped where he found himself, and waited for daylight to put things to rights. Some of the Tenth New York went to the river before stopping."[104] The beleaguered troopers of the First Pennsylvania did not reach safety at Charles City Court House until almost 11:00 that night. Once they arrived, they stood to horse all night, wary for a Confederate pursuit. The men of the Second Division had had an exhausting day that they would not soon forget.[105]

A Federal field hospital had been established approximately one mile behind the main line of battle. As the fighting raged, wounded soldiers trickled into the hospital, but it soon became obvious that the position was untenable and that the wounded men had to be moved. As the regimental surgeons labored, one of Gregg's staff officers spurred up, crying out, "Get out of here!" as the pursuing enemy was about to fall on their position. Dr. Alonzo D. Rockwell, chief surgeon of the Sixth Ohio Cavalry, recalled, "A few bursting shells gave emphasis to these words, and with no delay, the wounded were once again hustled into the waiting ambulances." The ambulances pulled out, and Rockwell was about to follow when four men showed up, bearing a wounded man on a shutter.

Rockwell paused. He learned that the desperately injured man was his friend the regimental adjutant, Lt. Henry Baldwin. The surgeon quickly realized that the adjutant would not survive. When Baldwin, in halting tones, inquired if he had a mortal wound, Rockwell tried to be cheerful, but the wounded man understood, saying, "My time, then, has come; I must die." As the doctor ministered to the dying man, Hampton's pursuing cavalry could be seen on a crest of ground not far away. Fleeing Yankee horse soldiers soon surrounded Rockwell. The winded Federals refused to leave Baldwin behind and carried him off on foot.

A few moments later, the sound of hoof beats pounding behind them told the Federals that the pursuing Confederates were almost on top of them. Rockwell recalled, "There was not a moment to lose; recognizing this, the adjutant, raising himself on his elbow with a last effort, gazed wildly at the approaching foe and exclaimed, 'Leave me, boys, leave me,' and he was dropped and left to his fate." The pursuing Rebel horsemen somehow avoided trampling Baldwin, who lived just a few moments longer. The next day, Rockwell found the adjutant's body lying alongside the road. He learned that a "kindly old negro" had ministered to the mortally wounded man. Baldwin's unselfish act deeply moved Rockwell, who recalled it emotionally for the rest of his life.[106]

Gregg had to leave many of his other wounded behind because of the lack of adequate transportation to move all of them to safety, a situation that Gregg regretted deeply. Gloating, one of the Richmond newspapers reported, "We felt sorry for when we saw wounded horses lying on the field—for the horse is a noble animal—but the cries of Sheridan's thieves and house burners was music to our ears, and we saw with satisfaction that many of these plunderers had met their just dues for their many outrages."[107] Most of the wounded Federals fell into the hands of the Confederates, who, in turn, left them in the hands of the local populace.[108] When the Southerners withdrew to pursue Wilson's raiders, the returning Union troopers recovered many of the bodies. That night Gregg told a friend that his fight might be considered successful if he lost no more than 1,000 men that day.[109]

Men straggled into camp near Charles City Court House almost all night. All told, and to his pleasant surprise, Gregg's division suffered 357 commissioned officers and enlisted men killed, wounded, or captured. The Confederates surrounded and captured Colonel Huey and a few men he had rallied.[110] One of the Richmond papers reported finding thirty dead Yankees clumped together on one portion of the battlefield.[111] Major Cilley, second-ranking officer of the First Maine Cavalry, was also wounded that day, meaning that the First Maine's two senior officers were left unfit for further duty.[112] The First Maine, which bore the brunt of the fighting, went into battle that day with approximately 260 officers and men. It lost 10 officers and 56 enlisted men killed, wounded, or captured, for 26 percent losses, a staggering toll, particularly considering the short duration of the fight.[113] A Georgia newspaper claimed, "Most of the enemy were killed after they had been driven from their works and were in retreat, when we fired into them from rear and flank."[114]

In this brief engagement, the Pennsylvanian's division suffered heavier casualties than Sheridan's entire command did on the second day at Trevilian Station.[115] Colonel Stokes of the Fourth South Carolina Cavalry reported that the Confederates had captured two of Gregg's artillery pieces, but Gregg never mentioned losing any of his guns, something that was a matter of great embarrassment to any general officer.[116] The prisoners were sent to Richmond under command of Capt. "Pick" Butler, younger brother of the Confederate brigade commander.[117]

Lt. Col. George H. Covode of the Fourth Pennsylvania Cavalry was mortally wounded while leading his regiment in battle. As the Confederates pursued Gregg's precipitous retreat, Butler and his staff trotted along behind. The general spotted a large man with long red sideburns lying by the roadside on an improvised stretcher made up of an army blanket with two poles on either end. Butler halted, and when Covode learned the identity of his caller, said, "This is the fate of Sheridan's raiders, but, General, I have the consolation of knowing that I have done nothing dishonorable on this raid."

Butler responded, "However that may be, sir, I certainly would not remind you of it under present conditions," and inquired as to how badly hurt the Pennsylvanian was. Covode replied, "Yes, my left arm is shattered, and our litter bearers dropped me here when your cavalry charged and overtook us." Butler took pity on the injured man, sending Dr. B. W. Taylor, chief surgeon of Hampton's division, to bring some apple brandy to Covode. Taylor then examined Covode and found that he had also been shot in the back. Covode died a little while later in a Confederate field hospital at Samaria Church. Butler later speculated that Covode had not admitted to having been wounded in the back for fear that he would be considered a coward. The historian of Butler's brigade wrote, "no such inference can be drawn from such a wound, as in a cavalry melee a man is apt to be shot in the back as in the breast or forehead. This wound of Colonel Covode's was no badge of dishonor or cowardice." The colonel was buried near Samaria Church in an unmarked grave.[118]

The victorious Confederates roamed the field looking for prizes of war. One of the South Carolinians complained, "As soon as we drive the enemy from the field the Virginia troops run in and plunder it, consequently our boys get very little. I passed a fine saddle on a dead horse, that I wanted, but did not have time to get it and when we turned back from the pursuit everything was gone. A bridle and halter is all that I have gotten yet."[119]

Having plundered the field, the exhausted Confederates camped near Salem Church. One of Butler's men recalled, "When a halt was made the men dropped on the ground and were soon asleep. I thought I was sleeping by a log but it proved at daylight to be one of the enemy's dead. One poor fellow, terribly shot, begged the boys to end his suffering, which one of them did with the stock of his gun." The same trooper described an unfortunate case of mistaken identity: "One of our boys I helped to bury, and marked his name on a piece of plank for the headboard. Greatly to our surprise, a short time after we saw him in camp. Said I, 'By Ned, I helped to bury you this morning.' 'Well,' he replied, 'I'm the livest dead man you ever saw.' They looked exactly alike, and that was the opinion of everyone else."[120]

Hampton's force did not escape scot-free. Colonel Massie of the Twelfth Virginia Cavalry was badly wounded during the pursuit. Hampton reported that his division suffered six killed and fifty-nine wounded that day; a review of newspaper reports of his casualties indicates that these figures are badly understated, and that his actual loss was close to 200.[121] The Fourth South Carolina, as an example, suffered 2 killed and 6 wounded out of only 100 men engaged. The Confederates evacuated their wounded to Richmond, where the friendly local population cared for them tenderly.[122] Gregg's stubborn resistance had cost him heavy casualties, but he had also inflicted punishment on Hampton's much larger force.

Waring lamented, "Had the attack been begun sooner . . . or had the dust been less we would have ruined the Yankees."[123] Despite the failure to destroy the Second Division, Hampton praised the performance of the two brigades sent to augment his weary divisions, writing, "Brigadier-General Chambliss, with his brigade, rendered most efficient service, as did Brigadier-General Gary, both of these commands contributing largely to the success at Samaria Church."[124]

Butler's South Carolinians had once again performed stellar service. Butler's keen eye for terrain and his foresight in ordering a reconnaissance of Gregg's line spotted the fatal weakness in the Union position. Stokes proudly announced, "Our brigade stands high as fighters both with the enemy and our troops. Our Enfield Rifles are the things to do the work. We have captured nearly enough carbines, sharps, etc. to arm our Regiment, but I prefer the Enfield."[125] In fact, the severe fire of Butler's Enfields again persuaded some of the Federals that they faced a combined force of both cavalry and infantry, and not just dismounted horse soldiers.[126]

Wickham's troopers also did well, prompting Fitz Lee to claim, "Our troops fought splendidly." Fitz noted, "I have again to draw the attention of the commanding General to Major James Breathed, of my Horse Artillery, who was very conspicuous in a cavalry charge, and, killed in a personal encounter, Col. Covode of the Fourth Pennsylvania Cavalry."[127] Lee's officer corps did not escape unscathed. Lt. J. Lucius Davis, son of the commanding officer of the Tenth Virginia Cavalry of Chambliss's brigade, stood atop the Federal breastworks, cheering on his comrades. A Federal bullet killed him instantly.[128] Davis was quickly avenged, though. The pursuing Confederates cut off the soldier who fired the fatal shot when his comrades fled. The Yankee found himself surrounded by angry Virginians. Terrified, the blue-clad trooper threw down his weapons and tried to surrender. An angry Southerner of Davis's company replied, "I never take prisoners," and, placing his carbine against the man's head, "blew his brains out."[129] A member of the First Virginia Cavalry reported that Wickham's brigade suffered forty men killed or wounded that hot June day.[130]

Gregg had sent couriers to try to reach Torbert, looking for reinforcements. However, all of those couriers were captured, meaning that Gregg's men got no support from the First Division. It also meant that the Confederates had full knowledge of Gregg's plight. This intelligence probably affected Hampton's tactical decisions that afternoon. When Sheridan wrote his memoirs years later, he claimed, "I remained in total ignorance till dark of the strait that his division was in."[131] For some reason, the sounds of battle might not have reached Sheridan's headquarters, as nobody there heard any of the firing of the intense battle raging just a few miles away.[132]

At least one of the Federals criticized Little Phil's conduct that afternoon: "This retreat never would have happened had it not been that Sheridan and the other division were in entire ignorance of what was going on in their rear."[133] Sheridan praised the steady Pennsylvanian's performance in protecting the wagon train's passage to safety on the James River. In 1866, when he prepared his official report of the Trevilian raid, Sheridan commented, "This very creditable engagement saved the train, which should never have been left for the cavalry to escort."[134] Years later, Little Phil wrote that Gregg's "steady, unflinching determination to gain time for the wagons was characteristic of the man, and this was the third occasion on which he had exhibited a high order of capacity and sound judgment since coming under my command." He continued, "The firmness and coolness with which he always met the responsibilities of a dangerous place were particularly strong points in Gregg's make-up, and he possessed so much professional though unpretentious ability that it is to be regretted that he felt obliged to quit the service before the close of the war."[135]

While the men of the Second Division did not play a major part in the fighting at Trevilian Station, they more than made up for their comparatively light losses by their heavy casualties at Samaria Church. A member of the Tenth New York Cavalry noted, "To the members of the Second Cavalry Division, the 24th of June, 1864, will always stand out in bold relief. . . . It was the first and only time the colors of the Second Division were lowered."[136] Another New Yorker called it "the most desperate fighting ever done by Gregg's gallant Second Division. . . . We realized for the first time how it felt to get a good thrashing and then be chased for our lives."[137] A member of the First Pennsylvania Cavalry observed, "on the 24th of June the 2d Cav Division met with a defeat such as it never did heretofore. . . .

It was the greatest fight I ever witnessed."[138] "We did not need to be told that we were cleaned up in this fight," observed Matthew W. King, an eighteen-year-old Ohio trooper.[139] Sergeant Webb of the First Maine Cavalry, a seasoned veteran, recorded in his diary the next day, "the affair . . . was decidedly the hottest engagement I ever was in."[140]

In spite of the magnitude of the defeat, an officer of the Twelfth Virginia Cavalry wrote that Samaria Church was "the best fight made by Gregg's Division."[141] Despite the ferocity of the fight and the fearful losses suffered by the Second Division, the men were proud of their performance. "General Gregg himself was as cool and as stern as a post. General Davies was everywhere, as usual," marveled an officer of the First Massachusetts.[142]

As the fighting raged at Samaria Church, Lt. Col. C. Ross Smith, of the Sixth Pennsylvania Cavalry, who served as the Cavalry Corps's provost marshal, arrived at Ulysses S. Grant's headquarters to report the safe arrival of the wagon train at Wilcox's Wharf along the James River. Smith also reported that Hampton was in Sheridan's front in force and asked for direction as to where and when to cross.

By stark contrast, Torbert's men had a fairly easy day on June 24th. Reveille sounded at 2:30 A.M., and the column had moved out by ten. It reached Charles City Court House around 4:00 P.M., with elements of Devin's brigade and six companies of U.S. Colored Troops encountering about 200 men of Lomax's brigade, who were quickly scattered.[143] Hillman A. Hall of the Sixth New York Cavalry recalled that "the dust was almost stifling, while the heat was intense, the sun blazing down in all its fierceness. The writer well remembers it, for he dropped like a shot from his saddle, and but for the prompt help of his comrades another grave might have been made on the road to the James."[144] Lt. Robert Wallace of Torbert's staff noted, "We were not attacked. . . . The command reached the James River in good time without losing a wagon. The trains covered many miles of road and it was a wonder some of them were not lost."[145] In fact, most of the Michigan Brigade spent the day in a handsome field of clover, their hungry horses enjoying good forage for the first time in days. Two of its regiments and Pennington's battery went out on picket as dusk began setting in. All things considered, it had been a pleasant day for the Michigan men.[146]

Just before dark, firing rang out in front of Torbert's position, and the Sixth New York Cavalry picketed the road. They soon encountered the fleeing remnants of Gregg's division. Several hours later, Capt. James F. McQuesten, one of Merritt's staff officers, out riding the picket line, stumbled on an enemy vidette and nearly rode into the Southern camp. McQuesten beat a hasty retreat and reported the nearness of the enemy troopers to Merritt, who deployed the Reserve Brigade. "Boots and saddles was at once sounded, and, rousing ourselves from deep slumber, we saddled our weary horses and stood to horse all night," grumbled a member of the Sixth Pennsylvania Cavalry.[147]

Not long after, Devin's brigade reported to General Getty, and the entire First Division stood to horse all night awaiting an assault that never came.[148] The men were tense, knowing that they still were not safe, and would not be until they made it across the James River the next morning. They briefly formed line of battle until they determined that Lomax's troopers had withdrawn and that the road to the landing was clear.[149] "Fell back into our own breast works & laid in line of battle all day. Not a reb to be seen," noted one of the Wolverines in his diary.[150]

When Grant learned from a skittish Sheridan that Gregg had been thoroughly beaten at Samaria Church, he fired off a note to Maj. Gen. Benjamin F. Butler, the commander of the Army of the James. Grant instructed Butler to send 1,000 to 1,500 men to Douthat's Wharf before daylight, as Sheridan expected "another attack at daylight, and would be much assisted if some infantry could reach him in time." Butler promptly responded, sending two regiments to Sheridan's aid. Butler inquired, "Cannot Sheridan fall back to Wilson's Wharf, about 4 miles? He will have the cover of our work and 1,500 men to assist him. There are also two gun-boats there to aid him. A boat from City Point can reach Wilson's Wharf in an hour and fifteen minutes." Butler also inquired as to Sheridan's precise location.[151]

Grant responded, "Charles City Court House is the place where our troops are, and where the enemy is confronting them. The wagons and one division of cavalry have come through to Wilcox's Wharf, but have been moving during the night to Charles City Court House." Grant issued instructions to Brig. Gen. Rufus Ingalls, the army's chief quartermaster, to send flatboats to the landing, to ferry the men across the James River.[152]

Early on the morning of Saturday, June 25, two weeks after the fighting began at Trevilian Station, Sheridan's train passed through Charles City Court House en route to Douthat's Landing on the James. Ingalls's flatboats ferried the train across the James to safety. It was another brutally dry, hot day, and the men stood to horse all day in the blazing sun, waiting for the passage of the wagons.[153] Before leaving, the Federals tore up nearly nine miles of the track of railroad, carrying the rails off with them.[154] A member of the Ninth New York Cavalry wrote home, "Our Cavalry is crossing the river here now on transport to join Grant's Army but where they are I do not know."[155] As the wagons crossed the river, a small contingent of the Sixth Ohio Cavalry returned to the Samaria Church battlefield with an ambulance, looking for wounded men. They retrieved a few severely injured Federals.[156]

Private Tuton of the Tenth New York found his way to Charles City Court House. After tying his horse to a rail, Tuton lay down and fell asleep instantly, using a rail for a pillow. On the morning of the 25th, a cacophony of shouts roused him: "10th New York, this way!"; "6th Ohio, over there"; "1st Maine, here"; "1st Massachusetts, yonder"; and "1st New Jersey, other side." Awakening, Tuton had some hot coffee and hardtack supplemented by some good Virginia tobacco. Realizing that he still had his horse and his weapon, Tuton took stock and found that a Confederate ball had struck him. Two old-fashioned daguerrotypes in cases, with glass on one side and cast iron on the other, saved the lucky New Yorker. To keep them safe, Tuton had wrapped the pictures in two folds of cloth and placed them in his coat pocket. The ball had imbedded itself in the cast iron case of one of them, saving Tuton from serious injury. Years later, he recalled, "At this day I consider it the best investment I ever made in life insurance, and am the proud possessor of that ball and the remains of those pictures." After seeing what had saved him, and lingering sense of demoralization quickly passed as Tuton realized he was safe.[157]

Later that afternoon, a relieved Rufus Ingalls announced to Meade, "I have returned from Douthat's Landing. General Sheridan is there with his command. His trains are all in without loss. They are in good condition."[158] The crossing was no picnic. Sgt. Thomas W. Smith of the Sixth Pennsylvania Cavalry observed, "We have to cross every thing in ferry Boats which is a verry tedious operation."[159] Once all the trains had safely crossed the river, the men of Sheridan's two weary, tattered divisions followed, prompting one Maine trooper to exclaim, "we were . . . again with the glorious old Army of the Potomac."[160] An Ohio man gratefully noted in his diary, "Drew five days' rations and two days' forage."[161] The regimental historian of the First Pennsylvania gratefully noted, "Here closed General Sheridan's second grand raid, the corps having been absent from the army nineteen days, and engaged in either marching or fighting the entire period, without a single day's respite."[162] An officer of the First Massachusetts Cavalry summed up the feelings of the men quite well: "I don't think these great raids amount to much."[163]

After finally crossing the James around noon on June 25, Cormany noted in his diary, "I take a swim—We feed and eat and . . . mail arrives." The next day, he inscribed, "Lay in reserve all day. Did some fine sleeping."[164] Sergeant Webb of the First Maine sat on the bank of the river, reflecting on the previous day's exertions. "Yesterday was a sad day in the history of the 2d Cav. Div. As I sit here on the banks of the James River, one of those who have miraculously escaped capture and death, I feel sad, very sad over a great calamity," he wrote.[165]

Rain finally fell on June 26, settling the dust and breaking the heat. The misery was over. It was almost like a furlough for the weary Northern horse soldiers, who got a few days of respite from the hardships of the field. They were grateful to be among familiar blue uniforms again and not among the hostile populace of the Old Dominion. "I feel just first rate this morning, have had a beautiful bath and a clean shirt and am going to be shaved in a few minutes," reported Lt. Thomas Lucas of the First Pennsylvania, "If I had something good to eat now, some change from the Army ration."[166]

The Confederates followed the Yankees toward the James River, but could not press another attack. The Union position was simply too strong, and the Rebel horsemen were too worn down to make another all-out assault. One historian commented, "it was beyond the bounds of possibility for Hampton to prevent this with his small force."[167] Private Gallagher of the First Virginia summed up the state of affairs nicely: "I was so stiff and sore from the running fight yesterday I could hardly saddle my horse and mount him."[168] Afraid of the strong Union artillery position atop Malvern Hill, they detoured around it, delaying their arrival. Instead, they watched the crossing, their prey slipping away after a chase of nearly 150 miles.[169]

The filthy Rebels crossed the James and camped near Drewry's Bluff, where they tried to rest a bit. "Took a bath after night fall. It was perfectly delicious," fondly recalled Colonel Waring.[170] The next day, they got their first full day of rest in nearly fifty days.[171] They knew, though, that the respite would be brief. "The news is that Grant is recrossing the James again is why we are awaiting orders," reported Stokes, "so I have no idea where we will go, but am sure we will go somewhere tomorrow morning, but we ought not to go anywhere if it could be avoided for the next three or four days at least, for we are perfectly worn out both man and horse."[172]

On June 25, Robert E. Lee wrote to Hampton. "I am rejoiced at your success. I thank you and the officers and men of your command for the gallantry and determination with which they have assaulted Sheridan's forces and caused his expedition to end in defeat. So soon as Sheridan crosses the river, I wish you to join me." A proud Hampton consulted with the Confederate high command, and Lee decided that after a brief rest, Hampton's weary troopers would set off after Wilson's and Kautz's raiders.[173] One of Fitz Lee's men gloated, "Having settled accounts with Sheridan, we next moved to pay our attention to the great raiders on the south side."[174] Another of the Southerners was less eloquent: "We have whipped the Enemy's Cav'ly so badly that they are back recruiting new horses."[175]

On June 26 Meade reported to Grant that he had not heard from Sheridan. Grant responded by telling him about the crossing of Sheridan's command. He then informed the commander of the Army of the Potomac that "Sheridan is now safe in as comfortable a place as he can be for recruiting his men and horses. You can send him such orders as you deem best. I think he should be got up leisurely to your left, where he can rest and at the same time add strength to your position."[176] Later that day, Sheridan reported to Meade for the first time in more than two weeks. Meade directed Little Phil to move his command to a position outside of Petersburg along the Petersburg and Jerusalem Plank Road. After nearly three long weeks of hard marching and even harder fighting, the Trevilian Raid had ended. The ordeal of the Northern horsemen had ended.[177]

Notes

1. Darryl Holland, *24th Virginia Cavalry* (Lynchburg, Va.: H. E. Howard Co., 1997), 78.

2. E. Scott Carson, "Hampton's Legion," in *The Gray Riders: Stories from the Confederate Cavalry*, comp. Lee Jacobs (Shippensburg, Pa.: Burd Street Press, 1999), 33.

3. Warner, *Generals in Gray*, 102. Gary's command would be the last organized

Confederate unit to evacuate Richmond in April 1865. The final meeting of the Confederate cabinet took place in Gary's mother's house in Cokesbury, South Carolina. Although Mart Gary was a protégé of Hampton and followed his mentor into politics in postwar South Carolina, Gary vigorously advocated the cause of white supremacy. Hampton and Gary had a major falling out after Gary ran for the U.S. Senate against both Hampton and Matthew C. Butler. The Bald Eagle died on April 9, 1881, and was buried in his home town of Cokesbury.

4. John Michael Priest, ed., *Stephen Elliott Welch of the Hampton Legion* (Shippensburg, Pa.: Burd Street Press, 1994), 36.

5. Wells, *Hampton and His Cavalry*, 218–19. While not quite a two-to-one advantage, Wells's point is nevertheless well taken.

6. O.R., vol. 36, part 3, 791.

7. John C. Donohoe diary, entry for June 24, 1864.

8. O.R., vol. 36, part 3, 791.

9. Union accounts of this battle call the church St. Mary's Church. However, the Confederate accounts all refer to it as Samaria Church. The actual name of the church is Samaria Church, which is the name that will be used in this account. The current location of Samaria Church is not the same location as the wartime location. The present location is about eight-tenths of a mile to the southeast of the wartime site of the Church. Today, an auto body repair shop stands on the site of the church. Visitors to the site should be aware that the present location of Samaria Church is not the historic location.

10. O.R., vol. 36, part 1, 1096.

11. William M. Davis, "St. Mary's Church, Va.: A Rattling Fight by One of Gregg's Cavalry Brigades," *The National Tribune*, June 12, 1890.

12. King, *To Horse*, 13.

13. E. M. Tuton, "St. Mary's Church: As Seen by a Private Soldier of the 10th N.Y. Cav.," *The National Tribune*, July 3, 1890.

14. O.R., vol. 36, part 1, 869.

15. Tobie, *First Maine Cavalry*, 293.

16. Tuton, "St. Mary's Church."

17. Crowninshield, *History of the First Regiment*, 225.

18. Webb diary, entry for June 25, 1864.

19. O.R., vol. 36, part 1, 855. One member of the Second Virginia Cavalry claimed that there was also a swamp between the Confederate line and Gregg's position, but there is not one that appears on the topographical maps and not one that this author found during his visit to the battlefield. Driver, *Second Virginia Cavalry*, 125.

20. Tuton, "St. Mary's Church."

21. Crowninshield, *History of the First Regiment*, 225; O.R., vol. 36, part 3, 791–92.

22. Athens, Georgia, *Southern Banner*, July 13, 1864.

23. Rockwell, *Rambling Recollections*, 152–53.

24. Brooks, *Butler and His Cavalry*, 268–69.

25. Allen, *Down in Dixie*, 390.

26. O.R., vol. 36, part 1, 855.

27. *Ibid.*, 1096.

28. George W. Beale, *A Lieutenant of Cavalry in Lee's Army* (Boston: Gorham Press, 1888), 162.

29. *Ibid.*

30. Rufus H. Peck, *Reminiscences of a Confederate Soldier of Company C, 2nd Virginia Cavalry* (Fincastle, Va.: n.p., 1913), 52.

31. O.R., vol. 36, part 1, 855; Allen, *Down in Dixie*, 388.

32. Beale, *A Lieutenant of Cavalry*, 162.

33. Webb diary, entry for June 25, 1864.

34. *Ibid.*

35. *Richmond Examiner*, July 1, 1864.

36. Beale, *History of the Ninth Virginia*, 130–31.

37. Vogtsberger, *The Dulanys of Welbourne*, 200.

38. Maryus Jones, "Colonel William Todd Robins: A Confederate Hero," *Southern Historical Society Papers*, 34 (Jan.–Dec. 1906), 276.

39. O.R., vol. 36, part 1, 1097.

40. Tobie, *First Maine Cavalry*, 294.

41. Davis, "St Mary's Church."

42. Crowninshield, *History of the First Regiment*, 225.

43. Allen, *Down in Dixie*, 390–91.

44. Mohr and Winslow, *The Cormany Diaries*, 437.

45. Allen, *Down in Dixie*, 391.

46. Webb diary, entry for June 25, 1864.

47. Smith is another of those great stories of the American Civil War, an unschooled natural warrior who found his real calling in the cauldron of combat. Born in Hollis, Maine, on November 1, 1827, Smith graduated from Washington (now Colby) College in Waterville, Maine, in 1856. After a brief stint as a law student, he took a teaching position before being commissioned colonel of the First Maine Cavalry. He would receive a brevet to brigadier general of volunteers for his conduct on June 24, 1864, and further brevets to major general of volunteers as well as brigadier general and major general, U.S. Army, for his gallant and meritorious service in the Civil War. He remained in the army after the war, and finally retired as a colonel in 1891. General Smith was buried in Arlington National Cemetery in 1902. See Hunt and Brown, *Brevet Brigadier Generals in Blue*, 565.

48. Webb diary, entry for June 25, 1864.

49. Tobie, *First Maine Cavalry*, 294.

50. Merrill, *Campaigns of the First Maine and First District of Columbia Cavalry*, 217.

51. David M. Gregg to the secretary of war, March 28, 1895 and Medal of Honor citation for Charles H. Smith Medal of Honor file, RG94, Entry 496, Box 1235, the National Archives, Washington, D.C.

52. *Ibid.*

53. Webb diary, entry for June 25, 1864.

54. Thomas, *Personal Reminiscences*, 19.

55. Sheridan, *Personal Memoirs*, 1:434.

56. Crowninshield, *History of the First Regiment*, 225.

57. Pyne, *Ride to War*, 226.

58. Driver, *Second Virginia Cavalry*, 126.

59. Mohr and Winslow, *The Cormany Diaries*, 437.

60. Peck, *Reminiscences*, 52.

61. Gallagher, *A Diary*, 6. The officer is unidentified.

62. O.R., vol. 36, part 1, 869.

63. *Ibid.*, 855.

64. Nelson, *If I am Killed*, 16; Stiles, *Fourth Virginia Cavalry*, 55–6.

65. Preston, *History of the Tenth New York*, 213–14.

66. Tuton, "St. Mary's Church."

67. Pyne, *Ride to War*, 226.

68. Crowninshield, *History of the First Regiment*, 225.

69. Beale, *A Lieutenant of Cavalry*, 162.

70. O.R., vol. 36, part 1, 856.

71. Davis, "St. Mary's Church."

72. Lloyd, *History of the First Pennsylvania Reserve Cavalry*, 103–104.

73. Pyne, *Ride to War*, 226–27.

74. Torlief S. Holmes, *Horse Soldiers in Blue: First Maine Cavalry* (Gaithersburg, Md.: Butternut Press, 1985), 175.

75. Halliburton, *Saddle Soldiers*, 150.

76. O.R., vol. 36, part 1, 870.

77. Mohr and Winslow, *The Cormany Diaries*, 437–38.

78. Rockwell, *Rambling Recollections*, 153.

79. J. C. Boice, M.D., "St. Mary's Church Fight: Interesting Reminiscence of a Stiff Little Engagement," *The National Tribune*, April 4, 1929.

80. O.R., vol. 36, part 1, 856.

81. Crowninshield, *History of the First Regiment*, 225–26.

82. Mohr and Winslow, *The Cormany Diaries*, 437.

83. Beale, *A Lieutenant of Cavalry*, 163.

84. Leiper Moore Robinson memoirs, Virginia Historical Society, Richmond, Virginia, 16.

85. O.R., vol. 36, part 1, 856.

86. Beale, *A Lieutenant of Cavalry*, 163.

87. Preston, *History of the Tenth Regiment*, 213–15.

88. Pyne, *Ride to War*, 229.

89. Henry C. Meyer, *Civil War Experiences under Bayard, Gregg, Kilpatrick, Custer, Raulston, and Newberry, 1862, 1863, 1864* (New York: Knickerbocker Press, 1911), 99. Weir's father was a celebrated artist and served as the West Point drawing instructor for more than thirty years. Henry C. Weir was not a West Pointer, but was well known to the high command of the Federal cavalry as a result of his father's prominent role in campus life. This may explain why he quickly received a coveted staff position with Brig. Gen. George D. Bayard in the early days of the war. His brother Gulian commanded Battery C of the Fifth U.S. Artillery at Gettysburg, and was one of the heroes of the repulse of Pickett's Charge. Gulian Weir later committed suicide, perhaps to avoid the pain of a lingering battle with melanoma. For more on Gulian Weir's heroic role at Gettysburg and on his tragic death, see David Shultz, "Gulian V. Weir's 5th U.S. Artillery, Battery C," *Gettysburg: Historical Articles of Lasting Interest* 18 (July 1998): 77–95.

90. David M. Gregg to Russell A. Alger, August 22, 1898, Henry C. Weir Medal of Honor File, RG 94, File No. 1465CB1866, the National Archives, Washington, D.C.

91. Col. J. P. Taylor to Russell A. Alger, December 14, 1897, Weir Medal of Honor File.

92. Pyne, *Ride to* War, 229; Heitman, *Historical Dictionary*, 1:1015. The Medal of Honor citation reads, "On this occasion, the Division being hard-pressed and falling back, this officer dismounted, gave his horse to a wounded officer, thus enabling him to escape, and afterward, on foot, rallied and took command of some stragglers and, with pistol in hand, helped to repel the last charges of the enemy."

93. In fact, an officer of the Fourth Pennsylvania Cavalry noted that "The majority of the horses in the command were either killed or wounded in this engagement. My horse was disabled here." Hyndman, *History of a Cavalry Company*, 131.

94. Pyne, *Ride to War*, 229–30.

95. Webb diary for June 25, 1864; Beale, *A Lieutenant of Cavalry*, 163; Wells, *Hampton and His Cavalry*, 220.

96. Wells, *Hampton and His Cavalry*, 220.

97. Baylor, *Bull Run to Bull Run*, 225.

98. Halliburton, *Saddle Soldiers*, 151.

99. Vogtsberger, *The Dulanys of Welbourne*, 200.

100. Gallagher, *A Diary*, 6.

101. Crowninshield, *History of the First Regiment*, 226.

102. O.R., vol. 36, part 1, 859.

103. Webb diary, entry for June 25, 1864.

104. Crowninshield, *History of the First Regiment*, 226.

105. Lloyd, *History of the First Regiment Pennsylvania Reserve Cavalry*, 104.

106. Rockwell, *Rambling Recollections*, 153–54.

107. *Richmond Daily Dispatch*, July 4, 1864.

108. James D. Ferguson diary, entry for June 25, 1864.

109. Pyne, *Ride to War*, 230.

110. Preston, *History of the Tenth Regiment*, 214.

111. *Richmond Whig*, June 27, 1864.

112. Like his colonel, Charles H. Smith, Cilley later received a brevet to brigadier general of volunteers in 1865, later serving at adjutant general of Maine. Hunt and Long, *Brevet Brigadier Generals in Blue*, 111.

113. Holmes, *Horse Soldiers in Blue*, 176.

114. *Southern Banner*, July 13, 1864.

115. Preston, *History of the Tenth Regiment*, 856. While Sheridan lost about 250 men on the second day, Gregg lost more than 350 at Samaria Church.

116. Halliburton, *Saddle Soldiers*, 150.

117. Brooks, *Butler and His Cavalry*, 269.

118. *Ibid.*, 269–70. Brooks later reported: "We learned afterwards that Colonel Covode was one of the most gallant, meritorious officers in Gregg's division. Colonel Covode's father was a distinguished member of Congress from Pennsylvania, extremely radical towards the South, and referred to the death of his son in the most bitter and relentless terms, as we afterwards learned, and among other things said, they had never been able to find or recover his body. No doubt he is buried with other dead near Samaria Church, and if the Confederates had been approached in a proper manner, his grave could have been identified and his body recovered. We were certainly not to blame for his death. He only met the fate of thousands of good men who take their lives into their hands when they go to war and into battle." See 270. However, Capt. William Hyndman of the Fourth Pennsylvania recounted, "It was found, months afterwards, stripped entirely naked, and had apparently been mutilated by the enemy. From the description we obtained from an old negro, who found him on the field, it appeared that he had been entirely undressed before he had expired, and that he had been left in that stark condition to die on the field. The colored man said, "He told me his name was George, and that his father was a big man in the North," meaning of course, that his father was a man of great influence. I was one of the parties who searched for the body afterwards, at the solicitation of his father—Hon. John Covode. We found the darkey living in the vicinity of where the fight took place, and naturally supposed that he must know something of the circumstances." Hyndman, *History of a Cavalry Company*, 131.

119. Halliburton, *Saddle Soldiers*, 150–51.

120. Calhoun, *Liberty Dethroned*, 132.

121. O.R., vol. 36, part 1, 1097. Various newspaper reports provide much different, greater casualty figures. Wickham's brigade reported eight men killed and fifty-

three wounded, for losses of sixty-one. *Richmond Dispatch*, July 1, 1864. Chambliss reported ten men killed and thirty-three wounded, for losses of forty-three. *Richmond Sentinel*, September 6, 1864 and *Richmond Dispatch*, July 1, 1864. Butler reported six men killed, thirty-four wounded, and two missing, for total losses of forty-two. *Charleston Daily Courier*, July 7, 1864. Gary reported five men killed, twenty men wounded, and five missing, for total losses of thirty. *Richmond Daily Examiner*, July 30, 1864. No figures are available for Rosser's brigade. The total losses reported in the newspapers for five of Hampton's six brigades were twenty-nine men killed, one hundred twenty-eight wounded, and seven men missing, for total casualties of one hundred sixty-four, significantly more than what Hampton reported to Robert E. Lee. Of the Confederate loss on June 24th, the *Richmond Examiner* states, "One hundred will cover our casualties." *Richmond Examiner*, June 27, 1864.

122. *Richmond Daily Examiner*, June 29, 1864.

123. Waring diary, entry for June 25, 1864.

124. O.R., vol. 36, part 1, 1097.

125. Halliburton, *Saddle Soldiers*, 150.

126. Mohr and Winslow, *The Cormany Diaries*, 437.

127. Fitzhugh Lee to Robert E. Lee, December 20, 1866.

128. Robert J. Driver, Jr., *Tenth Virginia Cavalry* (Lynchburg, Va.: H. E. Howard Co., 1982), 56.

129. *Richmond Dispatch*, July 9, 1864.

130. Driver, *Second Virginia Cavalry*, 126.

131. Sheridan, *Personal Memoirs*, 1:434.

132. Hagemann, *Fighting Rebels and Redskins*, 247.

133. Thomas, *Personal Reminiscences*, 19.

134. O.R., vol. 36, part 1, 799.

135. Sheridan, *Personal Memoirs*, 1:435. Indeed, Gregg resigned his commission in February 1865. He gave no explanation other than that pressing personal business required his attention. This man, who led a division of cavalry longer, and perhaps more competently, than any other Federal cavalry commander, thus missed the great moments of the Union cavalry and was not there for the final victory and the Grand Review through the streets of Washington, D.C. that occurred in May 1865. To this day, there has been no good explanation tendered as to the reasons why Gregg resigned his command. Historian Edward G. Longacre has suggested that Gregg suffered from posttraumatic stress disorder that forced his resignation, but this is unsubstantiated. Perhaps a better explanation would be that Gregg finally grew weary of army politics and with dealing with Phil Sheridan and George G. Meade.

136. Preston, *History of the Tenth Regiment*, 211–12.

137. *Ibid.*, 213 and 215. Interestingly, Capt. George Vanderbilt, the author of these statements, compared the thrashing and headlong flight to that suffered by the Confederates at Trevilian Station.

138. Wilmer Hall to his sister, June 26, 1864, Wilmer C. Hall Letters, Pennsylvania State Archives, Harrisburg, Pennsylvania.

139. King, *To Horse*, 13.

140. Webb diary, entry for June 25, 1864.

141. Baylor, *Bull Run to Bull Run*, 226.

142. Crowninshield, *History of the First Regiment*, 227.

143. Cheney, *Ninth New York Cavalry*, 191.

144. Hall, *History of the Sixth New York Cavalry*, 202–03.

145. Wallace, *A Few Memories of a Long Life*, 39.

146. Fitch diary, entry for June 24, 1865.

147. Gracey, *Annals of the Sixth Pennsylvania Cavalry*, 267.

148. Hall, *History of the Sixth New York Cavalry*, 202; Moyer, *Seventeenth Pennsylvania Cavalry*, 87.

149. Lloyd, *History of the First Pennsylvania Reserve Cavalry*, 104.

150. Grommon diary, entry for June 25, 1864.

151. O.R., vol. 36, part 3, 792–93.

152. *Ibid.*, 793.

153. Gracey, *Annals of the Sixth Pennsylvania Cavalry*, 267.

154. *Richmond Sentinel*, June 25, 1864.

155. Taylor, *Saddle and Saber*, 161.

156. Davis, "St. Mary's Church."

157. Tuton, "St. Mary's Church."

158. O.R., vol. 36, part 3, 793.

159. Eric J. Wittenberg, ed., *"We Have It Damn Hard Out Here": The Civil War Letters of Sgt. Thomas W. Smith, Sixth Pennsylvania Cavalry* (Kent, Ohio: Kent State University Press, 1999), 126.

160. Edward P. Tobie, *Service in the Cavalry of the Army of the Potomac, Personal Narratives of Rhode Island Soldiers and Sailors* (Providence, R.I.: N. Bangs Williams & Co., 1882), 34.

161. King, *To Horse*, 13.

162. Lloyd, *History of the First Pennsylvania Reserve Cavalry*, 104.

163. Crowninshield, *History of the First Regiment*, 227.

164. Mohr and Winslow, *The Cormany Diaries*, 438.

165. Webb diary, entry for June 25, 1864.

166. Lucas to his wife, June 26, 1864.

167. Wells, *Hampton and His Cavalry*, 223.

168. Gallagher, *A Diary*, 7. Gallagher noted that the men of Lee's division fully expected to be attacked that day, and he stated that he was entirely too tired to even resist if threatened with capture: "So I took off my jacket, fastened it to my saddle and took off a gold ring my mother had given me and told the boy holding my horse that I did not expect to get back again and give or send the ring to my

mother for me, and told him to send my horse home and that he could have my other things."

169. Ferguson diary, entry for June 25, 1864.

170. Waring diary, entry for June 25, 1864.

171. Gallagher, A Diary, 7.

172. Halliburton, Saddle Soldiers, 151.

173. O.R., vol. 36, part 3, 903.

174. "Narrative of Cavalry Operations," Richmond Sentinel, July 13, 1864.

175. Horace M. Wade to his sister, July 3, 1864, Lewis Leigh Collection, United States Army Military History Institute, Carlisle, Pennsylvania.

176. O.R., vol. 36, part 3, 794.

177. Ibid., 795.

⊹⊱ 11 ⊰⊹

An Assessment of the Trevilian Raid and the Battle of Trevilian Station

The Battle of Trevilian was the most important cavalry fight that occurred during the war.

After resting for a few days, Sheridan's two weary divisions set out to rescue Wilson's raiders on June 29. They arrived too late to do any good. The two weary divisions finally rejoined the main body of the Army of the Potomac on July 2, four weeks after departing on the Trevilian raid.[1] Thus, Meade lost the eyes and ears of the army for almost a month during some of the toughest campaigning of the American Civil War. The First and Second Cavalry Divisions, the cream of the Army of the Potomac's Cavalry Corps, suffered heavy casualties during those four weeks. In the two long, brutal days at Trevilian Station, Little Phil's two divisions sustained 95 men killed, 445 men wounded, and 410 men missing or captured, for total losses of 955, representing 10 percent of the 9,286 engaged.[2]

In addition, Gregg's Second Division lost another 357 men killed, wounded, or missing out of 2,147 men engaged on June 24 at Samaria Church.[3] He lost 17 percent of his total force engaged in a period of only two hours, and the actual percentage might have been significantly higher. The fight on June 24 cost Gregg's division 30 percent greater casualties than the First Division suffered on June 12, 10 percent greater casualties than Torbert took in a full day of fighting along the Fredericksburg Road on June 11, and only 10 percent fewer casualties than Custer's melee that day. The Confederates outnumbered Gregg by nearly two to one at Samaria Church. Gregg faced much greater odds than those faced by the other Federal commanders at Trevilian Station. In spite of those long odds, his men successfully covered Sheridan's flank, taking frightful losses in the process. A Confederate historian gleefully wrote, "So sorely was General Gregg's division handled in this affair that it required some time to recruit and mend up."[4] The Second Division never fully recovered.

In only three days of heavy fighting on June 11, 12, and 24, the two divisions of Union horsemen lost 14 percent of their total strength. These losses must be augmented by the losses sustained along the way, as well as by the breakdown of their mounts. It is nearly impossible to determine the exact number of men lost during the marches to and from Trevilian, and in the small skirmishes along the way. In short, the two excellent divisions of Federal cavalry lost nearly 20 percent of their effective strength in those nineteen days of hard campaigning, high losses for infantry, and virtually unheard of for horse soldiers.[5]

The fighting took a fearful toll in the Union officer corps. Sheridan lost six regimental commanders killed, wounded, or captured, as well as heavy casualties among his field- and company-grade officers.[6] In addition, the toll taken on their horses during this expedition left Sheridan's two divisions hors de combat. Sheridan's unforgiving order to destroy all broken-down animals, most of which could have been nursed back to health under different circumstances, meant that hundreds and even thousands of veteran horse soldiers were left combat ineffective because they had no mounts. The regimental surgeon of the Sixth Ohio Cavalry recounted, "there was always a rear guard, and when the disabled horses fell back, they were immediately shot. On one very hot day during a terrible march I remember counting some forty-five horses that had been thus disposed of along a course of less than five miles."[7] Clement Hoffman of the Sixth Pennsylvania Cavalry wrote, "We have lost more men on this raid than on the [May Richmond Raid], and especially horses, nearly one 4th of our horses played out and a great many of our men dismounted. I had two horses to play out but I am still mounted. We are all pretty well tired out and will gladly accept a rest to fix and get ourselves cleaned up once more if Grant does not hunt up another long journey for us to perform."[8]

Capt. Zimmerman Davis of the Fifth South Carolina Cavalry claimed that he counted 2,000 dead Union horses lining the retreat route, most of them shot in the head.[9] If Davis counted correctly, more than 20 percent of Sheridan's command was dismounted during the retreat alone, more than double the number lost on the march to Trevilian. Another 20 percent of the Sixth Ohio Cavalry lost their horses during the debacle at Samaria Church, and a trooper of the Sixth Ohio also reported that all of Randol's horses were killed during the brutal fight that day.[10] Dismounted cavalry is not terribly useful in fulfilling the traditional roles of scouting, screening, and intelligence gathering. While Sheridan received 1,900 fresh horses in July, most of these inexperienced animals needed training to be useful cavalry mounts.[11] As Custer succinctly put it, "Our men and horses are completely wearied out."[12] When the Confederates crushed Wilson's troopers at Reams's Station, the Third Division also was left hors de combat. In short, the Army of the Potomac's entire Cavalry Corps remained combat ineffective for weeks as a result of the Trevilian Raid.

Custer's brigade of Michigan cavalry suffered tremendous losses on June 11, 1864. He lost 22 percent of his command, mostly missing or captured. The Boy General lost twenty-seven men missing or captured for every man killed. These statistics plainly demonstrate that Custer lost control of the Fifth Michigan Cavalry on June 11, leading to the tremendous losses in missing and captured. The losses left the Michigan Cavalry Brigade combat ineffective on June 12, and for weeks to come. Custer's brigade lost another forty-seven men on the second day of the battle, representing 19 percent of the total Federal casualties that day. In short, Custer's losses represent 43 percent of Sheridan's total casualties at Trevilian Station, a staggering number. It is no wonder that Custer could not commit wholeheartedly to the futile assaults on the Confederate line on the bloody second day of the battle, or that little more was heard of him or his troopers until mid-August. It is also no wonder that the Michigan Brigade was never the same again. It never recovered and was never again the potent offensive force that it had been before the First Last Stand.

The heavy losses taken by Custer's brigade skew the casualty figures for the First Division on the first day of the battle. Fully 58 percent of Torbert's losses that day are attributable to Custer's decision to attack Hampton's wagon park and the resulting desperate struggle that ensued. The statistics also demonstrate that four separate, distinct battles occurred on the first day: Wickham's skirmish with the Wolverines along the Marquis Road, the meeting engagement at Bibb's Crossroads, Custer's foray for the wagons and his subsequent stand, and Torbert's prolonged dismounted fight on the Fredericksburg Road. An analysis of the casualties resulting from the two phases of the fight on the Fredericksburg Road indicates that the Northern losses are higher than the level of losses demonstrated in typical infantry fights of the Civil War.[13] Given the intensity of the fighting between the South Carolinians and Merritt's Regulars, much of it at close range, these statistics are not surprising at all.

The fighting on the second day was even heavier than the first. If Custer's disproportionate casualties on June 11 are considered as a separate battle, analysis of the Federal casualty statistics indicates that nearly 45 percent of the Federal losses occurred on the second day of the battle. Merritt took 244 casualties in about four hours that day, as compared to 294 men lost in a twelve-hour-long fight on June 11. This demonstrates the futility of repeated assaults against the stubborn resistance of Butler's South Carolinians at the Bloody Angle.

Despite the heavy losses in both men and horseflesh, Sheridan persistently claimed victory in the Trevilian Raid, and Grant's memoirs perpetuated this myth. In 1866, when he wrote his lengthy report of the Cavalry Corps's activities in the spring and early summer of 1864, Sheridan claimed "The result was constant success and the almost total annihilation of the rebel cavalry. We marched when and where we pleased; were always the attacking party, and always successful."[14] Within days of the Battle of Trevilian Station, Sheridan submitted his initial report of the fighting and claimed victory. Numerous Northern and Southern newspapers published his boasts. Most of Little Phil's biographers have latched onto this false claim. One early biography stated that Hampton's troopers "broke in considerable confusion," a statement far from the truth. The same biography also claimed that Hampton's victory over Wilson and Kautz at Reams's Station "was the only defeat of any portion of our Potomac cavalry after Sheridan assumed command," clearly an inaccurate contention.[15]

Wilson, who commanded the Third Cavalry Division during this period of time, keenly observed fifty years after the war that Sheridan "never failed in a doubtful situation to contend to the utmost for victory, *nor to claim it strenuously whether he had won it clearly or not.*"[16] His vigorous attempts to recast the debacle of the Trevilian raid failed. Although Sheridan won a tactical victory on June 11, he nevertheless failed to accomplish Grant's strategic objective, negating the outcome. No matter how positive a spin Little Phil tried to put on things, the Trevilian raid was an unmitigated disaster for his troopers. "This disaster which was called by our papers a victory," accurately complained Col. Luigi Palma Di Cessnola of the Fourth New York Cavalry, "is due to the bad management of our cavalry by the Generals in command."[17] Nothing about the Battle of Trevilian Station can be considered to be a Union victory.

Sheridan failed to make the junction with Hunter and obviously failed to bring Hunter's army east to link with the Army of the Potomac. More important, he failed to put the Virginia Central Railroad out of commission. Years after the war, Wilson, who was no admirer of Sheridan, wryly commented, "After striking the railroad at Trevilian's, it is claimed that he broke it up thoroughly, but I think it is a question of doubt whether he succeeded in breaking the track at all." He continued, "Be this as it may, it is certain that, if he did, it was broken in such an inadequate manner that it was repaired in a few hours by an ordinary railroad force, and that consequently for all practical purposes, the raid was a failure."[18]

Rosser summed things up quite nicely, although his memory of the participants seems a bit cloudy: "The Battle of Trevilian was the most important cavalry fight that occurred during the war. The entire cavalry force of the opposing armies in Virginia met there, many miles away from the support of other troops; each commander was thrown entirely on his own resources. Had Sheridan won the battle he would have gone on to Lynchburg, or wherever he desired, as there would have been no one to oppose him. He could have destroyed railroads, canals, depots, and, indeed, cut General Lee off and starved him out of Petersburg and Richmond."[19]

Jubal Early, sent to counter Hunter's thrust on June 13, marched west for a few miles, briefly moving along the route of the Virginia Central. On the 13th, when Early learned of the fight at Trevilian Station, he asked permission to march "by Louisa Court-House" in order to "try to smash up Sheridan and then turn off to Charlottesville."[20] Early's troops passed right through the battlefield at Trevilian Station just three days after the battle ended. Early did not mention any continuing damage to either the railroad or the telegraph there, noting only that "the railroad and telegraph . . . had been, fortunately, but slightly injured by the enemy's cavalry, and had been repaired."[21] Early's army continued to Charlottesville and boarded trains to carry them to Lynchburg, arriving there on June 16, just in time to repulse the slow advance of Hunter's army. Hunter withdrew into West Virginia, effectively withdrawing from the war for nearly a month. Early's victorious Confederates advanced down the Shenandoah Valley. They made it all the way to the northern environs of Washington, D.C., on July 12, before finally pulling back.[22]

If Sheridan had destroyed the railroad as ordered, Hunter's expedition to capture Lynchburg might have succeeded, because Early probably would have gone after Sheridan instead of Hunter. If Lynchburg fell, Lee's army would have been deprived of this critical supply and transportation center. Instead, Hunter declined to give battle and withdrew into West Virginia, temporarily removed from action. In short, Sheridan's failure to destroy the Virginia Central Railroad likely extended the war in the east by as much as six months. There were few truly decisive cavalry battles in the Civil War, but Hampton's victory at Trevilian Station must be counted as one because of its far-reaching implications.

Maj. Frederic C. Newhall of the Sixth Pennsylvania Cavalry was Sheridan's assistant adjutant general and one of Little Phil's staunchest supporters. Not even Newhall, who spent years defending his hero's actions in the Civil War, could agree with Sheridan's claims of victory at Trevilian Station. A number of years after the war, Newhall wrote, "Fair-minded troopers on our side call the fierce engagement between Sheridan and Wade Hampton at Trevilian a drawn battle." He continued, "We . . . think there is something rather fine in the aspect of our troopers stalking through so many miles of hostile territory directly afterward, unimpeded by the enemy's cavalry, who were close at hand and had us somewhat at a disadvantage." Newhall concluded with a damning and candid comment about the Trevilian raid, a sentiment undoubtedly shared by most of the First and Second Divisions. "We freely admit anything that anybody can say of the expedition, as to its futility, barrenness, and general worthlessness, of which we were conscious and heartily tired long before we saw the end of it."[23] Major Kidd likewise reported, "the expedition failed, for we did not reach Gordonsville and were certainly repulsed . . . we were unable to force a passage through his breastworks."[24] Surgeon John B. Coover of the Sixth Pennsylvania observed on June 25, "Altogether I think this last raid was something of a failure though as a matter of course, one in my position cannot know what the precise results of the movements are."[25]

In fact, some of the Northern newspapers quickly realized that Sheridan's claims of victory rang hollow. As early as June 20, 1864, the editor of the Pittsburgh *Evening Chronicle* observed, "If he was as successful as he reports, the inquiry arises why did he not, if Gordonsville was unattainable, advance on Charlottesville, or destroy the railroad between that and Gordonsville and then join Hunter, as was his original intention?" He continued, "We fear that Sheridan has not been so successful as was desired or expected, and that his failure to unite with our other forces in that region may lead to serious complications, and preserve to the enemy, not only Gordonsville and Charlottesville, but also Lynchburg. The next reports from there will be awaited with anxiety."[26] The next day, the same newspaper editor stated, "From the exceedingly meager reports furnished by the rebel papers it may be inferred that the raid is considered of very little importance, or else that it has met with greater success than the rebels are willing to acknowledge."[27]

Predictably, the Southern newspapers mocked Sheridan's claims that he had won the battle at Trevilian Station. The *Charleston Mercury* crowed, "We have received a more detailed account of the defeat of Sheridan's forces by our cavalry, under Generals Hampton and Fitz Lee, which not only confirms previous intelligence, but shows that the enemy were thoroughly beaten and demoralized."[28] "The Philadelphia *Inquirer* like a number of other Yankee papers, pleads very hard to show that Sheridan won a 'great victory'. This was done by one way only—a way the Yankees understand perfectly—*by lying*; infamous, atrocious lying," sneered the editor of the *Richmond Examiner*, who wrote, "If Sheridan won a 'victory'—if the Yankees take delight in such treatment as his men received at the hands of Hampton and his men, we wish them joy, and plenty more of the same sort of comfort."[29]

Rosser was far harsher in his assessment: "Sheridan was fairly and completely beaten, and all of his apologies for his retreat, 'ammunition exhausted and presence of infantry,' are unworthy of a great soldier. Why was he there without ammunition? Didn't he expect to have some fighting? If he had found a large force of infantry in his path he should have destroyed the railroad, each side of it, and thus compelled it to march back, which he could have ridden off unmolested upon the duties for which he was sent. These excuses are really too ridiculous to be discussed."[30]

Rosser gave an even more acid analysis of Sheridan's performance at Trevilian in a speech to Confederate veterans years after the war. The Texan claimed, "Sheridan concentrated his force and exerted his entire strength to the driving of Hampton out of his way, but he could not move him. The fight was conducted more like an infantry battle than a cavalry fight." He continued, "Sheridan displayed no skill in maneuvering; it was simply a square stand up fight, man to man, and Hampton whipped him—defeated his purposes and turned him back. The history writers of the North are endeavoring to make a great general of Sheridan, but the impartial historian, who will write for future generations to read, will overturn their feeble and foundationless structure." Rather, Rosser claimed that Little Phil had been routed and panicked on June 12th. He concluded, "So much afraid was he of pursuit and further disaster that he ran off and hid in the wilderness and changed his course only after learning that he was not followed by Hampton in force. Still to make assurance certain and safety sure, he has-tened across the Mattapony, putting that river, as well as the Pamunkey, between him and Hampton. Finally he got back to Grant after a long and tedious march."[31]

Ulysses R. Brooks, one of Butler's troopers, said of Little Phil's perfor-mance: "Sheridan was not by nature well suited to the command of cavalry. He was a dull man, and his mind worked too slowly for the quick maneuvers of the cavalry. As an infantry officer Sheridan possessed fair ability, as a cavalry officer he was the most absolute failure of all the many failures which, one after another, was laid aside by Mr. Lincoln." Brooks concluded, "Nothing saved Sheridan from the bleak, dreary, shores of oblivion but the exhausted condition of the Confederate cavalry, when he was assigned to the command of the Federal cavalry. Few in number, short of forage, short of rations, and constantly growing weaker as the enemy grew stronger, the Confederate cavalry maintained itself as an equal, if not more than a match, for its adversary until the end. Its raids were always successful and its battles were victorious."[32]

John B. Jones, a clerk in the Confederate War Department, echoed similar sentiments. On June 12, as the battle raged at Trevilian Station, Jones noted in his diary, "It is rumored that Sheridan has cut the road between Gordonsville and Charlottesville, and between that place and Lynchburg. If this be true, he will probably strike south for the Danville Road. Then we shall have *confusion here, and the famine intensified.*"[33] Such was the nature of the opportunity lost. In spite of their commander's poor performance, Sheridan had a true gift for inspiring the men who served under him. Even though Hampton had thrashed him twice, Sheridan "had secured our confidence thoroughly," leading one Maine man to claim that he and his comrades would follow the bandy-legged little Irishman anywhere "without hesitation."[34] This simple statement sums up the electric effect that Sheridan's presence had on the Federal Cavalry Corps.

Even infantrymen who were not present at Trevilian believed Hampton had won the battle. One Texan reported home, "Maj. Genl. Hampton, with two divisions of cavalry, met Mr. Sheridan's party near Trevilian's Depot; routed him, making large captures, and causing him to retrace his steps in hot haste, and take refuge at Whitehouse on the York River."[35] The Confederate cavalry's victory over Sheridan's horsemen garnered them respect among even the most weary infantrymen. After learning of the magnitude of Hampton's embarrassment of Little Phil, a Confederate foot soldier wrote, "The Cavalry have done & are doing very hard fighting. It is no longer an easy place."[36] A Georgian of Cobb's Legion boasted, "The boys have been so successful and have so much confidence in their own skill and valor, and in their officers, as to think it impossible for them to be whipped by Mr. Sheridan, as they call him. Gen. Hampton has won the admiration and esteem of all his men; they are in fine spirits—ready and willing to meet the enemy, by day or by night, and at any point."[37]

The performance of Sheridan's subordinate commanders during the Trevilian raid was mixed at best. Torbert did well on June 11. The grueling, close fight on the Fredericksburg Road played out more like the hard-fought battle in the Wilderness, not a cavalry battle. Torbert's experience in commanding infantry served him well that day, and his troopers fought long and hard before they finally forced Hampton's men from the field. However, Torbert did a poor job on the second day of the battle. He fed his men in piecemeal, in uncoordinated and seemingly poorly planned attacks against a very strong defensive position. With no real plan for the fight other than headlong rushes into Butler's Bloody Angle, Torbert's assaults there were bound to fail, and fail they did. Like Sheridan, Torbert deserves his fair share of the blame for that failure.

David Gregg's performance, however, is an enigma. Perhaps plagued by the division commander's poor health during the two days at Trevilian Station, Gregg's division did not play a decisive role in either day's fighting, although the attack by J. Irvin Gregg's brigade drove Hampton's men from their stubborn hold on Trevilian Station. On the second day of the battle, his division was no factor at all. Only Davies's brigade was lightly engaged, discouraging an enemy pursuit. However, Gregg's division performed splendidly at Samaria Church on June 24. Given the important mission of protecting Sheridan's flank in the face of superior numbers, Gregg made a determined stand at the cost of heavy casualties. Only that determined stand prevented Hampton's pursuing horse soldiers from falling upon Sheridan's flank and wreaking havoc on it. Evidently, the Federal high command realized the importance of Gregg's dogged stand at Samaria Church, as Gregg received a brevet to major general of volunteers on August 1, 1864, in recognition of that severe fight.[38]

The rest of the Northern subordinate command also gave spotty performances. Custer and his Wolverines were nearly destroyed on the morning of June 11, when the Boy General's reckless abandon caught them in a trap and nearly caused the annihilation of a fine brigade. As a consequence of the heavy losses taken by Custer's brigade that day, the Wolverines were not a factor for the balance of the raid. Custer nevertheless tried to put a positive slant on his performance. He bragged to his wife Libbie, "As usual, the Michigan Brigade was detached from the main body, for the purpose of turning the enemy flank and, if possible, attacking him in the rear. I was ordered to go to Trevilian Station, there to form a junction with two other brigades. I carried out instructions to the letter, but the others were three hours behind me."[39] Although Custer tried to carry out Sheridan's orders, his foray failed for a variety of reasons, not the least of which was the Boy General's audacity. Custer's mendacious bragging has deceived his admirers ever since—he nearly destroyed his beloved Michigan Brigade on June 11, 1864.

Only a portion of Davies's brigade was engaged on the first day at Trevilian, and his troopers only did rearguard duty on the second day. Devin's command performed well on both days. Given Devin's experience and reputation as a hard fighter, Torbert erred by failing to use this fine brigade to its full capacity. J. Irvin Gregg's brigade played the decisive role on the first day of the Battle of Trevilian Station, its determined attack driving Hampton's men from the field of battle. They were not engaged at all on the second day and suffered heavy losses at Samaria Church. Like his cousin, J. Irvin Gregg was a quiet, modest, competent soldier who could be depended upon in any emergency.

Many historians claim that Custer was Sheridan's protégé and that Sheridan turned to Custer in every crisis. Such is not the case. In fact, Sheridan leaned most heavily on Merritt and his Regulars. In nearly every fight, Sheridan gave the toughest assignments to Merritt, and the steady Reserve Brigade generally performed well. Sheridan groomed Merritt for higher command, and the quiet New Yorker did not disappoint. By the end of the Civil War, Merritt commanded the Cavalry Corps, a remarkable accomplishment for a man who had been out of West Point for less than a year when the war broke out.

Sheridan's horse artillery performed extraordinary service at Trevilian Station. The young Regulars who commanded those batteries were extremely capable, brave officers whose batteries provided the sturdy backbone of Sheridan's Cavalry Corps. The performance of Pennington's and Williston's batteries, in particular, was the linchpin of Sheridan's fight on the first and second days of the battle of Trevilian Station, respectively. Indeed, the bravery and magnificent performance of Williston's gunners gave Torbert his chance to break the Confederate lines at the Bloody Angle in front of the Ogg farm.

With Sheridan's two divisions out of action even before crossing the James River, Hampton's force fell upon the combined commands of Wilson and Kautz. On June 29, supported by a division of infantry and Fitz Lee's horse soldiers, Hampton pounced on the two Federal cavalry divisions near Reams's Station and thrashed them, sending them reeling south. After defeating the entire Federal cavalry force, the weary Confederate horse soldiers finally got a respite from their toils. They beat the blue-clad cavalry each time they faced it: at Trevilian Station, Samaria Church, and Reams's Station. A captain of the Phillips Legion pointedly wrote, "I think Gen. Hampton has convinced them that raiding is an unprofitable investment."[40] And so it was.

A few days later, an obviously proud Hampton penned a letter to his sister, Fisher. "For twenty five days, my men were in pursuit of the Yankees fighting six days often without food and sometimes marching all night," wrote the gratified South Carolinian. But they have behaved magnificently, and they have done better service than ever before." He continued, "In those 25 days we killed, wounded, or captured nearly if not quite 5000 Yankees, whipping them in every fight. They have left their dead all over the country, as well as their wounded. My own loss is about 900."[41]

But for Hampton's decisive victory at Trevilian Station, Early probably would not have made his foray across the Potomac River that summer. Thus, the panic generated in the national capital at Washington by the Confederate advance probably would not have happened, and marauding Confederate cavalry might not have burned the town of Chambersburg, Pennsylvania. Sheridan probably would not have been dispatched to the Shenandoah Valley and the Valley would not have been laid waste by his advancing forces.

Early's expedition into Maryland and Pennsylvania also meant that the entire Southern cavalry force never again operated as a cohesive unit in the Eastern Theater of the Civil War. Soon, Rosser, Lomax, and Wickham went to the Shenandoah Valley to try to hinder the advance of Sheridan's Army of the Shenandoah. Instead, they watched helplessly as the Northern horse soldiers enjoyed almost free rein in the Valley. At the Battle of Tom's Brook, fought on October 9, 1864, the Union horsemen inflicted the worst defeat ever experienced by the gray-clad mounted arm, the Northern horse soldiers utterly routing the Southerners. They chased them more than twenty miles in an action known derisively as "The Woodstock Races."

The Trevilian raid, followed by the entrapment of Wilson and Kautz, marked the emergence of Hampton as the preeminent Confederate cavalry officer in the Eastern Theater. Munford correctly observed that the fight at Trevilian "has been regarded by the Confederates as the proudest achievement of their cavalry during the war."[42] James G. Holmes, Hampton's adjutant general, remembered, "Gen. Hampton never lost his head, as was shown at Trevilian Station, . . . when Gen. Fitz Lee allowed General Custer to get in the rear of Butler's and [Wright's] brigades, fighting Sheridan under Hampton's immediate command. Here Hampton's coolness and fearlessness allowed him . . . to turn a probable rout into an assured success."[43]

The modest Hampton did not claim the credit for himself in his report of the campaign. "When the general commanding takes into consideration the disparity in numbers of the troops engaged," he wrote, "the many disadvantages under which my men labored, their hard marches, their want of supplies, their numerous privations, and the cheerfulness with which these were borne, he will, I trust, be satisfied with the results accomplished."[44]

Hampton's command also took heavy casualties on those two hot days in Louisa County. Of approximately 6,700 men engaged at Trevilian, Hampton suffered 813 casualties, including 59 men killed and 268 wounded, representing 12 percent of his total force involved. He lost a number of regimental commanders and one brigade commander.[45] The majority of the losses were in his own division; only 161 of those killed, wounded, or captured came from Fitz Lee's division. Butler's South Carolinians bore the brunt of the fighting on both days of the battle. They suffered 299 casualties in the two days of the battle, including 41 killed, 172 wounded, and 86 captured, representing 23 percent of his brigade's strength. These losses demonstrate the degree of faith placed in Butler and his troopers by Wade Hampton.[46]

Further, the raid wore down the brigade's horses. At the beginning of the Trevilian Raid, the Fourth South Carolina probably numbered about 400 officers and men; by June 25, 1864, fewer than 100 of them were fit for duty.[47] Nevertheless, and in spite of the significant losses at Trevilian Station, a member of Gary's Brigade wrote after the fight at Samaria Church, that Hampton "has a splendid command."[48]

The casualty statistics for Wright's brigade reflect the hammering that it took on June 11 and 12. Of the 1,900 men engaged, 273 were killed, wounded, or captured, representing losses of 14 percent for the brigade. The Seventh Georgia Cavalry, in its first engagement, suffered severely, including 11 men killed, 33 wounded, and 182 missing, for 38 percent of those engaged. The regimental commander, McAllister, was killed and the Seventh Georgia was left largely ineffective as a result of the losses that it sustained at the hands of Torbert's horse soldiers. Despite the heavy losses, the largely untried Georgians demonstrated that "they would . . . be depended upon under any and all circumstances."[49]

Rosser's brigade had the lowest casualties, reflecting the nature of its engagement on the 11th—the Laurel Brigade served as a shock force, intended to break up Custer's foray into the wagons. It succeeded, with virtually no casualties. After Rosser's wound, the Laurels played little part in the fighting at Trevilian. Lee's division also took relatively light casualties during the two days of fighting at Trevilian Station. Of 1,800 men engaged, his 161 casualties in the two-day battle reflect Lee's lackluster performance.

Hampton also conducted a brilliant fight at Samaria Church on June 24. He planned and executed a well-coordinated attack that drove Gregg's veterans from the field. Gary's charge on the end of Gregg's line began the process, and Fitz Lee's well-timed attack staggered the Federal line.

Committing his mounted reserve at just the right moment, Hampton split Gregg's line in two and drove it from the field. Only the heat and exhausted condition of his men and horses prevented Hampton from destroying Gregg's two brigades that day.

Hampton was brilliant that hot, dry summer. Demonstrating his prowess as a fighter and only slightly restrained by the toll taken on his horses and men, he chased the Union cavalry all over Virginia and thrashed it each time they met. An early Confederate cavalry historian proclaimed that the Trevilian Raid "demonstrated anew that the Confederate cavalry under Hampton was just as enterprising, as valiant, as enthusiastic, and as brave and dauntless as when it fought under Stuart."[50] Robert E. Lee wrote to President Davis on July 2: "You know the high opinion I entertain of Gen. Hampton and my appreciation of his character and services. In his late expedition he has displayed both energy and good conduct, and though I have feared that he might not have the activity and endurance so necessary in a cavalry commander . . . I request authority to place him in command."[51] With Davis's approval, Lee elevated the courtly South Carolinian to corps command on a permanent basis in August 1864.

The promotion ended the awkward arrangement that had been in place since Jeb Stuart's death in May. There were no longer three independent commands of cavalry with Robert E. Lee as titular head. While Hampton had none of the style or panache of Stuart, he was every bit as competent. Indeed, few soldiers on either side of the Civil War accomplished more or performed better during the last twelve months of the war than Wade Hampton did. He must occupy a position at the top of the ranks of the corps commanders on either side of the Civil War. His rise to prominence began at First Manassas, culminated three years later, and peaked in South Carolina before the war ended.

Not every member of the Confederate cavalry corps appreciated Hampton's performance or his promotion. Sgt. Jerry Haden of the First Virginia Cavalry commented, "[W]hat General Stuart was going to do, he would do before General Hampton got ready. But when Hampton got ready he was there. Stuart did his work with a rush, while Hampton never made an attack until he had made thorough preparation, and consequently, was generally successful, unless he was contending with overwhelming numbers." Haden concluded, "When the enemy left Trevilians, General Stuart would have been on them like a duck on a June bug."[52]

Col. Richard Dulany, acting commander of the Laurel Brigade, echoed similar sentiments in a letter home, written several months after the battle. "Hampton I think is superior to Stuart in prudence, good judgment and in military [affairs but] not the extreme dash (sometimes costly as at Dranesville) and perseverance for which Genl. Stuart was remarkable."[53] The criticism was unfair. Hampton's mounts were just as jaded as Sheridan's, and in no better shape to make a vigorous pursuit than those of the Federals. His brigade made as aggressive a pursuit as it could have been under the circumstances. To expect anything more simply is not reasonable.

Fitzhugh Lee was the odd man out. While the ever-courteous Hampton went out of his way to praise Lee's role in defeating Sheridan during the Trevilian Raid, the praise was faint. "I beg to express my entire satisfaction at the conduct of officers and men in my command. Maj. Gen. Fitzhugh Lee co-operated with me heartily and rendered valuable assistance," wrote Hampton.[54] Wells of the Fourth South Carolina Cavalry observed about the language of Hampton's report: "The words from General Hampton's official report . . . refer only to the fighting in the evening of the second day, as anyone can perceive who reads the entire report." He continued, "Those words were correct as applied to the assistance rendered by Fitzhugh Lee's division on the evening of the second day, and they were inserted in the report of General Hampton, with his invariable generosity and magnanimity, in order to shield Fitzhugh Lee from the personal consequences, which would otherwise have resulted from his failure to execute the orders referred to."[55] In fact, Lee did little during the fighting at Trevilian Station, although he managed the battle at Samaria Church well at the end of the expedition.

Rosser wrote, "Up to the time I was wounded there appeared to have been very little cooperation between General Fitz Lee and General Hampton, and while I am not prepared to say whose fault it was I felt then, and all of us who were in the fight on the 11th felt, that it was very unfortunate that General Lee did not unite with us this day. He did join General Hampton the next morning, and united, they successfully repulsed Sheridan and caused him to abandon his plans and return to General Grant." He concluded, "After the death of General Stuart no chief of the cavalry was appointed. When the divisions were together General Hampton, who was the senior officer, took command. I very much question whether General R. E. Lee put the entire force of his army under General Hampton when he sent it in pursuit of General Sheridan. If he did, I am surprised that Hampton did not bring Fitz Lee to him on the first day's fight at Trevilian."[56]

Indeed, it appears that Lee was less than aggressive on the morning of June 11, 1864. His sortie up the Marquis Road appears inept. In fact, Wickham apparently broke off the engagement and withdrew without pressing the fight. Then, Lee dawdled in moving to the sound of the battle raging to the west. He arrived several hours later, after the engagement had already raged for most of the day. Hampton's chief of horse artillery, Major Chew, observed, "If Fitz Lee had known the situation, with two brigades, we could have gobbled up the whole of [Custer's] command." Chew compared the failure to coordinate attacks at Trevilian Station to the lack of coordination that he believed cost the Confederates victory at the Battle of Gettysburg the year before.[57]

Edward Wells, who spent the rest of his life chronicling the accomplishments of Hampton's cavalry in the summer of 1864, had even harsher words for Lee's performance. "[Fitz Lee's] Division was in the desired position in time, and was ordered to operate on the right of Hampton's line," he observed. "This was not effectually done, and as a consequence of the failure to do so, Custer passed through the gap thus caused between Hampton's Division's right and Fitzhugh Lee's left." Wells saved his harshest words for his conclusion. "In this manner [Custer] reached the rear of Hampton's Division, and opened the way for the other Federals, and Fitzhugh Lee's Division was cut off, isolated and rendered useless for over twenty-four hours."[58]

Perhaps Lee pouted because his uncle had passed him over for command of the Army of Northern Virginia's cavalry. Perhaps he was ill that day, or perhaps the travails of the long march to Trevilian Station had left him exhausted and sluggish. Perhaps his command was hors de combat from the rigors of the march. Regardless, Lee's performance at Trevilian Station was unsatisfactory, and his lack of aggressiveness on the first day of the battle likely cost Hampton the opportunity to destroy Custer's vaunted Michigan Brigade. He could have split Davies's and J. Irvin Gregg's brigades at Samaria Church but did not do so. Fitz also disappointed Hampton at the end of June at Reams's Station, leaving Hampton complaining about Lee's second failure to coordinate his attacks with his. Fitz's unsatisfactory performances prompted Butler and Rosser to urge Hampton to ask for a court-martial of Lee.[59]

Fitz's biographer tried to put the best possible face on the Virginian's performance, claiming, "If Fitz had any ambitions [about succeeding Stuart], he remained quiet about it. Indeed, relations between Hampton and Fitz were as cordial as ever, and Hampton praised Fitz's cooperation at Trevilians."[60] Hampton's biographer, Manly Wade Wellman, recognizing the General's frustration after the dual failures quite correctly observed, "At Trevilian and again at Reams's Station, Fitz had seemed slow and stupid. Butler and one or two others suggested to Hampton that Fitz was jealous, calculating, wishful that Hampton might meet disaster and so be cleared from the way to his own promotion as Stuart's successor." He continued, "Hampton . . . mistrusted Fitz Lee, but his admiration for Robert E. Lee was too warm to allow such an accusation of the commander's nephew. After that, Hampton used Fitz as little as possible in his campaigns. That was all."[61]

The Battle of Trevilian Station marked Butler's ascent to prominence. Hampton praised his protégé lavishly: "Butler's defense at Trevilian was never surpassed." He added, "He was as good a soldier as we had."[62] The South Carolina lawyer was the hero of the entire campaign. His brigade bore the brunt of the fighting on both days of the Battle of Trevilian Station and also made a critical attack at Samaria Church. While on the return march from Trevilian, Hampton praised the performances of Butler and his men to Robert E. Lee, writing, "Butler's brigade held their ground against seven desperate charges under as heavy fire, artillery and musketry, as troops are often subjected to, without even giving back a foot. Their losses . . . both of prisoners and by casualties, came only from the want of experience in the field."[63]

Butler's brigade took the bulk of the casualties during the two days of fighting at Trevilian. Their effective and accurate fire persuaded Torbert that several regiments of infantry from Gordonsville had reinforced Hampton, and that he faced a strong force of foot soldiers and not dismounted cavalry on June 12.[64] One of the South Carolinians wrote that Butler "smacked Sheridan into pulp" in the summer of 1864, crediting the short-barreled Enfield rifles carried by Butler's brigade with the success of the summer campaign.[65] A member of the Laurel Brigade praised their performance lavishly: "The soldiers of Butler's brigade are worthy of all honor, for their gallant repulse, almost single-handed of Sheridan's whole force. The honor of South Carolina is bright with the lustre of their deeds."[66] The Federals quickly gained respect for the South Carolinians. Upon his return to the Army of the Potomac, Sheridan reportedly said, "I have met Butler and his cavalry, and I hope to God I never meet them again."[67] Later that summer, after the debacle at Reams's Station, Sheridan bitterly grumbled about Butler, "That damned man has caused me more trouble than all the rest of the 'Rebel cavalry' put together."[68]

When Hampton assumed corps command, Butler took over Hampton's division. He was promoted to major general in September 1864.[69] From that point forward, Butler was the most effective subordinate cavalry commander in the Army of Northern Virginia until his division went to South Carolina during the late fall of 1864. The performance of Butler and his brigade during the Trevilian raid was the great untold story of the spring and summer of 1864.

The rest of Hampton's subordinate commanders also performed well. Col. Gid Wright did good service at Trevilian in spite of the heavy casualties suffered by his command. Rosser and his Laurel Brigade recaptured Custer's prize and nearly destroyed his brigade. When Rosser went down with a wound, his brigade ceased having a significant role in the rest of the campaign. One member of the Laurel Brigade wrote, "We missed on the field the brilliant dash and energy of our old commander . . . we missed the inspiring voice and example of Rosser, after his wound, but the inspiration remained with his own 'people' and animated all."[70] Despite his failures in the Shenandoah Valley in the fall of 1864, Rosser received a promotion to major general and command of a division. Likewise, Lomax was promoted to major general and took command of all of Early's cavalry in the Valley after Fitz Lee received a combat wound. Although Wickham had been elected to the Confederate Congress in 1863, he did not resign his commission to assume his congressional seat until November 1864. He then entered a different arena of combat than the one to which he had been accustomed.

The Confederate horse artillery did good service, despite being outnumbered by Sheridan's superior force of gunners. Working under some extremely adverse circumstances, Chew's and Breathed's gunners provided a strong counterbalance to the effective Northern batteries. Despite this fact, the days of dominance by the Southern horse artillery were over. While the Southern batteries had been eclipsed by the powerful Northern batteries, they still provided good service for the balance of the war.

What then, was the net result of the Battle of Trevilian Station and Sheridan's second raid?

Analysis of the first day's fight at Trevilian shows that there were four distinct fights. The first was the skirmish between Wickham and Custer. The second was the meeting engagement that began at Bibb's Crossroads. While there was a brief mounted melee between Merritt's Regulars and a squadron of South Carolinians, the bulk of this fight was dismounted, much like an infantry battle. The difficult terrain dictated that the heavy combat had to be at close quarters.

The third distinct phase began at 8:00 that morning with Custer's foray into Hampton's wagon train and the resulting fracas that led to the creation of the "living triangle" and the near destruction of the Michigan Brigade. It included both vigorous mounted combat interspersed with dismounted action while Custer fought a lonely and protracted battle. While Custer tried to carry out Sheridan's plan, that plan was doomed to fail for a variety of reasons. The fourth phase occupied most of the afternoon, with Torbert launching an all-out assault along his entire battle line that not only saved Custer's brigade but also drove the Confederates from the field. These four fights could have been far more effective had they been coordinated and effectively directed by Sheridan, who probably should have taken personal command of the field.

The second day's fight was the best evidence of the poor command and control that plagued the Federals at Trevilian Station. Sheridan and Gregg did not participate in the determined assaults on the Bloody Angle in front of the Ogg farm. Instead, Torbert left Merritt to his own devices. Merritt sent for reinforcements and hit Butler's strong line repeatedly. Torbert did not exercise personal command that day. Instead of trying to flank Hampton out of a very strong position, Torbert instead permitted Merritt to launch seven uncoordinated and unsupported frontal assaults on a position that probably could not be taken by frontal assault. Only three things could have made a difference in the outcome of the second day's fighting. First was a flanking move by Gregg's division. Second was an assault by Custer's Wolverines. Third was such protracted combat that the Confederates would have run out of ammunition and been forced to withdraw, an unlikely result at best. Torbert's tactics resembled infantry tactics but showed no creativity or initiative and cost the Union horsemen heavy casualties in a fight that could not be won.

From a tactical standpoint, the bloody fights at Trevilian and Samaria Church accomplished little but the battering of a superbly equipped and mounted force of Federal cavalry and a heavy toll on the Union's horses. Sheridan lost every engagement during the expedition and suffered heavy casualties in the process. His failure to exercise personal command at any time during the two-days' fighting at Trevilian Station evidences Sheridan's inexperience in commanding large bodies of mounted men in battle. Neither his strategy nor his tactics for the campaign were imaginative, and he did not demonstrate any real leadership until the final days of the campaign when a desperate race to save the Federal wagon train from destruction developed. Only then did Sheridan, a former quartermaster, demonstrate any real prowess, and he deserves credit for safely delivering the wagon trains to safety. In the meantime, Hampton rose to prominence and never relinquished that role.

More tangible results may be traced from a strategic standpoint. By sending Torbert's and Gregg's veteran divisions on an extended raid, Grant drew off the Confederate cavalry force and made his crossing of the James River largely unmolested. His unhindered advance on Petersburg might have hastened the end of the war if his infantry corps commanders had executed his orders quickly and without hesitation. When they failed to do so, the Confederates built a defensive position strong enough to allow Lee's Army of Northern Virginia to reach Petersburg, and the war degraded into a siege. Early's advance down the Shenandoah Valley pulled away some of Grant's force. It ultimately led to the destruction of the beautiful valley and failed to break Grant's stranglehold on the critical rail junction at Petersburg. The fact that it took Grant another ten months to break the will of Lee's army only highlights the importance of the two critical failures that occurred.

First, had Sheridan succeeded, he would have cut Lee's link to the west and captured the critical supply depot at Lynchburg. This would have brought Hunter's army east. With Hunter converging from the north, the Army of the James holding the eastern front, and the Army of the Potomac squeezing the Confederates between them, the war undoubtedly would have ended much faster. In short, Sheridan's failure to carry out Grant's orders for the Trevilian raid bought the Confederacy another ten months. Second, the failure to capitalize on the distraction caused by Sheridan's raid prevented Grant from seizing a nearly undefended Petersburg. Thus, Hampton's performance during the Trevilian raid produced one of the Civil War's truly decisive victories. "I think anyone who will investigate this matter will conclude that, instead of gaining a victory, General Sheridan simply succeeded in rescuing his force from destruction, and in getting it back to the army much the worse for the wear," observed Wilson, quite accurately.[71]

Indeed, while Sheridan claimed that his cavalry enjoyed an unbroken string of victories over the Confederate horse soldiers, the truth does not bear him out. In fact, his use of the mounted arm was neither imaginative nor especially effective. Instead, because it operated without its eyes and ears, the main body of the Army of the Potomac could not protect its flanks as well as they should have been. While the participants on both sides of the Trevilian raid remembered it as the hardest expedition and the hardest cavalry fight of the Civil War, it did nothing to contribute to the Northern victory and actually harmed the Union's prospects for success, because Sheridan failed to carry out Grant's orders.

Wilson, an astute observer whose command also suffered as a result of Sheridan's inability to contain Hampton north of the James, concluded, "General Sheridan . . . had gained much reputation from the fact that his cavalry had not been driven out of the field, and he was credited with having beaten the enemy every time he had come in contact with him. It is true we were fairly successful in every skirmish and battle, but it is well to observe that we had no fight where our cavalry was fairly matched against the Confederate cavalry except at Yellow Tavern, and that was only an affair of two or three brigades, and was soon over."[72] The Battle of Trevilian Station, the largest all-cavalry battle of the Civil War, was the exception. Well advised and well planned, but poorly executed by Sheridan, the Trevilian raid was doomed because Lee did exactly what Grant tried to prevent him from doing—he countered Hunter.

The net result of the Battle of Trevilian Station is that Hampton's stellar performance extended the war for at least six months. While some might argue that Hampton could have been more aggressive during the retreat from Trevilian Station, his exhausted men and horses were not up to the task. The raid had taken the same toll on his command as it had on Sheridan's, prompting one Southern horse soldier to write, "All honor . . . to the whole cavalry, which, amid toils, privation, and suffering, still have hearts unshaken and hands ever ready to strike down invasion."[73] The eminent Confederate horse artillerist Roger Chew summed it up nicely in a postwar speech: "the Battle of Trevilians . . . was perhaps the most important fight of the war . . . because, if lost, General Lee and his whole army would have been without supplies. Trevilians was so important to General Lee that he was enabled thereby to stay in Petersburg for nearly a year longer."[74] The ascendance of Hampton's star had much farther reaching implications than anyone who participated in the expedition could have known. The tragedy is that this critical battle, in which good men of both sides suffered and died, has been largely forgotten by history.

Notes

1. O.R., vol. 36, part 1, 799.

2. Hampton claimed that he captured 570 Federals at Trevilian Station. See O.R., vol. 36, part 1, 1096. Sheridan claimed that only 175 of his men were taken prisoner, but this figure is clearly inaccurate. Ibid., 796. The data presented herein were researched and prepared by Bryce A. Suderow, and differ from the figures indicated in the Official Records.

3. The stated strength of 2,147 is an estimate. It does not take into account any losses of stragglers or casualties sustained in the various skirmishes along the way. It is impossible to pin down the precise strength of Gregg's division that day, as no statistics exist to demonstrate the actual strength. This figure was derived from Gregg's reported strength before the Battle of Trevilian Station and subtracting the losses taken in the two days of fighting. It is quite likely that the effective strength of Gregg's division was significantly less than 2,147 as a result of straggling, dismounted men, and casualties taken in the skirmishing on the retreat. For purposes of this analysis, I have used the higher number. The casualty figures are still staggering regardless of what the actual strength of the Second Division was on June 24.

4. Young, Confederate Wizards of the Saddle, 365. In fact, the odds faced by Gregg at Samaria Church matched those faced by Butler on June 12, but Butler had greater success in managing those odds than did Butler.

5. The casualty statistics for the Battle of Trevilian Station, which were in part compiled by Bryce A. Suderow of Washington, appear as appendixes B and C to this volume. These statistics differ from those set forth in the Official Records to some degree, as they were compiled from regimental casualty returns and not from official reports. The totals are somewhat different, but not by a great degree. The losses along the route of march and in the many skirmishes that marked the expedition are virtually impossible to ascertain.

6. The regimental commanders lost included Rodenbough, Loeser, Sackett,

Smith, Covode, and Huey. Huey was a former brigade commander under David Gregg.

7. Rockwell, *Rambling Recollections*, 154.

8. Clement Hoffman to his mother, June 23, 1864, Clement Hoffman letters, United States Army Military History Institute, Carlisle, Pennsylvania.

9. Brooks, *Butler and His Cavalry*, 253.

10. A trooper of the Sixth Ohio scrawled in his diary on June 24, "The Sixth Ohio lost 60 horses out of 300, the writer's being one of the number." King, *To Horse*, 13.

11. O.R., vol. 36, part 1, 801.

12. Merington, *The Custer Story*, 105.

13. Maj. Gen. Andrew A. Humphreys, Meade's chief of staff, suggested that losses in killed of approximately 18 percent were the norm for infantry battles of the Civil War. See Humphreys, *The Virginia Campaign of 1864 and 1865*, 1:72, n. 1. By simple arithmetic, that means 82 percent of those men lost but not killed, captured or missing, were lost to wounds.

14. O.R., vol. 36, part 1, 801.

15. Frank A. Burr and Richard J. Hinton, *Little Phil and His Troopers: The Life of Gen. Philip H. Sheridan: Its Romance and Reality: How a Humble Lad Reached the Head of an Army* (Providence, R. I.: J. A. & R. A. Reid, 1888), 173–74.

16. Carswell McClellan, *Notes on the Personal Memoirs of P. H. Sheridan* (St. Paul, Minn.: Press of Wm. E. Banning Jr., 1889), 24. The gist of McClellan's little book is that Phil Sheridan was a liar. McClellan points to three different episodes in the Civil War and demonstrates, rather persuasively, that Sheridan frequently failed to tell the truth in order to make himself look better in the harsh light of history.

17. Di Cessnola to Wood, July 7, 1864.

18. James Harrison Wilson, "The Cavalry of the Army of the Potomac," *Papers of the Military Historical Society of Massachusetts, Civil and Mexican Wars 1861, 1846*, 13 (Boston: Military Historical Society of Massachusetts, 1913), 58.

19. Rosser, *Riding with Rosser*, 38.

20. O.R., vol. 51, part 2, 1012–1013; Duncan, *Lee's Endangered Left*, 264.

21. Jubal A. Early, *Autobiographical Sketch and Narrative of the War Between the States* (Philadelphia: J. B. Lippincott, 1912), 373. According to Richard Duncan, repair crews were working on the railroad when Early's little army arrived there on the 15th.

22. For a detailed analysis of the fight at Lynchburg, and its implications, see Duncan's fine book, *Lee's Endangered Left*.

23. Frederic C. Newhall, "The Battle of Beverly Ford," included in *The Annals of the War Written by Leading Participants, North and South* (Dayton, Ohio: Morningside, 1988), 135. A year after the end of the war, Newhall penned a book titled, *With*

General Sheridan in Lee's Last Campaign, the primary purpose of which was to defend Sheridan's actions in relieving Maj. Gen. G. K. Warren of command at the Battle of Five Forks, fought April 1, 1865. Perhaps the wisdom of the passing years gave Newhall the ability to be more objective in his assessment of Philip Henry Sheridan by the time he wrote the passages quoted herein.

24. Kidd to his father, June 21, 1864.

25. John B. Coover to Dear Sister, June 23, 1864, John B. Coover letters, George F. Scott Collection, Mt. Carmel, Pennsylvania.

26. *Pittsburgh Evening Chronicle,* June 20, 1864.

27. *Ibid.,* June 21, 1864.

28. *Charleston Mercury,* June 22, 1864.

29. *Richmond Examiner,* June 24, 1864.

30. Rosser, *Riding with Rosser,* 39.

31. Brooks, *Butler and His Cavalry,* 256–57.

32. *Ibid.,* 257.

33. John B. Jones, *A Rebel War Clerk's Diary,* vol. 2 (New York: Sagamore Press, 1958), 390.

34. Edward P. Tobie, *Personal Recollections of General Sheridan* (Providence, R.I.: privately published, 1889), 17.

35. Edward B. Williams, ed., *Rebel Brothers: The Civil War Letters of the Truehearts* (College Station: Texas A & M University Press, 1995), 97. Of course, White House Landing is on the Pamunkey, not the York.

36. Power, *Lee's Miserables,* 79.

37. "Letter from Cobb's Legion," *Augusta Daily Constitutionalist,* July 10, 1864.

38. Burgess, *David Gregg,* 74.

39. Merington, *The Custer Story,* 104.

40. Milledgeville, Georgia *Southern Reporter,* July 26, 1864.

41. Charles E. Cauthen, ed., *Family Letters of the Three Wade Hamptons, 1782–1901* (Columbia: University of South Carolina Press, 1953), 105.

42. Thomas T. Munford, "A Confederate Cavalry Officer's Views on 'American Practice and Foreign Theory,'" *Journal of the United States Cavalry Association* 4 (1891): 202.

43. Holmes, "The Fighting Qualities."

44. O.R., vol. 36, part 1, 1098.

45. The brigade commander was Thomas L. Rosser, badly wounded in the leg in the closing action on June 11, and the lost regimental commanders included Aiken, Carter, and McAllister.

46. Unfortunately, the casualty statistics for the Confederates are not as reliable or as detailed as those for the Union. The Union strengths and losses are well documented and fairly easy to pull together, as the records are grouped together in the National Archives. The Southern statistics, however, are not compiled anywhere, and pulling them together often requires searching through obscure news-

papers for random reports. The lack of comprehensive and uniform records on Confederate strengths and losses is indeed unfortunate.

47. Halliburton, *Saddle Soldiers*, 145–51.

48. Priest, *Stephen Elliott Welch*, 38.

49. *Savannah Morning News*, October 5, 1930.

50. Young, *Wizards of the Saddle*, 365.

51. Douglas Southall Freeman, ed. *Lee's Dispatches* (New York: G. P. Putnam's Sons, 1915), 268.

52. Driver, *First Virginia Cavalry* (Lynchburg, Va.: H. E. Howard Co., 1989), 89.

53. Vogtsberger, *The Dulanys of Welbourne*, 219. At the Battle of Dranesville in December 1861, Stuart had enthusiastically pitched into a large force of Union infantry at Dranesville and had not done well there. His impulsive charge nearly destroyed his force.

54. Driver, *First Virginia Cavalry*, 89; O.R. vol. 36, part 1, 1097.

55. Edward L. Wells to Frank Dorsey, January 8, 1904, Wells Correspondence.

56. Rosser, *Riding with Rosser*, 38–39.

57. Chew, "The Battle of Trevilians," 11. Chew wrote, "If Hampton had not reached Rosser when he was about to charge, we would undoubtedly have captured Custer, and there was nothing Rosser would have done, either, for he was always anxious to capture Custer. They went to West Point together. But we could not pull it together."

58. Edward L. Wells to the Editor, *Richmond Dispatch*, January 12, 1900, Wells Correspondence.

59. Wellman, *Giant in Gray*, p. 151. Hampton wrote, "Had there been proper concert of action between the forces at Ream's and my own, there would have been no difficulty in cutting off the party." O.R., vol. 40, part 1, 807.

60. James L. Nichols, *General Fitzhugh Lee: A Biography* (Lynchburg, Va.: H. E. Howard Co., 1989).

61. Wellman, *Giant in Gray*, 151.

62. Brooks, *Butler and His Cavalry*, 254.

63. O.R., vol. 51, part 2, 1014.

64. *Ibid.*, vol. 36, part 1, 809.

65. Edward L. Wells to Mr. Haussman, December 2, 1898, Wells Correspondence.

66. *Petersburg Daily Register*, June 29, 1864.

67. Brooks, *Butler and His Cavalry*, 212.

68. *Ibid.*, 213.

69. Warner, *Generals in Gray*, 41.

70. *Petersburg Daily Register*, June 29, 1864.

71. Wilson, "The Cavalry of the Army of the Potomac," 58–9.

72. *Ibid.*, 76–7.

73. *Petersburg Daily Register*, June 29, 1864.

74. Chew, "The Battle of Trevilians," 10.

⇒ Epilogue ⇒

On July 12, 1864, Mrs. William Sackett, whose husband had received a mortal wound a month earlier on the first day of the Battle of Trevilian Station, arrived at Grant's headquarters. Via a flag of truce, Mrs. Sackett applied to Lee for permission to travel to Trevilian Station to find her husband. Lee initially denied the request to let her pass the lines, but also suggested that further inquiries would be made, and that she would be advised of her husband's condition. Two days later, Mrs. Sackett received a communication from Lee's chief surgeon, a Dr. Breckinridge, reporting that her husband had died on the evening of June 14 from wounds to the abdomen. Breckinridge further related that the colonel had been buried next to Mrs. Bibb's log cabin at Bibb's Crossroads, a short distance from Trevilian Station. He was buried almost on the spot where the first shots of the battle were fired.

Mrs. Sackett then visited the Christian Commission at City Point and obtained a large load of supplies. She brought an ambulance load of canned and dried fruits, canned meats, condensed milk, farina, cocoa, butter, and so forth to the camp of the Ninth New York Cavalry and distributed these treats to her husband's men. After completing her mission of mercy, Mrs. Sackett finally received permission to pass through the Confederate lines by flag of truce. She went to Richmond and then on to Trevilian Station, obtained a metal coffin, disinterred the remains of her heroic husband, and lovingly placed them in the coffin. She carried his remains back through the enemy lines under flag of truce, "and took all that was mortal of her gallant husband to his home." He was interred in Restvale Cemetery in his hometown of Seneca Falls, New York. A Union officer commented that Mrs. Sackett's "conduct was considered notable at the time."[1]

Within a few years of the end of the war, most of the Union graves that could be identified had been exhumed, and the bodies taken to various locations for burial in their final resting places. Some of the Federals rest in the National Cemetery at Spotsylvania, and others in the National Cemetery at the big Cavalry Corps hospital at City Point. Still others were taken to their hometowns for burial. A few rest in Louisa. Local lore has

328 Glory Enough for All

it that a number of soldiers still lie on the battlefield at Trevilian Station in unmarked graves, but the veracity of these legends cannot be determined.

However, nearly 100 horse soldiers who died as a result of the two days of combat at Trevilian Station were buried at Oakland Cemetery in Louisa. Lt. Col. Joseph McAllister of the Seventh Georgia Cavalry rests under a stone that reads, "Soldier-Scholar-Gentleman." Capt. John P. Hines of Bryan County, Georgia, who commanded Company H of the Seventh Georgia Cavalry, and who was killed in action during the fight for the wagons, lies next to his commanding officer.[2]

A short distance away rest Rev. John Towles's three sons, all of whom served in the Fourth Virginia Cavalry, and all of whom were killed in combat during the Civil War. The third son, Robert, received a mortal wound during the fighting on June 11, 1864. A resident of Louisa, who nursed the dying "noble boy," wrote to his mother, "He is more perfectly resigned than any one I ever saw, says he has always tried to live right, and is now resigned to the Will of the Lord, that all he cares to live for is to be a comfort to his parents. . . . He seems very much afraid you will not be able to bear the shock of his being so badly wounded. Says you have seen so much trouble since the War commenced."[3] One can only imagine the intense pain that must have plagued Reverend and Mrs. Towles. A genuine pride that their sons had died in the service of a cause they believed in probably tempered that pain. Death reunited the three brothers, who were all buried together in Oakland Cemetery.[4]

Very few of the Confederate and Union battle dead were identified and most of them rest in graves marked only by small granite markers that say "unknown." On June 12, 1982, on the 118th anniversary of the second day of the Battle of Trevilian Station, the Mineral Chapter of the United Daughters of the Confederacy dedicated a monument in Oakland Cemetery. Capped by the crossed flags of the United Daughters of the Confederacy, the top of the monument states, "Love Makes Memory Eternal." The front of it reads, "This monument is dedicated with affection, reverence and undying remembrance to the memory of the men who gave their lives at the Battle of Trevilians, June 11–12, 1864 and who were interred here."

Although this solemn and respectful monument pays tribute to the hundreds of men who gave their lives at the Battle of Trevilian Station, nothing is more moving or more poignant than standing among those quiet rows of small stones marked "unknown." Those graves represent just a small portion of the men who gave the last full measure of devotion during the Civil War. These men died with honor, defending a cause that they believed in. Because of the way they died, they were forever rendered missing in action for their families at home, who never found out what had happened to their loved ones. The silent graves of the Confederate and Union dead resting in Oakland Cemetery provide the most striking and most important reminder of the ferocity of those two days in June 1864. These graves represent just a few of the unknown soldiers who died in just one American war—still missing in action. The final resting places of soldiers who fought and died at Trevilian Station bear mute witness to the sacrifices made by the hot, parched horse soldiers of both sides who clashed in the largest all-cavalry battle of the American Civil War.

Notes

1. Cheney, *Ninth New York Cavalry*, 189–90; Bean, "Sheridan at Trevilian"; Hunt and Long, *Brevet Brigadier Generals in Blue*, 530.

2. Unfortunately, Capt. Hines's grave marker states only "Captain Hines." For many years, his first name was lost to history. Through intensive research, his name is now known once again. See Service Record of Capt. John P. Hines, M266, Roll 37, Compiled Service Records of Confederate Soldiers who Served in Organizations from Georgia, the National Archives, Washington, D.C.

3. Sallie Conner to Mrs. Towles, June 13, 1864.

4. Reverend and Mrs. Towles do not rest with their three sons. Instead, they rest in Prince William County, Virginia, where the family resided. Fittingly, their three sons rest on a battlefield far from home, bearing bleak witness to the human toll of war. Keith Kehlbeck to the author, February 7, 2000.

⊱ Appendix A ⊰

Order of the Battle

SHERIDAN'S TREVILIAN STATION RAID
THE BATTLE OF TREVILIAN STATION
JUNE 11–12, 1864

ARMY OF THE POTOMAC
CAVALRY CORPS
Maj. Gen. Philip H. Sheridan
Escort: Sixth U.S. Cavalry (Capt. Ira W. Claflin)

First Cavalry Division
Brig. Gen. Alfred T. A. Torbert

First Brigade
Brig. Gen. George A. Custer

First Michigan Cavalry (Lt. Col. Peter Stagg)
Fifth Michigan Cavalry (Col. Russell A. Alger)
Sixth Michigan Cavalry (Maj. James H. Kidd)
Seventh Michigan Cavalry (Lt. Col. Melvin Brewer—wounded;
    Maj. Alexander Walker)

Second Brigade
Col. Thomas C. Devin

Fourth New York Cavalry (Col. Luigi Palma DiCessnola)
Sixth New York Cavalry (Lt. Col. William H. Crocker)
Ninth New York Cavalry (Col. William Sackett—mortally wounded;
    Lt. Col. George S. Nichols)
Seventeenth Pennsylvania Cavalry (Lt. Col. James Q. Anderson)

Reserve Brigade (Third Brigade)
Brig. Gen. Wesley Merritt

First U.S. Cavalry (Capt. Nelson B. Sweitzer)
Second U.S. Cavalry (Capt. Theophilus F. Rodenbough—wounded;
    Capt. Charles McK. Loeser—captured; Capt. Daniel S. Gordon)
Fifth U.S. Cavalry (Capt. William K. Arnold)
Sixth Pennsylvania Cavalry (Capt. J. Hinckley Clark)
Nineteenth New York Cavalry (First New York Dragoons)
    (Col. Alfred Gibbs)

Second Cavalry Division
Brig. Gen. David M. Gregg

First Brigade
Brig. Gen. Henry E. Davies

First Massachusetts Cavalry (Lt. Col. Samuel E. Chamberlain)
First New Jersey Cavalry (Lt. Col. John W. Kester)
Sixth Ohio Cavalry (Col. William Stedman)
First Pennsylvania Cavalry (Col. John P. Taylor)
Tenth New York Cavalry (Maj. M. Henry Avery)

Second Brigade
Col. J. I. Gregg

First Maine Cavalry (Col. Charles H. Smith)
Second Pennsylvania Cavalry (Lt. Col. Joseph P. Brinton)
Fourth Pennsylvania Cavalry (Lt. Col. George H. Covode)
Eighth Pennsylvania Cavalry (Col. Pennock Huey)
Thirteenth Pennsylvania Cavalry (Maj. Michael Kerwin)
Sixteenth Pennsylvania Cavalry (Lt. Col. John K. Robison)

Horse Artillery Brigade
Capt. James M. Robertson

First U.S. Artillery, Batteries H & I (Capt. Alanson M. Randol)
Second U.S. Artillery, Batteries B & L (Lt. Edward Heaton)

Second U.S. Artillery, Battery D (Lt. Edward B. Williston)
Second U.S. Artillery, Battery M (Lt. Alexander C. M. Pennington Jr.)

Total strength: Approximately 9,200 men and 20 guns.

ARMY OF NORTHERN VIRGINIA
CAVALRY CORPS
Maj. Gen. Wade Hampton

Hampton's Division
Maj. Gen. Wade Hampton

Young's Brigade
Col. Gilbert J. Wright

Seventh Georgia Cavalry (Lt. Col. Joseph L. McAllister—killed in
    action; Maj. Edward C. Anderson, Jr., wounded and captured;
    Maj. John N. Davies)
Cobb's Georgia Legion (Col. Gilbert J. Wright)
Phillips Georgia Legion (Lt. Col. William W. Rich)
Twentieth Georgia Cavalry (Partisan Rangers Battalion)
    (Lt. Col. Samuel B. Spencer)
Jeff Davis Mississippi Legion (Lt. Col. Joseph F. Waring)

Rosser's Brigade (Laurel Brigade)
Brig. Gen. Thomas L. Rosser—wounded; Col. Richard H. Dulany

Seventh Virginia Cavalry (Col. Richard H. Dulany)
Eleventh Virginia Cavalry (Col. Oliver R. Funsten)
Twelfth Virginia Cavalry (Lt. Col. Thomas B. Massie)
Thirty-fifth Battalion Virginia Cavalry (Col. Elijah V. White)

Butler's Brigade
Brig. Gen. Matthew C. Butler

Fourth South Carolina Cavalry (Col. B. Huger Rutledge)
Fifth South Carolina Cavalry (Maj. Joseph H. Morgan)
Sixth South Carolina Cavalry (Col. Hugh K. Aiken—wounded;
    Maj. Thomas B. Ferguson)

Fitzhugh Lee's Division
Maj. Gen. Fitzhugh Lee

Wickham's Brigade
Brig. Gen. Williams C. Wickham
Col. Thomas T. Munford

First Virginia Cavalry (Lt. Col. William A. Morgan)
Second Virginia Cavalry (Col. Thomas T. Munford)
Third Virginia Cavalry (Col. Thomas H. Owen)
Fourth Virginia Cavalry (Col. William B. Wooldridge)

Lomax's Brigade
Brig. Gen. Lunsford L. Lomax

Fifth Virginia Cavalry (Capt. Ruben Boston)
Sixth Virginia Cavalry (Col. John S. Green)
Fifteenth Virginia Cavalry (Col. Charles R. Collins)

Independent Command
First Maryland Cavalry Battalion (Col. Bradley T. Johnson)
Baltimore Light Artillery (Lt. John McNulty)

Breathed's Horse Artillery Battalion
Maj. James Breathed
Maj. Roger Preston Chew

Washington Artillery of South Carolina (Hart's Battery)
   (Maj. James Hart)
Ashby Virginia Artillery of Virginia (Chew's Battery)
   (Lt. James W. Thomson)
Lynchburg Beauregards (Shoemaker's Battery) (Capt. John J. Shoemaker)
First Stuart Horse Artillery of Virginia (Capt. Phillip P. Johnston)

Total Strength: Approximately 6,450 men and 14 guns.

Note: The Third Cavalry Division, Army of the Potomac (Brig. Gen. James
H. Wilson), along with a horse artillery battalion, remained with the Army

of the Potomac during most of the raid. The Division of Maj. Gen. William H. F. "Rooney" Lee, also assigned to the Army of Northern Virginia's cavalry command, the independent cavalry command of Brig. Gen. Martin Gary, and the balance of the Confederate horse artillery battalion remained with the Army of Northern Virginia during most of the raid.

⊶ Appendix B ⊷

Union Strengths and Losses at the Battle of Trevilian Station

June 11, 1864

Unit Strength	% Loss	K	W	C	T
1st Cavalry Division (Brig. Gen. Alfred T. A. Torbert)					
First Cavalry Brigade (Brig. Gen. George A. Custer)					
F & S		0	1	0	1
7					
First Michigan		1	5	59	65
540					
Fifth Michigan		4	6	136	146
441					
Sixth Michigan		5	22	60	87
342					
Seventh Michigan		1	17	44	62
323					
Total:		11	51	299	361
1653	22%				
Second Cavalry Brigade (Col. Thomas C. Devin)					
F & S		0	0	0	0
7					
Sixth New York		0	3	13	16
351					
Ninth New York		4	40	3	47
428					
Fourth New York		0	4	0	4
252					
Seventeenth Pennsylvania		0	0	0	0
549					

Unit Strength	% Loss	K	W	C	T
Second Cavalry Brigade (Con't.)					
Total:		4	47	16	67
1587	4.2%				
Reserve Brigade (Brig. Gen. Wesley Merritt)					
F & S		0	0	0	0
7					
First U.S.		2	12	2	16
372					
Second U.S.		8	28	2	38
288					
Fifth U.S.		0	0	4	4
158					
Sixth Pennsylvania		5	27	0	32
343					
First New York Dragoons		8	26	3	37
435					
Total:		23	93	11	127
1604	7.9%				
First Division total		38	191	326	555
4844	11.5%				

Second Cavalry Division (Brig. Gen. David M. Gregg)

First Brigade (Brig. Gen. Henry E. Davies)					
F & S		0	0	0	0
6					
Sixth Ohio		0	0	0	0
665					
First New Jersey		0	1	0	1
673					
First Massachusetts		0	0	2	2
368					
Tenth New York		4	15	0	19
441					
Total:		4	16	2	22
2633	0.08%				

Unit Strength	% Loss	K	W	C	T
Second Brigade (Brig. Gen. J. Irvin Gregg)					
First Maine		0	3	0	3
446					
Second Pennsylvania		1	3	0	4
544					
Fourth Pennsylvania		2	28	2	32
406					
Eighth Pennsylvania		3	17	5	25
412					
Sixteenth Pennsylvania		2	11	0	13
420					
Total:		8	62	7	77
2228	3.4%				
Horse Artillery Brigade					
Battery M, Second U.S. Artillery		2	5	37	44
125					
Battery D, Second U.S. Artillery		0	0	0	0
131					
Battery I, First U.S. Artillery		1	1	0	2
125					
Total:		3	6	37	46
381	12%				
June 11 Cavalry Corps total:		53	274	372	699
9286	7.5%				

The material in this table was produced by Bryce A. Suderow, of Washington, D.C., and is used with his permission.

⊱ Appendix C ⊰

Union Strengths and Losses at the Battle of Trevilian Station
June 12, 1864

Unit Strength	% Loss	K	W	C	T
1st Cavalry Division (Brig. Gen. Alfred T. A. Torbert)					
First Cavalry Brigade (Brig. Gen. George A. Custer)					
F & S		0	0	0	6
First Michigan		11	16	2	29
Fifth Michigan		0	3	0	3
Sixth Michigan		1	1	0	2
Seventh Michigan		1	8	3	12
Total:		13	28	5	52
Second Cavalry Brigade (Col. Thomas C. Devin)					
F & S		0	0	0	0
Sixth New York		2	5	11	18
Ninth New York		0	1	0	1
Fourth New York		5	26	8	39
Seventeenth Pennsylvania		5	19	2	26
Total:		12	51	21	84
Reserve Brigade (Brig. Gen. Wesley Merritt)					
F & S		0	0	0	0
First U.S.		4	21	0	25
Second U.S.		0	9	0	9
Fifth U.S.		1	0	0	1
Sixth Pennsylvania		1	29	5	35
First New York Dragoons		7	32	6	45
Total:		13	90	11	115
First Division total		38	169	37	246

Unit Strength	% Loss	K	W	C	T
Second Cavalry Division (Brig. Gen. David M. Gregg)					
First Brigade (Brig. Gen. Henry E. Davies)					
F & S		0	0	0	0
Sixth Ohio		0	0	0	0
First New Jersey		2	1	1	4
First Massachusetts		0	0	0	0
Tenth New York		0	0	0	0
Total:		2	1	1	4
Second Brigade (Brig. Gen. J. Irvin Gregg)					
Not engaged					
Horse Artillery Brigade					
Battery D, Second U.S. Artillery		0	1	0	1
Total:		0	1	0	1
June 12 Cavalry Corps total:		42	171	38	251
Grand total, Union Cavalry Corps:					
June 11		53	274	372	699
June 12		42	171	38	256
Grand total:		95	445	410	955
9286	10.3%				

The material in this table was produced by Bryce A. Suderow, of Washington, D.C., and is used with his permission.

⇥ Appendix D ⇤

Confederate Strengths and Losses at the Battle of Trevilian Station

Unit Strength	% Loss	K	W	C	T
Hampton's Division					
Butler's Brigade (Brig. Gen. Matthew C. Butler)					
June 11					249
June 12					50
Total:					299
Fourth South Carolina		14	38	53	105
Fifth South Carolina		6	41	8	55
Sixth South Carolina		21	93	25	139
500					
Total:					
1300	23%	41	172	86	299
Wright's Brigade (Col. Gilbert J. Wright)					
June 11					250
June 12					50
Total:					300
Seventh Georgia		11	33	182	226
600	38%				
Phillips Legion					10
200					
Cobb Legion					10
200					
Twentieth Georgia Cavalry Battalion		2	3	3	8
400					
Jeff Davis Legion					10
200					

Unit Strength	% Loss	K	W	C	T
Love's Alabama Battalion		1	7	1	9
300					
Total:					
1900	14%				273

Rosser's Brigade (Brig. Gen. Thomas L. Rosser)

June 11					20
June 12					0
Total:					20

Seventh Virginia
Eleventh Virginia
Twelfth Virginia
First Maryland Cavalry (independent command)

Total:					
1250	1%				20
Division Total:		59	258	295	612
4450	14.5%				

Lee's Division

Wickham's Brigade (Brig. Gen. Williams C. Wickham)

June 11

	K	W	C	T
First Virginia	0	2	0	2
Second Virginia	0	5	0	5
Third Virginia	1	7	0	8
Fourth Virginia	0	19	4	23
Total:	1	33	4	38

June 12

	K	W	C	T
First Virginia	0	0	0	0
Second Virginia	1	8	0	9
Third Virginia	1	18	1	20
Fourth Virginia	1	3	0	4
Total:	3	29	1	33
Grand total:	4	62	5	71

	% Loss				
1300	5%				

Unit Strength	% Loss	K	W	C	T
Lomax's Brigade (Brig. Gen. Lunsford L. Lomax)					
June 11					50
June 12					40
Total:					90
500					
Fifth Virginia					
Sixth Virginia					
Fifteenth Virginia					
Division Total:					161
1800	8.9%				
Chew's Artillery Battalion (Maj. Roger P. Chew)					
June 11					21
June 12					10
Hart's South Carolina Battery		0	9	3	12
Thomson's Battery					9
Shoemaker's Battery					5
Johnston's Battery					5
Total:					31
412	8%				
Grand Totals:					
Hampton's Division		59	258	295	622
4450					
Lee's Division					161
1900					
Artillery					30
412					
TOTAL:					813
6762	12.3%				

The material in this table was produced by Bryce A. Suderow, of Washington, D. C., and is used with his permission.

⊱ Bibliography ⊰

Primary Sources:

Newspapers:

Atlanta Sunny South

Augusta (Georgia) *Daily Constitutionalist*

Boston Journal

Camden (South Carolina) *Journal*

Cavalier (Yorktown, Virginia)

Charleston Daily Courier

Charleston Mercury

Charlottesville Chronicle

Columbia South Carolinian

Cortland (New York) *Gazette & Banner*

Daily Southern Guardian (Columbia, South Carolina)

Detroit Advertiser & Tribune

Detroit Free Press

Daily Register (Petersburg, Virginia)

Fredonia (New York) *Censor*

Lewistown (Pennsylvania) *Gazette*

National Tribune

New York Herald

New York Times

Philadelphia Inquirer

Philadelphia Press

Pittsburgh Evening Chronicle

Raleigh Daily Progress

Raleigh Weekly Progress

Reading Eagle

Richmond Daily Dispatch

Richmond Daily Examiner

Richmond Examiner

Richmond Sentinel

Richmond Times-Dispatch

Richmond Whig

Savannah Morning News

Savannah Republican

Southern Banner (Athens, Georgia)

Southern Recorder (Milledgeville, Georgia)

Utica (New York) *Weekly Herald*

Washington, D.C., *Daily Morning Chronicle*

Unpublished Manuscripts:

Albany Institute of History and Art, McKinney Library, Albany, New York:
    Philip Neher Collection

American Antiquarian Society, Worcester, Massachusetts:
    Charles M. Munroe Diary for 1864

Atlanta History Center, Atlanta, Georgia:
    McClatchie Family Papers

Berks County Historical Society, Reading, Pennsylvania:
    David M. Gregg Papers

John C. Calhoun Collection, Indianapolis, Indiana:
    John Bauskett Memoir

Central Michigan University, Clarke Historical Library, Mount Pleasant, Michigan:
    Ebenezer Gould Letters
    Dexter Macomber Diary

Connecticut Historical Society, Hartford, Connecticut:
    Norman Ball Journal for 1864

Duke University, Special Collections Library, Durham, North Carolina:
    James D. Ferguson Diary
    Robert E. Lee Papers
    Munford/Ellis Family Papers (Thomas T. Munford Division)
    Frank E. White Diary and Memoirs

Georgia Department of Archives and History, Civil War Miscellany,
    Personal Papers, Atlanta, Georgia:
    Diary of Charles Paine Hansell
    Andrew J. Perkins Papers

Georgia Historical Society, Savannah, Georgia:
    Wayne–Stiles–Anderson Family Papers

Gettysburg National Military Park, Gettysburg, Pennsylvania:

Gregory Coco Collection:
   Robert Boyce Diary
   Lewis Fitch Diary
John Gilmer Collection, Louisa, Virginia:
   Hand-drawn map of Trevilian Station battlefield by Capt. Anderson
Historical Society of Pennsylvania, Philadelphia, Pennsylvania:
   Lewis Henry Carpenter Letters From the Field, 1862–64
   Simon Gratz Collection
   Thomas W. Smith Letters
Karla Jean Husby Collection, Marysville, Washington:
   James Henry Avery Memoir
Ernest A. Iler Jr. Collection, Newton, Georgia:
   Adam J. Iler Letters
Jefferson County Museum, Jefferson County, Virginia:
   Roger Preston Chew Papers
Jones Memorial Library, Lynchburg, Virginia:
   Samuel Burns Rucker Recollections
Keith Kehlbeck Collection, Marshall, Michigan:
   Towles Family Papers
Library of Congress, Manuscripts Division, Washington, D.C.:
   David M. Gregg Papers
   Wade Hampton Letters
   William G. Hills Diary for 1864
   Jedediah Hotchkiss Papers
   Lucius Manigault Papers
   Charles McVicar Diary for 1864
   Alexander Newburger Diary for 1864
   Howard M. Smith Letters
Louisa County Courthouse, Louisa, Virginia:
   Chancery Court records for 1974
   Louisa County land records
Louisa County Historical Society, Louisa, Virginia:
   Oral History of James Braxton
   Diary of Pattie Ann Carter Detter
Michigan State Archives, Lansing, Michigan:
   Adjutant General's Reports for 1864
Monroe County Historical Museum/Archives, Monroe, Michigan:
   Dr. Lawrence A. Frost Collection of Custeriana
Museum of the Confederacy, Eleanor S. Brockenbrough Library,
   Richmond, Virginia:

D. E. Gordon Letters
John D. Imboden Papers
Fitzhugh Lee Papers
Williams C. Wickham Papers
Recollections and Reminiscences, 1861–65, South Carolina United Daughters
    of the Confederacy
Confederate Reminiscences and Letters 1861–65, Georgia Division of the United
    Daughters of the Confederacy

The National Archives, Washington, D.C.:
    Congressional Medal of Honor files, RG 94
    Consolidated Service Records
    Consolidated Pension Records
    Cavalry Corps casualty reports, RG 94

New Jersey State Archives, Trenton, New Jersey:
    Memorials of Officers, Box 132 (First New Jersey Cavalry)

Pennsylvania State Archives, Harrisburg, Pennsylvania:
    Wilmer C. Hall Correspondence

Pennsylvania State University, Fred Lewis Pattee Library, State College,
    Pennsylvania:
    Luke Davis Diary for 1864

Rhode Island Historical Society, Providence, Rhode Island:
    George N. Bliss Letters
    George N. Bliss Reminiscences
    William Turner Scrapbook

Donna Sauerberger Collection, Gambrills, Maryland:
    Thomas Bayard Lucas Letters

Savannah Public Library, Savannah, Georgia:
    Thomas Gamble Collection

George F. Scott Collection, Mt. Carmel, Pennsylvania:
    John B. Coover Letters

South Carolina Department of Archives and History, Columbia, South Carolina:
    Zimmerman Davis Papers

South Carolina Historical Society, Charleston, South Carolina:
    Edward L. Wells Correspondence
    Edward L. Wells Memoirs

South Caroliniana Library, University of South Carolina, Columbia,
    South Carolina:
    James Earle Hagood Papers
    Wade Hampton Papers
    Thomas Cassells Law Papers

McLure Family Papers
United States Army Military History Institute, Carlisle, Pennsylvania:
    Civil War Miscellaneous Collection
    Civil War Times Illustrated Collection
    Harrisburg Civil War Roundtable Collection
    William S. Keller Letters
    Lewis Leigh Collection
    Wiley Sword Collection
    Michael Winey Collection
    Samuel B. M. Young Papers
    Clement Hoffman Letters
University of California at Santa Barbara, Santa Barbara, California:
    Wyles Collection
University of Michigan, Michigan Historical Collections, Bentley Historical
    Library, Ann Arbor, Michigan:
    Frank D. Grommon Diary for 1864
    James H. Kidd Papers
    John R. Morey Diary for 1864
    Walter H. Jackson Diary for 1864
University of Michigan, William L. Clements Library, Ann Arbor, Michigan:
    Schoff Civil War Collection
    Jonathan Dayton Papers, Louis Palma Di Cessnola Letters
    Nathan B. Webb Diary
University of North Carolina, Southern Historical Collection, Chapel Hill,
    North Carolina:
    Noble Brooks Diary
    William B. Burroughs Letters
    James D. Ferguson Papers
    William Penn Lloyd Papers
    Edward H. McDonald Reminiscences
    Joseph F. Waring Diary
University of Virginia Library, Special Collections Department, Alderman Library,
    Charlottesville, Virginia:
    Richard T. Davis Letters
    Jasper Hawse Diary
    Porter C. Wright Papers
    Jacob Greene Papers
Virginia Historical Society, Richmond, Virginia:
    William Ball Reminiscences
    Holmes Conrad Papers

Leiper Moore Robinson Memoirs
Gilbert J. Wright Papers

Virginia Military Institute, Archives, Lexington, Virginia:
A. C. L. Gatewood Recollections
John J. Shoemaker Papers

Virginia State Library and Archives, Richmond, Virginia:
Carter Family Papers, 1817–92
John C. Donohoe Diary
Daniel Grimsley Papers
James F. Wood Diary for 1864
Work Projects Reports

Mary Ball Washington Museum, Lancaster, Virginia:
John Chowning Diary
Dandridge William Cockrell Letters

Western Michigan University, Archives and Regional History Collections, Kalamazoo, Michigan:
John Hill Diary

Western Reserve Historical Society, Cleveland, Ohio:
Carlos P. Lyman Letters

Eric J. Wittenberg Collection, Columbus, Ohio
Miscellaneous correspondence

Jim Wood Collection, Howell, Michigan:
Oscar Wood Diary

Periodicals/Articles

Arehart, W. H. "Diary of W. H. Arehart." *The Rockingham Recorder* 1, no. 7 (1948): 224–25.

Ball, Mottrom D. "Rosser and His Critics: A Comrade-in-Arms Reviews the Attacks of Early and Munford." *Philadelphia Weekly Times*, July 12, 1884.

Bean, Theodore H., "Sheridan at Trevilian," *Philadelphia Weekly Times*, June 11, 1887.

Blackford, Charles M. "The Campaign and Battle of Lynchburg," *Southern Historical Society Papers* 30 (1903).

Boice, J. C., M.D. "St. Mary's Church Fight: Interesting Reminiscence of a Stiff Little Engagement." *The National Tribune*, April 4, 1929.

Bray, Joseph B. "Trevilian Station: Horse Artillery in the Sheridan Raid of 1864." *The National Tribune*, February 9, 1888.

Butler, Matthew C. "The Cavalry Fight at Trevilian Station." In *Battles and Leaders of the Civil War*, 4 vols. Edited by Robert U. Johnson and Clarence C. Buel. New York: Century, 1884–88, 4:237–39.

Carpenter, Louis Henry. "Sheridan's Expedition around Richmond, May 9–25, 1864." *Journal of the United States Cavalry Association* 1 (1888): 300–324.

Cook, M. B. "The Trevilian Raid." *National Tribune*, September 5, 1912.

Cooke, John Esten. "General Wade Hampton and His Cavalry." *Philadelphia Weekly Times*, February 21, 1880.

Cralle, G. T. "The Bold Horsemen." *Richmond Dispatch*, January 7, 1900.

Crowninshield, Benjamin W. "Cavalry in Virginia during the War of Rebellion." *Papers of the Military History Society of Massachusetts*, vol. 13, read February 12, 1886.

Cummings, W. G. "Six Months in the Third Cavalry Division Under Custer." *Military Order of the Loyal Legion of the United States, Iowa Commandery*, vol. 1, 1893, 296–313.

Daniel, John W. "General Jubal A. Early." *Southern Historical Society Papers*, vol. 22 (1895).

Davis, William M. "St. Mary's Church, Va.: A Rattling Fight by One of Gregg's Brigades." *National Tribune*, June 12, 1890.

Deck, D. M. "Captured at Trevilian Station." *Confederate Veteran* 24 (1916): 123–24.

Ferguson, R. H. "Seeks Lost Cornet." *Richmond Times-Dispatch*, August 23, 1914.

Grimsley, Daniel A. "Trevilian Again: Another Account of the Great Cavalry Fight." *Richmond Times-Dispatch*, January 21, 1900.

Hall, James O., ed. "An Army of Devils: The Diary of Ella Washington." *Civil War Times Illustrated* (February 1978).

Harper, Martha R. "Trevilian Station: Remembrances of an Aged Virginia Woman of the Battle." *National Tribune*, March 15, 1917.

Harris, Moses. "The Union Cavalry." *Military Order of the Loyal Legion of the United States, War Papers, Wisconsin Commandery*, read February 4, 1891.

Holmes, James G. "The Fighting Qualities of Generals Hampton, Butler and Others Related by Adjutant-General Holmes of Charleston." *The Sunny South* (June 13, 1896).

Isham, Asa B. "The Cavalry of the Army of the Potomac." *Military Order of the Loyal Legion of the United States, War Papers, Ohio Commandery* 5 (1903): 301–27.

———. "Through the Wilderness to Richmond." *Sketches of War History, 1861–1865: Papers Prepared for the Ohio Commandery of MOLLUS* 1 (1884).

Johnson, Bradley T. "My Ride around Baltimore in Eighteen Hundred and Sixty-Four." *Journal of the United States Cavalry Association* 2 (1889): 250–60.

Jones, Maryus. "Colonel William Todd Robins: A Confederate Hero." *Southern Historical Society Papers* 34 (Jan.–Dec. 1906): 275–77.

Kelly, John. "Trevilian Station: How Custer Saved the Flag and How His Brigade Was Helped out of a Tight Place." *National Tribune*, August 12, 1886.

Kennedy, G. W. "Trevilian Station: The 10th N.Y. Cav. In That Famous Charge." *National Tribune*, April 19, 1888.

Lawyer, Eli H. "Sheridan's Trevilian Raid." *National Tribune*, April 13, 1911.

Loeser, Charles McK. "Personal Recollections: A Ride to Richmond in 1864." In *From Everglade to Canon with the Second Dragoons*. Edited by Theophilus F. Rodenbough. New York: D. Van Nostrand & Co., 1875.

Lowden, J. K. "A Gallant Record: Michigan's 5th Cavalry in the Latter Period of the War." *National Tribune*, July 30, 1886.

McCabe, W. Gordon. "Defence of Petersburg." *Southern Historical Society Papers* 2 (1874).

McCrady, Edward, Jr. "Heroes of the Old Camden District, South Carolina, 1776–1861." *Southern Historical Society Papers*, 16 (1889).

McDonald, Carlos. "Diary." *Report of the Forty-Sixth Annual Reunion of the Sixth Ohio Volunteer Cavalry Association*. Warren, Ohio: Wm. Ritezel & Co., 1911.

"Memorandum of Information as to Battle, &c., in the Year 1864, Called for by the Honorable Secretary of War." *Southern Historical Society Papers* 2 (1874).

Merritt, Wesley. "Personal Reminiscences of the Civil War." In *From Everglade to Canon with the Second Dragoons*. Edited by Theophilus F. Rodenbough. New York: D. Van Nostrand, 1875.

Mettam, Henry Clay. "Civil War Memories of the First Maryland Cavalry, C.S.A." *Maryland Historical Magazine* 58 (1963).

Mitchell, Frederick W. "An Irish Lieutenant of the Old Second Dragoons." *Military Order of the Loyal Legion of the United States, War Papers, District of Columbia Commandery*, no. 77.

Munford, Thomas T. "A Confederate Cavalry Officer's Reminiscences." *Journal of the United States Cavalry Association* 4 (1891): 276–88.

———. "A Confederate Cavalry Officer's Views on 'American Practice and Foreign Theory.'" *Journal of the United States Cavalry Association* 4 (1891): 201–13.

———. "Reminiscences of Cavalry Operations." Paper No. 3, *Southern Historical Society Papers* 13 (1886).

Newhall, Frederic C. "The Battle of Beverly Ford." In *The Annals of the War Written by Leading Participants, North and South*. Dayton, Ohio: Morningside, 1988.

Orme, H. C. "Who is the Lady?" *Richmond Times-Dispatch*, August 1, 1915.

Parks, Robert E. "Diary of Robert E. Parks, Macon, Georgia, late Captain Twelfth

Alabama Regiment, Confederate States Army." *Southern Historical Society Papers* 1 (1873).

"The Twelfth Alabama Infantry, Confederate States Army." *Southern Historical Society Papers* 33 (1906).

Preston, Noble D. "The Battle of Trevilian." *Philadelphia Weekly Times*, August 28, 1880.

———. "On to Richmond: Capt. Preston Says Comrade Bray Got Things Wrong." *National Tribune*, March 22, 1888.

———. "Trevilian Station: Comrade Preston Explains His Former Communication." *National Tribune*, May 3, 1888.

———. "Trevilian Station: The Most Stubborn Cavalry Fight of the War." *National Tribune*, January 5, 1888.

"Reunion of Company D, First Regiment Virginia Cavalry, C.S.A." *Southern Historical Society Papers* 20 (1893).

Robinson, A. F. "The 1st N.Y. Dragoons." *National Tribune*, October 14, 1886.

Robinson, Frank. "The 1st N.Y. Dragoons." *National Tribune*, September 16, 1886.

Rodenbough, Theophilus F. "Sheridan's Richmond Raid." In *Battles and Leaders of the Civil War*. 4 vols. Edited by Robert U. Johnson and Clarence C. Buel. New York: Century, 1884–88, 188–93.

———. "Sheridan's Trevilian Raid." In *Battles and Leaders of the Civil War*, vol. 4. Edited by Robert U. Johnson and Clarence C. Buel. New York: Century, 1884–88, 233–36.

———. "Some Cavalry Leaders." In *Miller's Photographic History of the Civil War*, vol. 4. New York: Review of Reviews Co., 1911, 262–88.

Rust, Bushrod. "Met His Death in Last Fight." *Southern Historical Society Papers* 34 (1907).

Scott, Col. John. "The Black Horse Cavalry." In *The Annals of the War Written by Leading Participants, North and South*. Dayton, Ohio: Morningside, 1988.

"Second Congress, Second Session, Bill to Increase the Efficiency of the Cavalry." *Southern Historical Society Papers* 52 (1925).

Sisson, Nat. "Sheridan's Trevilian Raid." *National Tribune*, April 13, 1911.

Smith, B. F. "The Trevilian Raid." *National Tribune*, August 8, 1912.

Smith, Hiram R. "St. Mary's Church: A Desperate Little Cavalry Fight in June 1864." *National Tribune*, October 17, 1907.

Stanton, C. W. "Sheridan's Trevilian Raid." *National Tribune*, November 30, 1911.

"The Campaign from the Wilderness to Petersburg." *Southern Historical Society Papers* 14 (1887).

Tobie, Edward P. "Service in the Cavalry of the Army of the Potomac." *Personal*

Narratives of Events in the War of the Rebellion: Papers Read before the Rhode Island Soldiers and Sailors Historical Society 14 (1882).

Tuton, E. M. "St. Mary's Church: As Seen by a Private Soldier of the 10th N.Y. Cav." *National Tribune*, July 3, 1890.

Vest, Charles B. "Lost Arm at Trevilian." *Richmond Times-Dispatch*, August 23, 1914.

Wells, Edward Laight. "A Morning Call on Kilpatrick." *Southern Historical Society Papers* 12 (March 1884): 144–48.

Wiles, C. W. "On Horseback: Leaves from the Record of the 10th N.Y. Cavalry" *National Tribune*, November 4, 1886.

Williams, L. Eustis. "Charge of the Clarke Cavalry at Trevelyan Station." *Southern Bivouac* 3 (September 1884–May 1885): 217–19.

Wilson, James Harrison. "The Cavalry of the Army of the Potomac." *Papers of the Military Historical Society of Massachusetts* 13 (1913): 35–88.

Books

Adams, Charles Francis. *A Cycle of Adams Letters 1861–1865.* 2 vols. Edited by Worthington C. Ford. Boston: Houghton-Mifflin, 1920.

Agassiz, George R. *Meade's Headquarters, 1863–1865: Letters of Colonel Theodore C. Lyman from the Wilderness to Appomattox.* Boston: Atlantic Monthly Press, 1922.

Allen, Stanton P. *Down in Dixie: Life in a Cavalry Regiment in the War Days.* Boston: D. Lothrop Co., 1888.

Barr, James Michael. *Let Us Meet in Heaven: The Civil War Letters of James Michael Barr, 5th South Carolina Cavalry.* Edited by Thomas D. Mays. Unpublished book manuscript.

Baylor, George. *Bull Run to Bull Run: Four Years in the Army of Northern Virginia, Containing a Detailed Account of the Career and Adventures of the Baylor Light Horse, Company B, Twelfth Virginia Cavalry, C.S.A.* Washington, D.C.: Zenger, 1983.

Baynes, Richard C., ed. *The Life and Ancestry of John Thistlethwaite Baynes (1833–1891).* Irvine, Ca.: privately published, 1987.

Beach, William H. *The First New York (Lincoln) Cavalry, from April 19, 1861 to July 7, 1865.* New York: The Lincoln Cavalry Association, 1902.

Beale, George W. *A Lieutenant of Cavalry in Lee's Army.* Boston: Gorham Press, 1888.

Beale, Richard L. T. *History of the Ninth Virginia Cavalry in the War between the States.* Richmond: B. F. Johnson, 1899.

Biler, Daniel V., III., ed. *A Soldier's Journey: An Account of Private Isaac Bobst, from Antietam to Andersonville.* Gettysburg, Pa.: Thomas Publications, 1990.

Black, John L. *Crumbling Defenses; or Memoirs and Reminiscences of John Logan Black, C.S.A.* Edited by E. D. Swain. Macon, Ga.: J. W. Burke Co., 1960.

Booth, George Wilson. *Personal Reminiscences of a Maryland Soldier in the War between the States 1861–1865.* Baltimore, Md.: privately published, 1898.

Bowen, James R. *Regimental History of the First New York Dragoons, with Lists of Names, Post-Office Addresses, Casualties of Officers and Men, and Number of Prisoners, Trophies, &c.* Washington, D.C.: Gibson Bros., 1865.

Bradshaw, Ada Bruce, ed. *The Civil War Diary of Charles William McVicar.* Privately published, 1977.

Bradshaw, William T. *The Ninth N.Y. Cavalry: A Forlorn Hope June 11th, 1864, Trevillian Station, Va.* Washington, D.C.: privately published, 1864.

Brooke-Rawle, William, ed. *History of the Third Pennsylvania Cavalry, Sixtieth Regiment Pennsylvania Volunteers, in the American Civil War, 1861–1865.* Philadelphia: Franklin Printing Co., 1905.

Brooks, U. R. *Butler and His Cavalry in the War of Secession 1861–1865.* Columbia, S.C.: The State Company, 1909.

———. *Stories of the Confederacy.* Columbia, S.C.: The State Company, 1912.

Calhoun, Charles M. *Liberty Dethroned: A Concise History of Some of the Most Startling Events before, during, and since the Civil War.* Greenwood, S.C.: privately published, 1903.

Carpenter, James Edward. *A List of the Battles, Engagements, Actions, and Important Skirmishes in which the Eighth Pennsylvania Cavalry Participated during the War of 1861–1865.* Philadelphia: Allen, Lane & Scott's, 1886.

Carroll, John M., ed. *Custer in the Civil War: His Unfinished Memoirs.* San Rafael, Ca.: Presidio Press, 1977.

Carson, William Clark. *My Dear Jennie.* Blake W. Carson, ed. Richmond, Va.: The Dietz Press, 1982.

Carter, William R. *Sabres, Saddles and Spurs: The Diary of Lt. Col. William R. Carter, 3rd Virginia Cavalry.* Walbrook D. Swank, ed. Shippensburg, Pa.: Burd Street Press, 1998.

Cauthen, Charles E., ed. *Family Letters of the Three Wade Hamptons, 1782–1901.* Columbia: University of South Carolina Press, 1953.

Cheney, Newell. *History of the Ninth Regiment, New York Volunteer Cavalry.* Poland Center, N.Y.: Martin Mere & Son, 1901.

Conrad, Thomas Nelson. *The Rebel Scout: A Thrilling History of Scouting Life in the Southern Army.* Washington, D.C.: The National Publishing Co., 1904.

Crowninshield, Benjamin W. *A History of the First Regiment of Massachusetts Volunteer Cavalry.* Boston: Houghton-Mifflin Co., 1891.

Davies, Henry E. *General Sheridan.* New York: D. Appleton & Co., 1895.

Doster, William E. *A Brief History of the Fourth Pennsylvania Veteran Cavalry*. Pittsburgh, Pa.: n.p., 1891.

Dowdey, Clifford, and Louis N. Manarin, eds. *The Wartime Papers of Robert E. Lee*. Boston: Little, Brown & Co., 1961.

Early, Jubal Anderson. *Autobiographical Sketch and Narrative of the War between the States*. Philadelphia: J. B. Lippincott Co., 1912.

Evans, Clement Anselm, ed. *Confederate Military History: A Library of Confederate States History in Thirteen Volumes Written by Distinguished Men of the South*. 13 vols. Atlanta. Ga.: Confederate Publishing Co., 1899.

Flint, Joseph N. *Regimental History of the First New York Dragoons, with a List of Names, Post-Office Address, Casualties of Officers and Men, and Number of Prisoners, Trophies, &c*. Washington, D.C.: Gibson Brothers, 1865.

Foster, Alonzo. *Reminiscences and Record of the Sixth New York V.V. Cavalry*. Brooklyn, N.Y.: privately published, 1892.

Freeman, Douglas Southall, ed. *Lee's Dispatches*. New York: G. P. Putnam's Sons, 1915.

Gallagher, DeWitt C. *A Diary Depicting the Experience of DeWitt Clinton Gallagher in the War between the States while Serving in the Confederate Army*. Reorganized Co. E., First Virginia Cavalry, 1961.

Goldsborough, W. W. *The Maryland Line in the Confederate Army, 1861–1865*. Baltimore, Md.: Guggenheim, Weil & Co., 1900.

Gordon, John B. *Reminiscences of the Civil War*. New York: Charles Scribner's Sons, 1903.

Gracey, Samuel L. *Annals of the Sixth Pennsylvania Cavalry*. Philadelphia: E. H. Butler & Co., 1868.

Grant, Ulysses S., *Personal Memoirs of U.S. Grant*. 2 vols. New York: Charles L. Webster & Co., 1885.

Grimsley, Daniel A. *Battles in Culpeper County, Virginia, 1861–1865 and Other Articles by Major Daniel A. Grimsley of the Sixth Virginia Cavalry*. Culpeper, Va.: Raleigh Travers Green, 1900.

Hagemann, E. R., ed. *Fighting Rebels and Redskins: Experiences in Army Life of Colonel George B. Sanford 1861–1892*. Norman: University of Oklahoma Press, 1969.

Hall, Hillman A., ed. *History of the Sixth New York Cavalry (Second Ira Harris Guard), Second Brigade, First Division, Cavalry Corps, Army of the Potomac 1861–1865*. Worcester, Mass.: The Blanchard Press, 1908.

Halliburton, Lloyd, ed. *Saddle Soldiers: The Civil War Correspondence of General William Stokes of the 4th South Carolina Cavalry*. Orangeburg, S.C.: Sandlapper Publishing Co., 1993.

Harris, Samuel. *Personal Reminiscences of Samuel Harris*. Chicago: The Robinson Press, 1897.

Haskins, William L. *The History of the First Regiment of Artillery from Its Formation in 1821, to January 12, 1876*. Portland, Maine: B. Thurston, 1879.

Heitman, Francis E. *Historical Register and Dictionary of the United States Army*. 2 vols. Washington, D.C.: United States Government Printing Office, 1903.

History of the Eighteenth Regiment of Cavalry, Pennsylvania Volunteers, 1862–1865. New York, Publication Committee, Eighteenth Pa. Cavalry Assoc., 1909.

Howard, Wiley C. *Sketch of Cobb Legion Cavalry and Some Incidents and Scenes Remembered*. Atlanta, Ga.: privately published, 1901.

Humphreys, Andrew A. *The Virginia Campaign of 1864 and 1865. The Army of the Potomac and the Army of the James*. 2 vols. New York: Charles Scribner's Sons, 1883.

Husby, Karla Jean, and Eric J. Wittenberg, eds. *Under Custer's Command: The Civil War Journal of James Henry Avery*. Washington, D.C.: Brassey's, 2000.

Hyndman, William. *History of a Cavalry Company: A Complete Record of Company A, Fourth Pennsylvania Cavalry*. Philadelphia: James B. Rogers Co., 1870.

Isham, Asa B. *Historical Sketch of the Seventh Regiment Michigan Volunteer Cavalry*. New York: Town Topics Publishing Co., 1893.

Jones, John B. *A Rebel War Clerk's Diary*. 2 vols. New York: Sagamore Press, 1958.

Kidd, James H. *Historical Sketch of General Custer*. Monroe, Mich.: Monroe County Library System, 1978.

———. *Personal Recollections of a Cavalryman in Custer's Michigan Brigade*. Ionia, Mich.: Sentinel Printing Co., 1908.

King, Matthew W. *To Horse: With the Cavalry of the Army of the Potomac, 1861–65*. Cheboygan, Mich.: n.p., 1926.

Lee, William O. *Personal and Historical Sketches and Facial History of and by Members of the Seventh Regiment Michigan Volunteer Cavalry, 1862–1865*. Detroit: Ralston Co., 1901.

Lloyd, William P. *History of the First Regiment Pennsylvania Reserve Cavalry, from Its Organization, August 1861, to September 1864, with List of Names of All Officers and Enlisted Men Who Have Ever Belonged to the Regiment, and Remarks Attached to Each Name, Noting Change*. Philadelphia: King & Baird, 1864.

McClellan, Carswell. *Notes on the Personal Memoirs of P. H. Sheridan*. St. Paul, Minn.: Press of Wm. E. Banning, Jr., 1889.

McDonald, William N. *A History of the Laurel Brigade*. Baltimore, Md.: Sun Job Print Office, 1907.

McKinney, Edward P. *Life in Tent and Field, 1861–1865*. Boston: Richard G. Badger, 1922.

Meade George, ed. *The Life and Letters of General George Gordon Meade*. 2 vols. New York: Charles Scribner's Sons, 1913.

Merrill, Samuel H. *The Campaigns of the First Maine and First District of Columbia Cavalry*. Portland, Maine: Bailey & Noyes, 1866.

Merington, Marguerite, ed. *The Custer Story: The Life and Letters of General George A. Custer and His Wife Elizabeth*. New York: The Devin-Adair Co., 1950.

Meyer, Henry C. *Civil War Experiences under Bayard, Gregg, Kilpatrick, Custer, Raulston, and Newberry, 1862, 1863, 1864*. New York: Knickerbocker Press, 1911.

Mohr, James C., and Richard E. Winslow, eds. *The Cormany Diaries: A Northern Family in the Civil War*. Pittsburgh, Pa.: University of Pittsburgh Press, 1982.

Moncure, E. C. *Reminiscences of the Civil War*. Caroline County, Va.: privately published, 1924.

Moyer, Henry P. *History of the Seventeenth Regiment, Pennsylvania Volunteer Cavalry*. Lebanon, Pa.: n.p., 1911.

Mulligan, Abner B. *"My Dear Mother and Sisters": Civil War Letters of Capt. A. B. Mulligan, Co. B, 5th South Carolina Cavalry—Butler's Division of Hampton's Corps, 1861–1865*. Spartanburg, S.C.: Reprint Co., 1992.

Myers, Frank M. *The Comanches: A History of White's Battalion, Virginia Cavalry, Laurel Brig., Hampton's Div., A.N.V., C.S.A.* Baltimore, Md.: Kelly, Piet & Co., 1871.

Neese, George M. *Three Years in the Confederate Horse Artillery*. New York: Neale Publishing Co., 1911.

Nelson, Horatio. *If I Am Killed on This Trip I Want My Horse Kept for My Brother: The Diary of the Last Weeks in the Life of a Young Confederate Cavalryman*. ed., Harold E. Howard. Lynchburg, Va.: H. E. Howard Co. and Manassas Chapter, U.D.C., 1980.

Nevins, Alan, ed. *A Diary of Battle: The Personal Journals of Colonel Charles S. Wainwright, 1861–1865*. New York: Harcourt, Brace & World, 1962.

Newhall, Frederic C. *With General Sheridan in Lee's Last Campaign*. Philadelphia: J. B. Lippincott, 1866.

Opie, John N. *A Rebel Cavalryman with Lee, Stuart, and Jackson*. Chicago: W. B. Conkey Co., 1899.

Peck, Rufus H. *Reminiscences of a Confederate Soldier of Company C, 2nd Virginia Cavalry*. Fincastle, Va: n.p., 1913.

Pond, George E. *The Shenandoah Valley in 1864*. New York: Charles Scribner's Sons, 1883.

Porter, Horace. *Campaigning with Grant*. Bloomington: Indiana University Press, 1951.

Preston, Noble D. *History of the Tenth Regiment of Cavalry, New York State Volunteers, August 1861 to August 1865*. New York: D. Appleton, 1892.

Priest, John Michael, ed. *Stephen Elliott Welch of the Hampton Legion*. Shippensburg, Pa.: Burd Street Press, 1994.

Pyne, Henry. *Ride to War: The History of the First New Jersey Cavalry*. New Brunswick, N.J.: Rutgers University Press, 1961.

Reid, Whitelaw, *Ohio in the War*. 2 vols. Cincinnati, Ohio: Robert Clarke Co., 1895.

Report of the Forty-fifth Annual Reunion of the Sixth Ohio Veteran Volunteer Cavalry Association. Privately published: 1910.

Reynolds, Arlene, ed. *The Civil War Memories of Elizabeth Bacon Custer*. Austin: University of Texas, 1994.

Robertson, James I., Jr., ed. *The Civil War Letters of General Robert McAllister*. New Brunswick, N.J.: Rutgers University Press, 1964.

Rockwell, A. D., M.D. *Rambling Recollections: An Autobiography*. New York: Paul B. Hoeber, 1920.

Rodenbough, Theophilus F., ed., *From Everglade to Canon with the Second Dragoons*. New York: D. Van Nostrand, 1875.

Rosser, Thomas L. *Riding with Rosser*. Edited by Roger S. Keller. Shippensburg, Pa.: Burd Street Press, 1997.

Sheridan, Philip H. *Personal Memoirs of P. H. Sheridan*. 2 vols. New York: Charles L. Webster & Co., 1888.

Shoemaker, John J. *Shoemaker's Battery, Stuart Horse Artillery, Pelham's Battalion, Army of Northern Virginia*. Memphis, Tenn.: S. C. Toof & Co., 1908.

Stevenson, James H. *"Boots and Saddles": A History of the First Volunteer Cavalry of the War, Known as the First New York (Lincoln) Cavalry, and also as the Sabre Regiment. Its Organization, Campaigns and Battles*. Harrisburg, Pa.: Patriot Publishing Co., 1879.

Strang, Edgar B. *Sunshine and Shadows of the Late Civil War*. Philadelphia: privately published, 1898.

Summers, Festus P., ed. *A Borderland Confederate*. Pittsburgh, Pa.: University of Pittsburgh Press, 1962.

Sumner, Merlin E., ed. *The Diary of Cyrus Comstock*. Dayton, Ohio: Morningside, 1987.

Supplement to the Official Records of the Union and Confederate Armies, Reports, Addendum, Series 1, vol. 6. Wilmington, N.C.: Broadfoot Publishing Co., 1997.

Swank, Walbrook D., ed. *Sabres, Saddles and Spurs: Lieutenant Colonel William R. Carter, C.S.A.*. Shippensburg, Pa.: Burd Street Press, 1998.

Taylor, Gray Nelson. *Saddle and Saber: The Letters of Civil War Cavalryman Corporal Nelson Taylor*. Bowie, Md.: Heritage Books, 1993.

Thomas, Hampton S. *Some Personal Reminiscences of Service in the Cavalry of the Army of the Potomac*. Philadelphia: L. R. Hamersly, 1889.

Tobie, Edward P. *History of the First Maine Cavalry, 1861–1865*. Boston: Press of Emory & Hughes, 1887.

————. *Personal Recollections of General Sheridan*. Providence, R. I.: privately published, 1889.

————. *Service in the Cavalry of the Army of the Potomac, Personal Narratives of Rhode Island Soldiers and Sailors*. Providence, R.I.: N. Bangs Williams & Co., 1882.

Tremain, Henry Edwin. *The Last Hours of Sheridan's Cavalry*. New York: Bonnell, Silvers & Bower, 1904.

Veil, Charles H. *The Memoirs of Charles Henry Veil: A Soldier's Recollections of the Civil War and the Arizona Territory*. New York: Orion Books, 1993.

Vogtsberger, Margaret Ann, ed. *The Dulanys of Welbourne: A Family in Mosby's Confederacy*. Lexington, Va.: Rockbridge Publishing, 1995.

Wallace, Robert C. *A Few Memories of a Long Life*. Fairfield, Wash.: Ye Galleon Press, 1988.

War Department, Office of the Chief of Staff. *Field Service Regulations, United States Army, 1910*. War Department Document No. 363. Washington, D.C.: United States Government Printing Office, 1910.

The War of the Rebellion: A Compilation of the Official Records of the Union and Confederate Armies, 70 vols. in 4 series. Washington, D.C.: United States Government Printing Office, 1889–1904.

Watson, George William. *The Last Survivor*. Edited by Brian Stuart Kesterson. Washington, W.V.: Night Hawk Press, 1993.

Wells, Edward L. *A Sketch of the Charleston Light Dragoons*. Charleston, S.C.: Lucas, Richardson & Co., 1888.

————. *Hampton and His Cavalry in '64*. Richmond, Va.: B. F. Johnson Publishing Co., 1899.

Williams, Edward B., ed. *Rebel Brothers: The Civil War Letters of the Truehearts*. College Station: Texas A & M University Press, 1995.

Williamson, James J. *Mosby's Rangers: A Record of the Operations of the Forty-third Battalion Virginia Cavalry, from Its Organization to the Surrender*. New York: Ralph B. Kenyon, 1896.

Wittenberg, Eric J., ed. *One of Custer's Wolverines: The Civil War Letters of Bvt. Brig. Gen. James H. Kidd, Sixth Michigan Cavalry*. Kent, Ohio: Kent State University Press, 2000.

————. *At Custer's Side: The Civil War Writings of Bvt. Brig. Gen. James H. Kidd*. Kent, Ohio: Kent State University Press, 2001.

———. *"We Have It Damn Hard Out Here": The Civil War Letters of Sgt. Thomas W. Smith, Sixth Pennsylvania Cavalry*. Kent, Ohio: Kent State University Press, 1999.

Secondary Sources

Periodicals/Articles

Jones, Pat. "Mother's Race across Battlefield is Recalled: Mrs. Lucy Hughson Carried Baby in Arms across Field at Trevilians in 1864 during Bitter Engagement," *Richmond Times-Dispatch* Sunday magazine section, date unknown, copy in files of Louisa County Historical Society.

Longacre, Edward G. "Long Run for Trevilian Station." *Civil War Times Illustrated* 18 (November 1979): 28–39.

Meyers, Jerry. "Trevilian!" *Louisa County Historical Magazine* 30, no. 1 (Spring 1999): 29–50.

Monaghan, Jay. "Custer's First Last Stand: Trevilian Station, 1864." In *The Custer Reader*. Edited by Paul Andrew Hutton. Lincoln: University of Nebraska Press, 1992.

Morris, Roy, Jr. "Sweltering Summer Collision." *Military History* 19, no. 2 (February 1993).

Ryckman, W. G. "Clash of Cavalry at Trevilians." *Virginia Magazine of History and Biography* 75, no. 4 (1967): 443–58.

Shultz, David. "Gulian V. Weir's 5th U.S. Artillery, Battery C." *Gettysburg: Historical Articles of Lasting Interest* 18 (July 1998): 77–95.

Suderow, Bryce A. "The Battle of Trevilian Station, June 11–12, 1864." Unpublished manuscript, Washington, D.C.

White, John C. "A Review of the Services of the Regular Army during the Civil War." Serialized article from an unknown periodical in files at U.S. Army Military History Institute, Carlisle, Pennsylvania, 1909.

Books

Alberts, Don E. *Brandy Station to Manila Bay: A Biography of General Wesley Merritt*. Austin, Tex.: Presidio Press, 1980.

Allardice, Bruce S. *More Generals in Gray*. Baton Rouge: Louisiana State University Press, 1995.

Armstrong, Richard L. *Eleventh Virginia Cavalry*. Lynchburg, Va.: H. E. Howard Co., 1989.

———. *Seventh Virginia Cavalry*. Lynchburg, Va.: H. E. Howard Co., 1992.

Baker, Gary R. *Cadets in Gray: The Story of the Cadets of the South Carolina Military*

Academy and the Cadet Rangers in the Civil War. Columbia, S.C.: Palmetto Bookworks, 1989.

Balfour, Daniel T. *Thirteenth Virginia Cavalry*. Lynchburg, Va.: H. E. Howard Co., 1986.

Bates, Samuel P. *History of the Pennsylvania Volunteers, 1861–1865*. 5 vols. Harrisburg, Pa.: D. Singerly, State Printer, 1869.

———. *Martial Deeds of Pennsylvania*. Philadelphia: T. H. Davis & Co., 1875.

Brown, Dee Alexander. *Grierson's Raid: A Cavalry Adventure in the Civil War*. Urbana: University of Illinois Press, 1954.

Burgess, Milton V. *David Gregg: Pennsylvania Cavalryman*. Privately published, 1984.

Burr, Frank A., and Richard J. Hinton. *Little Phil and His Troopers: The Life of Gen. Philip H. Sheridan: Its Romance and Reality: How a Humble Lad Reached the Head of an Army*. Providence, R.I.: J. A. & R. A. Reid, 1888.

Burnett, William G. *Better a Patriot Soldier's Grave: The History of the Sixth Ohio Volunteer Cavalry*. Ridgewood, Ohio: privately published, 1982.

Bushong, Millard K., and Dean M. Bushong. *Fightin' Tom Rosser*. Shippensburg, Pa.: Beidel Printing House, 1983.

Carter, Samuel, III. *The Last Cavaliers: Confederate and Union Cavalry in the Civil War*. New York: St. Martin's Press, 1979.

Carter, William H. *From Yorktown to Santiago with the Sixth U.S. Cavalry*. Baltimore, Md.: Lord Baltimore Press, 1900.

———. *The Life of Lieutenant General Chaffee*. Chicago: University of Chicago Press, 1917.

Catton, Bruce. *Grant Takes Command*. Boston: Little, Brown & Co., 1968.

———. *Never Call Retreat: The Centennial History of the Civil War*. New York: Doubleday, 1965.

———. *The Army of the Potomac: A Stillness at Appomattox*. New York: Doubleday, 1953.

Chisholm, Claudia Anderson, and Ellen Gray Lillie. *Old Home Places of Louisa County*. Louisa, Va.: Louisa County Historical Society, 1979.

Davis, Julia. *Mount Up: A True Story Based on the Reminiscences of Major E. A. H. McDonald of the Confederate Cavalry*. New York: Harcourt, World & Brace, 1967.

Divine, John E. *35th Battalion Virginia Cavalry*. Lynchburg, Va.: H. E. Howard Co., 1985.

Doumato, Lamia. *Frank Furness, 1838–1912*. Monticello, Ill.: Vance Bibliographies, 1980.

Driver, Robert J., Jr. *Fifth Virginia Cavalry*. Lynchburg, Va.: H. E. Howard Co., 1997.

———. *First Virginia Cavalry*. Lynchburg, Va.: H. E. Howard Co., 1989.

————. *First and Second Maryland Cavalry, C.S.A.* Lexington, Va.: Rockbridge Publishing, 1999.

————. *Second Virginia Cavalry.* Lynchburg, Va.: H. E. Howard Co., 1995.

————. *Tenth Virginia Cavalry.* Lynchburg, Va.: H. E. Howard Co., 1982.

Duncan, Richard R. *Lee's Endangered Left: The Civil War in Western Virginia, Spring of 1864.* Baton Rouge: Louisiana State University Press, 1999.

Eanes, Greg. *"Destroy the Junction": The Wilson–Kautz Raid and the Battle for the Staunton River Bridge, June 21, 1864–July 1, 1864.* Lynchburg, Va.: H. E. Howard Co., 1999.

Final Report of the Commission to Provide for a Monument to the Memory of Wade Hapmpton. Columbia, S.C.: Gonzales and Bryan, 1906.

Foote, Shelby. *The Civil War: A Narrative.* 3 vols. New York: Random House, 1958–1974.

Fortier, John. *Fifteenth Virginia Cavalry.* Lynchburg, Va.: H. E. Howard Co., 1993.

Freeman, Douglas Southall. *Lee's Lieutenants: A Study in Command.* 3 vols. New York: Charles Scribner's Sons, 1942.

————. *R. E. Lee: A Biography.* 4 vols. New York: Charles Scribner's Sons, 1934.

Frye, Dennis E. *Twelfth Virginia Cavalry.* Lynchburg, Va.: H. E. Howard Co., 1988.

Hackley, Woodford B. *The Little Fork Rangers: A Sketch of Company D 4th Virginia Cavalry.* Richmond, Va.: Press of the Dietz Printing Co., 1927.

Holland, Darryl. *24th Virginia Cavalry.* Lynchburg, Va.: H. E. Howard Co., 1997.

Holmes, Torlief S. *Horse Soldiers in Blue: First Maine Cavalry.* Gaithersburg, Md.: Butternut Press, 1985.

Hopkins, Donald A. *Horsemen of the Jeff Davis Legion: The Expanded Roster of the Men and Officers of the Jeff Davis Legion, Cavalry.* Shippensburg, Pa.: White Mane, 1999.

————. *The Little Jeff: The Jeff Davis Legion, Cavalry Army of Northern Virginia.* Shippensburg, Pa.: White Mane, 1999.

Hunt, Roger D., and Jack R. Brown. *Brevet Brigadier Generals in Blue.* Gaithersburg, Md.: Olde Soldier Books, 1989.

Hutton, Paul Andrew, ed. *The Custer Reader.* Lincoln: University of Nebraska Press, 1992.

Jacobs, Lee, comp. *The Gray Riders: Stories from the Confederate Cavalry.* Shippensburg, Pa.: Burd Street Press, 1999.

Johnson, Alvin Jewett. *New Illustrated Family Atlas, with Descriptions, Geographical, Statistical, and Historical.* New York: Johnson & Ward, 1859.

Johnston, Angus James, II. *Virginia Railroads in the Civil War.* Chapel Hill: University of North Carolina Press, 1961.

Joslyn, Mauriel. *The Biographical Roster of the Immortal 600*. Shippensburg, Pa.: White Mane, 1992.

Judge, Joseph. *Season of Fire: The Confederate Strike on Washington*. Berryville, Va.: Rockbridge Publishing Co., 1994.

Keen, Hugh C., and Horace Mewborn. *43rd Battalion Virginia Cavalry: Mosby's Command*. Lynchburg, Va.: H. E. Howard Co., 1993.

Kester, Donald E. *Cavalryman in Blue: Colonel John Wood Kester of the First New Jersey Cavalry in the Civil War*. Hightstown, N.J.: Longstreet House, 1997.

Kinsley, D. A. *Favor the Bold: Custer, the Civil War Years*. Kansas City, Mo.: Promontory Press, 1967.

Knapp, David Jr. *The Confederate Horsemen*. New York: Vantage Press, 1966.

Krick, Robert K. *Lee's Colonels: A Biographical Register of the Field Officers of the Army of Northern Virginia*. Dayton, Ohio: Morningside, 1992.

———. *Ninth Virginia Cavalry*. Lynchburg, Va.: H. E. Howard Co., 1982.

Langellier, John P., Kurt Hamilton Cox, and Brian C. Pohanka, eds. *Myles Keogh: The Life and Legend of an "Irish Dragoon" in the Seventh Cavalry*. El Segundo, Ca.: Upton and Sons, 1998.

Lewis, Michael J. *Frank Furness: Architecture and the Violent Mind*. New York: W. W. Norton, 2001.

Longacre, Edward G. *The Cavalry at Gettysburg: A Tactical Study of Mounted Operations during the Civil War's Pivotal Campaign, 9 June–14 July, 1863*. Rutherford, N.J.: Fairleigh-Dickinson University Press, 1986.

———. *Custer and His Wolverines: The Michigan Cavalry Brigade 1861–1865*. Conshohocken, Pa.: Combined Books, 1997.

———. *Jersey Cavaliers: A History of the First New Jersey Volunteer Cavalry, 1861–1865*. Hightstown, N.J.: Longstreet House, 1992.

———. *Lincoln's Cavalrymen: A History of the Mounted Forces of the Army of the Potomac*. Mechanicsburg, Pa.: Stackpole Books, 2000.

———. *Mounted Raids of the Civil War*. South Brunswick, N. J.: A. S. Barnes, 1975.

Magner, Blake A., ed. *At Peace with Honor: The Civil War Burials of Laurel Hill Cemetery, Philadelphia, Pennsylvania*. Collingswood, N.J.: C. W. Historicals, 1997.

Matter, William D. *If It Takes All Summer: The Battle of Spotsylvania*. Chapel Hill: University of North Carolina Press, 1988.

McFeely, William S. *Grant: A Biography*. New York: W. W. Norton & Co., 1982.

Mitchell, Lt. Col. Joseph B. *The Badge of Gallantry: Recollections of Civil War Congressional Medal of Honor Winners, Letters From the Charles Kohen Collection*. New York: The MacMillan Company, 1968.

Morgan, James A., III. *Always Ready, Always Willing: Battery M, Second U.S. Artillery*. Gaithersburg, Md.: Olde Soldier Books, no date.

Morris, Roy, Jr. *Sheridan: The Life and Wars of General Phil Sheridan*. New York: Crown Publishers, Inc., 1992.

Murray, J. Ogden. *The Immortal Six Hundred: A Story of Cruelty to Confederate Prisoners of War*. Winchester, Va.: Eddy Press Corp., 1905.

Musick, Michael. *Sixth Virginia Cavalry*. Lynchburg, Va.: H. E. Howard Co., 1990.

Nanzig, Thomas. *Third Virginia Cavalry*. Lynchburg, Va.: H. E. Howard Co., 1989.

Nichols, James L. *General Fitzhugh Lee: A Biography*. Lynchburg, Va.: H. E. Howard Co., 1989.

Northern, William J., ed. *Men of Mark in Georgia*. 6 vols. Atlanta, Ga.: A. B. Caldwell, 1907–12.

O'Connor, Richard. *Sheridan the Inevitable*. Indianapolis, Ind.: Bobbs-Merrill, 1953.

O'Gorman, James F. *Architecture of Frank Furness*. Philadelphia: Philadelphia Museum of Art, 1987.

Poirer, Robert G. *"By the Blood of Our Alumni": Norwich University Citizen Soldiers in the Army of the Potomac*. Mason City, Iowa: Savas Publishing, 1999.

Power, J. Tracy. *Lee's Miserables: Life in the Army of Northern Virginia from the Wilderness to Appomattox*. Chapel Hill: University of North Carolina Press, 1998.

Rhea, Gordon C. *The Battle of the Wilderness, May 5–6, 1864*. Baton Rouge: Louisiana State University Press, 1994.

———. *The Battles for Spotsylvania Court House and the Road to Yellow Tavern, May 7–12, 1864*. Baton Rouge: Louisiana State University Press, 1997.

———. *To the North Anna River: Grant and Lee, May 13–25, 1864*. Baton Rouge: Louisiana State University Press, 2000.

Rhodes, Charles D. *History of the Cavalry of the Army of the Potomac, including that of the Army of Virginia*. Kansas City, Mo.: Hudson-Kimberly Pub. Co., 1900.

Roll of Officers and Members of the Georgia Hussars and of the Cavalry Companies, of which the Hussars Are a Continuation with Historical Sketch Relating Facts Showing the Origin and Necessity of Rangers or Mounted Men in the Colony of Georgia from Date of Its Founding. Atlanta, Ga.: privately published, 1906.

Slade, A.D. *A. T. A. Torbert: Southern Gentleman in Union Blue*. Dayton, Ohio: Morningside, 1992.

Starr, Stephen Z. *The Union Cavalry in the Civil War*. 3 vols. Baton Rouge: Louisiana State University Press, 1976–85.

Stiles, Kenneth C. *Fourth Virginia Cavalry*. Lynchburg, Va.: H. E. Howard Co., 1985.

Swank, Walbrook Davis. *The Battle of Trevilian Station: The Civil War's Greatest and Bloodiest All Cavalry Battle*. Shippensburg, Pa.: Burd Street Press, 1994.

————. *Confederate Letters and Diaries, 1861–1865*. Mineral, Va.: privately published, 1988.

————. *The War in Louisa County, 1861–1865*. Charlottesville, Va.: Papercraft Printing & Design Co., 1986.

Swiggart, Carolyn Clay. *Shades of Gray: The Clay and McAllister Families of Bryan County, Georgia During the Plantation Years*. Darien, Conn.: Two Bytes Publishing, 1999.

Sword, Wiley. *Mountains Touched with Fire*. New York: St. Martin's Press, 1995.

Thomas, Emory M. *Bold Dragoon: The Life of J. E. B. Stuart*. New York: Random House, 1986.

Thomas, George E., Michael J. Lewis, and Jeffrey A. Cohen. *Frank Furness: The Complete Works*. New York: Princeton Architectural Press, 1991.

Thomas, William H. B. *Gordonsville, Virginia: Historic Crossroads Town*. Gordonsville, Va.: Green Publishers, Inc., 1971.

Townsend, George Alfred. *Major General Alfred Torbert: Delaware's Most Famous Civil War General*. Bowie, Md.: Heritage Books, 1991.

Turner, George Edgar. *Victory Rode the Rails: The Strategic Place of the Railroads in the Civil War*. Wesport, Conn.: Greenwood Press, 1972.

Trudeau, Noah Andre. *Bloody Roads South: The Wilderness to Cold Harbor, May–June 1864*. Boston: Little-Brown & Co., 1989.

Urwin, Gregory J. W. *Custer Victorious: The Civil War Battles of General George Armstrong Custer*. Rutherford, N.J.: Combined University Presses, 1983.

Van de Water, Frederic F. *Glory-Hunter: A Life of General Custer*. Indianapolis, Ind.: Bobbs-Merrill, 1934.

Vandiver, Frank E. *Jubal's Raid*. Lincoln: University of Nebraska Press, 1960.

Warner, Ezra J. *Generals In Blue: The Lives of the Union Commanders*. Baton Rouge: Louisiana State University Press, 1964.

————. *Generals In Gray: The Lives of the Confederate Commanders*. Baton Rouge: Louisiana State University Press, 1959.

Wellman, Manly Wade. *Giant In Gray: A Biography of Wade Hampton of South Carolina*. New York: Charles Scribner's Sons, 1949.

Wert, Jeffry D. *Custer: The Controversial Life of George Armstrong Custer*. New York: Simon & Schuster, 1996.

Whittaker, Frederick. *A Complete Life of General George A. Custer*. 2 vols. Lincoln: University of Nebraska Press, 1993.

Young, Bennett H. *Confederate Wizards of the Saddle*. Boston: Chapple Publishing Co., 1914.

⊷ Index ⊷

Abercrombie, Gen. John J., 242, 248n.146
Adams, Lt. William, 84
Aiken, Col. Hugh K., 73–74, 178, 333
Aldrich, Lt. Alfred, 139
Alger, Col. Russell A., 331
Alger, Lt. Col. Russell, 101, 102, 108–09; at Battle of Bloody Angle, 185; resigns commission, 126n.23
Allen, Lt. James, 109
Allen, Sgt. Stanton P., 269–70
Allen, Wash, 199
Almond, Lt. Charles H., 116
ambulances (retreat from Samaria Church), 280, 283
ammunition, 26, 187, 197–98, 199, 274
Anderson, Lt. Col. James Q., 331
Anderson, Maj. Edward C., Jr., 80, 333
Anderson, Maj. Ned, 147, 148, 222; on Wright, 149
Army of Northern Virginia, 11; Second Corps, 224
Army of Northern Virginia, Cavalry Corps, units:
  DIVISIONS: Fitzhugh Lee's, 46, 49, 54 map, 61, 72, 99 map, 113, 142, 156, 159 map, 160, 254, 259, 260n.28, 313, 334, 344, 345; Hampton's, xiii–xiv, 46, 49, 156, 159 map, 179, 249, 251–52, 253, 259, 298n.121, 304, 312–13, 313–14, 316, 333, 343, 345; William Lee's, 233, 335. See also individual listings
  BATTALIONS, BRIGADES: Breathed's Horse Artillery Battalion (Chew's), 334, 345; Butler's Brigade, 61, 70 map, 72–73, 80, 83–84, 85 map, 86, 87, 99 map, 142, 145 map, 155, 176, 190, 193–97, 240, 260n.28, 265, 276 map, 286, 298n.121, 333, 343; Chambliss' Brigade, 233, 241, 270, 286, 298n.121; Dulaney's (Laurel Brigade), 257, 265, 269, 276 map; First Maryland Cavalry Battalion, 334; Lomax's Brigade, 99 map, 113, 118, 120, 125, 203, 205 map, 236, 264, 267, 334; Rosser's (Laurel Brigade), 45, 54 map, 61, 82, 105–06, 107, 108–09, 112, 117, 145 map, 154, 176, 313, 333; Thirty-fifth Battalion Virginia Cavalry (Comanches), 98 map, 107, 108, 333; Wickham's Brigade, 97–98, 99 map, 100, 115, 118, 125, 141, 199, 203, 204, 205 map, 236, 260n.28, 265, 268, 276 map, 286, 316, 319, 334; Wright's Brigade, 61, 70 map, 72, 79, 80, 81, 84, 85 map, 86, 87, 99 map, 100, 102, 110, 125, 142, 145 map, 150, 176, 186, 205 map, 265, 276 map, 313; Young's Brigade, 333. See also individual listings
  CAVALRIES: Seventh Georgia, 66n.67, 70 map, 79–80, 81, 87–88, 102, 110, 145 map, 147–49, 222, 313, 333, 343; Twentieth Georgia, 50, 80, 81, 107, 110, 177, 187, 333; First Maryland Battalion, 212n.71, 221, 334; Fourth South Carolina, 70 map, 71, 73, 74, 79, 82, 87, 176, 184, 199, 201, 205 map, 206, 285, 313, 333, 343; Fifth South Carolina, 70 map, 73, 81, 86, 139, 140, 176, 198–99, 205 map, 240, 260n.28, 333, 343; Sixth South Carolina, 50, 70 map, 71, 73–74, 80, 89, 105, 139, 140, 152, 169, 170, 176, 188, 189, 190, 194–95, 199, 200, 202, 205 map, 343; Seventh South Carolina, 268; First Virginia, 282, 334, 344; Second Virginia, 99 map, 116, 268, 272,

CAVALRIES, *continued*
334, 344; Third Virginia, 203, 204, 260n.28, 334, 344; Fourth Virginia, 98, 99 map, 115, 119–20, 236, 334, 344; Fifth Virginia, 334, 345; Sixth Virginia, 99 map, 115, 120–22, 121–22, 152, 334; Seventh Virginia, 168, 218, 257, 333, 344; Ninth Virginia, 257; Eleventh Virginia, 107, 172, 333, 344; Twelfth Virginia, 108, 276 map, 281, 333, 344; Fifteenth Virginia, 113, 334, 345; Twenty-fourth Virginia Cavalry, 276 map; Thirty-fifth Battalion Virginia (Comanches), 99 map, 107, 108, 177, 333; Gary's Independent, 263, 268, 270, 286, 292n.3, 298n.121, 335. *See also* individual listings
ARTILLERIES: Baltimore Light, 334; Breathed's Horse Battalion (Chew's), 112, 124, 145 map, 149, 150, 151, 154–55, 196, 240, 241, 334, 345. *See also* individual listings
LEGIONS: Cobb's Georgia, 70 map, 81, 87–88, 334, 343; Jeff Davis Mississippi, 70 map, 81, 105, 106–07, 195, 276 map, 281, 334; Phillips Georgia, 70 map, 105, 141, 276 map, 281, 334. *See also* individual listings
INDEPENDENT COMMAND: Baltimore Light Artillery, 221, 334; First Maryland Cavalry Battalion, 212n.71, 221, 334. *See also* Gary's Independent cavalry brigade
BATTERIES: Hart's (Washington Artillery of South Carolina), 79, 84, 85 map, 141, 145 map, 191, 193, 196, 241, 334, 345; Johnston's (First Stuart Horse Artillery of Virginia), 82, 334, 345; Shoemaker's (Lynchburg Beauregards), 151, 203, 207, 334; Thomson's (Ashby Virginia Artillery of Virginia), 82, 85 map, 104, 106, 107, 154, 190–91, 196, 205 map, 334, 345. *See also* Breathed's Horse Artillery
Army of the James, 2; Butler links with Meade to move on Petersburg, 223; Wilson-Kautz raid, 253
Army of the Potomac, 3; combines with Army of the James to move on Petersburg, 223; size of Sheridan's command, 25, 34n.94; U.S. Colored Troops, 257, 288
Army of the Potomac, Cavalry Corps, units:
DIVISIONS: First, 5, 39, 83, 85 map, 99 map, 137, 142, 145 map, 155, 179, 183, 200, 205 map, 254–55, 267, 289, 301, 303, 319, 331–32, 337, 341. *See also* Torbert's Division; Second, xiii–xiv, 5, 20, 37, 70 map, 137, 158, 236, 238, 250, 258, 264, 268–75, 276 map, 277–84, 301, 309–10, 313–14, 319, 322n.3, 332–33, 338, 342. *See also* Gregg's Division; Third, 3, 5, 253, 303, 311. *See also* Wilson's Division
BRIGADES: First, First Division, 59, 145 map, 159 map, 183, 187, 250, 288, 301, 303, 316, 319, 331, 337, 341. *See also* Custer's Brigade; First, Second Division, 54 map, 150, 158, 159 map, 208, 217, 250, 251, 258, 264, 266–67, 275, 310, 332, 338, 342. *See also* Davies' Brigade; Horse Artillery, 332. *See also* Robertson's Brigade; Second, First Division, 53, 70 map, 82–83, 89, 94n.49, 99 map, 137, 145 map, 156, 159 map, 178, 187, 190, 193, 204, 205 map, 217, 218, 224, 241, 250–51, 257–58, 288, 331, 337. *See also* Devin's Brigade; Second, Second Division, 54 map, 83, 89, 99 map, 142, 145 map, 159 map, 208, 250, 309–10, 332, 339, 341, 342. *See also* Gregg's Brigade; Third (Reserve), 41, 54 map, 70 map, 72, 84, 85 map, 99 map, 135, 137, 145 map, 156, 159 map, 183, 187, 190, 193, 196, 203, 205 map, 289, 304, 311, 319, 332, 334, 338, 341. *See also* Merritt's Brigade
CAVALRIES, 212n.71; First Maine, 49, 57, 58, 83, 89, 145 map, 149, 178–79, 207, 217–18, 233, 251–52, 265–66, 270–71, 284, 332, 339; First Massachusetts, 207, 266, 269, 278, 332, 338, 342; First Michigan, 98, 99 map, 100, 104, 113, 184–85, 205 map, 331, 337, 341; Fifth Michigan, 97, 99 map, 100, 101, 108, 109, 125, 157, 184–85, 205 map, 331, 337, 341; Sixth Michigan, 99 map, 100, 102–03, 104, 117–18, 183–85, 205 map, 253, 331, 337, 341; Seventh Michigan, 97, 98, 99 map, 100, 104, 117, 118, 122, 123, 124, 145 map, 151, 184–86, 205 map, 331, 337, 341; First New Jersey, 49, 150, 218, 332, 338, 342; First New York Dragoons, 70 map, 76, 77–78, 82–83, 138,

155, 198. *See also* Nineteenth New York; Fourth New York, 82–83, 86, 155, 190, 194, 205 map, 241, 257, 331, 337, 341; Sixth New York, 84, 94n.49, 133, 137, 190, 193–94, 205 map, 238, 250, 258, 288, 331, 337, 341; Ninth New York, 82, 86, 155, 158, 187, 189, 233, 250, 327, 331, 337, 341; Tenth New York, 39, 41, 58, 142–44, 145 map, 236, 273–74, 279, 282, 332, 338, 342; Nineteenth New York, 332. *See also* First New York Dragoons; Sixth Ohio, 206–07, 238, 242–43, 253, 277–78, 290, 303, 323n.10, 338, 342; Thirteenth Ohio Dismounted, 257; First Pennsylvania, 217, 237, 251, 254, 275, 282, 332; Second Pennsylvania, 332, 339; Fourth Pennsylvania, 145 map, 147, 241, 254, 332, 339; Sixth Pennsylvania, 41, 70 map, 76, 78, 192, 196–98, 205 map, 206, 237, 289, 332, 338, 341; Eighth Pennsylvania, 146, 150, 238, 265, 273, 332, 339; Thirteenth Pennsylvania, 332; Sixteenth Pennsylvania, 145 map, 146, 172, 219, 231, 275, 332, 339; Seventeenth Pennsylvania, 49, 156, 190, 205 map, 250, 257, 331, 337, 341; First U.S., 70 map, 76–77, 79, 83, 205 map, 332, 338, 341; Second U.S., 70 map, 72, 73, 74, 76, 78, 83, 134, 192, 205 map, 332, 338, 341; Fifth U.S., 70 map, 76, 205 map, 332, 338, 341; Sixth U.S., 188, 231–32, 331; Regular Army, 5, 136, 158, 183, 184–85, 188, 217, 250, 311, 319. *See also* Merritt's Brigade. *See also* individual listings

ARTILLERIES: First U.S., 83, 332; Regular Army, 5; Second U.S., 100, 192, 332–33; Third U.S., 196. *See also* Robertson's Brigade

BATTERIES: Denison's Battery, 275, 276 map; Heaton's Batteries (B, L), 83, 85 map, 88, 137, 205 map, 238, 332; Pennington's Battery (M), 99 map, 100, 107, 108, 116, 120–21, 123, 124, 311, 333, 339; Randol's Batteries (H, I), 83, 85 map, 89, 142, 145 map, 149, 273, 274, 275, 276 map, 303, 332, 339; Williston's Battery (D), 76, 85 map, 192–93, 203, 205 map, 217, 311, 333, 342. *See also* Robertson's Brigade

Arnold, Capt. William K., 332

artilleries, guns (Confederate). *See also* individual listings

Baltimore Light, 334

Breathed's Horse Battalion (Chew's), 112, 124, 145 map, 149, 150, 151, 154–55, 334

artilleries, guns (Federal), 34n.97. *See also* Robertson's Brigade

First U.S., 83, 332

Regular Army, 5

Second U.S., 100, 192, 332–33;

Third U.S., 332–33;

Averell, Brig. Gen. William W., 261n.46

Avery, Maj. M. Henry, 48, 142, 143

Avery, Sgt. Marvin, 184, 185

Avery, Sgt. James Henry, 128n.63, 332

Baggs, William, 187

Baker, Dr. Joe, 55

Baldwin, Lt. Henry, 283

Ball, William, 45, 46, 51

Baltimore Light Artillery, 221, 334

Banks, Maj. Gen. Nathaniel P., 2

Barr, James M., 81

battalions (Confederate)

FITZHUGH LEE'S DIVISION: Breathed's Horse Artillery (Chew's), 79, 84, 85 map, 88, 104, 106, 107, 112, 116, 145 map, 149, 150, 176, 190–91, 196, 203, 204 map, 240, 318, 334, 335, 345; First Maryland Cavalry, 199, 212n.71, 221, 334

battalions (Confederate), *continued*
   HAMPTON'S DIVISION: Love's Alabama, 344; Thirty-fifth Virginia Cavalry, 99 map, 107, 108, 333
batteries (Confederate): Chew's (Ashby Virginia Artillery of Virginia), 334; Hart's (Washington Artillery of South Carolina), 79, 84, 85 map, 141, 145 map, 191, 193, 196, 241, 334, 345; Johnston's (First Stuart Horse Artillery of Virginia), 82, 334, 345; Shoemaker's (Lynchburg Beauregards), 151, 203, 207, 334, 345; Thomson's (Ashby Virginia Artillery of Virginia), 82, 85 map, 104, 106, 107, 154, 190–91, 196, 202, 205 map, 334, 345. *See also* Breathed's Horse Artillery
batteries (Federal): Denison's Battery, 275, 276 map; Heaton's Batteries (B, L), 83, 85 map, 88, 137, 205 map, 238, 332; Pennington's Battery (M), 99 map, 100, 107, 108, 116, 120–21, 123, 124, 311, 333; Randol's Batteries (H, I), 83, 85 map, 89, 142, 145 map, 149, 273, 274, 275, 276 map, 303,332; Williston's Battery (D), 76, 85 map, 192–93, 203, 205 map, 217, 311, 333, 342. *See also* Robertson's Brigade
Battle of Dranesville, 325n.53
Battle of Tom's Brook, 312
battles. *See* Bloody Angle; Hampton's wagons; Samaria Church; Trevilian Station
Bauskett, Lt. John, 50, 74, 140, 170; at Battle of Bloody Angle, 188, 189, 194, 195, 199–200, 207–08
Baxley, J. V., 71, 80–81
Baylis, Lt. George, 281
Baylis, Lt. Richard, 124
Baylor, Capt. George, 154
Beale, Col. Richard L. T., 257
Beale, Lt. George W., 268, 278
Bean, Capt. Theodore H., 34n.94, 49, 133, 156, 231; on shooting of horses, 52–53
Beauregard, Gen. P. G. T., 207, 223
Beloir, Sgt. Mitchell, 124
Bentley, Maj. Wilbur G., 251
Bibb, Richard, 146
Bibb's Crossroads, 71, 72, 319; location (maps), 85, 159, 205
Bibbet, Capt. A. H., 251–52
Birge, Capt. Manning D., 103
Bloody Angle, Battle of, xi, 193, 196–98, 203–04, 206–07; assessment of, 319; Butler's Brigade reinforced by Fitzhugh Lee's Division, 195; casualties, 185, 186, 187, 189, 190–92, 199–202, 208; Chew on, 194; closing engagement, 204; map, 205; opening engagement, 184
Boice, Sgt. James C., 277–78
Boston, Capt. Ruben, 116–17, 334
Bowen, James R., 138
Bowling Green, 229 map, 231
Bradshaw, William, 84, 86
Breathed, Maj. James, 286, 334
Breathed's Horse Artillery (Chew's, various batteries), 318, 334; battle at White House Landing, 240; Battle of Bloody Angle, 190–91, 196, 203, 205 map, 207; Battle of Trevilian Station (June 11), 79, 82, 84, 85 map, 106, 107, 145 map, 149, 150; casualties, 345; Fight for Hampton's Wagons, 104, 112, 116; positions morning of June 12, 176
Breckinridge, John Cabell, 48, 157
Brewer, Lt. Col. Melvin, 97, 122, 331

Brewster, Capt., 101

brigades (Confederate)

FITZHUGH LEE'S DIVISION: Lomax's, 99 map, 113, 118, 120, 125, 203, 205 map, 236, 264, 267, 334, 345; Wickham's, 97–98, 99 map, 100, 115, 118, 125, 203, 204, 205 map, 236, 260n.28, 316, 319, 334, 344

HAMPTON'S DIVISION: Butler's, 54 map, 61, 70 map, 72–73, 80, 83–84, 85 map, 86, 87, 99 map, 142, 145 map, 155, 176, 190, 193–97, 205 map, 240, 260n.28, 265, 276 map, 298n.121, 333; Dulaney's (Laurel Brigade), 226, 257, 265, 269, 276 map; Rosser's (Laurel Brigade), 45, 54 map, 61, 105–06, 107, 108–09, 112, 117, 145 map, 154, 176, 313, 333, 334; Wright's, 61, 70 map, 72, 79, 80, 81, 84, 85 map, 86, 87, 99 map, 100, 102, 110, 125, 141, 142, 145 map, 150, 176, 186, 205 map, 313, 343; Young's, 333

brigades (Federal)

FIRST CAVALRY DIVISION: First, 59, 145 map, 159 map, 183, 187, 250, 288, 301, 303, 310, 316, 319, 331, 337, 341. See also Custer's Brigade; Second, 54 map, 70 map, 82–83, 89, 94n.49, 99 map, 137, 145 map, 159 map, 178, 187, 190, 193, 204, 205 map, 224, 241, 250–51, 257–58, 288, 331, 337, 341. See also Devin's Brigade; Third (Reserve), 54 map, 70 map, 72, 84, 85 map, 99 map, 135, 137, 145 map, 156, 159 map, 183, 187, 190, 193, 196, 203, 205 map, 289, 304, 311, 319, 331, 338, 341. See also Merritt's Brigade

SECOND CAVALRY DIVISION: First, 54 map, 150, 158, 159 map, 208, 250, 251, 258, 264, 266–67, 275, 310, 332. See also Davies' Brigade; Horse Artillery, 76, 89, 99 map, 100, 107, 108, 116, 120–21, 123–24, 137, 149, 192–93, 196, 202, 203, 205 map, 217, 238, 273, 274, 276 map, 311, 332, 332–33, 339, 342. See also Robertson's Brigade; Second, 54 map, 83, 89, 99 map, 142, 145 map, 159 map, 208, 250, 309–10, 332. See also Gregg's Brigade

Brinton, Lt. Col. Joseph P., 332

Brooks, Noble J., 65n.59, 87–88, 221

Brooks, Ulysses R., 88–89, 95n.77, 169, 202, 240; on gunboat artillery, 248n.138; on Sheridan, 308

Brooks, Whitfield, 189

Brown, Eliza, 97, 114

Buck, Capt. Thomas H., 257

Buford, Brig. Gen. John, 3, 7

Burgess, Anthony Beale, 191–92

burials, 221–22; Ogden, 174. See also dead, the; graves

Butcher, John, 78

Butler, Brig. Gen. Matthew C., 19–20, 50, 69, 101, 183, 333; at Battle of Bloody Angle, 184, 185, 190, 193, 196, 202, 207, 209; at Battle of Samaria Church, 267; at Battle of Trevilian Station (June 11), 79, 139–40, 141, 154–55; captures Loeser, 75; on condition of troops after Battle of Trevilian Station, 220; Covode and, 284–85; Hampton on, 317; Sheridan on, 318; on the terrain of Trevilian Station battlefield, 71; v. Fitzhugh Lee, 316

Butler, Capt. Nat "Pick," 75, 154, 284

Butler, Maj. Gen. Benjamin F., 2, 289

Butler's Brigade, xiv, xix, 260n.28; battle at White House Landing, 240; Battle of Bloody Angle, 190, 193–201, 205 map; Battle of Samaria Church, 265, 276 map, 286, 298n.121; Battle of Trevilian Station (June 11), 72–73, 80, 83–84, 85 map, 86, 87, 99 map, 142, 145 map; campsite (June 10), 54 map; Hampton's Trevilian Station defense plan and, 61; ordered to fall back from Torbert's attack, 155; position during opening engagements at Trevilian Station, 70 map; positions morning of June 12, 176

Cadet Rangers, 139–40, 200

Calhoun, Capt. John C., 184, 195

Calhoun, Charles M., 52, 74, 89; on Fitzhugh Lee, 152

captures (prisoners), 287; Anderson, 148; by Baker, 55; Battle of Samarian Church, 278; Boston, 116–17; Brown, 114; Conrad, 43; Ferguson, 146; by Fifth Michigan Cavalry, 101; Garnett, 232; Greene, 115; Hall, 39; by Hampton's Division at Trevilian Station, 322n.2; Hansell, 111; Hopkins, 148; Huey, 284; Iler, 148; Loeser, 75; Macomber, 118; by New York cavalries, 86; by Pendil, 143; Powell, 216; Rucker, 152; by Seventeenth Pennsylvania Cavalry, 156; by Seventh Michigan Cavalry, 185–86; by Veil, 79. See also intelligence; prisoners

Carpenter, Lt. Louis H., 39, 71, 138, 183, 209n.1; on Battle of Trevilian Station, 156

Carpenter's Ford, xix, xix–xx, 25, 67n.84, 218

Carter, Lt. Col. William R., 119–20, 131n.105

Carter, Pattie Ann, 167

casualties (killed, wounded), 143, 215, 260n.28, 302, 331, 332, 333; Adams, 84; Aiken, 178; ambulances and, 179, 181n.43; Baldwin, 283; Ball, 168; Barr, 81; Battle of Bloody Angle, 185, 186, 187, 188, 189, 190–92, 198, 199–202, 208; Battle of Samaria Church, 283–86, 297n.121, 301; Battle of Trevilian Station, 337–45; Baylis, 124; Beloir, 124; Bentley, 251; Carter, 119; Clowney, 89; Confederate Army, Trevilian Station, 158, 343–45; Confederate v. Union statistics, 323n.46; Custer's Brigade, 303, 310; Darlington, 224–25; Ellicott, 120; Fourth South Carolina Cavalry at Trevilian Station, 313; Gifford, 86; Hampton's Division at Battle of Trevilian Station, 312–13; Hayes, 110; Humphrey, 162n.22; Lining, 82; local civilians and, 167; Lucius, 286; McAllister, 147–48; Mc-Clatchey, 148–49; Nelson, 273; normal percentage for infantry battles during Civil War, 323n.13; O'Neill, 121; Official Records v. Suderow statistics, 322n.5; Ogden, 137; Pollard, 257; Preston, 143, 170; regimental commanders, 322n.6, 323n.45; retreat to White House Landing and, 216, 217; Rodenbough, 75–76, 90; Russell, 170; Sackett, 86, 86–87, 90, 216; Sixth Michigan Cavalry at Fight for Hampton's Wagons, 117–18; Stuart, xiii, 18; Tebbs, 272; the Towles brothers, 119; Trask, 149–50; Union Army, Trevilian Station, 157, 337–42; Wells, 88

cavalries, vi

cavalries (Confederate): Seventh Georgia, 66n.67, 70 map, 79–80, 81, 87–88, 102, 110, 145 map, 147–49, 222, 313, 333, 343; Twentieth Georgia, 50, 80, 81, 107, 110, 177, 187, 333; First Maryland Battalion, 212n.71, 221, 334; Fourth South Carolina, 70 map, 71, 73, 74, 79, 82, 87, 176, 184, 199, 201, 205 map, 206, 285, 313, 333, 343; Fifth South Carolina, 70 map, 73, 81, 86, 139, 140, 176, 198–99, 205 map, 240, 260n.28, 333, 343; Sixth South Carolina, 50, 70 map, 71, 73–74, 80, 89, 105, 139, 140, 152, 169, 170, 176, 188, 189, 190, 194–95, 199, 200, 202, 205 map, 333, 343; Seventh South Carolina, 268; First Virginia, 282, 334, 344; Second Virginia, 99 map, 116, 268, 272, 334, 344; Third Virginia, 203, 204, 260n.28, 334, 344; Fourth Virginia, 98, 99 map, 115, 119–20, 236, 334, 344; Fifth Virginia, 334, 345; Sixth Virginia, 99 map, 115, 120–22, 121–22, 152, 334; Seventh Virginia, 168, 218, 257, 333, 344; Ninth Virginia, 257; Eleventh Virginia, 107, 172, 333, 344; Twelfth Virginia, 108, 276 map, 281, 333, 344; Fifteenth Virginia, 113, 334, 345; Twenty-fourth Virginia, 281; Thirty-fifth Battalion Virginia (Comanches), 99 map, 107, 108, 177, 333; Gary's Independent, 263, 268, 270, 286, 292n.3, 298n.121, 335. See also individual listings

cavalries (Federal): First Maine, 49, 57, 58, 83, 89, 145 map, 149, 178–79, 207, 217–18, 233, 251–52, 265–66, 270–71, 284, 332, 339; First Massachusetts, 207, 266, 269, 278, 332, 338, 342; First Michigan, 98, 99 map, 100, 104, 113, 184–85, 205 map, 331, 337,

341; Fifth Michigan, 97, 99 map, 100, 101, 108, 109, 125, 157, 184–85, 205 map, 331, 337, 341; Sixth Michigan, 99 map, 100, 102–03, 104, 117–18, 183–85, 205 map, 253, 331, 337, 341; Seventh Michigan, 97, 98, 99 map, 100, 104, 117, 118, 122, 123, 124, 145 map, 151, 184–86, 205 map, 331, 337, 341; First New Jersey, 49, 150, 218, 332, 338, 342; First New York Dragoons, 70 map, 76, 77–78, 82–83, 138, 155, 198. *See also* Nineteenth New York; Fourth New York, 82–83, 86, 155, 190, 194, 205 map, 241, 257, 331, 337, 341; Sixth New York, 84, 94n.49, 133, 137, 190, 193–94, 205 map, 238, 250, 258, 288, 331, 337, 341; Ninth New York, 82, 86, 155, 158, 187, 189, 233, 250, 327, 331, 337, 341; Tenth New York, 39, 41, 58, 142–44, 145 map, 236, 273–74, 279, 282, 332, 338, 342; Nineteenth New York, 332. *See also* First New York Dragoons; Sixth Ohio, 206–07, 238, 242–43, 253, 277–78, 290, 303, 323n.10, 332, 338, 342; Thirteenth Ohio Dismounted, 257; First Pennsylvania, 217, 237, 251, 254, 275, 282, 332; Second Pennsylvania, 332, 339; Fourth Pennsylvania, 145 map, 147, 241, 254, 332, 339; Sixth Pennsylvania, 41, 70 map, 76, 78, 192, 196–98, 205 map, 206, 237, 289, 332, 338, 341; Eighth Pennsylvania, 146, 150, 238, 265, 273, 332, 339; Thirteenth Pennsylvania, 332; Sixteenth Pennsylvania, 146, 172, 219, 231, 275, 332, 339; Seventeenth Pennsylvania, 49, 156, 190, 205 map, 250, 257, 331, 337, 341; First U.S., 70 map, 76–77, 79, 83, 205 map, 332, 338, 341; Second U.S., 70 map, 72, 73, 74, 76, 78, 83, 134, 192, 205 map, 332, 338, 341; Fifth U.S., 70 map, 76, 205 map, 332, 338, 341; Sixth U.S., 188, 231–32, 331; Regular Army, 5, 136, 158, 183, 184–85, 188, 217, 250, 311, 319. *See also* individual listings

Cave, Reuben, 55

Chamberlain, Lt. Col. Samuel E., 266, 332

Chambliss, Brig. Gen. John, 233

Chambliss' Brigade, 233, 241, 298n.121; Battle of Samaria Church, 269, 270, 286; v. Devin's Brigade near Samaria Church, 257–58

Chapman, Col. George, 5

Charge of the Light Brigade, The (Tennyson), vi

Charles City Court House, 259, 267; arrival of Sheridan's wagon train, 289; location (maps), 229, 276; retreat of Gregg's Division from Samaria Church and, 278–79, 284; secured by Tobert, 288

Charleston Mercury, 307

Charlottesville, 22, 23, 40 map, 307

Charlottesville Road, 155, 183, 190; location (maps), 60, 173, 205

Chew, Maj. Roger Preston, 334; on Battle of Bloody Angle, 194, 209; on Battle of Trevilian Station, 316, 321–22; at Battle of Trevilian Station (June 11), 82, 106; on Custer v. Rosser, 325n.57

Chew's Horse Artillery. *See* Breathed's Horse Artillery

Chickahominy River, 253, 258; location (maps), 24, 229

Christian Commission at City Point, 327

Christiancy, Isaac P., 129n.79

Cilley, Maj. Jonathan P., 275, 284

Cisco, Johnnie, 97, 114

citizenry, 226; during Battle of Trevilian Station, 141–42; Federal foragers and, 39, 47, 48, 58–59, 179, 219, 233; horses and, 235; the wounded and, 167

City Point, 229 map, 249; National Cemetery, 327

Civil War: consequences of Hampton's victory at Trevilian Station, 311; normal percentage of infantry battle casualties, 323n.13; worst defeat of Confederate cavalry, 312

Claflin, Capt. Ira W., 232

Clark, Capt. J. Hinckley, 332

Clayton's Store, 53, 54 map

Clowney, John, 89

Cobb's Georgia Legion, 333; Battle of Trevilian Station (June 11), 81, 87–88; casualties, 343; position during opening engagements at Trevilian Station, 70 map

Cold Harbor, xi, 33n.84; Grant on, 21

Collins, Col. Charles R., 334

Comanches. See Thirty-fifth Battalion Virginia

communications, 49

Company Q, 11, 30n.42, 53, 242

Conrad, Capt. R. C., 120

Conrad, Capt. Thomas N., 42–43, 234

Conrad, Maj. Holmes, 124

contrabands, 38; retreat to White House Landing and, 217. See also fugitives

Cooper, Gen. Samuel, 263

Coover, John B., 306

Copeland, Joseph T., 101

Coppinger, Capt. John J., 157, 165n.98

Coppinger, Capt. Joseph J., 90

Cormany, Lt. Samuel, 55, 172, 254, 258, 291; at Battle of Samaria Church, 272; on Battle of Samaria Church, 270, 277; on Battle of Trevilian Station, 146; destruction of railroad tracks and, 177–78

Covode, Lt. Col. George H., 284, 286, 297n.118, 332

Crampton, Capt. Benjamin P., 257

Critcher, Lt. Col. John, 113, 128n.75

Crocker, Lt. Col. William H., 38, 331

Cryer, Lt. M. H., 277–78

Cuddebec, C. L., 77–78

Curtis, Isaac S., 43

Custer, Brig. Gen. George A., xix, 5, 26, 310, 311, 331; attempt to recapture Hampton's wagons, 151; at Battle of Bloody Angle, 186; at Fight for Hampton's Wagons, 98, 100, 107–08, 109–10, 112, 117, 122–25, 135, 136; at Haw's Shop, xiii; Kidd on, 6; loses contact with Torbert at Battle of Trevilian Station, 90–91; on the recapture of Hampton's wagons by the Fifteenth Virginia Cavalry, 112–13, 113–14; resources on, 29n.24; Rosser and, 15; Rosser on, 122; Torbert on, 158; v. Rosser's Laurel Brigade, 325n.57

Custer, Libbie, 114, 129n.79

Custer's Brigade (Wolverines), xix, 97, 158, 250, 288, 331; Battle of Bloody Angle, 187, 205 map, 319; campsite (June 10), 53; campsite (June 11), 159 map; casualties, 125, 301, 303, 310, 337, 341; reconnaissance (June 12), 183; Sheridan's Trevilian Station raid plan and, 59. See also individual listings of Michigan cavalries

    Fight for Hampton's Wagons: captures Hampton's wagons, 101; loses Hampton's wagons, 113; attempt to recapture Hampton's wagons, 151; isolates Fitzhugh Lee's Division from Hampton's, 100–103, 104, 316; Kelly on, 134; opening engagement, 98; position during capture of Trevilian Station, 145 map; reinforced by Merritt's Regular Army, 136; rendered hors de combat, 157, 310, 319; Torbert's attempts to contact (June 11), 133, 135; v. Conrad, 120; v. Rosser's Laurel Brigade, 105–06, 107, 108–09, 112, 115–16, 117; v. Sixth Virginia Cavalry, 121–22; v. Wickham's Brigade, 118–19

Dahlgren, Col. Ulric, 3, 234, 247n.102, 257

Dana, Capt. Amasa G., 135, 161n.6

Danne's Store, 176, 159 map, 197, 214n.127

Darlington, Maj. William B., 224–25

Davidson, Nathaniel, 26, 133, 216, 231, 232

Davies, Brig. Gen. Henry E., 4, 41, 280, 332

Davies' Brigade, 150, 158, 208, 217, 250, 264, 266–67, 275, 276 map, 310, 332; campsite (June 10), 54 map; campsite (June 11), 159 map; clearing Sheridan's path from White House Landing, 251

Davies, Maj. John N., 333

Davis, Capt. Zimmerman, 131n.105, 302

Davis, Jefferson, 46

Davis, Lt. J. Lucius, 286

dead, the, 216–17, 221, 284. See also burials; graves

Deck, D. M., 81–82

Deep Bottom, 229 map

Devin, Col. Thomas C., 6–7, 331; at Battle of Bloody Angle, 189–90; at Battle of Trevilian Station (June 11), 155, 158

Devin's Brigade, 178, 241, 250–51, 288, 331; Battle of Bloody Angle, 187, 190, 193, 204, 205 map; Battle of Trevilian Station (June 11), 82–83, 89, 94n.49, 99 map, 137, 145 map; campsite (June 10), 54 map; campsite (June 11), 156, 159 map; casualties, 258, 337, 341; position during opening engagements at Trevilian Station, 70 map; retreat to White House Landing, 218, 224; Sheridan's Trevilian Station raid plan and, 59; v. Chambliss' Brigade near Samaria Church, 257–58

Di Cessnola, Col. Luigi Palma, 155, 305, 331; on Battle of Bloody Angle, 190, 204, 206

divisions (Confederate). See also individual listings

    Fitzhugh Lee's, 46, 49, 54 map, 61, 72, 99 map, 113, 142, 156, 159 map, 160, 222, 254, 260n.28, 313, 334

    Hampton's, xiii–xiv, 46, 49, 156, 159 map, 179, 222, 249, 251–52, 253, 298n.121, 304, 312–13, 313–14, 316, 333

    William Lee's, 335

divisions (Federal)

    First Cavalry, 5, 39, 83, 85 map, 99 map, 137, 142, 145 map, 155, 179, 183, 200, 205 map, 254–55, 267, 289, 303, 319, 331–32, 337, 341. See also Torbert's Division

    Second Cavalry, xiii–xiv, 5, 20, 37, 70 map, 137, 158, 236, 238, 250, 258, 264, 268–75, 276 map, 277–84, 301, 309–10, 313–14, 319, 322n.3, 332–33. See also Gregg's Division

    Third Cavalry, 3, 5, 253, 303, 311, 334. See also Wilson's Division

doctors: Breckinridge, 327; Burton, 154; Pease, 179; Phillips, 179; Powell, 216; Rae, 216; Rockwell, 206, 283; Rulison, 179; Taylor, 285; Wilson, 157

Dodge, Capt. Horace, 109

Douthat's Landing, 289

Dowling, Sgt. W. H., 140, 168, 199, 202, 203

dragoons (Federal). See First New York Dragoons

Drake, Capt. George, 109

Dulaney, Col. Richard H., 154, 281, 333; on Hampton, 315

Dulaney's (Laurel Brigade), 226, 257; Battle of Samaria Church, 269, 276 map

Dunkelberger, Capt. Isaac Rothermel, 187–88, 210n.23

Dunkirk, 229 map, 236, 241

Early, Lt. Gen. Jubal A., 224, 305–06, 312, 320

Edens, Lt. Alan, 158, 206

Egan, Lt. William, 121

Eighth Pennsylvania Cavalry, 332; Battle of Samaria Church, 265, 273; Battle of Trevilian Station (June 11), 146, 150; casualties, 339; retreat to White House Landing, 238

Eldridge, Daniel, 117, 185

Eleventh Virginia Cavalry, 333; casualties, 344; Fight for Hampton's Wagons, 99 map, 107; at Gordonsville, 171

Ellicott, Thomas P., 119–20

Evening Chronicle (Pittsburgh), 307

Farnsworth, Sgt. Maj. Herbert, 144, 145

Ferguson, Maj. James D., 44, 113, 267

Ferguson, Maj. Thomas B., 74, 139, 333

Ferguson, R. H., 146

Fifteenth Virginia Cavalry, 334; casualties, 345; Fight for Hampton's Wagons, 113

Fifth Michigan Cavalry, 97, 331; Battle of Bloody Angle, 184–85, 205 map; Battle of Trevilian Station (June 11), 157; casualties, 125, 337, 341; Fight for Hampton's Wagons, 99 map, 100, 101, 108, 109

Fifth South Carolina Cavalry, 260n.28, 333; battle at White House Landing, 240; Battle of Bloody Angle, 198–99, 205 map; Battle of Trevilian Station (June 11), 73, 81, 86, 139, 140; casualties, 343; position during opening engagements at Trevilian Station, 70 map; position morning of June 12, 176

Fifth U.S. Cavalry, 332; Battle of Bloody Angle, 205 map; Battle of Trevilian Station (June 11), 76; casualties, 338, 341; position during opening engagements at Trevilian Station, 70 map

Fifth Virginia Cavalry, 334; casualties, 345

First Cavalry Division, 5, 39, 267, 289, 331–32; Battle of Bloody Angle, 200, 205 map, 208; Battle of Trevilian Station, assault along Fredericksburg Road, 85 map, 301; Battle of Trevilian Station, drives Confederates from the field, 155, 319; Battle of Trevilian Station, isolates Butler's Brigade from Fitzhugh Lee's Division, 142; casualties, 303, 337, 341; reconnaissance (June 12), 179, 183; securing Sheridan's path across the Chickahominy, 254–55; v. Chambliss' Brigade near Samaria Church, 257–58. *See also* Torbert's Division

Twentieth Georgia, 177

First Maine Cavalry, 49, 57, 58, 178–79, 207, 332; Battle of Samaria Church, 265–66, 270–71, 284; Battle of Trevilian Station (June 11), 83, 89, 145 map, 149; casualties, 284, 339; retreat to White House Landing, 217–18, 233

First Maryland Cavalry, 221, 334; Battle of Bloody Angle, 199, 212n.71

First Massachusetts Cavalry, 332; Battle of Bloody Angle, 207; Battle of Samaria Church, 266, 269, 278; casualties, 338, 342

First Michigan Cavalry, 331; Battle of Bloody Angle, 184–85, 205 map; casualties, 337, 341; clearing Sheridan's path from White House Landing, 251–52; Fight for Hampton's Wagons, 98, 99 map, 100, 104, 113

First New Jersey Cavalry, 49, 150, 332; casualties, 338, 342; retreat to White House Landing, 218

First New York Dragoons (Nineteenth New York Cavalry), 332; Battle of Bloody Angle, 198; Battle of Trevilian Station (June 11), 76, 77–78, 82–83, 138, 155; casualties, 338, 341; position during opening engagements at Trevilian Station, 70 map

First Pennsylvania Cavalry, 158, 217, 332; Battle of Samaria Church, 275; clearing Sheridan's path from White House Landing, 251, 254; retreat from Samaria Church, 282; retreat to White House Landing, 237

First U.S. Cavalry: Battle of Bloody Angle, 187–88, 205 map; Battle of Trevilian Station

(June 11), 76–77, 78, 83; position during opening engagements at Trevilian Station, 70 map

First Virginia Cavalry, 248n.137, 334; casualties, 344; pursuit of Gregg's retreat from Samaria Church, 282

Fitch, Sgt. Lewis, 98

Fitzgerald, John, 118, 130n.96

foraging: Confederates in pursuit of Sheridan, 226–27; Federals during march to Trevilian Station, 38–39, 41–42, 47, 48, 55, 56–57, 58–59; Federals during retreat to White House Landing, 219, 233, 234, 236; Federals morning of June 12, 179. *See also* citizenry

Forsyth, Maj. George, 232, 246n.96

Foster, Sgt. Alonzo, 194

Foster, Sgt. John T., 203–04

Fourth New York Cavalry: Battle of Bloody Angle, 190, 194, 205 map; Battle of Trevilian Station (June 11), 82–83, 86, 155; casualties, 331, 341; retreat to White House Landing, 241; v. Chambliss' Brigade near Samaria Church, 257

Fourth Pennsylvania Cavalry, 254, 332; Battle of Trevilian Station (June 11), 145 map, 147; casualties, 339; retreat to White House Landing, 241

Fourth South Carolina Cavalry, 333; Battle of Bloody Angle, 184, 199, 201, 205 map, 206; Battle of Trevilian Station (June 11), 71, 73, 74, 79, 82, 87; casualties, 285, 313, 343; position during opening engagements at Trevilian Station, 70 map; position morning of June 12, 176

Fourth Virginia Cavalry, 119–20, 236, 334; casualties, 344; Fight for Hampton's Wagons, 98, 99 map, 115, 119–20

Fowler, Thomas M., 203–04

Fredericksburg Road, 61, 122, 147, 301, 303–04; location (maps), 60, 70, 85, 99, 159; Sheridan's Trevilian Station raid plan and, 59

fugitives, 49; retreat to White House Landing and, 243n.9. *See also* contrabands

Fulk, John S., 277–78

Funsten, Col. Oliver R., 333

Furness, Capt. Frank H., 197–98, 211n.64, 212n.65

Gallagher, Dewitt C., 118, 282, 291, 299n.168; on Battle of Samaria Church, 272–73

Garnett, Capt. A., 232

Gary, Brig. Gen. Martin, 233, 335; Hampton and, 293n.3

Gary's Independent cavalry brigade, 292n.3, 335; Battle of Samaria Church, 268, 270, 286, 298n.121; reinforces Hampton near Samaria Church, 263

Gentry house, 205 map

Getty, Brig. Gen. George W., 242, 248n.146, 249, 256, 257

Gibbs, Col. Alfred, 77, 138, 332

Gifford, Sgt. Edward P., 86

Giles, Sgt. Andrew, 195

Gordon, Brig. Gen. James B., xiii, 14

Gordon, Capt. Daniel S., 332

Gordon, Lt. D. E., 152

Gordonsville, 22, 82, 170–71; location (maps), 24, 40, 229; Sheridan's failure to capture and, 306, 307

Gordonsville Road, 112, 153, 155, 176, 179, 183, 190, 209n.1; crossing of Custer's Brigade toward Hampton's wagons, 100; Hampton's Trevilian Station defense plan and, 61; location (maps), 60, 70, 85, 99, 145, 159, 173, 205

Grant, Ulysses S., 5, 20, 233, 238–39, 288, 292; advance on Petersburg and, 320; appointed lieutenant general of U.S. Army, 1–2; appoints Sheridan instead of Gregg as commander of the Cavalry Corps, 3; chief purpose in sending Sheridan to Trevilian Station, xiv; instructs Sheridan to unite with Hunter at Charlottesville, 22–23; memoirs of and Sheridan, 304; orders Maj. Gen. Butler to reinforce Sheridan at Douthat's Wharf, 289; orders Sheridan's march from White House Landing to City Point, 249; Overland Campaign and, xi; plan to capture Petersburg, 223; positions army across the Pamunkey, xiii; Robert Lee's assessment of purpose in sending Sheridan toward Chilesburg, 46–47; the Wilderness and, xii

graves: present-day cemeteries, 327–29; Spotsylvania battlefield, 227–28. See also burials; dead, the

Green, Col. John S., 334

Greene, Capt. Jacob L., 114–15

Green Spring Road, 183, 190; location (maps), 173, 205

Gregg, Brig. Gen. David M., 309–10, 332; on battle at Cold Harbor, 21; at Battle of Samaria Church, 288; as a commander, xi, 3, 8–9; preparations for Battle of Samaria Church, 265–67; relationship with Sheridan, 243n.2; resigns commission, 28n.10, 298n.135; Sheridan on, 271, 287; on Weir, 280

Gregg, Gen. J. Irvin, 9–10, 332

Gregg's (David) Division, 5, 37, 250, 309–10, 332–33; Battle of Bloody Angle, 319; Battle of Samaria Church, 264, 268–75, 276 map, 301, 313–14; Battle of Trevilian Station (June 11), 137, 158; camps at Samaria Church, 258; campsite (June 11), 156; casualties, 338, 342; destroys mill at Walkerton, 238; destruction of Virginia Central Railroad, 177; march to White House Landing, 236; number of troops at Battle of Samaria Church, 301, 322n.3; position during opening engagements at Trevilian Station, 70 map; reconnaissances morning of June 12, 178; retreat from Samaria Church, 275, 277–84; Sheridan's Trevilian Station raid plan and, 59; v. Hampton's Division at Haw's Shop, xiii–xiv, 20. See also Second Cavalry Division

Gregg's (Irvin) Brigade, 55, 208, 250, 309–10, 332; Battle of Samaria Church, 276 map; Battle of Trevilian Station (June 11), 83, 85 map, 89, 99 map, 142, 145 map; campsite (June 10), 54 map; campsite (June 11), 159 map

Grierson, Col. Benjamin, 22

Grimsley, Daniel A., 121, 122, 204

Grommon, Frank, 117

gunboats, 148; Brooks on artillery of, 248n.138; at White House Landing, 239–42

Hall, Hillman A., 288

Hall, Maj. William P., 39

Hampton, Maj. Gen. Wade, 11, 71, 221, 258, 325n.59, 333; at Battle of Bloody Angle, 203; on Battle of Bloody Angle, 206; at Battle of Trevilian Station, xviii, 81, 87, 105, 106, 110, 113, 125, 138, 139, 142, 155, 157; on Battle of Trevilian Station, 160; on Butler at Battle of Trevilian Station, 207, 317; as a commander, xii, xiv, 12–13; in comparison to Fitzhugh Lee, 32n.69; in comparison to Stuart, 314–15; on Fitzhugh Lee, 315; Gary and, 293n.3; Holmes on, 312; informed of Sheridan's advance, 43; learns that Grant has crossed the James, 233; Libbie Custer and, 129n.79; at opening engagement at Trevilian Station, 72; positions his division between Gordonsville and Sheridan, 51; positions his division between Westover and Sheridan, 259; preparations for Battle of Samaria Church, 264, 265, 267–68; on pursuit of Sheridan in retreat to White House Landing, 225–26; resources on, 30n.48; Robert Lee on, 315; Sheridan's Trevilian Station raid plan and, 59; size of command, 44; Trevilian Station defense plan, 61, 172; v. Wickham, 18, 32n.70

Hampton's Division, 39, 253, 256, 257, 259, 304, 309, 333; advance on White House Landing, 239–42; Battle of Bloody Angle, 205 map; Battle of Samaria Church, 276 map, 285, 298n.121, 310, 313–14; Battle of Trevilian Station, 145 map, 316; campsite (June 11), 156, 159 map, 179; casualties at Battle of Trevilian Station, 312–13, 343; condition of troops after Battle at Trevilian Station, 220; consequences of victory at Trevilian Station on remainder of Civil War, 311; Hampton on, 311; harassment of Federal advance from White House Landing, 251–52; march in pursuit of Sheridan's advance into Virginia, 46, 47–48, 49–51; pursuit of Gregg's Division in retreat from Samaria Church, 282; pursuit of Sheridan in retreat to White House Landing, 222, 228, 235; v. Gregg's Division at Haw's Shop, xiii, 20; withdraws from White House Landing, 249

Hampton's wagons, 70 map, 72, 85 map, 303, 319; captured by Fifth Michigan Cavalry, 101; recaptured by Fifteenth Virginia Cavalry, 113

Hansell, Sgt. Charles, 50, 107, 110, 111, 177, 221; at Battle of Bloody Angle, 187; at Battle of Trevilian Station (June 11), 80

Hare, John, 191

Harper, Martha, 167

Harrison, Lt. A. J., 140

Hart, Maj. James, 334

Hastings, Capt. Smith H., 100

Haw's Shop, xiii–xiv, 20

Hayes, William, 110

Heaton, Lt. Edward, 332

Heeth, Lt. Tom, 110

Hertz, John, 103–04, 127n.34

Hickey, Lt. Myron, 179

Hill, Lieut. Gen. Daniel Harvey, vi

Hills, William G., 56

Hines, Capt. John P., 148, 328, 329n.2

Holder, Ned, 199–200

Holmes, James G., 312

Holtzman, Lt. John D., 119

Horrigan, Lt. Patrick W., 77

horses, 10, 16, 37, 303; citizenry and, 235; Company Q and, 11; in Hampton's pursuit of Sheridan to White House Landing, 230; losses by Sixth Ohio Cavalry at Battle of Samaria Church, 323n.10; during march to Trevilian Station, 37, 38, 41, 52–53; during retreat to White House Landing, 236, 238; and shooting of, 19, 302; Smith and, 270–71; v. artillery, 147

hospitals, 179, 216, 221; Battle of Samaria Church, 282

Howard, Lt. Col. John B., 231, 232

Howard, Lt. Wiley C., 81, 88, 153, 186

Huey, Col. Pennock, 146, 273, 284, 332

Hughson, Lucy Dettor, 141–42, 167

Humphrey, Capt. Moses B., 139, 162n.22, 200

Hunter, Major Gen. David, 21, 22, 22–23, 157, 220, 223–24, 305–06; Sheridan's failure at Trevilian Station and, 320, 321

Hyndman, Capt. William, 297n.118

Iler, Sgt. Adam J., 148

Imboden, John D., 21

Ingalls, Brig. Gen. Rufus, 2, 289, 290

Inquirer (Philadelphia), 307
intelligence, 175, 232, 287. *See also* reconnaissance
Isham, Lt. Asa, 37–38

James River, 21, 264, 320; crossing of Sheridan's wagon train, 289–91; location (maps), 24, 40, 229
James River Canal, 23
Janeway, Maj. Hugh, 150
Jay, Samuel, 241
Jeff Davis Mississippi Legion: Battle of Bloody Angle, 195; Battle of Samaria Church, 276 map, 281; Battle of Trevilian Station (June 11), 81, 105, 106–07; casualties, 343; position during opening engagements at Trevilian Station, 70 map
Johnson, Col. Bradley T., 12, 221, 244n.44, 334
Johnston, Capt. Phillip P., 334
Johnston, Joseph E., 2
Jones, Brig. Gen. William E., 22
Jones, John B., 308–09
Jones, Lt. Frank, 186
Jones, Sgt. Joseph C., 133
Jones Bridge, 256
Jordan, Charles W., 252
Judson, Capt. Robert E., 108

Kautz, Brig. Gen. August V., 253
Keller, William, 254
Kelly, John, 134
Kendall, Cpl. Carthage, 191
Kennedy, George W., 143
Kennedy, John, 121, 131n.111
Kerwin, Maj. Michael, 332
Kester, Lt. Col. John W., 150, 332
Kidd, Maj. James H., 253, 331; at Battle of Bloody Angle, 184; on Battle of Trevilian Station, xvii, 306; on Custer, 6, 125; at Fight for Hampton's Wagons, 100, 102–03, 104–05, 117, 118; on Sheridan, 4–5
Kilpatrick, Gen. Judson, 3
King, Matthew W., 242, 288
King and Queen Court House, 229 map, 234

Laurel Brigade. *See* Dulaney's Brigade; Rosser's Brigade
Law, William A., 73
Lawyer, Eli, 75, 78
Lee, Cpl. Billie, 187
Lee, Gen. Robert Edward, 2, 18, 51–52; assessment of Grant's purpose in sending Sheridan toward Chilesburg, 46–47; on Hampton, 314; informed of Sheridan's advance, 43; informs Hampton that Grant has crossed the James, 233; Petersburg and, 320, 322; plan to defend Lynchburg, 223–24
Lee, Maj. Gen. Fitzhugh, xii, 11–12, 221, 236, 334; assessment of Grant's strategy upon information of Sheridan's advance, 46–47; at Battle of Samaria Church, 267, 269; at Battle of Trevilian Station, 97, 105, 316–17; Calhoun on, 152; Hampton on, 160–61,

315; orders Wickham's Brigade up Marquis Road, 97; plan to intercept Sheridan's retreat to White House Landing, 220–21; preparations to meet Sheridan, 44; on pursuit of Sheridan in retreat to White House Landing, 226; resources on, 30n.43; rivalry with Hampton, 18, 32n.69; at Wilson's Wharf, xiii

Lee, Maj. Gen. William H. F. "Rooney," xii, xiv, 11, 15, 335

Lee's (Fitzhugh) Division, 222, 254, 259, 334; Battle of Bloody Angle, 195, 205 map; Battle of Samaria Church, 276 map, 313; Battle of Trevilian Station, 72, 142, 155, 160; campsite (June 10), 54 map; campsite (June 11), 156, 159 map; casualties, 260n.28, 313, 344; Fight for Hampton's Wagons, 99 map, 113; Hampton's Trevilian Station defense plan and, 61; march in pursuit of Sheridan's advance into Virginia, 46, 49; march to reinforce Hampton's Division (June 12), 173 map, 174

Lee's (William) Division, 335; Chambliss' Brigade, 233, 241

Leeman, Capt. J. H., 275

legions (Confederate). *See also* individual listings
    Cobb's Georgia, 70 map, 81, 87–88, 334, 343
    Jeff Davis Mississippi, 70 map, 81, 105, 106–07, 195, 343
    Phillips Georgia, 70 map, 105, 141, 334, 343;

Lewis, John, 241

Lewis, Maj. Ivy F., 110, 111

Lincoln, Abraham, 1; on Sheridan, 5

Lining, Thomas, 82

Loeser, Capt. Charles, 74–75, 332

Loeser, Capt. James M., 169

Lomax, Brig. Gen. Lunsford L., 12, 128n.75, 318, 334; at Fight for Hampton's Wagons, 113

Lomax's Brigade, 236, 267; Battle of Bloody Angle, 203, 205 map; casualties, 345; Fight for Hampton's Wagons, 99 map, 113, 118, 120, 125; v. Ninth New York Cavalry, 264

Longstreet, Lt. Gen. James, 2

looting, 216

Louisa: location (maps), 99, 159; Oakland cemetery, 328

Louisa County, 61

Louisa Court House, 40 map, 59

Love's Alabama Battalion, 344

Lovell, Capt. Don G., 104, 117

Lowden, James K., 109

Lucas, Lt. Thomas, 158, 237, 291

Lyman, Lt. Col. Theodore, 2

Lynchburg, 22, 23, 224, 305, 306

Macomber, Dexter, 118, 175

Madden, Lt. Daniel, 231, 232

Manigault, Gabriel, 73–74

Manning, Wade Hampton, 196

maps: campsites of Confederate and Union forces (June 10), 54; positions of forces night of June 11, 159; route of Fitzhugh Lee's march to Hampton's Division, 173; Torbert's assault along Fredericksburg Road, 85; Trevilian Raid theater of operations, 24, 40; Trevilian Station, battlefields, 60; Trevilian Station, capture of, 145

marches
    Fitzhugh Lee to Hampton's Division, 173 map, 174, 214n.127
    Hampton and Fitzhugh Lee in pursuit of Sheridan into Virginia, 46, 47–48, 49–51

marches, *continued*
>   Sheridan to James River, 255–56; arrives at Wilcox's Landing, 266; crosses the Chickahominy, 258; crosses the James, 289–91
>   Sheridan to Trevilian Station, 25–26; Carpenter on, 46–47; foraging and, 39, 41–42, 56–57; Hampton's Iron Scouts and, 55, 56; horses and, 37, 38, 41, 52–53; Lee's assessment of Grant's strategy for, 46–47; rear guard and, 39; scouts inform Hampton of Sheridan's advance, 43
>   Sheridan to White House Landing, 206–07, 248n.146; arrival, 242; battle against Hampton prior to arrival, 239–42; casualties and, 216, 217; Hampton's pursuit of, 222, 228; map, 229; prisoners and, 231, 238, 242; Sheridan on, 227
>   War Department Field Service Regulations, 62n.4
Marks, Samuel J., 238
Marquis Road, 52, 218; Custer campsite (June 10), 97; Sheridan's raid plan and, 59
Mason, Maj. Robert, 236
Massie, Lt. Col. Thomas B., 281, 285, 333
Mattapony River, 229 map, 234–35, 238
McAllister, Lt. Col. Joseph L., 313, 328, 333; at Battle of Trevilian Station (June 11), 147–48
McClatchey, John, 148–49
McClellan, Lt. Col. Carswell, 32n.65
McDonald, Carlos, 26, 42
McDonald, Maj. Edward, 170–71
McGuire, Capt., 74
McIntosh, John B., 5
McKinney, Edward P., 38, 84
McNulty, Lt. John, 334
McQuestion, James F., 289
McVicar, Sgt. Charles, 104, 106, 154; on artillery shelling at White House Landing, 240; at Battle of Bloody Angle, 191; on Battle of Bloody Angle, 208; on pursuit of Sheridan in retreat to White House Landing, 239–40
Meade, Gen. George G., 2–3, 32n.65, 223, 231, 232, 292; as a cavalry commander, 31n.64; contact with Sheridan during Sheridan's retreat and, 233, 234–35; instructs Sheridan to march to Deep Bottom, 249, 259n.2; relieves Pleasonton, 3; v. Sheridan, xii, 16, 17
Merritt, Brig. Gen. Wesley, 7–8, 332; at Battle of Bloody Angle, 189, 192; on Battle of Trevilian Station, 160; at Battle of Trevilian Station (June 11), 77, 135–36, 158; on Ogden, 137; on Rodenbough, 76; Sheridan and, 311; on Williston at Bloody Angle, 193, 211n.39
Merritt's Brigade, 289, 311, 331; Battle of Bloody Angle, 187, 190, 193, 196, 197, 203, 205 map, 304, 319; Battle of Trevilian Station (June 11), 84, 85 map, 99 map, 135, 137, 145 map; campsite (June 10), 54 map; campsite (June 11), 156, 159 map; casualties, 338, 341; opening engagement at Trevilian Station, 72; position during opening engagements at Trevilian Station, 70 map; reconnaissance (June 12), 183. *See also* Regular Army
Meyers, Jerry, 61, 64n.35, 68n.114
Millar, Capt. A. R., 148
Miller, Cal, 191
Mitchell, Capt. Robert Walsh, 197–98
Moncure, E. C., 47
Moore, Capt. Thomas W., 231
Morgan, Lt. Col. William A., 334
Morgan, Maj. Joseph H., 333

Morrow, Col. Albert P., 212n.65

Moss, John and Matt, 201

Mulligan, Capt. Abner B., 71, 91n.5, 200, 221, 235, 239

Munford, Col. Thomas T., 12, 30n.45, 129n.79, 272, 334; on Battle of Trevilian Station, 312; at Fight for Hampton's Wagons, 115, 116

Myers, Capt. Frank, 107, 158

Navy, Sgt. John, 188

Neese, Sgt. George M., 45, 50, 89, 161, 165n.115, 240; at Battle of Bloody Angle, 191

Nelson, Horatio, 44, 98, 204, 273

Netherland Tavern, 69, 104, 105, 141, 142, 147, 158; captured by the Eighth Pennsylvania Cavalry, 146; location (maps), 70, 85, 99, 145, 159, 173

Nettles, Lt. William J., 139

Newburger, Alexander, 240

Newhall, Capt. Frederick C., 6, 261n.46, 306; on Sheridan's march to Douthat's Landing, 255, 256

New York Herald, 26, 47, 133, 160, 216

Nichols, Lt. Col. George S., 80, 331

Nichols, Lt. John H., 188

Nineteenth New York Cavalry, 332. See also First New York Dragoons

Ninth New York Cavalry, 250, 331, 337; Battle of Bloody Angle, 189, 205 map; Battle of Trevilian Station (June 11), 82, 86, 155, 158; casualties, 341; Mrs. Sackett and, 327; retreat to White House Landing, 233; v. Lomax's Brigade, 264

Ninth Virginia Cavalry, 257

North Anna River, xi, xiii, 218, 222; Carpenter's Ford and, xix–xx, 25, 67n.84; location (maps), 24, 40, 54, 229; Sheridan's course to Trevilian Station and, 25

Norton, Sgt. L. P., 274

Nunn's Creek Road, 99 map, 112

O'Neil, Charles, 121

Ogden, Lt. Frederick Callender, 136–37

Ogg's house, 176, 191, 195, 221; location (maps), 159, 205

Onweller, William, 117, 130n.95

Ordner, Capt. John, 143

Orme, Capt. C. H., 141–42

Overland Campaign, xi, 11

Owen, Col. Thomas T., 334

Padgett, Eddie, 195

Pamunkey River, 233; location (maps), 24, 40, 229

Pate, Lt. Col. Henry Clay, 31n.53

Peck, Rufus, 268

Pemberton, Lt. Gen. John C., 22

Pendil, Azil M., 143

Pennington, Lt. Alexander C. M., Jr., 131n.111, 333

Persons, Kimball, 143

Petersburg, 21, 223, 320, 322; location (maps), 24, 33n.84, 229

Phillips Georgia Legion, 333; Battle of Samaria Church, 276 map, 281; Battle of Trevilian Station (June 11), 105, 141; casualties, 343; position during opening engagements at Trevilian Station, 70 map picketing, 16, 57, 97, 150, 253, 258, 259; at Battle of Bloody Angle, 189; night of June 11, 168, 170; retreat to White House Landing and, 218; Sixth New York Cavalry, 288–89; Sixth Ohio Cavalry, 206–07

Piedmont, 22

Pierce, John "Jap," 190–91

Pleasonton, Maj. Gen. Alfred, xi, 3

Poindexter house, 84, 85 map

Point Lookout, 238

Pollard, Lt. James, 257

Pond, Thomas G., 187

Poore's Creek, 186, 205 map

Porter, Col. Horace, 4

Preston, Lt. Noble D., 27, 58, 143, 171

prisoners: Allen, 175; Loeser, 169, 174–75; Macomber, 175; retreat to White House Landing and, 216, 231, 238, 242; Rucker, 168. See also captures

railroads, 22, 290. See also Virginia Central Railroad

Randol, Capt. Alanson M., 332

rations, 26, 45

Ream's Station, Battle of, 311; Hampton on, 325n.59

rear guards, 39, 55, 264, 310; Battle of Trevilian Station (June 11), 105, 158; Bauskett and, 50; Fight for Hampton's Wagons, 100, 102, 104; retreat to White House Landing, 218, 230, 237, 241; shooting of horses, 53, 302; wagon train to Douthat's Landing, 256

reconnaissance, 178, 179, 183, 261n.46, 286. See also intelligence

regiments. See cavalries

Regular Army, 5, 53, 217, 250, 311, 319; Battle of Bloody Angle, 184–85, 188; Battle of Trevilian Station (June 11), 72, 77, 83, 86, 136, 158; reconnaissance (June 12), 183; Sheridan's Trevilian Station raid plan and, 59. See also Merritt's Brigade

Reno, Maj. Marcus A, 95n.88

Ressler, Capt. Isaac, 55, 146

retreats, withdrawals: Confederates at Trevilian Station, 154–55, 319; Confederates from White House Landing, 249; Federals from Samaria Church, 275, 277–84; Federals from Trevilian Station, 215–43

Rich, Lt. Col. William W., 333

Richardson, Sgt. A. R., 73, 202

Richmond Daily Dispatch, 258

Richmond Examiner, 114, 298n.121, 307

Robertson, Capt. James M., 332

Robertson's Brigade (Horse Artillery, various batteries), 217, 332–33; Battle of Bloody Angle, 192–93, 196, 202, 203, 205 map; Battle of Samaria Church, 273, 274, 276 map; Battle of Trevilian Station, 76, 89, 137, 149, 311; casualties, 339, 342; Fight for Hampton's Wagons, 99 map, 100, 107, 108, 116, 120–21, 123–24; horses and, 303; retreat to White House Landing, 238

Robison, Lt. Col. John K., 277, 332

Rodenbough, Capt. Theophoplis F., 8, 59, 90, 92n.9, 245n.65, 332; at Battle of Trevilian Station, 75–76; at Battle of Trevilian Station, opening engagement, 72

Rosser, Brig. Gen. Thomas L., xii, 31n.53, 69, 71, 318, 333; on Battle of Trevilian Station, 305; on cooperation between Hampton and Fitzhugh Lee, 315–16; on Custer, 122; Custer and, 15; informed of Sheridan's advance, 43; Loeser and, 174; on Sheridan, 307–08; v. Custer, 105–06, 108, 325n.57; v. Custer, wounded, 153–54; v. Fitzhugh Lee, 316; v. Stuart, 14

Rosser's Brigade (Laurel Brigade), 82, 313; campsite (June 10), 54 map; casualties, 344; Fight for Hampton's Wagons, 99 map, 105–06, 107, 108–09, 112, 115–16, 117, 125; Hampton's Trevilian Station defense plan and, 61; ordered to fall back from attack on Custer's Brigade, 154; position during capture of Trevilian Station, 145 map; position morning of June 12, 176

Rucker, Samuel B., 152

Russell, Capt. William D., 148

Russell, Maj. Whiteford D., 171

Rutledge, Col. B. Huger, 184, 201, 333; assumes command of Butler's Brigade, 176; at Battle of Trevilian Station, 79

Sackett, Col. William, 86–87, 90, 331; at Battle of Trevilian Station (June 11), 82, 84, 86; grave of, 327

Sackett, Mrs. Williams, 327

Samaria Church, 24 map, 258, 259; present location, 293n.9

Samaria Church, Battle of: casualties, 301; Confederate reserve units, 265, 268, 276 map; Federal retreat, 275, 277–84; Gregg's preparations for, 265–67; Hampton's preparations for, 264, 265, 267–68; horses lost by Sixth Ohio cavalry, 323n.10; map, 276; opening engagement, 268–69; terrain, 265

Sanford, Capt. George B., 76, 136–37, 210n.20, 227; on Sheridan, 87

Sceva, Lt. Col. B. F., 41

scouting, 47–48, 120, 226, 230, 234; Butler's Brigade (June 12), 183; Hampton's Iron Scouts, 55, 56; Hampton informed of Sheridan's advance, 43

Second Cavalry Division, 5, 37, 250, 309–10, 332–33; Battle of Bloody Angle, 319; Battle of Samaria Church, 264, 266–67, 268–75, 276 map, 287–88, 301, 313–14; Battle of Trevilian Station, 70 map; camps at Samaria Church, 258; destroys mill at Walkerton, 238; march to White House Landing, 236; number of troops at Battle of Samaria Church, 301, 322n.3; retreat from Samaria Church, 275, 277–84; v. Hampton's Division at Haw's Shop, xiii–xiv, 20. See also Gregg's (David) Division

Second Pennsylvania Cavalry, 332; casualties, 339

Second U.S. Cavalry, 332; Battle of Bloody Angle, 192, 205 map; Battle of Trevilian Station (June 11), 72, 73, 74, 76, 78, 83, 134; casualties, 338, 341; position during opening engagements at Trevilian Station, 70 map. See also Gregg's (David) Division

Second Virginia Cavalry, 334; Battle of Samaria Church, 268, 272; casualties, 344; Fight for Hampton's Wagons, 99 map, 116

Seddon, James, 43

Sego, Tom, 199

Seventeenth Pennsylvania Cavalry, 49, 156, 250, 331, 337; Battle of Bloody Angle, 190, 205 map; casualties, 341; v. Chambliss' Brigade near Samaria Church, 257

Seventh Georgia Cavalry, 333; Battle of Trevilian Station (June 11), 79–80, 81, 87–88, 145 map, 147–49; casualties, 222, 313, 343; Fight for Hampton's Wagons, 102, 110; position during opening engagements at Trevilian Station, 70 map; Waring on, 66n.67

Seventh Michigan Cavalry, 97, 331; Battle of Bloody Angle, 184–86, 205 map; Battle of Trevilian Station (June 11), 145 map, 151; casualties, 337, 341; Fight for Hampton's Wagons, 98, 99 map, 100, 104, 117, 118, 122, 123, 124

Seventh South Carolina Cavalry, 268

Seventh Virginia Cavalry, 168, 218, 257, 333; casualties, 344

Shanahan, Lt., 101

Shenandoah Valley, 312, 320

Sheridan, Lieut. Gen. Philip, xi, 3, 238–39, 247n.128, 292, 323n.16, 331; assessment of situation night of June 11, 157; at Battle of Bloody Angle, 187; on Battle of Bloody Angle, 208; at Battle of Trevilian Station (June 11), 87, 90, 133, 137; Brooks on, 308; on Butler, 318; on cavalry, vi; as a cavalry commander, xviii; contact with Meade during retreat to White House Landing, 234–35; decision to retreat to White House Landing, 215; on Gregg at Battle of Samaria Church, 271, 287; Hunter and, 320, 321; instructed at White House Landing to return to the Army of the Potomac at City Point, 249; instructions by Grant to unite with Hunter at Charlottesville and, 22–23, 160; Jones on, 308–09; Kidd on, 4–5; leadership of, 320; learns that Hampton is aware of his advance, 46; Lincoln on, 5; on march to White House Landing, 227; Merritt and, 311; Neese on, 161; reconnaissance morning of June 12 and, 179, 181n.44, 209n.1; relationship with Gregg, 243n.2; Rosser on, 307–08; sends word to Gregg to retire from Samaria Church, 266; size of command, 25, 34n.94; Trevilian Station raid plan, 59; v. Alger, 126n.23; v. Hampton at Haw's Shop, xiii–xiv, 20; v. Meade, xii, 16, 17, 32n.65; v. Stuart at Yellow Tavern, xii–xiii, 17–18, 19; Wilson on, 304, 305, 321

Sherman, William Tecumseh, 2, 22

Shoemaker, Capt. John J., 152, 334

Sigel, Maj. Gen. Franz, 2, 21

Sims, Leonard, 111, 187

Sixteenth Pennsylvania Cavalry, 219, 332; Battle of Samaria Church, 275; Battle of Trevilian Station (June 11), 145 map, 146; casualties, 339; retreat to White House Landing, 231

Sixth Michigan Cavalry, 253, 331; Battle of Bloody Angle, 183–85, 205 map; casualties, 337, 341; Fight for Hampton's Wagons, 99 map, 100, 102–03, 104, 117–18

Sixth New York Cavalry, 238, 250, 288, 331; Battle of Bloody Angle, 190, 193–94, 205 map; Battle of Trevilian Station (June 11), 84, 94n.49, 133, 137; casualties, 337, 341; v. Chambliss' Brigade near Samaria Church, 258

Sixth Ohio Cavalry, 206–07, 253, 332; Battle of Samaria Church, 273, 274–75, 290, 303, 323n.10; casualties, 338, 342; retreat from Samaria Church, 277–78; retreat to White House Landing, 238, 242–43

Sixth Pennsylvania Cavalry, 41, 289, 332; Battle of Bloody Angle, 192, 196–98, 205 map, 206; Battle of Trevilian Station (June 11), 76, 78; casualties, 338, 341; position during opening engagements at Trevilian Station, 70 map; retreat to White House Landing, 237

Sixth South Carolina Cavalry, 50, 89, 169, 333; Battle of Bloody Angle, 188, 189, 190, 194–95, 199, 200, 202, 205 map; Battle of Trevilian Station (June 11), 71, 73–74, 80, 105, 139, 140, 141, 152; casualties, 343; position during opening engagements at Trevilian Station, 70 map; position morning of June 12, 170, 176

Sixth U.S. Cavalry, 231–32, 331; Battle of Bloody Angle, 188

Sixth Virginia Cavalry, 334; Battle of Bloody Angle, 203–04; Fight for Hampton's Wagons, 99 map, 115, 120–22, 121–22, 152

Smith, Col. Calvin H., 332

Smith, Col. Charles H., 57, 149, 270–71, 294n.47

Smith, Lt. Harmon, 98, 123–24

Smith, Maj. Howard M., 138, 198

Smith, Sgt. Thomas W., 290

Spencer, Lt. Col. Samuel B., 333

Spotsylvania Court House, xi, xii, 17; graves of the battlefield, 227–28; location (maps), 24, 40, 229

Sproul, Capt. Robert J., 98

St. Mary's Church. See Samaria Church

Stagg, Lt. Col. Peter, 98, 185, 331

Stanton, C. W., 78–79

Stedman, Col. William, 332

Stevenson, Lt. Walter, 109

Stockweather, George, 198

Stokes, Lt. Col. William, 88, 141, 226, 236, 254, 259, 284, 286, 292; at Battle of Bloody Angle, 201; on the pursuit of Gregg's retreat from Samaria Church, 281

Strang, Edward B., 42, 206; at Battle of Trevilian Station (June 11), 78; on the graves of the Spotsylvania battlefield, 228; on retreat to White House Landing, 219

Stuart, Maj. Gen. James Ewell Brown, xi, xi–xii, 11; at Battle of Dranesville, 325n.53; on cavalry, vi; in comparison to Hampton, 314–15; v. Rosser, 14; v. Sheridan at Yellow Tavern, xii–xiii, 17–18

Suderow, Bryce A., 34n.96, 345

Sultana (Ship), 104

surgeons. *See* doctors

Sweitzer, Capt. Nelson B., 332

Taylor, Col. John P., 280, 332

Taylor, Giles, 269–70

Taylor, Nelson, 86

Tebbs, Capt. Willoughby W., 272

Tennyson, Lord Alfred, vi

Tenth New York Cavalry, 41, 58, 236, 332; Battle of Samaria Church, 273–74; Battle of Trevilian Station (June 11), 142–44, 145 map; casualties, 338, 342; retreat from Samaria Church, 279, 282

Terrill, John, 281

Third Cavalry Division, 253, 303; v. Hampton at Ream's Station, 311. *See also* Wilson's Division

Third Virginia Cavalry, 260n.28; Battle of Bloody Angle, 203; Battle of Trevilian Station, 204; casualties, 334, 344

Thirteenth Ohio Dismounted Cavalry, 257

Thirteenth Pennsylvania Cavalry, 332

Thirty-fifth Battalion Virginia (Comanches), 177, 333; Fight for Hampton's Wagons, 99 map, 107, 108

Thomas, Capt. Hampton, 271

Thomas, Wiley, 140

Thomson, Capt. James, 120, 153

Thomson, Lt. James W., 334

Thorp, Lt. Col. Thomas J., 77

Tobie, John P., 83

Todd's Tavern, xii, 17; location (maps), 24, 229

Torbert, Brig. Gen. Alfred T. A., xi, xiii, xiv, 56, 242, 250, 331; assigned to command First Cavalry Division, 5–6; at Battle of Bloody Angle, 187, 189, 317; on Battle of Bloody Angle, 208; at Battle of Trevilian Station, 82, 84, 90–91, 133, 151, 155, 309; on Custer, 158; on Devin, 257; Sheridan's Trevilian Station raid plan and, 59

Torbert's Division, 5, 39, 267, 331–32; Battle of Bloody Angle, 200, 205 map; Battle of Trevilian Station, 83, 85 map, 99 map, 137, 142, 145 map, 155, 301, 319; campsite (June 11), 156; casualties, 303, 337, 341; reconnaissance June 12, 179, 183; secures Charles City Court House, 288; securing Sheridan's path across the Chickahominy, 254–55. *See also* First Cavalry Division

Towles, James, Robert and Vivian, 119–20, 328

Trask, Thomas A., 149–50

Treichel, Capt. Charles, 178, 253

Treichel, Maj. William P. C., 181n.40

Trevilian, Charles Goodall, 170

Trevilian Station, xix; location (maps), 24, 40, 99, 173, 229

Trevilian Station, Battle of, xiv–xv, xviii, xix, 72–90, 133–41, 142, 147–53, 159–61; assessment of Fitzhugh Lee's performance at, 316–17; battlefields of, 60 map, 61–62; campsites of Confederate and Union forces (June 10), 54 map; capture of station, 145 map; casualties (June 11), 157–58; casualties in Fitzhugh Lee's Division, 313; casualties in Fourth South Carolina Cavalry, 313; casualties in Hampton's Division, 312–13; casualties in Seventh Georgia Cavalry, 313; Chew on, 321–22; Confederate brigades ordered to fall back, 154–55; consequences of Hampton's victory on remainder of Civil War, 311; corps hospital (Union), 179; Eighth Pennsylvania Cavalry captures Netherland Tavern, 146; engagements of, 303, 319; Federal troops captured by Hampton, 322n.2; Kidd on, xvii; opening engagements, 71; positions of forces during opening engagements, 70 map; positions of forces night of June 11, 156, 159 map; Rosser on, 305; Sheridan's raid plan, 59; terrain and, 61, 71; Torbert's assault along Fredericksburg Road (map), 85. *See also* Bloody Angle; Hampton's wagons

Truman, Harry S., 211n.38

Turner, Bill, 199

Tuton, Edmond M., 274, 290

Twelfth Virginia Cavalry, 154, 333; Battle of Samaria Church, 276 map, 281; casualties, 344; Fight for Hampton's Wagons, 108

Twentieth Georgia Cavalry, 333; Battle of Bloody Angle, 187; Battle of Trevilian Station (June 11), 80, 81; Fight for Hampton's Wagons, 107, 110

Twenty-fourth Virginia Cavalry, 276 map, 281

United Daughters of the Confederacy, 328

U.S. Colored Troops, 257, 288

Vanderbilt, Capt. George, 143, 273–74

Veil, Lt. Charles H., 79, 93n.34, 230; on battle of Bloody Angle, 188

Vinton, Capt. Harvey V., 103

Virginia Central Railroad, 23, 222; destruction of, 155, 177–78, 181n.36; Hampton positions on between Gordonsville and Sheridan, 51; location (maps), 24, 40, 54, 60, 70, 85, 99, 145, 159, 173, 205, 229; Sheridan's failure to destroy and, 215, 305–06

Wadsworth, Capt. Craig, 157

wagons, 26; number of in Sheridan's march to Douthat's Landing, 255. *See also* Hampton's wagons

wagon trains. *See* marches

Wainwright, Maj. Gen. Philip Henry, 3–4

Walker, Maj. Alexander, 124, 331

Walkerton, 229 map, 232

Wallace, Lt. Eustis, 122

Wallace, Lt. Robert C., 91, 133–34, 217, 288

War Department Field Service Regulations, 62n.4

Waring, Lt. Col. Joseph Fred, 45, 291, 333; at Battle of Bloody Angle, 191, 195; on Battle of Samaria Church, 286; at Battle of Trevilian Station (June 11), 81, 105, 106–07; on march to meet Sheridan, 49; on pursuit of Sheridan in retreat to White House Landing, 223, 230, 235; on the Seventh Georgia Cavalry, 66n.67

Warren, Maj. Gen. Gouverneur K., 20

Washburne, Rep. Elihu, 1

Washington, Ella, 39

Webb, Sgt. Nathan B., 57, 170, 172, 242, 291; at Battle of Samaria Church, 268; on Battle of Samaria Church, 271, 288; at Battle of Trevilian Station (June 11), 83, 90, 149

Weir, Capt. Henry C., 279–80, 296n.89

Wellman, Manly Wade, 317

Wells, Edward Laight, 10, 45, 50; at Battle of Trevilian Station, 71, 88, 222; on Battle of Trevilian Station, 316; as a biographer of Hampton, 65n.44, 94n.75

West Point, 238, 242

White, Col. Elijah V., 333

White, Col. Lige, 111–12

White House Landing, 27, 236, 239, 253; Sheridan's arrival, 242

Wickham, Brig. Gen. Williams C., 12, 18, 30n.45, 318, 334

Wickham's Brigade, 236, 260n.28, 316, 319; Battle of Bloody Angle, 199, 203, 205 map; Battle of Samaria Church, 265, 268, 276 map, 286, 297n.121; Battle of Trevilian Station, 204; casualties, 344; engages Custer's Brigade on Marquis Road, 97–98; Fight for Hampton's Wagons, 99 map, 100, 115, 118, 125

Wilcox's Landing, 266

Wilderness, the, xi, 16, 156

Williston, Lt. Edward B., 333; Merritt on, 193, 211n.39

Wilson, Brig. Gen. James H., xi, xii, 253, 334; assigned to command Third Cavalry Division, 5; on Sheridan, 304, 305, 321

Wilson's Division, 3, 5, 253, 303, 334; v. Hampton at Ream's Station, 311. *See also* Third Cavalry Division

Winn, Sgt. Hill, 195

Wolverines. *See* Custer's Brigade

Wood, James F., 45, 106, 168, 218, 241

Wood, Lt. O. L., 190

Wood, Oscar, 118

Woodridge, Col. William B., 334

Woodruff, Lt. Carle, 121–22

Woodstock Races, The, 312

Wright, Col. Gilbert J., 14, 52, 318, 333; Anderson on, 149

Wright, J. Russell, 20

Wright's Brigade: Battle of Bloody Angle, 186, 205 map; Battle of Samaria Church, 265, 276 map; Battle of Trevilian Station (June 11), 72, 79, 80, 81, 84, 85 map, 86, 87, 99 map, 141, 142, 150; casualties, 313, 343; Fight for Hampton's Wagons, 100, 102, 110, 125; Hampton's Trevilian Station defense plan and, 61; position during capture of Trevilian Station, 145 map; position during opening engagements at Trevilian Station, 70 map; position morning of June 12, 176

Yellow Tavern, xii–xiii, 17–18, 19, 40 map

Young, Brig. Gen. Pierce M. B., 13–14

⊱ About the Author ⊰

Eric J. Wittenberg has spent much of his adult life studying Union cavalry operations in the Civil War. A native of southeastern Pennsylvania, he became interested in the Union cavalry as a young boy. Mr. Wittenberg is a graduate of Dickinson College, Carlisle, Pennsylvania, and the University of Pittsburgh School of Law. His first book, *Gettysburg's Forgotten Cavalry Actions*, was named the winner of the third annual Bachelder-Coddington Literary Award as 1998's best new work interpreting the Battle of Gettysburg. He and his wife Susan live in Columbus, Ohio.